Explaining the Performance of Human Resource Management

Human resource departments increasingly use the statistical analysis of performance indicators as a way of demonstrating their contribution to organisational performance. In this book, Steve Fleetwood and Anthony Hesketh take issue with this 'scientific' approach by arguing that its preoccupation with statistical analysis is misplaced because it fails to take account of the complexities of organisations and the full range of issues that influence individual performance. The book is split into three parts. Part I deconstructs research into the alleged link between people and business performance by showing that it cannot explain the associations it alleges. Part II attributes these shortcomings to the importation of spurious 'scientific' methods, before going on to suggest more appropriate methods that might be used in future. Finally, Part III explores how HR executives and professionals understand their work and shows how a critical realist stance adds value to this understanding through enhanced explanation.

STEVE FLEETWOOD is Professor of Employment Relations and HRM in Bristol Business School, University of the West of England, Bristol. His research focuses on philosophy of science and methodology as it is applied in social science, especially in organisation and management studies and economics. He has written extensively on critical realism.

ANTHONY HESKETH is Senior Lecturer at Lancaster University Management School. His research focuses on capturing the impact of people and strategy on organisational performance.

Explaining the Performance of Human Resource Management

STEVE FLEETWOOD
University of the West of England

ANTHONY HESKETH
Lancaster University Management School

CAMBRIDGE
UNIVERSITY PRESS

CAMBRIDGE UNIVERSITY PRESS
Cambridge, New York, Melbourne, Madrid, Cape Town,
Singapore, São Paulo, Delhi, Tokyo, Mexico City

Cambridge University Press
The Edinburgh Building, Cambridge CB2 8RU, UK

Published in the United States of America by Cambridge University Press, New York

www.cambridge.org
Information on this title: www.cambridge.org/9780521699358

First published 2010
Reprinted 2011
First paperback edition 2011

A catalogue record for this publication is available from the British Library

Library of Congress Cataloguing in Publication data
Fleetwood, Steve, 1955–
   Explaining the performance of human resource management /
   Steve Fleetwood, Anthony Hesketh.
      p.   cm.
   Includes bibliographical references and index.
   ISBN 978-0-521-87599-8
   1. Personnel management.   1. Hesketh, Anthony.   11. Title.
   HF5549.F574 2010
   658.3–dc22
   2010008748

ISBN 978-0-521-87599-8 Hardback
ISBN 978-0-521-69935-8 Paperback

For Anne & Helen, Thea and Abby

Contents

Figures

Tables

Preface

For those who wish to be free from the difficulty it is profitable to go through the difficulties properly; for the subsequent freedom from difficulty is the resolution of the difficulties gone into, and those who are unaware of a knot cannot unite it.

(Aristotle, *The Metaphysics*)

In the summer of 2005 one of us was presenting at a conference arranged by one of the leading US consulting houses for senior executives. Like so many other conferences that litter today's global executive network, the topic of the conference was 'Making HR Transformation Work'. A partner of the consulting house had heard one of us speak at another conference and was intrigued by our alternative view that we should aim to understand how human resource management (HRM) achieves its impact, not through measurement and prediction, but through explanation, and using a philosophical approach called *critical realism*.

As is the wont at such conferences, a cartoonist had been hired at great expense to the hosts. The cartoonist was charged with the responsibility of capturing the essence of what was being said, which would appear on a huge screen behind the presenter. As one of us began to articulate our critique of the way in which businesses currently seek to 'measure' how HR unlocks the performance of people, the cartoonist first drew a picture of a giant canary blocking access to the shaft of a coalmine. In an instant, the cartoonist had captured what we were trying to say. In order to establish if a mine was filled with poisonous gas, miners would often release a canary into the mine. The hypothesis deployed was a simple one: were the canary to stop singing, it was deduced the mine was probably unsafe. The giant canary in the cartoon immediately depicted: a) how inappropriate for the task the canary was; and b) that we have now left this somewhat quaint practice behind and replaced it with much more sophisticated levels of understanding as to how gas collects in mines. Or at least we thought we had.

As the presentation continued, another cartoon appeared, this time to roars of laughter in the audience. The cartoonist had drawn a human egg being approached by millions of sperm in order to depict our view that we can run literally millions of regressions and still the results will be unsuccessful in terms of *explaining* how HR practices can either enable or disable the performance of people.

The quest to find 'the Holy Grail of establishing a causal link between HRM and performance' (Legge 2001: 23) appears to have united groups who usually manage to ignore one another. Many university-based empirical researchers, HRM consultants, HR managers, HR business partners, not to mention some government departments, trade unions and think tanks are united in their belief in the existence of a quantifiable, measurable, empirical and statistical link, connection, relation or association between HRM practices and organisational performance. Henceforth we will refer to this as the HRM–P link. And whilst each of these stakeholders has slightly different reasons for holding this belief, few doubt its existence.[1]

This belief has encouraged a small army of researchers who, armed with the very latest 'scientific' methods, empirical data and statistical techniques, seek to specify the link with ever more quantitative precision. Current HRM and related journals bulge with empirical studies, each one investigating a slightly different bundle of HRM practices, including this or that intervening variables, using slightly different measures of performance, and each one coming up with slightly different results. Whilst some find the evidence, at best, inconclusive, most are prepared to believe that the sought after link exists, and will be shown to exist with more, and better, empirical analysis. In a recent article taking stock of the paradigm, leading empirical researchers Becker and Huselid (2006: 906–7) claim that:

For example, on the basis of the results of five national surveys between 1991 and 2000 and data collected from more than 3,200 firms, we have estimated that 'the effect of a one standard deviation change in the HR system is 10–20% of a firm's market value' (Huselid & Becker, 2000: 851). More broadly, in a meta-analysis of 92 recent studies on the HR-firm performance relationship, Combs, Ketchen, Hall, and Liu (2006) found that an increase of one standard deviation in the use of high-performance work systems is associated with a 4.6% increase in return on assets (ROA).

Despite the fact that the belief in a quantifiable, measurable, empirical and statistical link between HRM practices and organisational performance is widely held, there are a few who remain unconvinced. And we are amongst their number. We do not believe that this kind of link exists in the simplistic form described by many writers; and as our fieldwork shows, many HR professionals agree with us. This brings us nicely to the purpose of this book.

Explaining the Performance of Human Resource Management focuses upon what we call *meta-theory*, which, for the time being, can be thought of as philosophy of science, methodology and research techniques. We argue forcefully that the meta-theory underpinning empirical research on the HRM–P link, along with the commonly used quantitative, empirical and statistical techniques, have extremely serious shortcomings. These shortcomings are so serious that they not only undermine almost all the empirical research, they also damage our ability to theorise matters adequately. Worse still, empirical researchers on the HRM–P link are not even aware of these shortcomings. The purpose of the book, then, is to initiate a scholarly debate about the most appropriate meta-theory to use to explain why HRM practices influence organisational performance. And now for some caveats.

First, we are aware that our book will make us extremely unpopular amongst the army of empirical researchers worldwide currently engaged in empirical research on the HRM–P link because, whether we are right or wrong, no one wants to have their entire meta-theoretical approach called into question. This is something we, as scholars in the field with an alternative view, just have to live with.

Second, although we do not believe that a quantifiable, measurable, empirical and statistical link between HRM and organisational performance exists, this does not mean that we think that HRM practices are unconnected to organisational performance. Indeed, we emphatically accept that a well-managed workforce does, in many circumstances, tend to increase organisational performance. What we do not accept is that this tendency will manifest itself in the kind of quantifiable, measurable, empirical and statistical link of the kind currently sought after by empirical researchers through techniques such as regression analysis. We take the fact that the empirical evidence is inconclusive to mean that social systems in general, and the workplace in particular, are multiply caused, complex, evolving and subject to the exercise of human agency. And this, in turn, means that they are not the kinds of systems where relatively mechanical chains of causality (i.e. '*x* causes *y*, causes *z*') are found. The problem is not necessarily that causal relations are absent; but rather the problem lies in the way causality is (mis)conceived in the literature.

Third, although we clearly do not believe our critique to be mistaken, we have given due consideration to the possibility that it might be. Even if we are mistaken, however, we do not believe the paradigm will be damaged by two dissenting voices out of scores of articles and now several books that claim (nearly) all is well in the paradigm. If our critique is not mistaken, then our two dissenting voices should make a valuable contribution to the paradigm.

Fourth, whilst we do sketch out our alternative meta-theory, we will no doubt be criticised for failing to put all this into practice and failing to offer a full-blown alternative theoretical model of the HRM–P system. Unfortunately, doing all this is probably beyond the ability of two researchers, and certainly beyond the scope of one book. Two researchers cannot possibly:

(1) identify the meta-theory underpinning empirical research on the HRM–P link;
(2) explain the meta-theoretical shortcomings;
(3) pinpoint their causes;
(4) introduce, explain and deploy an alternative meta-theory;
(5) generate an alternative theoretical model; and
(6) test these alternative theories.

A small army of empirical researchers are already engaged in some of this, and asking us to do it on our own is asking the impossible. Our task is to highlight the meta-theoretical problems that bedevil empirical research on the HRM–P link, give some hints as to how they might be resolved, and hope that others will join with us in developing alternatives.

Fifth, and related to the previous two points, we will no doubt be criticised for being largely negative, for deploying a strong critique whilst offering little by way of positive contribution. We are, of course, aware that this kind of strong critique often irritates those who see themselves as getting on with the real task of 'doing' empirical research on the HRM–P link. To them, we are likely to be viewed as 'wreckers' pursuing the 'easy option' of sniping from the sidelines. We reject this for two reasons. First, because we seriously believe that the meta-theoretical shortcomings are so serious that the likes of ourselves, who have taken the time and trouble to investigate meta-theory thoroughly, perform a valuable service by spelling the shortcomings out boldly. Second, because we do not believe that researchers should plough on regardless of known shortcomings, on the (mistaken) grounds that no alternative exists. Nascent alternatives, such as those we offer, will remain under-developed until some of the small army of researchers abandon the current meta-theoretical perspective and start engaging with alternatives. Where would science be today if we had remained with flat-earth theory on the grounds that, whilst we knew the earth was not flat, we were not exactly sure what shape it was?

Finally, this is not a kind of 'how to' book, where we prescribe an alternative meta-theory so HR professionals can get on with the job of 'doing' HR. The book is intended for several audiences. It should be of interest to academics working in the areas of HRM, Industrial and Employment Relations, Organisation and Management Studies, Economics of Personnel, Sociology of Work and Employment and to HR consultants, concerned to better understand in order to investigate the relationship between the way people are managed and the way organisations perform. It should be of interest to practicing HR managers, business partners and senior executives who suspect people – or, to use the in-vogue phrase, talent management – matter. It should be of interest to trade unions and their negotiators engaged in negotiating the introduction of HRM practices in ways that protect and promote the interests of their members. It should be of interest to those involved in government departments like the former DTI, now BERR, and the Treasury, not to mention employers' associations like the CIPD, CBI and various think tanks such as the Work Foundation dedicated to promoting better people management. It should also be of interest to a smaller number of academics interested in meta-theory, especially those who are critical of positivist meta-theory (or scientism as we prefer to call it) and seek alternatives. In sum, everyone gains from a plausible explanation of how HRM practices influence organisational performance – if indeed they do. Unless we need to identify a particular party, then, we will use the term 'HR stakeholders' to refer to all those who may have an interest in explaining how HRM practices influence organisational performance.

In addition, meta-theory is not 'for' any one in particular, and neither is the 'meta-theory of HRM'. Imagine a scenario where HR managers are engaged in negotiations with the trade unions over the introduction of performance-related pay. There is no meta-theory for, or relative to, HR managers which is distinct from that for, or relative to, trade unionists. In a later chapter we will claim that the workplace is an 'open system'. To the extent that this claim is true, then it is true for HR managers and for trade unionists, and indeed for other stakeholders. Whatever political implications follow from claims such as these, they do not invalidate the meta-theory that generated them, and to the extent they are true, they can only worry those who are afraid of the truth.

Acknowledgements

The long gestation period of *Explaining the Performance of Human Resource Management* has given rise to a correspondingly long list of people we need to thank. Our memories will inevitably be selective so we apologise now to those colleagues – academic and practitioners – whom we overlook below.

Those individuals whose contributions would be impossible to forget include Martin Hird, then HR Director at BAE Systems, and Tony McCarthy, now Group Director of People and Board Member at British Airways plc. Together with Tony, Martin opened the door for our original research with HR executives back in 2002. This was supported with a generous research grant from Lancaster University to enable us to undertake the research in the United States for the *Something Wicked This Way Comes* research project. This, together with Martin's voluminous knowledge of HR, and his corresponding-ly voluminous networks, not to mention Professor Cary Cooper's boundless energy – led the way to what has now become the £1.4 million Performance-Led HR Centre at Lancaster. So, it has been a long time in coming, but half a dozen papers and a book later, we can now claim seedcorn research money does lead to substantial output!

Together with these key players, additional support was provided by Carl Gilleard, Chief Executive of the AGR for the research *Adding Value Beyond Measure*, enabling us to try out some of our emerging findings. After this, a long list of people, in no particular order, have opened doors to and for us, and encouraged our work during some of the dark days when we felt the 'Quantum Force' of the statisticians was going to preclude us from publishing our work. Riding to our rescue was Rick Delbridge who edited a special issue of *Organization* and who was especially encouraging of our work, cajoling us to write 'just one more draft' in order to tease out the empirical and explana-tory insights our critical realism and *reflexive performance* could afford. Then follows a long list of people, including David Andrews,

Xchanging, Mark Blundell, McDonald's, David Brown, Shell, Paul Chesworth, Vodafone, Peter Clark, IBM, Guy Haines, CSC, John Hindle, Accenture, Professor Bob Jessop, Lancaster University, Guy-Joël de Lhoneux, Unilever, Deborah Kops, Deutsche Bank, Tim Palmer, PA Consulting, Bill Payne, IBM and John Whelan, BAE Systems. These few people gave their time and networks, giving us access to what is now a global network of HR and C-suite executives. The majority of this network has chosen to remain anonymous but here we thank you all the same! The usual disclaimer relating to the claims we make in this book being our own opinions applies.

We also have to thank our editor at Cambridge University Press, Paula Parish. As each deadline sailed by our inboxes and phone mailboxes were filled with nothing but kind and encouraging emails and messages to continue working on the manuscript. Never once did Paula show frustration with us. This made for a refreshing change in a world where an immediate response is demanded, let alone expected, proving Cambridge University Press is one of the few remaining publishing houses that still understands what academic research requires in order to flourish. Our greatest debts, as ever, are owed to Anne Fleetwood and Helen, Thea and Abby Hesketh who take outstanding performance to a level far beyond our powers of understanding on a daily basis! This is for you.

PART I

HRM *and organisational performance today*

1 | *Crisis? What crisis?*

Every HR professional should be able to pass this one-question exam: how does your work add value to this business in economic terms?

(Ulrich 1997: 246)

HR has become an answer to a very important question, how can we improve a firm's financial performance?

(Becker and Huselid 2006: 907)

Let's face it. After close to 20 years of hopeful rhetoric about becoming 'strategic partners' with a 'seat at the table' where the business decisions that matter are made, most human-resources professionals aren't nearly there. They have no seat, and the table is locked inside a conference room to which they have no key. HR people are, for most practical purposes, neither strategic nor leaders.

(Hammond 2005: 40)

These are heady days for the human resources department. Consider for a moment the magnitude of the debates over the war for talent, human capital management, intellectual capital and the centrality of intangibles in accounting for the competitive advantage of organisations, and you are left nothing short of awe-struck as to the commercial importance of the human resources (HR) department. Surely now we can claim HR is finally *at* the boardroom table and not *on* it, to paraphrase one of the leading publications of the now burgeoning field of measuring the link between HR and organisation performance – something we refer to as the *HRM–P link* (Becker *et al.* 2001)?

A decade after Ulrich's 'Bloody Question' at the beginning of *Human Resource Champions* (1997: 1), namely, 'should we do away with HR?', the HR department appears to have moved backwards in its bid for corporate recognition. The big-hitting business guru writers appear to agree. Rosebeth Moss Kanter has recently predicted 'the demise of the HR function' (Moss Kanter 2003: xi), merely bringing to organisational fruition the warning sounded by Jeffrey Pfeffer over a decade ago in which he warned the HR function was 'entering a game where winning is unlikely and playing by the rules set by others exposes human resource professionals to the possibility of at best short-term victories and long-term problems' (1997: 357).

These long-term problems now appear to be coming home to roost. Despite the powerful discourse of Ulrich's *Champions* and the thriving emergent industry surrounding the business partner role in HR, major analyses of the function's standing in the boardroom suggest HR is at rock-bottom. A multitude of reports – academic as well as more practitioner-based – suggest that the strategic people agenda is not being met by HR. For example, the consultancy Deloitte recently established that despite executives placing heavy emphasis on strategic people issues, less than half of all major organisations across the globe have a HR director on their board (Deloitte 2007). More worryingly perhaps, their research also revealed only one in four executives believed HR was capable of contributing to strategy formulation and delivering operational results.

A clear gulf has emerged, then, between the executive agenda for HR and those charged with the responsibility of its implementation or 'operational HR' (Ulrich 2007). Whilst top executives grapple with the complexities of human capital management and measurement at the corporate level, the majority of HR staff are engaged in 'back office' administration, which, in turn, is increasingly being outsourced to and delivered by a specialist third-party provider at lower cost. Little wonder, then, that Moss Kanter (2003: xi) has suggested that 'the senior HR executive is not endangered, but the HR department is'.

Coming in from the cold

The HR department has not been slow to respond. A thriving industry has grown up around the measurement of HR's contribution to the financial performance of host organisations. Consulting houses such as EP First Saratoga at Pricewaterhousecoopers (PwC) and The Hackett Group offer HR practitioners the opportunity to effectively measure their way to credibility. This increasing emphasis on measurement can be seen as a direct response to competitive pressures, which in turn have brought about an increased focus on cutting costs in an attempt to improve profitability. Significantly, an organisational myth of 'doing more with less' has emerged around the measurement of HR: namely, successful organisations spend *less* on particular aspects of delivering their HR processes than under-performing organisations.

A strategic triad has now emerged where driving through gains in efficiency complements the more laudable leadership pursuits of increased quality and innovation. Many would argue increased productivity is nothing new. There has always been the pressure to grow earnings per share to satisfy the capital markets (Pfeffer 1997). What is new, however, is the ascription of *causality* to cost cutting in generating world-class organisations. The logic implied here is diminishing year-on-year expenditure on HR is indicative of successful executive management and its ability to leverage more from less. Less has in fact become more. The following is typical of the genre:

Hackett's Book of Numbers™ research found that a significant cost gap exists between world-class and typical companies, with world-class companies now spending 25 percent *less* than their peers ($1,422 versus $1,895/company employee). World-class companies also now operate with 16 percent *fewer* staff (11.88 versus 14.11 HR Staff/1,000 employees). (The Hackett Group 2007, emphases added)

As increasingly available information has driven down some of the transaction costs within organisations (e.g. Davenport 2005), vertical integration is now giving way to dis-integration as executives build interdependent ecosystems of extended organisations in an attempt to shift costs away from delivery to new growth platforms (Demos *et al.* 2001). Where cost cutting was once a means to a strategic end, it has now become a strategic end in itself in the eyes of many executives.

The impact of profits earned on sales can be enhanced or 'leveraged' if fixed operating costs can be reduced. The cost of people to an organisation is increasingly the largest fixed cost on the company's balance sheet (e.g. see Barber and Strack 2005).[1] It follows from this that a reduction in the costs of people can enable greater flexibility to executives to obtain higher levels of operating leverage. The pressure brought to bear on executives' abilities to meet such demands through benchmarking is now staggering. So much so that a failure to keep downward pressure on costs is distinctly career-inhibiting to executives. In the words of one influential commentator, 'costs above the 90th percentile might be perilous to ignore' (Ghemawat 2007: 62).

New models of delivering HR services via technology-enabled Enterprise Resource Planning (ERP) systems have opened up new financial models and accounting opportunities to quite literally turn what are fixed (internal employee) costs to variable (external or third-party provider employee and service) costs through outsourcing. Paying third-party providers on a per-transaction-delivered basis, rather than a fixed salary for employees, affords executives major productivity gains and frees financial resource to be leveraged in different parts of their businesses, at least in theory (see, for example, Williamson 1975). Where the HR media sees such developments as an affront to the durability of HR's long-term professional status, executives see an external market for capabilities triggering them to ask questions as to what really is 'core' to their organisation and what of that which remains is 'peripheral' and can be pushed out into 'extended organisations' with which organisations partner to deliver services at agreed prices and levels of quality (Aron and Singh 2005).

Moreover, executives can now increasingly scale or 'commoditise' processes and capabilities to such an extent that many more complex services previously thought to be incapable of being outsourced in HR are now under the spotlight (Hesketh 2006, 2008a). For Davenport (2005: 102), 'a new world is coming, and it will lead to dramatic changes in the shape and structure of corporations [as] a broad set of process standards will soon make it easy to determine whether a business capability can be improved by outsourcing it'.

Enter the academy

It is the shape and structure of organisations where debate over the future of the HR department has been at its apex. Academic debate has recently switched course away from establishing a link between a particular human resources management practice and performance in favour of establishing the best 'fit' between different bundles, systems, strategic capabilities or architectures of HR processes that implement strategy and form the basis of HR's contribution to competitive advantage (cf. Becker and Huselid 2006: 899).

Significantly, this recent shift to HR's role in the development of strategic capability and competitive advantage stems from the belief amongst academics that the debate over the causal link between HR and organisational performance is deemed to have been won. Scores of studies now exist claiming to have 'demonstrated statistically significant relationships between measures of HR and firm profitability', or some other measure of performance (Wright *et al.* 2003: 21). There is a remarkable agreement here between studies generally supporting a pro-business agenda, and studies supporting a pro-employee agenda – both wings appear to have a vested interest in demonstrating statistical associations between the ways people are managed, and the organisation's performance. This means that the search for this statistical association crosses the organisational political divide. Brian Becker and Mark Huselid (2006: 921), two highly influential authors in both the academy and advisory worlds, reflect upon the current state of affairs:[2]

To a substantial degree, managers now 'get it' and do not have to be persuaded that the quality with which they manage the workforce has strategic impact. What they now need is help in understanding how to generate and sustain those potential returns.

It is at this point that alarm bells begin to ring. This is for at least three reasons. First, and as we have already flagged above, it is far from clear that senior executives 'get' the impact of HR. Much of the evidence aimed at this level of organisational management suggests the contrary is in fact the case. Second, if academic 'research has demonstrated statistically significant relationships between measures of HR and firm profitability', why then do practitioners still require help in understanding *how* HR generates returns? This is related to a third problem, namely the 'appliance of science' and the atrophied account it provides in relation to an *explanation* of how people unlock performance. As we will argue at length later in the book, research on the HRM–P link is dominated by what we will, for the time being, simply refer to as the 'scientific' approach. There is no harm in thinking of this as an approach that engages in quantification and measurement to obtain quantitative data, and then uses this data to test predictions via a battery of statistical tools and techniques. Despite its popularity, there are some, like us, who doubt the legitimacy of this approach. Not only do we think that this is a kind of spurious 'science' (hence we use scare quotations when referring to the 'scientific' approach), we also think this 'scientific' approach has serious shortcomings. The most important shortcoming lies in the fact that, whilst this 'scientific' approach might tell us *that* certain HR practices are positively associated with the enhanced performance of business units at different levels of an organisation, it does not explain to us – or to practitioners – *how* or *why* such practices enable the enhanced performance of people and the teams, units and organisations to which they belong. In other words, the 'scientific approach' states *that* a statistical relation exists; but it does not explain *how* and *why* such a relation exists. As one executive put it to us, 'we are still left twiddling our thumbs at our Monday morning meetings about *how* to improve performance through our HR'.

It will now be clear to the reader that we remain unconvinced about the veracity of the evidence deriving from the 'scientific' approach used to examine the link between HRM and organisational performance in helping managers with the everyday situations they find themselves in when seeking to improve the performance of their people and organisations. The primary reason for this concern revolves around the problems associated with what might be described as a very particular 'logic of science', or a 'scientific logic' that is at work here.

The logical song

Research on the HRM–P link carried out using the 'scientific' approach is rooted, ultimately, in a very specific notion of causality: *causality as regularity*. This notion of causality turns on the idea that if some event (event *y*) regularly follows some other event (event *x*), then some may assume that event *x* causes event *y*. It is not difficult to see how this translates into thinking about the HRM–P link. If increases in organisational performance regularly follow the introduction of some bundle of HRM practices, then some may assume that the introduction of the bundle of HRM practices caused the increase in organisational performance.

It is easy to see why this scientific logic strikes a chord with the HR community. A vast array of forces, accepting this logic, have been deployed on behalf of the HR department to protect it from wider executive forces (allegedly) keen to exert downward pressure on

costs, on the one hand, or even challenge the department's very existence (e.g. Hammond 2005). Indeed, forces have also been deployed
on behalf of employees to promote the idea that there is a business
case for treating employees well – much of this is found in the literature on so-called High Performance Workplaces, and variants, e.g.
employee engagement. Crucial to the deployment of these forces has
been the use of this logic of science. This 'scientific' logic affords three
advantages to those within the HR community who seek to justify
the operational budgets of HR functions. First, the very discourse of
'science' and 'scientificity' is seductive in the sense that it captures the
high ground – after all, those who challenge results that are arrived at
'scientifically' automatically gain the label of being 'un-scientific', or
perhaps not quite understanding the science, or some such. Second,
it places the massive volume of evidence at the disposal of academics,
practitioners, consultants, advisors, policy-makers, union negotiators
and executives, seeking to justify the operational budgets of HR functions.[3] Third, it heads off any potential charges of 'special pleading'
by those with an interest in maintaining the HR department. In short,
almost all stakeholders, it seems, have a vested interest in accepting
the logic of science that provides the quantitative data that in turn
provides evidence of an HRM–P link.

What little debate around the use of 'science' there has been, has
generated more empirical heat than theoretical light. Not that you
would be afforded even the faintest of whiffs of doubt as to the veracity of this data by advocates of the particular scientific logic underpinning research on the HRM–P. For example, drawing together
the now four decades' worth of research in the field, Becker and
Huselid (2006: 906–7) present the evidence everybody in HR wants
to hear, whilst at the same time, employing the seductive discourse of
'science':

[N]on-economists are influential when they, too, make 'novel prescriptions that are relevant to the marketplace' by focusing their research on
'economic outcome variables' (Bazerman, 2005: 27). This observation
is particularly applicable to [Strategic Human Resources Management]
research. For example, on the basis of the results of five national surveys
between 1991 and 2000 and data collected from more than 3,200 firms,
we have estimated that 'the effect of a one standard deviation change in
the HR system is 10–20% of a firm's market value' (Huselid & Becker,
2000: 851). More broadly, in a meta-analysis of 92 recent studies on

the HR-firm performance relationship, Combs, Ketchen, Hall, and Liu (2006) found that an increase of one standard deviation in the use of high-performance work systems is associated with a 4.6% increase in return on assets (ROA).

Contrary to the perceptions held by wider HR practitioners, this 'scientific' research has not taken place in a vacuum. Indeed, the media serving the HR world has been as equally quick to celebrate 'evidence' claiming to have found the 'Holy Grail' of a causal link between HR and organisational performance (e.g. Peacock 2008) as the wider business media has been to attack HR for a lack of 'convincing evidence' to support its business case (e.g. Donkin 2005; Hammond 2005). Nor has the academy been slow to recognise its opportunity in this malaise. As the debate over the utility of output from the academy to business rages on both sides of the Atlantic, leading scholars in the HRM–P link field have seized their opportunity. Turning to Becker and Huselid once again, 'financial effects such as an *x* percentage change in shareholder value or *y* percentage change in *ROA provide a compelling external validation to results that otherwise are simply "statistically significant"'* (2006: 907, emphasis added).

Note the italicised section. There is a view that the majority of chief executives do not require convincing over the much used, if now slightly cliché, axiom that 'people are their most important asset' (e.g. Cheese *et al.* 2008; Gratton 2000). But the majority of their boardroom colleagues do. What the research findings referred to by Becker and Huselid are really being used for, then, is to settle political debates within organisations over *who* should *own* HR architectures, *what* should be delivered and its *impact*. The logic of science is, paradoxically, both implicit and hidden, and explicit and centre stage in terms of establishing the veracity of the claims made by people at the echelons of organisations on both the positive and negative views over the link between HR and improved firm performance.

Two worlds, two takes, same problem

Servicing this organisational clamour for scientific validity has seen an endless stream of new ideas, formulas and paradigms in which emerging 'gurus' or 'fads' thrive with varying degrees of success in a world comparable to medieval medicine. It is not just the capacity of the academy and management consultancy business to continually construct and re-construct these new solutions that is staggering. Almost as amazing is the regularity with which organisations, their leaders and shareholders, if not beleaguered employees, continue to forgive the 'Jesuits of Capitalism' for their continued failings. Both the academy and consulting sectors have attempted to provide organisations with new solutions to answer the challenge set by Dave Ulrich: namely, to demonstrate not what HR does, but what HR delivers (cf. Ulrich 1997: vii). Claims and counter-claims are regularly exchanged between the two camps.

For the academy, the turn to the logic of 'science' has enabled researchers to jettison subjectivity, objectively scrutinise and largely refute the measurement products offered by the consultants, whose dazzling array of 'performance-transforming' interventions are dismissed as nothing more than effective storytelling which do not 'necessarily and immediately modify the actions of [their] audience, but ... alter their *beliefs, attitudes* and *feelings* towards [their] suggestions' (Huczynski 1993: 245, original emphases). The role of the academy in HR, then, has essentially been one of challenging the accuracy of fads and gurus and, 'establishing the credibility of HR as a science' (Dipboye 2007: 96). Such a task for the majority of academics working in the HRM–P field has meant dealing with 'the "black box" that describes the strategic logic between a firm's HR architecture and its subsequent performance' (Becker and Huselid 2006: 899). In short, to inject scientific evidence into what has largely been a rhetorical debate over the role of HR in driving the performance of organisations.

A staggering array of research papers, chapters and books now pervade the HRM–P debate. Almost without exception this work deploys the 'scientific' approach. A number of different schools within the field have emerged, each with a slightly different perspective on the side of the equation which brings together different HR systems and architectures, but nearly always the same dependent variable: the headline financial performance of the firm. There are slight variations in both independent and dependent variables, whether in terms of slightly different types of, and combinations between, HR processes, or the performance of business units in terms of productivity measures or self-reported performance, the latter of which is seen to be highly problematic (e.g. Wall and Wood 2005, for a discussion). Indeed, acknowledging the vast multitude of problems associated with using the scientific approach to the HRM–P link has almost become a field in its own right (see Gerhart *et al.* 2000; Wall and Wood 2005; Wright *et al.* 2001). That said, a great deal of discussion of these problems does not get anywhere near to the kinds of problems we raise in this book and are what we refer to below as 'technical' problems.

The simultaneous acknowledgement of possible (largely measurement-oriented) errors and movement away from individual reporting of performance is presented as a robust way in which the academy can distance its work from the problems of subjectivity associated with more interpretavistic and, crucially, less scientific, methods of (qualitative) research. As we shall see in what follows, there exists a substantial alternative body of work exploring the capacity of HR to enable people to improve their own performance (see Hesketh and Fleetwood 2006b), and subsequently that of their organisation, but this body of research is almost entirely overlooked by those academics working in the field of the HRM–P link. What is passed off as 'science' has in effect become the only game in town. Inserting financial performance into the dependent variable side of the equation has allowed the academy to empirically facilitate the HR practitioner requirement of being able to simultaneously 'talk strategy and walk profits' (Clegg and Ross-Smith 2003). Consequently, advocates of the 'scientific' approach focus on the relationships between systems or 'architectures' of HR and organisational performance rather than an examination of individual practices and their reflexive sense making. The following is typical of the genre:

The field of HR strategy differs from traditional HR management research in two important ways. First, SHRM [Strategic Human Resources Management] focuses on organizational performance rather than individual performance. Second, it also emphasizes the role of HR management *systems* as solutions to business problems (including positive and negative complementarities) rather than individual HR management practices in isolation. (Becker and Huselid 2006: 899, original emphasis)

The results of these analyses are regarded with a mixture of admiration and fear by many academics, let alone the practitioners whose daily work they are in part devised to facilitate. This has provided the consulting world with an open door to present their own analytical tools and techniques to a HR community, which doesn't know its *r*-squares from its R-squares, reeling from the signs and symbols of statistical tables apparently confirming how particular HR practices might be associated with variations in the performance of organisations.

A new industry within the human resources advisory and consulting sector has grown up, currently worth in the region of a staggering $25 billion annually and set to increase to $30 billion by 2011 (IDC 2006). In trying to overcome the complexities of the academy, and secure the large-scale custom of leading client organisations, the consulting industry has spawned a number of performance-measuring artefacts designed to help executives capture the impact of human capital on their profits or 'bottom lines'. Well known examples include *Economic Value Added* (EVA), Watson Wyatt's *Human Capital Index* (HCI), Mercer's *Human Capital Wheel*, Hackett's *World Class Performance Index* and Saratoga's benchmarking and return on investments (ROI) to human capital measures (see Mayo 2000).

Claim and counter-claim are exchanged between the academy and consulting camps. Consultants accuse academics of esoteric and irrelevant research that cannot be easily re-worked into organisational and practical settings. The academy rebukes the consultants for their atrophied view of performance and their failure to engage in rigorous, objective and 'scientific' research. Moreover, a third and new field has opened up where individuals step out of the academy and in to the consulting world and offer new measurement tools which combine the rigour and science of academic research with the clinical and impressive presentation and branding of consulting houses. It is the concepts and tools brought to market by these individuals which have arguably succeeded most. Examples here include the *Business Score Card* and *Strategy Maps* of Kaplan and Norton (1996, 2004), which have now been famously applied in an HR context by Becker *et al.* (2001) in the form of the *HR Scorecard*.

Significantly, whichever camp the majority of ideas emerge from, and whatever the variations in focus and application, their underpinning philosophy, almost without exception, remains the same: 'science'. For example, the authors of the *HR Scorecard* waste little time in illustrating the two primary reasons why they think researchers and practitioners should focus on measuring HR:

A sound performance-measurement system does two things. First it improves HR decision-making by helping you focus on those aspects of the organization that create value. In the process, it provides you with feedback that you can use to evaluate current HR strategy and predict the impact of future decisions ... Second, it provides a valid and systematic justification for resource-allocation decisions. HR can't legitimately claim its share of the firm's resources unless it can show it contributes to the firm's financial success. (Becker *et al.* 2001: 110–11)

The impact of the *HR Scorecard* on human resources directors and HR as a whole cannot be easily underestimated. Its success lies in the combination of the authors' recognition that the HRM–P link is difficult to measure for a number of technical reasons, and, crucially, that the majority of HR directors and HR professionals short on time and under considerable pressure from their executive colleagues to demonstrate how their departments contribute to the organisation's bottom-line, require a narrative with which to outline how they have overcome such problems, and convince their colleagues of the veracity of the results before them. Thus:

Ultimately, you must have a persuasive story about what's in the black box. You must be able to throw back the cover of that box and reveal a plausible process of value creation from HR to firm performance. The strategic HR architecture we have described, aligned with the strategy and implementation process, forms such a story. Telling this story – *through the measurement system you design* – will help you identify actionable goals and performance drivers. (Becker *et al.* 2001: 111, emphasis added)

A whole new performance lexicon has been constructed, enabling HR directors and their functional colleagues to articulate a clear and compelling case for the performance of HR. The feat achieved by the authors of the *HR Scorecard* has been to present this new language in relatively straightforward terms, which is simultaneously based on highly technical and sophisticated analytics.

So the authors present a case where politically sensitive HR directors understand the dangers of attempting to explain the technical argument in the boardroom, hence the rhetorical question from the authors (2001: 121), 'how would you interpret a correlation of .35? Has your CEO ever asked you to describe HR's contribution in terms of correlation, or its equivalent statistical term "explained variance"?'. HR executives are then presented with a two-page summary of the underlying categories of data, how they might be applied to HR and a two-sentence explanation as to how a multivariate rather than a bivariate perspective provides causal models that measure relationships in actionable terms. All this, for the authors, means: 'When you create the HR Scorecard, using the approach we describe, you are actually *linking HR to firm performance*. But you will also develop a new perspective on your HR function, practices, and professional development. In measurement terms, the benefits will far outweigh the costs' (Becker *et al.* 2001: 205, original emphasis).

Accounting for People

The new perspective advocated by the authors of the *HR Scorecard* has had far-reaching implications. Partly in response to the financial scandals of Worldcom, Enron and Arthur Andersen, and increasing recognition of the growing distance between the book value and market value of firms – so-called intangible value or intellectual capital (Lev 2001) – the political administrations of nation states have been tightening their grip on the financial valuation of businesses. The UK was particularly adventurous in this vein, calling, in 2003, for a timescale making it compulsory for all publicly listed organisations in the UK to provide a convincing account of the value of their people or human capital assets in their Operating and Financial Review (OFR). The OFR essentially represents the section of a company's annual report in which companies detail their policies, strategies and performance.

Significantly, and perhaps reflecting the growing ebullience borne of the increasing research output from the academy claiming to have established a causal link between high-performance HR architectures and actual firm financial performance, the original legislation released in 2003 suggested that the review should shift from annual statements in companies' annual reports which are 'true and fair' to a 'due and careful enquiry' where the latter would include legislation for a new criminal offence with unlimited fines for directors who 'recklessly approved an OFR'.

Alongside the new OFR requirement was an additional government-sponsored taskforce into how the value of HR would be captured by companies in their narrative accounting. This investigation had been triggered by the chair of the new Accounting for People Task Force, Diane Kingsmill, who had recently completed a separate report on women's participation in the labour market but had concluded in passing that, 'although good human capital management was a crucial element in organizations' performance and productivity', it was routinely underreported (Kingsmill 2003: 56).

Accounting for People caused a huge wave through the UK HR professional sector, enveloping consultants, advisors, the HR media and academics, who all contributed to the debate. Kingsmill concluded that, 'Human Capital Management [was] an approach to analyze, measure and evaluate how people policies and practices create value [and was] winning recognition as a way of creating long-term sustainable performance in an increasingly competitive world' (Kingsmill 2003: 3). Significantly, Kingsmill advocated that such human capital management should sensibly ride on the back of the legislation already being put in place by government concerning the OFR. The government agreed and debate over which metrics and techniques might be used to measure the performance of people and their contribution to overall business performance and future strategies commenced.

By the end of 2004, with the legislation relating to the OFR due to come into force in April of the following year, the then Chancellor Gordon Brown announced that he was postponing the delay of the launch of the new-look OFR to widen consultation, which many took for code meaning the civil service had not been convinced of the validity of the measurement techniques relating people to strategy and business performance. The implementation of the OFR was again postponed at the end of 2005, and subsequently abandoned as a form of compulsory legislation in early 2006. Although not openly stated, many commentators, consultants and academics again took this change of heart on the part of the Prime Minister as conceding that intangible value, such as that of people working inside organisations, could not be adequately measured, at least certainly not to the level that would stand up in the courts were directors to be viewed to be disingenuous over articulating the contribution of, amongst other things, their people to their businesses.

Like Kingsmill and others, including those academics adopting a 'scientific' approach to investigating the HRM–P link, we recognise that people and their competent management and support systems constitute competitive advantage – including above average financial performance – for those organisations excelling in this area. We do

not, however, subscribe to the view that the simple mimetic replication of particular HR systems or architectures will generate such
financial returns for those organisations making the investment in
such systems. Nor do we think the returns to such investments –
whether surpluses or losses – can be directly measured and read off
in the way depicted by those advocating the 'scientific' approach to
examining the HRM–P link. Which brings us neatly to the reasons
why we have undertaken the writing of *Explaining the Performance
of Human Resource Management*.

Underlying theses

Underpinning our thesis are four major strands of thinking. These
are:

(1) *The logical song*: at present the overwhelming discourse per-
vading HR's capacity to contribute to above-norm business performance can be best understood in terms of a technical puzzle
through which the association between certain combinations or
bundles of HR processes – or architectures – and business performance can be measured 'scientifically' in order to *predict* the
impact of HR on future firm performance. Our primary contention is that such a discourse is at best limiting in terms of its
utility to both the academy and to practitioners, and, at worst,
is extremely misleading. Nevertheless, to adopt a dissenting tack
is heretical for academics and positively career inhibiting for HR
executives. This is a deleterious state of affairs, which can only
hurt the HR department and those connected with it. We will
pick up this theme in Chapter 2.

(2) *The people–performance split*: largely due to the importation of
such 'scientific' methods into the debate over the causal impact
of HR on business performance, the complexities of the role
of individuals in shaping the performance of organisations has
become decoupled from the HR systems put in place to manage
them. This is largely the consequence of the focus of investigation
moving away from people and their capabilities to establishing
the impact of particular bundles of HR processes – or architectures labelled high-performance work systems – in generating
above-norm business returns. Our primary contention is that the

causal impact of such HR bundles and architectures has been reified. It is people, not systems (albeit people working in systems), who enable performance. We will set out our reasoning for this in Part II of the book which explores the fundamental shortcomings of the 'scientific' approach to research on the HRM–P link. This is an unashamedly philosophical exploration of the problems associated with the 'scientific' method as it is applied in the social setting of the organisation. Readers short on time, or less inclined to such deeper philosophical debate, might like to move straight to Part III, where we explore how HR executives and professionals understand their work and how our meta-theoretical stance adds value to this understanding through enhanced explanation.

(3) *Moving from causality to enablement through explanation*: rather than seeking to *predict* the impact of HR on organisational performance as advocated by the 'scientific' approach, we advocate a move from prediction to *explanation* in keeping with the philosophical position of *critical realism* (Archer 2003; Bhaskar 1978; Sayer 2000). Crucial to this position is the recognition that all explanation and understanding of social realities have to be mediated through a process of conceptualisation. Our primary contention is that such a process requires a shift to what we call 'reflexive performance' in which the cause of an event is not assumed to simply be the event(s) that preceded it (i.e. causality as regularity), but rather is the conflux of many interacting causal phenomena (i.e. complex or thick causality). Far from measuring and predicting how HR causes performance outcomes, we follow Archer's (2003) prescription of a process of reflexive deliberation through which the role of HR in *enabling*, as opposed to mechanically causing, certain organisational outcomes is *explained*. This argument is articulated in Chapter 7.

(4) *Resonance with practice*: we are convinced that the approach advocated by reflexive performance not only provides us with insights into and explanation and understanding of the role played by HR in enabling performance, but that such an approach resonates strongly with the executive and middle management respondents we have interviewed in our work exploring HR's relationship with high performance. In Part III we develop a theoretical and discursive lexicon with which HR professionals can

articulate their role in shaping the activities of their organisations. We undertake this largely through the in vivo experiences of HR professionals themselves.

The structure of the book

The book is essentially in three parts. Part I explores the current state of the HR profession and the evolution of the different academic fields – or schools of thought – which have arisen in what has become the HRM–P link school. Some of this material is heavily laden with academic discourse, having arisen from different schools of thought in the wider management literature. To offset part of this complexity we have in Chapter 2 deployed several metaphors to illustrate and clarify the primary insights each different perspective adopts. In some cases we use existing metaphors deployed by the schools themselves – such as the 'black box' by the universal school. There is no intention to dismiss or dilute the specific claims articulated within each perspective; on the contrary, our aim is to make what are complex issues more accessible to the reader. Many writers conflate the different schools and use them interchangeably to justify their approach. We hope the remainder of Part I clarifies the differences in methods deployed by the various schools.

The third chapter hints that the fundamental problems afflicting the contemporary empirical research on the HRM–P link are rooted in its commitment to what appears to be 'science' – but is more accurately referred to as 'scientism'. The aim of this chapter is to elaborate, at some length, what this current research involves and, more importantly, the problems it faces – which are often referred to generically as the *problem of under-theorisation*. Whilst some of those who study the HRM–P link recognise empirical research is under-theorised, we are not aware of any who are prepared to take the problem seriously, or of any who are willing to consider just how deep it runs. And we think the problem runs so deep as to seriously undermine the whole paradigm.

The first three chapters of Part II delve deeply into the philosophy of science to arrive at the conclusion that scientism has some serious shortcomings. Because we recognise philosophy of science is a new area for many, we offer a brief overview that can be seen as either a substitute or a preparation for these three chapters. It is aimed specifically at practicing HR managers, business partners and senior executives; trade unionists and trade union negotiators; those involved in government departments (e.g. BERR and the Treasury); employers' associations (e.g. CIPD, CBI and various think tanks such as the Work Foundation). It will be of less interest to HR consultants and academics, who ought to be, at the very least, familiar with key aspects in the philosophy of science, even if they do not write about it explicitly. In short, it is aimed at that group we will call '*HR practitioners*'. Why should HR practitioners bother with the philosophy of science? Leaving aside the appeal to intellectual curiosity, there remains an issue of self-interest: without some awareness of the philosophy of science, HR practitioners run the risk of being sold snake oil and not even knowing it! Whilst this overview minimises specialist terminology, there is no avoiding the following terms: *ontology* (i.e. a theory of the way the world, generally speaking, is); *epistemology* (i.e. a theory of what constitutes knowledge of this world); and *methodology* (i.e. a theory of how we gain this knowledge). Whilst terms like these can appear daunting, they are often less difficult to understand than many of the technical terms routinely found in statistical work on the HRM–P link – e.g. *Varimax Rotation* or *Structural Equation Modelling*.

Chapter 4 works its way through the deductivist method, the ontology of events and their alleged regularities, closed systems, prediction and the quantification of qualities, not only to show the philosophy of science underpinning empirical research on the HRM–P link, but also to identify its shortcomings.

Scientism's method is the called the *deductive method* or simply *deductivism*, whereby to 'explain' something is to predict that something as a deduction from a set of initial conditions, assumptions and law(s) or some other regular pattern of events. Water expands when frozen; there is water in my radiator; therefore if the temperature falls below freezing, my radiator will spring a leak. At some point, of course, we did not know this, so had to conduct experiments that eventually allowed us to predict what regularly happens to water in radiators when it freezes. In the HRM context, we do not really know what causes increases in organisational performance, although we suspect HRM practices will be involved. Empirical researchers seek a statistical link between HRM and performance so they can predict what regularly happens to performance when HRM practices are introduced. The attentive reader might already have started to doubt the wisdom of transposing techniques that work in natural science settings to social science settings.

From the perspective of scientism, *observable events* are the building blocks of empirical research: they are the things of interest that happen in the social world and about which researchers collect their data. An event might be the introduction of team working, the duration of a training programme, the strength of employee commitment to organisational culture, an increase in productivity and so on. If and when these events are observed, recorded, counted or measured they become variables. The social world, or at least that part of it that is amenable to scientism, is presumed to consist of observed events. To put it crudely, 'what you see is what there is', and what you see are events.

From this *ontology of events*, an epistemology follows. If particular knowledge is gained through observing events, more general or scientific knowledge is gained only if these events manifest themselves in some kind of pattern; a flux of totally arbitrary events would not result in knowledge of any kind. Not just any old pattern will do, though, as these events must manifest themselves as *event regularities*. The paradigm case of event regularity is a 'law' such as Ohm's Law. Notice that this kind of knowledge is completely reliant upon the existence and ubiquity of *event regularities*. These event regularities do a lot of work for scientism, but they are also its Achilles heel.

These event regularities form the basis upon which predictions or hypotheses are formulated and tested. Predictions are arrived at *inductively*, that is to say, they are based on researchers observing that event X is regularly succeeded by event Y, thereby allowing them to predict that the next time X occurs, Y is likely to follow. Testing a hypothesis means testing a prediction about what researchers think will happen to the magnitude of one variable (e.g. productivity) when the magnitude of another variable (e.g. the composition of a team) changes. The key point is that predictions and hypotheses are derived from, and dependent upon, *regularities* between events (as variables). Henceforth, we will generalise and style regularities between events as 'whenever event X then event Y'.

According to critical realists, however, event regularities occur only in specific systems called *closed systems*. Closed systems are characterised by event regularities and open systems are characterised by a lack of such regularity. The car radiator mentioned above is an example of a closed system, as is a hi-fi system. A change in the volume control of the hi-fi (event X) is regularly conjoined with a change in volume (event Y). Whilst empirical researchers on the HRM–P link never state matters in this way, they nevertheless implicitly presuppose that the workplace wherein an HRM practice is implemented (event X), and changes in performance occur (event Y), is a closed system. Whilst event regularities and closed systems are fundamental to scientism, the deductive method and empirical research on the HRM–P link, they are exceptionally rare phenomena. There appear to be very few spontaneously occurring closed systems in the natural world, and virtually none in the social world. There are, however, compelling reasons to reject the idea that the social world is a closed system. We offer a priori, empirical and practical evidence to support our claim.

Whilst empirical researchers on the HRM–P link cannot be totally unaware of problems involved with quantification, their commitment to scientism encourages them to turn a blind eye. Indeed, when questioned about the problems of quantifying qualitative things, the usual replies are: 'well it's the best we can do' or 'well how would *you* measure it' – and our answer is simple: 'we wouldn't try to measure it'. Given the range of phenomena that has been measured, many empirical researchers clearly presume that (virtually) anything can be measured with sufficiently sophisticated measuring instruments and proxies. Indeed, the nostrum 'if it cannot be measured, it cannot be managed' has its origin in the idea of the ubiquity of quantification. Empirical research on the HRM–P link is, of course, based upon quantification and measurement. Yet most of the important features of HRM practices and organisational performance are *naturally qualitative, inherently complex, multidimensional, evolving and often subjective*. The basic problem, as we see it, is that whilst much of the social world can often (albeit with great difficulty) be understood, it often *cannot* be measured, at least not *meaningfully* measured. Taking naturally qualitative, inherently complex, multidimensional, evolving and often subjective phenomena and reducing them to the single dimension of a variable so that they can be measured, means they are emptied of virtually all meaning. Commitment to scientism and the deductivist method, with their imperative to quantify and measure, forecloses non-quantitative avenues of investigation and analysis. Is it really possible to *meaningfully* measure something as complex as (say) organisational culture by asking people to respond to a Likert Scale of 1–5?

Chapter 5

This chapter shows that empirical research on the HRM–P link is characterised by a preoccupation with prediction to the neglect of explanation; serious confusion surrounding, and between, the concepts of prediction and explanation; and a lack of clarity vis-à-vis the nature and purpose of theory.

Explanation

Whilst many researchers on the HRM–P link presume they are actually explaining something, this may not be the case. This is because many of the concepts deriving from scientism *look like* explanations, but when scrutinised, are not really explanations at all. A bona fide explanation is an answer to a 'Why' question. Let us consider some of these cases.

Explanation is not 'explanation of variance'. In the lexicon of statistics, to 'explain' is to use some 'explanatory' variables to 'explain' some proportion of the variance (i.e. spread of the measured values) in another variable. Whilst this is perfectly legitimate for technical use, it does not translate well from this technical context. Such an 'explanation' does not actually explain *why* the 'explanatory' variables account for this proportion of variance. That is, it does not provide an account of the actual operation of the causal mechanisms that the explanatory variables are assumed to reflect.

Explanation is not statistical association. At best, a statistical association describes a state of affairs, or suggests *that* something is the case; it does not reveal *why* it is the case. Knowing *that* the overall effects of some bundle of HRM practices on organisational performance is 20 per cent does not explain *why* this might be the case.

Explanation is not regularity. We do not explain why the bus was late today by stating that it is always, or regularly, late. Neither do we explain why some bundle of HRM practices causes an increase in organisational performance by stating that this bundle of HRM practices always, or regularly, causes an increase in organisational performance.

Explanation is not prediction. Explanation is often confused with prediction but prediction does not constitute explanation. Even in those cases where successful prediction can be made (almost never in the social world), it is often possible to predict *without explaining anything at all.* Whilst doctors can predict the onset of measles following the emergence of Koplik spots, the latter does not explain measles. An adequate explanation of measles would involve an account of underlying causal mechanisms such as the virus that causes both the spots and the illness. Similarly even if we could predict that organisational performance would increase following the introduction of some bundle of HRM practices, the regression equation used to make the prediction would not contain the explanation and we would simply be left asking: why?

Unfortunately, research on the HRM–P link, rooted as it is in scientism, remains committed to many, if not all, of these concepts. They *look like* explanations, but when looked at closely, turn out not to be bona fide explanations at all.

Chapter 6

Chapter 6 changes key as we shift from using critical realism in critical mood to offering it as a potentially more fruitful philosophy of science with which to investigate the effects of HRM on organisational performance. Let us start with what, for critical realists, is the keystone: ontology.

Critical realists claim the social world is not only *open* (as we have seen) but also *layered* and *transformational.* It is *layered* in the sense that it consists not only of actual and observed events, such as changes in HRM practices and changes in organisational performance, but of a series of underlying structures and mechanisms. Underneath the events we see are a set of structures and mechanisms we often do not see. These structures and mechanisms, when set in motion by human beings, or 'agents', give rise to the events we observe. In open systems like the workplace, these structures and mechanisms are in operation alongside many other structures and mechanisms and often have complicated effects. If we think of team working and performance-related pay as underlying structures and mechanisms, then not every instance of team working causes an increase in organisational performance, because team working may be (negatively) influenced by individual performance-related pay – or by some other factor.

The social world is also thought to be *transformational* in the sense that these structures and mechanisms are only reproduced and transformed via the activity of agents. These structures and mechanisms enable and constrain agents' actions but, importantly, do not determine these actions. In this agency-structure framework, neither agency nor structure are privileged or ignored, and both must be fully explored before we can claim to be offering a bona fide explanation.

Critical realists reject the notion of causality as event regularities (i.e. where X is said to cause Y, when event Y regularly follows event X) in favour of a notion of causality as the exercise powers. Most things have powers which enable certain outcomes, but not others. Water has the power to slake thirst but not prevent sunburn. Humans have the power to hold a conversation and plant crops, but not read people's minds or levitate. Bureaucratic organisations have the power to handle downward information flows, but not upward flows. The powers possessed by phenomena make them causally efficacious. Causal powers (not event regularities) are the basic components of causality. Whilst many phenomena have causal powers, we are particularly interested in the powers of human beings and the powers of HR practices.

Critical realists use the notion of *tendency* to replace scientism's notion of law-like event regularity. Many empirical researchers probably have a notion of tendency in mind which involves some kind of rough and ready event regularity. For critical realists the term 'tendency' does not refer to an outcome, result or pattern qua events, which is precisely what a rough and ready event regularity would refer to. Rather the term 'tendency' refers to the *force* that causes some outcome, result or pattern. Metaphorically speaking, a force drives, propels, pushes, thrusts, asserts pressure and so on, and whether or not this results in some outcome, result or pattern of events, the force must be differentiated from its effects. Now, to write that a causal phenomenon P, has a tendency to Q, does not mean that it will Q.

In an open system, one phenomenon does not exist in isolation from other phenomena, rather there is usually a multiplicity of phenomena each with their own tendencies – and counter-tendencies. And these tendencies and counter-tendencies converge in some space–time location. Understanding the relation between a causal phenomenon and its tendency, then, requires us to understand that the phenomenon does not always bring about certain effects, but it *always tends to*. If a person has a tendency to play music, the tendency does not vanish the moment they put down their instrument.

Social entities such as organisations, workplaces, departments, work-teams or whatever, exist as configurations of components that endow them with powers and tendencies. A workplace consists of a configuration of social structures, mechanisms, institutions, rules, conventions, resources and (non-human) powers. Entities usually do whatever it is they do, not in virtue of any individual component, but in virtue of the *interaction* of all constituent components – not to mention external causal factors, but we leave them out of the picture for the moment. A string quartet generates a piece of music in virtue of the interaction of, for example, violins, viola and cello. The term we use to refer to the entity as a whole is a *causal configuration*. This insight is, of course, recognised in the concept of synergy.

It is causal configuration, then, that generate tendencies and these tendencies can counteract, or augment, one another in complex ways. The causal configuration that constitutes a work-team with the tendency to resist control, co-exists simultaneously with the configuration that constitutes a management team with the tendency to assert control. The outcome, however, depends upon the relative strengths of the tendencies. To know what tendencies and counter-tendencies are in operation, we need to know the make up of the causal configuration that generates it.

Causality and explanation

It is possible to identify two conceptions of causality, which we call *thin* (which we reject) and *thick* (which we accept). It is also possible to identify two corresponding conceptions of explanation, which we call *thin* (which we reject) and *thick* (which we accept). It is, furthermore, possible to 'map', as it were, the two conceptions of explanation to the two conceptions of causality. *Thin* causality maps onto *thin explanation* and *thick* causality maps onto *thick explanation*.

Let us consider *thin causality* and *thin explanation*. Providing a causal history, or account, of a phenomenon, and hence explaining it, could be interpreted to mean providing knowledge simply about the event(s) that preceded it. We refer to this notion of explanation as *thin*. Thin explanation is based upon thin causality, as explanation is reduced merely to providing knowledge about a succession of events. If and when causality is thin, something like the explanation of a lamp's illumination simply requires knowledge that 'a finger flicked a switch'. Any further information about the finger, the switch, or anything else, adds no more information than is necessary and is, therefore, superfluous. If this can be said to constitute an explanation at all, then it is a very weak one: indeed most of us would not even recognise this as a bona fide explanation, because it would simply leave us asking: why? It would be a curious 'explanation' indeed that left us with little or no *understanding* of the phenomenon it purported to explain.

Now let us consider *thick causality* and *thick explanation*. Providing a causal history of a phenomenon, and hence explaining it, could be interpreted to mean providing knowledge about the underlying mechanisms and structures, along with (if we are dealing with social phenomena) the human agents that reproduce and transform these mechanisms and structures. That is, explanation could be based upon thick causality. If and when causality is complex, then explanation of the lamp's illumination does not reduce to merely providing knowledge about a succession of events but rather requires knowledge about the wider conflux of interacting causal phenomena. Knowledge about the nature of the glass, the gas, the filament, the wire, the switch, the plug, the electricity, as well as the finger that flicked the switch and the intentions of the human whose finger it is, all add to the richness of the explanation and are, therefore, not superfluous but absolutely necessary. There is little doubt that most of us would recognise this immediately as constituting a very rich, robust or thick explanation as it would (at the very least go some way to) answer the question: why?

To exemplify *thick causality* and *thick explanation* in context, consider how we might robustly explain an increase in productivity following the introduction of teamworking. A thick explanation would demand two kinds of knowledge. First, it requires what we might call *hermeneutic* knowledge. That is, knowledge relating to a range of human cognitive activities such as understanding, intention, purpose, meaning, interpretation, reasons and so on, borrowed from the *verstehen* tradition in sociology. Hermeneutics is the discipline concerned with phenomena like these. Notice that gaining access to this kind of qualitative, hermeneutic knowledge is impossible via the quantitative, empirical, statistical techniques used in empirical research on the HRM–P link. Second, a thick explanation requires knowledge about a significant (but not infinite) set of interacting causal phenomena through which agents initiate this action. This might, for example, include information on: the social, political, economic and spatial environment of the industry and/or the firm; the industrial relations system; the composition of the team; the experiences and wishes of individuals comprising the team; the nature of the new jobs, tasks and skills (if any); the relationship between team members; the relationship between team members and line managers, and between both of these and corporate strategy; the nature of control in the firm; the nature of any synergies (or dis-synergies) created by the interaction of these causal phenomena and so on. Whilst this is far easier said than done, simply finding a statistical association between teamworking and productivity does not deliver an explanation at all.

The objective of the *causal-explanatory method* is to *explain*, and it does so by providing a thick *causal* history. The result is a causal-explanatory theory or account based on explanation (which encapsulates human understanding) not prediction. Most researchers, indeed most HRM stakeholders, are likely to balk at the prospect of abandoning the goal of prediction. The *desire* to (inductively) predict, however laudable, cannot be transformed into the *ability* to predict if the social world lacks event regularities – i.e. is an open system. Whilst we share the desire to make practical recommendations, we are steadfastly unwilling to reject the logic of our conclusions. There is, however, a way out of this seeming dilemma. And the key lies with explanation.

Explanation, and by this we mean *thick* explanation, can guide practice: indeed, it is probably our only guide to practice in open systems. To the extent that we can successfully uncover the underlying structures and mechanisms that, along with the actions of agents, causally govern workplace performance (and there is no denying the difficulty of this) we have a theory that explains this phenomena. To the extent we have a theory and an explanation, we have knowledge of the tendencies and counter-tendencies in operation. To the extent that we have knowledge of these tendencies and counter-tendencies, we can make (fallible) judgments about workplace performance. Whilst we hesitate to call this a prediction because it is not an *inductive* prediction of any kind, it is nevertheless a prediction, albeit one driven by explanatory power, rooted in tendencies and heavily qualified. Reluctantly, and in the absence of an alternative, we call it a *tendential prediction*. HR professionals and trade union representatives frequently have to make (fallible) judgment calls like this. They constantly have to judge whether any change in HRM practices will result in a tendency to increase organisational performance, a tendency to improve pay and conditions of workers or whatever. That they are able to make judgment calls of this nature, even if they are fallible ones, implies that they have some explanation of the way the workplace operates. In other words, they operate on the basis of tendencies and tendential predictions, not law-like regularities and inductive predictions.

In sum, then, critical realism offers an alternative to scientism. If only a small part of the army of empirical researchers hunting for a statistical association between HRM practices and organisational performance stopped trying to 'hunt the Snark' and started considering alternative philosophical approaches, it would only take a few years to know whether or not alternatives like critical realism are any better – they certainly cannot be any worse.

With this alternative end in mind, Chapter 7 brings the book to its final part, and to a conclusion with empirical insights drawn from our research with senior HR professionals and their executive colleagues in their organisations. It is not the purpose of this final chapter to demonstrate how professionals in organisations view their organisational experiences through the lens of meta-theory. What we do achieve, however, is a demonstration of how the alternative ontology of critical realism sits more 'comfortably' with the descriptions by executives of organisational life in general, and complex causality in particular.

In short, individual managers and researchers have explored and applied their knowledge through a process of first, retroduction, and then second, retrodiction. What is striking about the daily experiences of many HR professionals are their experiences of circumnavigating the processes used to manage the metrics used to 'measure' their interventions to introduce the mechanisms their experience has taught them works, not simply in a pragmatic way, but because they have a basic understanding of why it works. It soon becomes apparent that where the quantum form of performance data ends, the process of explanation and understanding begins.

We combine the poetic praxeology of Hari Tsoukas with the internal conversation and critical realism of Margaret Archer to enable us to acknowledge the complicated motives of human action and its dialectical and temporal development on the one hand, whilst acknowledging the relativity and reflexivity of human intentionality captured by Archer's notion of the internal conversation on the other.

A key process in our fieldwork has been the development of what Archer calls 'reflexive determination', to which we give a slight twist and refer to as 'reflexive performance'. Reflexive performance is a specific case of reflexive determination, where agents reflect specifically upon some aspect of their performance, or the performance of others. Indeed, Archer recognises this, referring to 'our performative achievement in the practical order' (2003: 120) as one of humanity's key concerns. We incorporate what are labelled 'predicates' (e.g. thinking, deliberating, believing, loving, etc.) into the reflexive processes engaged in by individuals when deliberating over some specific personal or agential project.

This reflexive determination represents the personal process by which individuals identify the enablements and constraints of social structure, and link them to *their* agency. For Archer, some social structures enable or constrain the execution of particular processes. The key to reflexive performance, therefore, is identifying the structures and mechanisms deemed to enable or constrain wider organisational performance and constructing personal emergent properties to formulate strategies and processes to use them to pursue their personal goals. Reflexive determination, or reflexive performance, affords two critical observations in examining the HRM–P link: namely, the *transfactuality* of HR practices and their impact upon wider organisational performance, and, second, the *contingency*, and hence *variability*, in the capacity of certain HR practices to generate the outcomes expected.

Drawing on our fieldwork, we contextualise and illustrate how the various building blocks of critical realism can be used by researchers to open up a deeper ontology of reflexive performance. The reader will see at work tendencies, structures, mechanisms and how an entire conflux of interacting causal phenomena operate in a more complex form: what we label *complex causality*. From this we then move to explain how it is open systems are both tendential – certain outcomes cannot always be predicted in a scientistic form, but we can begin to uncover and explain why certain processes generate certain outcomes (and not others) and how the influences of social structures, institutions, mechanisms, rules, resources etc. that human agents draw upon in order to initiate action, *can* be *retroduced* and their operation uncovered and ultimately *explained*.

Conclusion

We hope that after reading *Explaining the Performance of Human Resource Management*, readers will come to realise that empirical research on the HRM–P link not only has some serious shortcomings, but also that these shortcomings are unlikely to be easily resolved. Indeed their roots go deep into scientistic philosophy of science, the deductive method, and the quantitative, empirical, statistical research techniques that scientism encourages. We hope that, with the appetite whetted, some HR practitioners may now be tempted to cast an eye over Chapters 3, 4 and 5. They are not an 'easy read', but they are no more difficult than chapters found in any introductory book on the use of statistical methods.

As we have stated above, for many HR stakeholders, what follows will verge on the heretical. The HR department has spent the best part of thirty years trying to establish its credibility in the eyes of executives leading other departments within our major organisations. Our view, as will become clear as we move through our argument, is that much of what we read about HR's capacity to drive the performance of organisations falls victim to what we have named after one of our least favourite management contacts, *Lambért's Law*.

Lambért's Law celebrates proof over intuition, the general over the particular, stability over fluidity, the abstract over concrete experience and, above all else, the (alleged scientific) logic over the narrative of verisimilitude. Lambért's Law requires – nay, demands – straightforward language that all managers can understand. Lambért's Law labels the complex as gobbledegook. This is the reduction and dilution of the rich, albeit complex, world of talent and its management to simple and clear formula, the kind of deductivistic reasoning that leads HR directors – and perhaps more importantly their colleagues round the boardroom table, if they are indeed *at* the table – to think if we invest x in our people, we can look forward to y in return. Only y is rarely reported, and boardrooms, the business media and wider stakeholders are beginning to ask why.

Our principle aim, then, in writing *Explaining the Performance of Human Resource Management* is to help all involved in understanding how people – *not* the HR department itself – enable the performance of their organisations. If, by demonstrating how many executives do not actually use 'scientistic' methods but their own reflexive deliberations to understand and explain the performance of their people, we will have achieved this Herculean task.

2 | Tracking the emergence of the HRM–P link paradigm

[T]hose who still wait for a Newton are not only waiting for a train that won't arrive, they're in the wrong station altogether.

(Giddens 1975: 13)

And still they wait. The information boards on the HRM–P station announce long delays, and yet those passengers advocating the measurement of the HRM–P link continue to wait on their platforms for the *'train of science'* to arrive. The train has yet to emerge from a very long and dark tunnel in which the entrance and exit are clearly visible, but the train has somehow lost its way in the 'black box' in between. Meanwhile, on platforms across the station, there are additional passengers fully expecting to board the train. At one platform they are not at all concerned. They saw the train enter the blackness of the tunnel at one end, and they have observed that their platform is clearly in line with the track exiting the tunnel at the other end; and because this regularly occurs, they predict the imminent arrival of the train. Not so far away at another platform, passengers are aware of the delay but have deduced from the complexity of tracks around their platform that the train will eventually reach them – even if they are not sure how or when. On another platform they have resorted to a 'safety in numbers' approach and concluded that given so many passengers are waiting for trains on other platforms, they cannot all be mistaken about the train eventually arriving ... can they? Word of the delay has, however, spread to other platforms where they suspect the train might never arrive and are making their feelings known to the station's staff. Meanwhile, a small number of passengers are leaving the station and heading for their cars and bicycles. They already know the train of 'science' is never going to arrive.

In this chapter we provide an account of the emergence of the academic and practitioner 'platforms' or methods of research devoted to examining the link between HRM and organisational performance.

Our starting point is one suggesting the academy's insistence on adopting a 'scientific' approach to establish a causal link is ultimately flawed. We explain why weaknesses in the HRM–P paradigm continue despite constant iterations of the examination of the 'causal chain' between HR and organisational performance. We conclude the chapter by suggesting what has been described as the quest for the Holy Grail of the HR field represents nothing more than an empirical wild goose chase. An alternative perspective is required if academic researchers, consultants and even HR practitioners are to be saved from themselves and their quest for that which ultimately does not exist in the material form that they seek.

The appliance of science

We have previously made no secret of our frustrations at the serious meta-theoretical problems underpinning the HRM–P link paradigm (e.g. Fleetwood and Hesketh 2004, 2006, 2008; Hesketh and Fleetwood 2006a and 2006b). Moreover, this meta-theoretical shortfall is not limited to our particular focus of study. The management field as a whole is predicated on a commitment to the 'scientific' or, as we prefer to call it, 'scientistic' approach which we think is fundamentally and irreparably flawed. What makes this all the more frustrating from our perspective is the continuing insistence of the academy to leave its collective head firmly inserted in the meta-theoretical sand. This is the case despite (most)[1] academics themselves being aware not just of the theoretical and meta-theoretical limitations brought about by their scientism (see, for example, Bennis and O'Toole 2005; Clegg and Ross-Smith 2003; Ghoshal 2005), but also their awareness of an apparent research–practice gap, which manifests itself in the lack of demand from practitioners for their 'best available scientific evidence' (Rynes *et al.* 2007: 1001). HR practitioners, it seems, do not want what is on offer from the academy. We think this research–practice gap is very revealing.

Let us take some time to reflect upon this gap via a recent special edition of *The Academy of Management Journal* devoted to exploring the research–practice gap in HRM (Rynes *et al.* 2007). 'It's hardly news', remarks the special edition's editor and colleagues in the opening article, 'that many organizations do not implement practices that research has shown to be positively associated with employee productivity and firm financial performance [and it] has been observed in nearly every field ... there is separation between those who conduct research and those who are in a position to implement research findings' (Rynes *et al.* 2007: 987). It is worth remarking that the authors in the special edition like to collectively refer to themselves as being engaged in 'science'.

A whole host of possible reasons as to why practitioners do not often take academic research into consideration are offered by each of the ten articles comprising the special issue. Not one of them, however, even contemplates the possibility that the problem might lie with the meta-theoretical claims made by the swathes of empirical 'science' each contributor cites. 'Science', it appears, is not at fault. Instead, the fault is placed firmly at the door of practitioners who consume the snake oil of consultants, or aimed at the unscientific, 'bridging' publications which unite research and practice such as the *Harvard Business Review*, which, we are told, need 'to move towards a higher level of sophistication' (Rynes *et al.* 2007: 987).

Cascio (2007: 1009) suggests that 'academics, consultants, and journalists live in different "thought worlds"', and hardly contributes to a reduction in hostilities between the opposing camps with his observation, 'practices that academics regard as technically meritorious are sometimes not adopted [because] managers frame HR practices as matters of administrative style rather than as technical innovations [and] as a result, they may choose technically ineffective HR interventions'. This observation will hardly ingratiate academic science to HR practitioners, even if Cascio's other observations regarding the over-emphasis on technical solutions by academics and the realities of organisational politics for managers overshadowing technical merit might well resonate with HR professionals.

The primary reason for the research–practice gap lies, then, in the inability of 'science' to compete effectively with consultants, who, 'without the best available evidence, will continue to baffle and not [be] a conduit between organizational science and practice' (Rousseau 2007: 1041). Consultants, they suggest, are incapable of carrying out their own research to a requisite level. Moreover, moving beyond the snake oil offered by consultants will only happen 'when the quality of our research evidence is made more evident to practitioners' (Rousseau 2007: 1041). If only practitioners would seek, so the logic goes, they would then find the truth laid before them by the 'scientists' of the academy.

There are various strategies for revealing these truths. One is a request for more work illustrating how 'one approach is X percent [better] than that of those selected by another and that this has a financial benefit of X dollars' (Lawler 2007: 1035). The common strategy, however, seems to be to call for more 'science'. One contributor to the special edition (Saari 2007), a consultant, no less, suspects that there is a 'nugget of relevant findings for the HR practitioner' in academic work, but it is buried so deep it is hard to find. This criticism notwithstanding, she goes on to ask for more science in her request for additional research in areas in which 'the most powerful and clear-cut ROI can be shown for organizations' (2007: 1043). Another practitioner also puts in a request for additional science, whilst at the same time revealing an apparent inability to spare the time to consult a business textbook written during the last decade with her prescription that, 'textbooks should be steeped in scientific evidence but written for the average student; they should include insights from practitioners as well as scholarly information' (Cohen 2007: 1018). We can almost hear the collective sigh of disbelief emanating from the publishing houses of Prentice Hall, Thomson, Wiley and Harvard Business School Press.

Peppered throughout the special edition are references to the superiority of academic theory and, most notably, 'science'. 'There is nothing', we are reminded, 'so practical as good theory', although what constitutes 'good theory' is left tantalisingly undefined by all of the ten articles comprising the special edition. Moreover, as we will show in what follows, one of the problems facing empirical researchers on the HRM–P link is not that there are too few theories, but that there are too many: a veritable embarrassment of riches. One suggestion is that the 'key strength of our field is our ability to conduct empirical research' (Latham 2007: 1029). Echoing another matter we discuss below, Rynes (2007) argues that better theory is to come from more empirical, perhaps 'bigger' science. Indeed, more of the same is very much the order of the day. Only David Guest raises doubts about the approach with his call for HRM researchers to 'not forget that evidence in the social sciences is always likely to be contested [and that]

... given the available evidence, evidence-based practice in HR management may be a step too ambitious' (2007: 1025).

Such an observation is clearly not entertained by Rynes, who pulls together the observations of her colleagues in a final article making no fewer than twenty-six recommendations (see Rynes 2007: 1047, Table 1). None heeds Guest's warning call, nor contains a request for an adequate definition of what constitutes a theory explaining how HRM affects organisations. Indeed, and flying in the face of what we will argue later, Rynes even goes as far as to suggest the field should 'relax theory requirements' (2007: 1047, Table 1)!

Crucially, a final suggestion from the editor as to one possible future course for the academy is to employ alternative methods such as case studies and ethnography. Such methods, she suggests, are more likely to resonate with practitioners, more likely to capture the complexities of organisational life and more likely to reveal the dynamics sitting behind what are at first the counter-intuitive findings of quantitative analysis (cf. Rynes 2007: 1048). What this appears to ignore, however, is the fact that methods such as these are avoided in empirical research on the HRM–P link because they are seen as 'unscientific' in the sense that they do not make use of the usual empirical, quantitative, statistical techniques. One commentator understands this clearly. The problem lies with *the appliance of science* as it were, in which 'we have adopted the "scientific" approach of trying to discover patterns and laws, and have replaced all notions of human intentionality with a firm belief in causal determinism for explaining all aspects of corporate performance' (Ghoshal 2005: 77).

Our primary claim in *Explaining the Performance of Human Resource Management* is that it does not have to be this way. In the following chapters we will be articulating how research in business and management more widely, and in the paradigm of the HRM–P link in particular, can move out of the shadows of 'science' into alternative forms of explanation and inquiry. But before we can suggest ways out of the mess in which the paradigm now finds itself, we want to reflect on how we got into this mess in the first place, and this requires a succinct overview of the history of empirical research on the HRM–P link. This overview will also serve another purpose. It will show that despite the evolution of slightly different approaches, they all share a basic commitment to the general idea that a statistically demonstrable link exists between HRM practices and organisational performance. In the next section we use the metaphors of Russian dolls, Rubik's Cubes and black boxes to consider the three basic approaches to empirical research on the HRM–P link well known to researchers within the field, namely, the Contingency, Configurational and Universalistic approaches. It is at these platforms where passengers continue to wait for the train of 'science'.

Russian dolls, Rubik's Cubes and black boxes

Wind the clock back to 1981. Charles marries Diana, the first space shuttle, Columbia, launches, and Harvard Business School does something it has not done for twenty years: it introduces a new course. This new programme, the first since managerial economics was introduced in the 1960s, is in the groundbreaking area of human resource management (see Beer *et al.* 1984; Walton and Lawrence 1985).

Armed with the benefit of hindsight Beer *et al.*'s *Managing Human Assets* was strikingly advanced. At its heart were the four Cs of *commitment* – captured in the contemporary debate over discretionary effort or engagement; *competence* – underlined by the debate now taking place over talent and human capital management; *congruence* – which has grown into the debate over strategic human resources management and; *cost effectiveness* – where measuring the return on investment to human resources was first mooted, and where a quarter of a century later, the debate over how best to capture the ROI to human resources still continues.

It was a debate Beer and his colleagues had seen coming. 'The 4Cs', they informed us, 'do not provide managers with actual measurement methods and data for assessing the effects of their firm's HRM policies. These methods are numerous, and they differ depending on the level of analysis chosen' (Beer *et al.* 1984: 19–20). All the warning signs to HRM–P link scholars were there, be it in the form of phrases such as 'cost effectiveness may appear to be easier to measure, but that appearance can be deceiving', or 'accounting efforts, while potentially very useful, have fallen short of their promise' (Beer *et al.* 1984: 20–1). With unerring prophecy, the answers to the problems of measurement were also included:

In the final analysis, assessment of HRM outcomes is a matter of judgement informed by data from a variety of sources and in a variety of forms (qualitative and quantitative) and evaluated by various stakeholders. (Beer *et al.* 1984: 21)

This of course did not preclude researchers from beginning the quest for the Holy Grail of establishing the *causal* link between HRM and performance. Within months of the publication of the Harvard texts, researchers were already building on Walton and Lawrence's (1985) high commitment work systems and 'extending the personnel function well beyond the limits of its traditional activities ... to stake a claim on the strategic planning process, arguing that participation in the "front end" of business planning is essential to meeting the long-run needs of the enterprise' (Miles and Snow 1984: 36–7). And so the Contingency School within the HRM–P link paradigm was born.

The Russian dolls of the Contingency School

Staying with Raymond Miles and Charles Snow, the Contingency School's approach to the HRM–P link can be neatly summed up by their prescription that 'essentially, we argue that the human resources management system must be tailored to the demands of business strategy' (1984: 37). Two versions of the Contingency School rapidly emerged. One, which we have already alluded to, originated in Harvard and extolled the virtues of aligning human resource management into a coherent whole that meshes with other aspects of the firm's operations (Beer *et al.* 1984: 177). For the Harvard, or 'soft', school of HRM (Legge 2005), managing certain human resources would 'enhance the performance of the organization [through] the well being of employees' (Beer *et al.* 1984: 19).

Another mode of thought within the Contingency School, which has grown to dominate thinking during the last three decades, originated out of Michigan. Whilst the developmental humanism of Harvard was recognised, writers from the alternative, or what Karen Legge (1995) refers to as the "hard", school of HRM suggested the alternative of focusing 'on human resources management in terms of its strategic role in both the formulation and the implementation of long-run plans' (Tichy *et al.* 1982: 47). Significantly, moving away from the wellbeing of employees per se, the strategic debate of human resources became one in which 'clearly, the dependent variable is performance: the human resource elements are designed to impact performance at both the individual and the organizational levels'. It is worth citing the Michigan School's wrapping of performance around what they called the Human Resource Cycle in full:

Performance, in other words, is a function of all the human resource components: selecting people who are best able to perform the jobs defined by structure; motivating employees by rewarding them judiciously; training and developing employees for future performance; and appraising employees in order to justify the rewards. In addition, performance is a function of the organizational context and resources surrounding the individual. Thus strategy and structure also impact performance through the ways jobs are designed, through how the organization is structured, and through how well services or products are planned to meet environmental threats and opportunities. (Tichy *et al.* 1982: 49–50)

Three additional key pillars supporting the emergence of the Contingency School's application within the HRM–P link paradigm need to be recognised. First, the theoretical construct of contingency was imported from the wider and, significantly, contemporary organisational studies of the time. The antecedents to the Contingency School can be traced back to the early statistical work of those like Mason who demonstrated how an organisation's performance was contingent upon its response to wider market conditions (Mason 1939). Second, a structural-contingency school was already well established at the beginning of the human resources management field's birth in the 1980s, which had already concluded high-performing firms appeared to adopt particular structures or combinations of differentiation and integration that were consistent with wider environmental or market demands (e.g. Burns and Stalker 1961; Lawrence and Lorsch 1967). This work was extended by writers such as Miner (1979) and Argyris (1973) who established that a tight fit between strategy and structure was essential. Third, and crucial to our main discussion, by the early 1980s writers such as Lenz were making observations that:

In general, there is sufficient evidence to conclude that structure affects performance. This stems, in part, from the administrative efficiency of structural arrangements and their impact upon human behaviour and social interaction. There is some evidence indicating the use of grossly inappropriate structure entails certain costs. *Beyond these generalizations*

the going gets tough and the need to qualify one's remarks is essential.
(Lenz 1981: 142, emphasis added)

Note the italicised section. Despite Lenz's obvious caveats, the emerging Contingency School within the HRM–P link wasted little time in 'tailoring personnel and human resource management practices to specific strategies based on employee characteristics necessary to meet strategic demands' (Schuler 1987: 1 n.b., 10, 1). Miles and Snow (1984: 43) were quick to tell us that 'the basic services provided by human resources units are well known to most organizations'. But as they went on to suggest, 'although most organizations need the services listed, the priorities assigned to each and the manner in which they are performed may, and in many instances, should, vary in accordance with the organization's strategy' (Miles and Snow 1984: 43). It was no longer *what* human resources managers did but the *way* in which they did it.

Before long, à la carte 'menus' of human resources practices and processes were on offer (Schuler 1987; Schuler and Jackson 1987a, 1987b) in which the activities of the HR department could be tightly aligned with an organisation's overarching strategy. One influential paper offered no less than twenty-four such 'menus' or propositions (Schuler 1987), effectively comprising a myriad of choices for the 'linking of human resource management with strategy' (p. 1). Matching human resources menus to organisational strategy was effectively like constructing a set of Russian dolls in which the outer doll of strategy would neatly encase the inner dolls comprising the menu of human resource components on offer. The trick was to ensure each of the dolls (human resource components) were 'integrated' in the correct order. This is effectively where the empirical hunt for the most efficient integration of human resources components began. After searching through two decades' worth of research for this publication we have still to establish what the most 'efficient integration' might be, or even how we might identify what constitutes *inefficient* integration.

It appears authors working in the Contingency School have had similar problems. Returning to Schuler and Jackson once more, 'although a fit between HRM practices and organizational strategy is likely to be more effective than a lack of fit, this remains to be empirically examined' (Schuler and Jackson 1987a: 139). Another paper by the same authors concluded, 'although only a beginning, the success of these firms [under analysis] suggests that HRM practices for all levels of employees are affected by strategic considerations' (Schuler and Jackson 1987b: 215).

A decade later, and citing what had previously been seen as subject to further 'empirical examination' and representing 'only a beginning' in terms of a suitable body of evidence, the same authors suggested that there was 'broad agreement that a strategic approach to human resources management involves designing and implementing a set of internally consistent policies and practices that ensure a firm's human capital (employees' collective knowledge, skills and abilities) contributes to the achievement of its business objectives' (Huselid *et al.* 1997: 171). Fast-forwarding another decade and the impact of the Contingency School's thinking on the performance of the human resources function remains as elusive as it is enticing. In setting out their framework for a new decision science of talent management Boudreau and Ramstad (2007: 29) allocate human resources, organisational resources and overarching business strategy into a sequential, causal chain (or Russian dolls) for talent and organisation decisions in the following order:

Investments → Programme and Practices (efficiency) → Performance of Organization Elements and Talent Pools (effectiveness) → Organization's Sustainable Strategic Success (impact)

The outer doll of impact, then, has a smaller doll within it comprising the effectiveness of the talent pools, which in turn has a smaller doll made up of the efficiency of the programme and practices put in place by the human resources function to drive the creation and performance of such talent pools. So far, so good, but how this logic aids our understanding of the role played by human resources in driving the performance of organisations is left unexplained. At the heart of Boudreau and Ramstad's logic is an assumption that human resource processes affect people and their performance in a similar way to the decision sciences comprising the finance and marketing functions. They justify this causal logic in terms of the appliance of science:

Why use the term science? Because the most successful professions have decision systems that follow scientific principles and that have a strong capacity to quickly incorporate new scientific knowledge into practical applications. Disciplines such as finance, marketing and operations not only provide leaders with frameworks and concepts that describe how those resources affect strategic success; they also reflect the findings from universities, research centres, and scholarly journals. Their decision models are compatible with the language and structure of the scholarly science that supports them. (Boudreau and Ramstad 2007: 27)

The authors are careful to circumnavigate the accusation of prescribing business leaders with yet more numbers to manage. Boudreau and Ramstad even go as far as to suggest that 'a fixation on measurement can prove to be very dysfunctional' (2007: 188). Indeed, many organisations are identified as having well-implemented human resource management measures but suffering from 'hitting a wall in HR measurement', and rarely understanding what drives true strategic change, 'despite ever more comprehensive databases, and ever more sophisticated data analysis and reporting' (2007: 189). For Boudreau and Ramstad, the other side of the measurement wall, where it would appear they imply organisations should aspire to be, is characterised by an understanding of what causes strategic impact with indicators that are valid and rigorous (Boudreau and Ramstad 2007: 189, Figure 9.1). Establishing such an analytical framework is a time-consuming process where the maturity of metrics revolving around key or 'anchor points' comprising variables in areas such as investments in human resources, systems and wider human capital. Again, so far, so good, only other researchers have adopted similar logical models and they too have hit measurement walls.

In an authoritative review of the output of the Contingency School, Becker and Huselid (1998: 65–6) suggest that 'there is surprisingly little analysis of data that would provide corroborative support for the "external fit" hypothesis', despite their expecting 'to see a strong empirical relationship between a firm's strategic choices and the nature of its HRM system'. The reasons for this lack of empirical confirmation are in part down to the 'continuing challenges of the literature', represented by 'the need to measure the actual extent to which the HRM system is embedded in the firm's operations in a way that is appropriate for that firm's particular strategic goals' (Becker and Huselid 1998: 66). The possible solutions proposed by the authors are, in their words, 'unrealistic', and remain 'a considerable obstacle'.

Other researchers have reached similar conclusions and have sought alternatives, which brings us nicely to the Configurational School.

In sum, then, despite recognition of the complex relation between the HRM system and wider corporate strategy, empirical researchers operating under the rubric of the Contingency School are still part of what we call the HRM–P paradigm. That is, they seek a link, association or empirical relation between HRM practices, in this case, when appropriately aligned or integrated with corporate strategy, and organisational performance. And they presume this link is quantifiable and measurable with appropriate metrics, and discoverable using the usual range of quantitative, empirical and statistical research techniques.

The Rubik's Cubes of the Configurational School

Like the Contingency School before it, the Configurational School had antecedents in extant wider management literature. If the 1980s were about looking externally for a fit between organisational practices and strategy, the 1990s began with a switch to the internal integration of the Configurational School. At its most elementary, 'organisational configuration' was used by researchers 'to denote any multidimensional constellation of conceptually distinct characteristics that commonly occur together' (Meyer *et al.* 1993: 1175).

Whereas contingency theory was seen as fragmented, reductionistic and largely deterministic, the configuration approach offered holistic synthesis and equifinality. The latter construct was particularly appealing to researchers within the HRM–P link paradigm: organisations had continually defied the adoption of similar or 'universal' components in their human resource practices, making claims correlating causality with performance and wider strategic enablement problematic. Suddenly, the equifinality assumption presented the opportunity to researchers for the variety of systems they encountered to be accommodated by the claim that 'a system can reach the same final state from differing initial conditions and by a variety of paths' (Katz and Kahn 1978, cited in Doty *et al.* 1993: 1201). Empirically speaking, there was now more than one way to skin a cat. Variation and complexity were no longer challenges to the longevity of the human resources department: different organisations could, and *should*, implement processes in ways to best meet their own idiosyncratic strategic and human resource needs. Similar to the solving of a Rubik's Cube, human resource components comprising employment systems could be configured and re-configured in many different ways to reach the same high (or average, or even low) performance outcomes.

The primary level of analysis for the Configuration School was the *system* of human resource components rather than examining in isolation individual practices and policies. Multiple paths of HRM systems could be evaluated, while capturing their alignment in both internal (HRM policies) and external (with wider organisational policies and goals) contexts. For Becker and Huselid (1998: 55–6) this meant that 'the focus on alignment necessarily invokes the possibilities for complementarities or synergies within an appropriately aligned system [in which] these complementarities can be positive, where "the whole is greater than the sum of the parts," or negative, where elements of the system conflict (internally or externally) and actually destroy value rather than create value'. With this logical deduction in place, the search for empirical models to discover the optimal configuration of human resource components began in earnest.

Opening up such variation to analysis meant that the Configuration School correspondingly opened up a significant opportunity for researchers in the HRM–P link paradigm to dovetail with the emerging debate in the 1990s over the resource-based view (RBV) originally articulated by Barney (1991). A distinction could now be made between an emerging *behavioural* perspective represented by the Contingent School, suggesting how competitive advantage lay in adopting the right human resource processes to acquire, develop and retain the requisite human capital for existing strategy, and the new *resource-based view of the firm* which combined the *internal* analysis of hard-to-replicate, if not unique, components and activities in organisations with the analysis of their *external* and competitive environments. Critically, the RBV recognised how 'no two companies [or their HR systems] are alike because no two companies have the same set of experiences, acquired the same assets and skills, or built the same organizational cultures' (Collis and Montgomery 1995: 119).

By the close of the 1990s three major pieces of work had been completed exploring the contribution of configurational theory to the HRM–P link paradigm. By far the most heavily cited HRM–P link paper in the Configurational School is that by Delery and Doty (1996). This in part stems from Doty's particular contribution to theorising within the wider literature devoted to configurational theory (e.g. Doty and Glick 1994; Doty *et al.* 1993). Notwithstanding this pivotal role in theory-building, the centrality of the Delery and Doty paper to the Configurational School is all the more perplexing when the three separate hypotheses developed within the paper to 'operation-alise' the configurational nature of human resource systems support the null hypothesis in each case (see Delery and Doty 1996: 823–5). In what amounts to an empirical scraping of the bottom of the bar-rel, the authors suggest an alternative, more parsimonious configur-ational theory for a single, more advanced type of employment system than others (cf. Delery and Doty 1996: 824). A statistically significant difference was at last found between the so-called market (advanced high-performance work systems) and internal (implied to be less advanced) employment systems concepts introduced by the authors when hierarchical regressions with Return on Assets (ROA) and Return on Equity (ROE) were run. This final test enabled the authors to claim 'the configurational results suggest that some configurations of HR practices are better than others', although they were quick to point out that their 'interpretations of the configurational results are the most speculative ... and thus, we cannot make strong arguments that synergy among HR practices under investigation enhance organ-izational performance' (Delery and Doty 1996: 827). Despite this important caveat, the paper is routinely cited (if not read) as evidence for the impact of configurational or internal best fit models on organ-isational performance by different types of human resource systems (e.g. Paauwe 2004).

A second paper investigated 'the hypothesis that "bundles" of inter-related and internally consistent HR practices, rather than individual practices, are the appropriate unit of analysis for studying the link to performance, because they create the multiple, mutually reinforcing conditions that support employee motivation and skills acquisition' (MacDuffie 1995: 198). Central to this analysis was the claim that the combination of human resource practices into bundles offered a better explanation of how managers and employees interacted within organisations to affect high performance. In order to validate the bundles in question three tests were used. Five out of the seven stand-ardised reliability scores were lower than conventional acceptance standards, although as is convention in the HRM–P link paradigm when Cronbach alpha scores are low, they are simply reported, not commented on (see MacDuffie 1995: 210). A second validation method, namely factor analysis, revealed the emergence of strong factors, 'but each factor combined variables ... in ways that were not readily interpretable' (MacDuffie 1995: 210). A third instrument, cluster analysis, did apparently underpin statistically distinct clusters but the author decided not to report these crucial data. These limitations notwithstanding, the combination of data on bundles of work practices with independent data obtained from manufacturing plans on quality and productivity led MacDuffie to conclude that 'these results provide the strongest statistical evidence to date of a positive relationship between innovative human resource practices and economic performance' (1995: 218).

A third paper effectively represented the taking of an econometric hammer to a theoretical or logical nut in order to establish that 'out of 78 possible bivariate correlations among the 13 HRM variables listed, 71 are positive and 48 are positive and [statistically] significant' (Ichniowski *et al.* 1997: 295). Dazzling econometric analysis was deployed using a vast array of impressive financial data to uncover empirical nuggets such as, 'workers' performance is substantially better under incentive pay plans that are coupled with supporting innovative work practices – such as flexible job design, employee participation in problem-solving teams, training to provide workers with multiple skills, extensive screening and communication, and employment security' (Ichniowski *et al.* 1997: 311–12). What human resource executives already knew had now become empirical fact. Very few executives could make sense of the befuddling array of statistical analyses contained in the paper but nobody in human resources was going to challenge the 'scientificity' of an econometric model which 'shows that innovative HRM practices raise worker productivity' (Ichniowski *et al.* 1997: 311). A new mandate for human resources, to paraphrase the subtitle of one well-known book of the same year, had been offered to a grateful HR department.

The primary problem of the Configurational School lies in the unsophisticated notion of causality assumed to be at work in different high-performance work practices. The starkest version of this critique reduces the statistical differences detected between the 'impact' of different working systems to nothing more than the mathematical equivalent of reading patterns in tea leaves (see Fleetwood and Hesketh 2008). More sympathetic critiques point to the wild variations in which work systems are investigated and the problems associated with using subjective perceptions of employees as proxies for organisational performance (Legge 2005). For example, Stavrou and Brewster label as 'business performance' a subjective measure that turns out to be nothing more than 'the perceptions of study participants as to the performance of their organization in comparison with that of other competitors' (2005: 191). Similarly, Perry-Smith and Blum (2000: 1110) also use a performance proxy they describe as 'a four-item measure (α = .85) of perceived market performance assessed relative to that of other firms and includes items related to marketing and market share'. Note here the spurious scientificity, masquerading as something far more important in the form of the alpha scores (α) which are, when all is said and done, merely an expression of subjective perceptions. Moving beyond the confines of subjectivity represented the central challenge to the HRM–P link paradigm. Which brings us to the Universalistic School.

In sum, then, despite recognition of the complex relation between the HRM practices themselves, empirical researchers operating under the rubric of the Configurational School are still part of what we call the HRM–P paradigm. That is, they seek a link, association or empirical relation between bundles of HRM practices when (horizontally) integrated or aligned with one another, and organisational performance. And they presume this link is quantifiable and measurable with appropriate metrics, and discoverable using the usual range of quantitative, empirical and statistical research techniques.

The black box of the Universalistic School

Despite the observation by Beer and colleagues, alluded to above, that human resources and high-performance work systems did not lend themselves to accounting measures, a number of researchers have sought to relentlessly pursue this Holy Grail of the HRM–P link. Most of the empirical crusades have been conducted in the regions of establishing a causal link between certain common or 'universalistic' human resource components or 'best practices' and the financial bottom line of the organisation. This represents an extension of the work by Pfeffer (1994) who made the simple observation that 'what successful firms tend to have in common is that for their sustained advantage, they rely not on technology, patents, or strategic position, but on how they manage their workforce' (Pfeffer 2005: 96). Pfeffer went on to identify thirteen specific workforce management techniques that have become largely the foundation stones of modern human resource department architectures. It is these same practices that have been subjected to continuing empirical scrutiny from both the Contingency and Configurational Schools (e.g. Kinnie *et al.* 2005; Perry-Smith and Blum 2000; Stavrou and Brewster 2005). Pfeffer certainly advocated the measurement of the implementation of these activities, largely because of his recognition of the political ramifications of not being seen to capture the contribution to organisational performance made by HR:

In a world in which financial results are measured, a failure to measure human resource policy and practice implementation dooms this to second class status, oversight, neglect, and potential failure. (Pfeffer 2005: 104)

But Pfeffer also added several words of caution. Like those researchers before him, Pfeffer was quick to acknowledge that 'which practice is critical does depend in part on the company's particular technology and market strategy' (Pfeffer 1995: 104). Implementation issues were also seen to be potentially highly problematic. Crucially, Pfeffer cautioned that this 'Baker's Dozen' of HR should not be seen as a universalistic panacea of practice. Notwithstanding his acknowledgement that the implementation of the thirteen practices was very much a 'horses for courses' selection process, Pfeffer conceded that 'it is possible for a company to do all of these things and be unprofitable and unsuccessful, or to do a few or none of them and be quite successful' (Pfeffer 1995: 104). The cat was already out of the bag, however: research had already commenced to establish the 'proof' that best practice processes were unequivocally linked to organisational performance.

The most celebrated paper in the Universalistic School is the seminal work by Huselid (1995). The paper forwarded three major advances within the HRM–P link paradigm. First, the work departed from previous literature insofar as 'the level of analysis used to estimate the firm-level impact of HRM practices is the system, and the perspective is strategic rather than functional' (Huselid 1995: 636). Exactly how this work can be described as any more strategic than other papers in the HRM–P link paradigm is left unclear.

Second, it was claimed that the analysis provided one of the first empirical explorations of the 'prediction that the impact of High Performance Work Practices on firm performance is contingent on both the degree of complimentarity, or internal fit, among these practices and the degree of alignment, or external fit, between a firm's system of such practices and its competitive strategy' (Huselid 1995: 636). On this showing, the Universalistic School does not represent a departure from the Contingency and Configurational Schools, but an extension of their thinking principally because of the application of a third, and primary, advance offered by Huselid's paper, namely, the dependent variable being firm-level measures of truly *independent* and *actual* financial performance.

The paper transformed the standing of human resources (be it academic research or their practitioner equivalents) overnight. The commotion was largely attributable to Huselid's achievement of being able to illustrate that 'in terms of market value, the per employee effect of increasing such practices one standard deviation was $18,641' (Huselid 1995: 659). Nobody thought to ask what a standard deviation increase in high-performance work systems might look like, or how it might be implemented inside organisations. Human resources directors were too seduced by claims such as 'a one-standard-deviation increase in such practices is associated with a relative 7.05 percent decrease in turnover and, on a per employee basis, $27,044 more in sales and $18,641 and $3,814 more in market value and profits, respectively' (Huselid 1995: 667). Huselid did not stop there. In what must have represented manna from heaven to the heavily scrutinised HR director under constant downward pressure on costs, Huselid suggested his results urged organisations to consider constant levels of investment on an annual basis, thus ensuring both the longevity of the HR department, and even alluding to the wider returns on investment being enjoyed by employees. On these terms, all stakeholders, organisations, their employees and the HR department, were *financial* beneficiaries. Huselid's paper was lauded in practitioner publications for finally providing HR directors with the financial evidence to underpin their claims of an empirical, *quantifiable, statistical* and, above all else, *financial* return on investment to the HR department. The academy too was impressed, awarding the prestigious Best Paper

Award by the American Academy of Management. Academic science in general, and researchers in the field of human resources in particular, had now secured their ticket to boardroom significance.

Certain alarm bells were, however, ringing in the distance. Lurking deep in the paper, which nobody appeared to notice, let alone cite, was the empirical equivalent of the death toll of the Contingency and Configurational Schools, where Huselid observed, 'despite the strong theoretical expectation that better internal and external fit would be reflected in better financial performance, on the whole results did not support the contention that either type of fit has any incremental value over the main effects associated with the use of High Performance Work Practices' (Huselid 1995: 665–6). This pattern of evidence was replicated a year later by Delery and Doty (1996). Again, nobody seemed too perturbed by the latter paper's finding that 'we cannot make strong arguments that synergy amongst HR practices under investigation enhance organizational performance' (Delery and Doty 1996: 827). The HRM–P link bandwagon was now in full swing and nobody was going to let any contrary evidence stand in the way of HR's march to credibility.

A year later saw the publication of Dave Ulrich's *Human Resource Champions* (Ulrich 1997). Ulrich masterfully appealed to the continuing insecurity of the human resources community with his observation that the HR department undersold itself. It was time for 'a new agenda for both HR practices and HR professionals [to] emerge' (Ulrich 1997: 1). Armed with the findings of Huselid, Delery, Doty, Ichiowski, Shaw and Prennushi, HR could now afford to be ebullient enough to 'focus less on what HR professionals do and more on what they *deliver*' (Ulrich 1997: vii, original emphasis).

Champions set out new and multiple roles for human resources professionals absorbing the configurational details of the thirteen high-performance work practices under the umbrella of administrative experts and the aspects of fit from the Contingency School under the much-hailed strategic or business partner. The magnitude of the changes that followed is difficult to comprehend. Within months, organisations were moving to the so-called '3-Box Model' of HR business partners, HR experts and HR transactional services to enable HR departments to best align themselves with emergent organisational strategy, or, as many suspected, the downward pressure on back office costs. The debate over the adequacy or otherwise of the 3-Box Model is still far from resolved. Nevertheless, the contribution of empirical research on the HRM–P link in justifying the now massive investments made in the new model of delivery is unquestionable.

The impact of the Universalistic School has been profound. Riding on the wave of the huge success of *Champions*, during which Ulrich reached the dizzy heights of a leading *Fortune Magazine* Business Guru, and the analytical work of Huselid, who had been joined by Brian Becker (e.g. Becker and Huselid 1998), the three leading authors of the HRM–P link paradigm combined forces to release the *HR Scorecard* (Becker *et al.* 2001). At the heart of the book was the continuing debate over the strategic contribution made by human resources. 'It's up to HR', observed the authors, 'to develop a new measurement system that creates real value for the firm and secure human resources' legitimate place as a strategic partner' (Becker *et al.* 2001: 11). The authors tapped into a parallel business tool – the *Balanced Scorecard* of Kaplan and Norton (1996), which was gaining in popularity – 'because it incorporates measures that describe the actual value-creation process rather than focusing on just the financial *results* that traditional accounting methods assess' (Becker *et al.* 2001: 1). We had come full circle: we were now to concentrate once more on what HR did, not on the results delivered. The authors, then, were systemically attempting to balance the need to retain the humanism of the original Harvard School of human resources with the harder, more measurement orientation of the Michigan School.[2]

Although couched in the discourse of human resources the *HR Scorecard* is unequivocally a book with measurement at its centre. There is acknowledgement of the Contingency School's requirement that the right competencies are in place, as there is to the Configurational School in the recognition that the organization of human resources processes, or HR architecture, is implemented to ensure HR is a strategic asset, not a hindrance. Ultimately, however, the book is about how HR contributes to organisational performance and, therefore, is firmly rooted in the HRM–P paradigm. The authors place their cards on the table in the opening pages of the book: 'the bottom line is this: If current accounting methods can't give HR professionals the measurement tools they need, then they will have to develop their own ways of demonstrating their contribution to firm performance' (Becker *et al.* 2001: 11). Executives are treated to an essay on the principles of good measurement. What they (mis)understand as 'Causality', the conceptual foundation stone of the Universalistic School, is given a particularly lengthy exposition against the backdrop of specific HR examples. Echoing Huselid's original paper, we are then presented with the goal of the *HR Scorecard*:

Ideally, you will develop a measurement system that lets you answer questions such as, how much will I have to change x in order to achieve our target change in y? To illustrate, if you increase training time by 20 percent, how much will that change employee performance and, ultimately, unit performance? Or, if you reduce turnover among key technical staff in R&D by 10 percent, how long before that action begins to improve the new-product-development cycle time? (Becker *et al.* 2001: 119)

The authors were effectively attempting to open up the 'black box' of the causal relationship between HR components (x) and unit or organisational performance (y). The opacity of the relationship between two variables, although clearly acknowledged, was dismissed as executives 'have to make decisions, and [their] colleagues expect those decisions to produce results' (Becker *et al.* 2001: 121). Ultimately, suggest the authors, executives 'need to know whether the system in question will produce a change in employee performance and, if so, by how much' (Becker *et al.* 2001: 121). At no point are the difficulties of the black box acknowledged as a major empirical problem. On the contrary, we are informed that, 'you must have a persuasive story about what's in the blackbox. You must be able to throw back the cover of that box and reveal a plausible process of value creation from HR to firm performance' (Becker *et al.* 2001: 111). We are reassured that 'if it can be measured, it's much less of a problem', that we can draw distinctions between the different levels of causality yielded by different HR systems because 'all other causes are not created equal', and informed that this variation in causal impact should not be cause for concern because, ultimately, 'you can account for joint influences' (Becker *et al.* 2001: 125). Thinking they have provided some insight into causality, when they have merely recognised the multi-causal nature of the world, and drawing the methodological claims about 'causal linkages' of the book together, the authors conclude:

So you *can* operationalize your causal inferences – you just need to carefully consider the plausible alternatives to the HR effect you are interested in. For *x* to be the cause of *y*, for example, you have to be confident that the effect on *y* is not due to some other influence other than *x*. If you can keep those other influences from varying, your confidence in your causal inference will increase. You will also be able to express your inference in actionable terms. (Becker *et al.* 2001: 122, original emphasis)

Other researchers who have more recently examined the 'black box' are less ebullient. Nevertheless, despite Purcell and colleagues referring to the problem of 'unlocking the black box' in the title of their six-year study of the HRM–P link, and their observation that despite the work of Pfeffer, Huselid, Guest and others, 'we do not know why or how HR policies translate into performance' (Purcell *et al.* 2003: 2), the authors could still conclude from their study that, 'in some organisations it was possible to demonstrate a clear association between people management and performance' (Purcell *et al.* 2003: x–xi). Performance in this study, however, refers to the correlations between staff evaluations and attitudinal outcomes (see Purcell *et al.* 2003: 18, Table 2). Elsewhere, performance is explored 'by looking at linear correlations in individual case study organisations to explore the links between front-line leadership and satisfaction with other aspects of policy and practice identified in the Bath People and Performance model' (Purcell *et al.* 2003: 18). Closer analysis of this study ultimately reveals the researchers did not study organisational performance at all: the dependent variables were constructs obtained from a questionnaire to operationalise the concepts of motivation, job satisfaction and commitment. Indeed, the authors suggest, 'pure financial measures of the sort reported publicly for the whole corporation are much more remote, and numerous other factors cloud the relationship between input and output' (Purcell *et al.* 2003: 53). We agree entirely.

No such problems of visibility are apparent in the latest large-scale research from the Universalistic School (Tamkin *et al.* 2008). Although the researchers caution that 'it is important to note that statistical analysis of a cross sectional sample can only show the various factors of people management practice are correlated with performance, *it cannot provide evidence that they cause changes in performance*' (2008: 14), they are also at pains to point out that a rise in their 4A index score by one would provide 'an increase in gross profits per employee of between £1,083 and £1,568' (2008: 57, our emphasis). As we will elaborate upon below, there is an element of duplicity at work here: on the one hand they state that correlation is not causality, whilst, on the other hand, hinting that causality is indeed present. Moreover, nobody appeared to notice that when factoring in the differences of relative value between Huselid's paper in 1995 and the 2008 study, the increased monetised contribution had fallen by at least half in real terms.[3] Comparison of these two seminal papers, therefore, now appeared to reveal the alleged return on investment to human resources had halved in little over a decade! This did not preclude *Personnel Today* from running the front-page headline, '100% proof: good HR will boost your company profits' (26 February 2008).

In sum, then, despite recognition that there may be some set of 'best practices', empirical researchers operating under the rubric of the Universalistic School are still part of what we call the HRM–P paradigm. That is, they seek a link, association or empirical relation between these best HRM practices and organisational performance. And they presume this link is quantifiable and measurable with appropriate metrics, and discoverable using the usual range of quantitative, empirical and statistical research techniques.

The kaleidoscope of the Contextual School

The different approaches that constitute the HRM–P paradigm have not been without their critics. Pointing to the vexed issue of the black box, Legge (2005: 30) suggests that 'it is widely recognised, even by adherents to this research agenda and its associated positivistic research designs that little has been done to unlock the "black box" of the processes that link HRM (however conceptualised) with organisational performance (however conceptualised)'. By alluding to the lack of conceptual clarity we feel Karen Legge is clearly on to something. One of the primary reasons for the failure to open up the black box in Legge's eyes has been the HRM–P link paradigm's inability to accommodate in a satisfactory way the complexities of organisational life which, in Legge's words, 'sits uneasily with the large-scale surveys and quantitative approaches of positivism' (2005: 31). An attempt to deal satisfactorily with such complexity is the defining hallmark of the emerging Contextual School most closely associated with the work of Paauwe (2004). This new contextually-based human resource theory of performance is essentially:

[A] theoretical framework that enables a complete overview of the factors influencing the shaping of HRM policies and practices. Moreover, the theory emphasizes different rationalities and resulting outcomes. It also takes into account the various actors involved and their interaction with strategy and the wider societal context. (Paauwe 2004: 100)

We attribute the metaphor of a kaleidoscope to the Contextual School partly because of this insistence on examining performance across a wide range of different indicators (see Paauwe 2005: 101–4), but primarily because of its insistence of moving from the triad of a perspective espousing the linear relationship between 'strategy → HRM → performance' into an alternative perspective advocating understanding human resources' contribution to performance through 'value-laden/ethical HRM → organizational viability → enabling strategic options' (cf. Paauwe 2004: 85). This different lens – or more accurately, perhaps, *lenses* – incorporates, in the author's words, 'elements of the contingency and configurational mode (Delery and Doty, 1996), institutionalism and RBV, and is inspired by the Harvard approach (Beer et al., 1984)' (Paauwe 2004: 90).

All of the problems we have already alluded to above in relation to the Configuration and Contingency Schools are imported into the Contextual School. Paauwe himself acknowledges this, albeit tucked away in an endnote, in his recognition that 'the distance between HRM practices or systems and financial performance indicators (e.g. sales, profits, and market value) is too large to enable valid and reliable statements to be made on (statistically) significant effects found in empirical research' (2004: 105, n. 6). Where Paauwe departs from previous writers in the HRM–P link paradigm, and moves closer to the position we advocate, is in his insistence on examining the wider relational rationalities shaping performance outcomes as well as the more economic rationalities of examining performance in quantitative form.

Table 2.1. *Summarising the HRM–P paradigm*

School	Metaphor	Perspective	Seminal example
Contingency	'Russian doll'	Performance contingent on alignment of different HR processes with organisational strategy and processes	Schuler and Jackson (1987a)
Universalistic	'Black box'	A linear relationship between organisational performance and certain HR practices	Huselid (1995)
Configurational	'Rubik's Cube'	How the pattern or configuration of multiple HR processes are related to each other and to organisational performance	Delery and Doty (1996)
Contextual	'Kaleidoscope'	A complete overview of the factors influencing the shaping of HRM policies and practices	Paauwe (2004)

Indeed, Paauwe suggests, 'just like Beer *et al.*'s famous Harvard model (1984), the framework in this respect is more about mapping relevant factors than a set of related testifiable hypotheses' (Paauwe 2004: 95). So far, so good. This is why we do not include the Contextual School as part of the HRM–P paradigm proper.

No sooner have we recognised this, however, than we have to acknowledge Paauwe's inability to break completely with 'scientism', as he suggests that 'it is possible to test for the availability and nature of (human) resources meeting the criteria of the RBV' (Paauwe

2004: 97). This notwithstanding, an important fissure in the wall of scientism dominating the HRM–P link has been opened up. Moreover, increasing the complexity of the patterns within the kaleidoscope it would also appear other researchers have been attracted to widening the scope of factors under analysis, including, for example, wider stakeholders (e.g. Edgar and Geare 2005), employee engagement (e.g. Cheese *et al.* 2008) and viability and competitive advantage (e.g. Boxall and Purcell 2000).

Yet with a wider and more complex lens comes a less clear picture. Given the continuing insistence on the part of Contextual School scholars to ground their work in scientism, manifested by using performance in its various guises as the dependent variable, the inclusion of multifarious and emergent aspects of human resources management in the independent variable side of the equation does nothing but present complex and beautiful patterns of possible outcomes, which nevertheless do nothing but turn in circles like a kaleidoscope. These weaknesses have been recognised by some of the researchers working within the different schools of HRM–P link paradigm. As we shall see in the next section of the book, however, this acknowledgement of the limitations of a scientisitc approach to measuring the performance of HRM amounts to nothing more than the prescription of more of the same, only on a larger scale.

Pause to take stock

A glance at the history of the discipline, then, shows that whilst the link between HRM and performance can be conceptualised in various ways (see Table 2.1 for a summary), there is nevertheless a common theme. The link is presumed to exist directly or indirectly (via mediating variables/mechanisms) between (a) an HRM practice or perhaps more plausibly a bundle of practices when (horizontally) integrated or aligned with one another; possibly when these practices are (vertically) aligned or integrated with corporate strategy; possibly when all this occurs in an appropriate context which may possibly involve a range of stakeholders and (b) organisational performance. Whilst this is an accurate way of putting matters because it includes the various ways in which the link has been conceived, it is also rather convoluted. For ease of exposition, henceforth, we refer simply to the *link between HRM practices and organisational performance,* yet always have in mind this more accurate conception. What we go on to argue in the rest of the book, therefore, is not altered by distinctions between the different approaches; our critique appertains to all four of these approaches. The quest for the Holy Grail of the link between different HRM practices and organisational performance may have opened up on four separate fronts but represents, at least for us as will become clear from what follows, nothing more than an empirical wild goose chase.

PART II

Meta-theorising the HRM–P link

3 | The state of contemporary research on the HRM–P link: a technical analysis

Introduction

Current empirical research on the HRM–P link is orientated around two key ideas. The first idea is that of a presumed link, association or empirical relation between HRM practices and organisational performance. Legge (2001: 23) is not exaggerating when she refers to 'the search for the Holy Grail of establishing a causal link between HRM and performance'. This link is conceptualised in various ways. It is presumed to exist directly or indirectly (via mediating variables/ mechanisms) between (a) an HRM practice or perhaps more plausibly a bundle of practices when (horizontally) integrated or aligned with one another; possibly when these practices are (vertically) aligned or integrated with corporate strategy; possibly when all this occurs in an appropriate context which may possibly involve a range of stakeholders, and (b) organisational performance. Whilst this is an accurate way of putting matters because it includes the various ways in which the link has been conceived, it is also rather convoluted. For ease of exposition, therefore, we refer simply to the *link between HRM practices and organisational performance*, yet always have in mind this more accurate conception. Second, this link is presumed to be quantifiable and measurable with appropriate metrics, and discovered using the usual range of quantitative, empirical and statistical research techniques. Whether these phenomena are measured at the level of the firm, business unit or individual makes no difference to our argument, and we leave this out of consideration.

The aim of this chapter is to elaborate, at some length, what this current research involves and, more importantly, the problems it faces – which are often referred to generically as the *problem of under-theorisation*. Whilst some of those who study the HRM–P link recognise empirical research is under-theorised, we are not aware of any who are prepared to take the problem seriously, or of any who are willing to consider just how deep it runs. And we think the problem runs so deep as to seriously undermine the whole paradigm.

The current 'state of play' in empirical research on the HRM–P link

Like Topsy, empirical research on the HRM–P link has 'just growed' – indeed, it is still growing. Rather than bombard the reader with dozens of references to empirical research on the HRM–P link, references that can be found in almost any article on the subject, we refer the reader to three recent reviews of the literature by Wall and Wood (2005); Godard (2004); Boselie *et al.* (2005); a slightly more 'theoretical' review by Wright and Boswell (2002); a recent overview of the main models by Zheng *et al.* (2006); and a meta-analysis by Combs *et al.* (2006).[1] HR consultants such as Accenture also contribute to the research, see Cantrell *et al.* (2005); Brakely *et al.* (2004); and Balageur *et al.* (2006).

To get a feel for the paradigm under investigation, we offer the following as a stylised version of a 'typical' piece of research on the HRM–P link. Whilst variations exist in this extensive literature we feel confident enough to suggest that this is a fairly accurate sketch.

A typical paper will open by referring to a list of seminal articles that have offered some empirical support for the idea that HRM practices and organisational performance are linked. Reference is commonly made to one, or a combination, of four main perspectives or approaches: the universalistic, internal fit, best practice or one size fits all; the bundling or internal fit; the contingency or external fit; and the configurational. All of these offer variations on the nature and context of the link between HRM practices and performance. Sometimes all this appears in sections on 'existing literature', sometimes there is a suggestion that this is the 'theoretical' part of the paper, and sometimes there is a specific section dedicated to 'theory', or 'theory and hypotheses'. Often a specific theory or theories will be mentioned, such as resource-based theory, although it is common to find a kind of 'name dropping' exercise where passing reference is made to several theories without a clear statement of which theory is actually underpinning the empirical analysis and how it underpins it. Whatever 'theory' is mentioned, the discussion is usually superficial, especially relative to the discussion of statistical techniques that come later in the paper. The paper will then move on, in some cases quite rapidly, and often in a relatively unsophisticated manner, to make a series of hypotheses stating that some specified HRM practices are associated with increased organisational performance. A section on 'methodology' then follows, usually with a considerably in-depth and highly sophisticated discussion of the statistical techniques used (e.g. regression, analysis of variance, correlation, structural equation modelling and factor analysis) explaining how the various HRM practices are measured, and empirical data is generated. The HRM practices commonly measured are: incentive pay, recruiting and selection, teamwork, employment security, flexible job assignment, communication and labour relations. Organisational performance is commonly measured via return on investment, growth or sales. The paper then presents the findings and discusses them, before concluding, often with comments on the limitations of the research, and comments about the direction of future research.

What becomes clear, even from a glance through some of this extensive research, is that it is preoccupied with, and dominated by, quantitative, statistical, empirical analysis of the kind that we characterised in the last chapter as scientistic. Impressionistic evidence is, however, not all we have to go on. A substantial review of HRM literature by Hoobler and Brown-Johnston 'took a discerning look at what is and is not being published in HR' (2005: 666) and found:

[S]tatistical regression was by far the method of choice, represented in a full 35 percent of the articles studied. Various analysis of variance and meta-analysis accounted for 9 percent and 5 percent respectively, while correlation and structural equation modeling or confirmatory factor analysis respectively amounted to 6 percent and 3 percent. (Hoobler and Brown-Johnston 2005: 668)

Boselie *et al.*'s (2005: 70) comprehensive survey of the HRM–P literature observed that despite calls 'for more use of qualitative methods to examine this relationship, we found only a few wholly qualitative studies'. Mitchell and James (2001: 531) found that around half of the articles in a sample of leading management journals use something like what we refer to as the scientistic philosophy of science.

Furthermore, empirical research on the HRM–P link appears to be largely devoid of insight and anything other than the most superficial discussion and reflection on the philosophy of science underpinning the quantitative techniques in use. Out of 467 articles sampled, Hoobler and Brown-Johnston (2005: 666) found just *one* article on philosophy of science. We managed to find another three articles by Wright and McMahan (1992), Brewster (1999) and Ferris *et al.* (2004) who mention philosophy of science in empirical research on the HRM–P link. We also found an article by McGoldrick *et al.* (2001) on theory and philosophy of science in HR development and an article by Kane (2001) who considers philosophy of science in HRM more generally.[2]

Researchers on the HRM–P link can be considered on a kind of continuum. At one end are those committed to scientism and quantitative, statistical, empirical methods and research techniques because they have no knowledge of alternatives. As Brewster puts it: 'Like the fish's knowledge of water ... researchers not only see no alternatives, but do not consider the possibility that there could be any' (Brewster 1999: 217). At the other end are those who are highly knowledgeable about the full range of alternative philosophies, methods and techniques, and whose commitments emerge from careful and conscious reflection and deliberation. We can find little evidence of this highly knowledgeable category in the HRM–P literature – which does not, of course, mean there are no such persons; they may simply choose not to make public their insights into philosophy, methodology and research techniques. Somewhere in the middle are those who are, to varying degrees, aware of alternatives and may be sympathetic to alternative techniques, perhaps even ethnographic research, yet who stick with scientism and its methods and techniques. It is our belief that most empirical researchers on the HRM–P link fall into this rather amorphous middle category. Their reasons for sticking with scientism and its methods and techniques are various, but most likely include the following.

First, a general preoccupation with quantification and measurement[3] grew as part of the Enlightenment, and is closely connected to the requirements of mathematics and statistics, not to mention scientism more generally. Lawson neatly summarises the point: 'in the euphoria of the achievements of the Enlightenment, indeed the "mathematization" of the social sciences became a major theme of contemporary Western culture' (2003: 259). The 'mathematisation' of the HRM–P paradigm is now accepted by empirical researchers, apparently, without question. According to Gallo and Thompson (2000: 242), 'Nearly everyone agrees that good measures are the key to determining results in HRM, as in just about everything else'. Wang *et al.* (2002: 208) refer to HRD as being 'in its infancy with largely descriptive rather than quantitative features' as opposed to 'the rigorous methodologies developed by economists and psychologists'.[4]

Second, in their postgraduate education, and with notable exceptions, the only brush most of these researchers are likely to have had with philosophy of science will probably be a rather narrow 'methodology' course, dominated by training in empirical research techniques, possibly with some mention of things like non-participant observation or ethnography. It is most unlikely they will have come across philosophical issues like ontology, epistemology and aetiology or *genuine* methodology. By 'genuine' methodology we mean a discussion that goes beyond learning how to measure and quantify the social world and then apply the usual statistical techniques, and takes alternative philosophies, methods and research techniques seriously.[5] In their recent book, Purcell *et al.* (2009: 4–8) have a section dedicated to 'methodological problems' afflicting empirical research on the HRM–P link. Whilst they are quite right in their identification of the few 'methodological problems' they mention, this is not a section on 'genuine methodology'.

Third, many empirical researchers see discussions of philosophy, methodology and research technique as wasteful distractions from 'doing' research.

Fourth, it is easier to get research published by sticking to scientism and the quantitative, statistical and empirical methods and research techniques it encourages. For reasons contained in the foregoing points, many, if not most, journal editors and journal referees now believe that using quantitative, statistical and empirical techniques is the only 'rigorous' or 'scientific' (we would say 'scientistic') approach to social science and other approaches are rejected as '*un*scientific'.

Finally, there is a kind of inertia stemming from the fact that most other researchers in the HRM–P paradigm are committed to scientism and the quantitative, statistical and empirical methods and research techniques it encourages. There is, therefore, no need to justify the approach taken or, indeed, even give it a second thought.[6]

We cannot agree, therefore, with commentators who claim to see fairly widespread discussion and debate of methodology in the HRM–P literature. Marchington and Zagelmeyer (2005: 3) refer to 'repeated discussion of more general methodological shortcomings'. Even critics like Paauwe and Boselie (2005: 987) suggest that 'methodological issues have been debated'. Whilst it is true that the term 'methodology' often gets a mention in the literature, this is not evidence of serious debate or discussion of *genuine* methodology. Indeed, discussion of 'methodology' is often no more than discussion of what we might call 'technical' problems with the metrics, measurement, estimating techniques and data.[7] We do not address these problems because our critique goes beyond such technicalities. To state the case boldly, even if these 'technical' problems were resolved, our critique would still retain its force because it is directed to more fundamental, meta-theoretical concerns. The almost obligatory, yet decidedly brief, discussions of the problem of reverse causality and the alleged need for longitudinal analysis to overcome this problem do not constitute serious methodological discussion.

As will become even clearer over the next three chapters, empirical research on the HRM–P link, rooted as it is in a scientistic philosophy of science, is dominated by, and preoccupied with, the application of quantitative, statistical and empirical techniques. Indeed, we would go as far as to say that *empirical research on the HRM–P link is being driven, not by theory, but by scientism, the deductive method and the quantitative, statistical and empirical techniques sponsored by scientism.* At least one leading empirical researcher on the HRM–P link is prepared to accept this point:

statistical sophistication appears to have been emphasized at the expense of theoretical rigour. (Guest 1997: 263)

the risk of following the empirical route is that *we allow ourselves to be dominated by statistical convenience.* Ideally we should be adhering more rigorously to a theoretical basis for combining variables, always assuming that such a theory is available … In future it might be useful to *combine practices on the basis of theory rather than statistical analysis.* (Guest 2001: 1099–100)

This is not a new observation. Way and Johnson (2005: 6) are able to cite the well-known work of Delery who, in 1998, recognised that:

The conceptual foundations of SHRM have been relatively weak and many of the empirical investigations have made assumptions not driven by, or consistent with, the theoretical base. (Delery, cited in Way and Johnson 2005: 6)

Although a minority, there are other researchers with an interest in HRM practices and organisational performance who are not dominated by, and preoccupied with, scientism and its quantitative, statistical and empirical techniques.[8] These contributions are characterised by (what they interpret as) a serious attempt to 'unlock the black box', that is, to *explain* the causal mechanisms and processes at work governing any relationship between HRM practices and performance. This does not mean that *all* these commentators reject quantitative, statistical and empirical analysis, but it does mean that *scientism and its techniques do not drive their analysis*. Gifford *et al.*'s (2005) report for the Institute for Employment Studies, whilst not exactly being mainstream HRM–P literature, nevertheless considers some of the usual drivers (i.e. independent variables). We mention it because its relatively in-depth case studies exemplify the kind of research necessary to make a start on opening the black box. In one place, for example, they mention the 'internal fit' approach. Instead, however, of simply being able to state that there is 'internal fit', which is all empirical research on the HRM–P link can do, they are in a position to explain *why* this is the case (2005: 83–4). We might add that there are also numerous case studies that investigate individual HR or HPW practices associated with increased performance – e.g. teamworking, empowerment, payment systems and so on. Whilst these do not seek to investigate the bundling effects of combined practices, they nevertheless open the black box by providing partial explanations of *why* the practice under investigation might influence performance. Examples include two classics by Delbridge (1998) and Scott (1994), plus articles by Bacon and Blyton (2003); Edwards and Collinson (2002); Geary and Dobbins (2001) and Liden *et al.* (2001).

Others operate from a perspective that is difficult to label, but is rooted in insights stemming from what is variously described as postmodernism, poststructuralism, social constructionism, continental philosophy, and the linguistic or discursive 'turn' in social science.[9] For ease we refer to this group as postmodernists. The main thrust of the postmodern critique of scientism or positivism is a critique rooted less in the *philosophy* of science and more in the *sociology and politics* of science. The critique aims to deconstruct the claims made by (natural and social) scientists to show that far from these claims being 'true' they are socially constructed as 'true' via a range of power-knowledge discourses. Far from being politically neutral, science serves power in many ways, not least by socially constructing individual identities and subjectivities, to produce what Townley (1994) has called the 'industrial subject' – a workforce that is not so much politically combative as 'out to lunch', as Hancock (1999: 168) puts it. Whilst we agree and disagree with various postmodern sentiments (and here is not the place to elaborate), the point is we are engaged in a different form of critique, namely, a critique aimed specifically at the underlying philosophy of science. We do, however, have significant differences with the ontological commitments of many (but not all) of these writers. As critical realists, we part company with the *strong* social constructionist ontology that postmodernists are often (but not always) committed to. Critical realists reject the tendency to downplay, fudge or, at the extreme, deny the existence of extra-linguistic or extra-discursive phenomena. We also worry that this *strong* social constructionist ontology can result in *philosophy* of science collapsing into sociology and politics of science, making it impossible to even discuss issues of what, for example, a plausible theory might look like. Whilst we think sociology and politics of science is a perfectly legitimate, indeed crucial, endeavour, there is still a job of work for the philosophy of science to do. Postmodernists Foley *et al.* (1999: 170) for example, claim that to seek underlying theories is to remain wedded to the 'modernist tradition' and is 'optimistic if not futile'. On the contrary, we think it *is* possible to provide theories, but this will require a completely different philosophical perspective to the existing scientism, one we will discuss in Chapter 6. For critical realist comments on *strong* social constructionist ontology see Fleetwood (2004 and 2005) and Potter and Lopez (2001).

Henceforth, when we refer to 'empirical research on the HRM–P link', or to 'the paradigm', we specifically exclude those commentators, postmodernists or otherwise, who are engaged in non-scientistic investigation of HRM practices and organisational performance. Henceforth, and unless inappropriate, we will also drop the suffix 'of science' and simply refer to philosophy for convenience.

Empirical evidence

A recent PricewaterhouseCoopers report concludes that: 'What we can say with confidence is that those businesses in which people strategy is aligned with the business strategy perform better' (2003: 24) . A recent review of studies carried out by the CBI reported that: 'More than 30 studies carried out in the UK and USA since the early 1990s leave no room to doubt that there is a correlation between people management and business performance, that the relationship is positive, and that it is cumulative: the more effective the practices, the better the result' (cited in Rafferty *et al.* 2005: 7). Whilst assertions like this are now commonplace in the literature, they are also open to question. Indeed, frequent (mis)reporting of findings from a small number of seminal research papers seems to have generated a powerful, yet misleading, discourse.[10] This discourse emerges via the gradual and subliminal sliding into first acceptance, then subsequent adoption into the paradigm, of 'myths'. The empirical evidence is made even harder to interpret by the fact that out of the scores of empirical studies undertaken in the last decade, virtually none attempt to replicate earlier findings, and they all end up testing slightly different hypotheses relating to slightly different bundles of HR practices, when aligned with strategy in slightly different ways, in slightly different contexts and using slightly different dependent and independent variables – something we elaborate upon in Chapter 5.

Rather than trawl through all the empirical research, it is more fruitful to make use of three recent surveys of the empirical research. Wall and Wood (2005: 454) conclude that 'existing evidence for a relationship between HRM and performance should be treated with caution'. Godard (2004: 355) writes: 'Overall, these concerns suggest that we should treat broad-brush claims about the performance effects of [High Performance Work systems], and about research findings claiming to observe them, with a healthy degree of scepticism'. Boselie *et al.* (2005: 81–2) conclude that: 'A steady body of empirical evidence has been accumulated since the pioneering days of the mid-1990s … Ten years on the "Holy Grail" of decisive proof remains elusive'. Most recently, Purcell *et al.* (2009: 3) repeat a similar sentiment, writing: 'Despite this extensive effort the goal of establishing a clear link between HR practices and performance still seems some way off'.

To this we have to add another important caveat. Hundreds of empirical researchers on the HRM–P have run, quite literally, thousands of regressions, using various model specifications and various data, and ended up with either inconclusive or even counter evidence. Because these (negative) results are never published, their omission only serves to generate the impression that empirical research that has been done supports the existence of a positive link between HRM and performance. This is, however, not the case. Even research carried out by those who 'believe' in the existence of the HRM–P link is often less than conclusive *when placed under close scrutiny*. Let us single out Huselid's seminal paper on the grounds that it is frequently cited as providing empirical evidence for the existence of an HRM–P link – as, for example, the PricewaterhouseCoopers report cited above. This is not our reading of Huselid, at least not when he is read closely.

Huselid (1995) tests four hypotheses:

(1a) systems of HRM practices will diminish employee turnover and increase productivity and financial performance;
(1b) employee turnover and productivity will mediate the relationship between systems of HRM practices and financial performance;
(2) complementarities among HRM practices will diminish employee turnover and increase productivity and financial performance;
(3) alignment of a firm's HRM practices with its competitive strategy will diminish employee turnover and increase productivity and financial performance.

Commenting on hypotheses 2 and 3 Huselid writes: 'despite the compelling theoretical argument that better internal and external fit will increase firm performance, I found only modest evidence of such an effect for internal fit and little evidence for external fit' (1995: 643). Huselid's empirical evidence does not, therefore, support the claim that there is a link between bundles of HRM practices and performance, or between HRM practices, when aligned, and performance. Turning to hypothesis 1a and 1b, a careful reading of the paper shows that these hypotheses are supported for eighteen out of twenty-four variables. Although Huselid claims there is 'strong support for the hypotheses predicting that High Performance Work Practices will affect firm performance and important employment outcomes' he does recognise that 'the results are not completely unambiguous' (1995: 640). In sum, the best we can legitimately say about one of the most frequently cited papers in the HRM–P literature is that the evidence is inconclusive. Indeed, this is the best we can, and should, say about the empirical evidence on the HRM–P link more generally.

The problem of under-theorisation

Many empirical researchers on the HRM–P link are aware of what can, generally speaking, be referred to as the 'problem of under-theorisation'. They sometimes complain, variously, that the paradigm lacks theory, lacks *good* theory, has made little theoretical progress, or lacks the theoretical foundations necessary to support and explain their empirical findings. Some, like Youndt and Snell (2004: 1004), even open their articles by stating this problem. We enter this debate by letting (a sample) of these researchers speak for themselves. This should make it clear that *we* are aware, that *they* are aware, of the problem.

With a few exceptions ... there has been little effort to extend SHRM theory in a way that formally integrates the mechanism through which the HR architecture actually influences firm performance. (Becker and Huselid 2006: 900)

Much of the writing in the field of SHRM has been concerned with either practical advice or presentation of empirical data. Without good theory, the field of SHRM could be characterized as a plethora of statements regarding empirical relationships and/or prescriptions for practice that fail to explain why these relationships exist or should exist. If, in fact, the criticism that the field of SHRM lacks a strong theoretical foundation is true, then this could undermine the ability of both practitioners and researchers to fully use human resources in support of firm strategy. (Wright and McMahan 1992: 297)

To understand as opposed to measuring the performance, we need to make these linkages. There may be an association between HRM practices and company profit, but without some linkages, we will not know why: we have no theory. This implies that we need a range of types of performance measures. (Guest 1997: 267)

[T]he mechanisms by which human resource decisions create and sustain value are complicated and not well understood ... It is difficult to grasp the precise mechanisms by which the interplay of human resource practices and policies generate value. To imitate a complex system, it is necessary to understand how the elements interact ... Researchers are a long way from understanding the precise nature of these interactions. (Becker and Gerhart 1996: 781–2)

If we are to improve our understanding of the impact of HRM on performance, we need a theory about HRM, a theory about performance, and a theory of how they are linked. (Guest 1997: 263)

[I]t is essential that we make progress in theory development ... Theory about performance has made only modest progress. (Guest 2001: 1092–3)

to date there is very little research that '*peels back the onion*' and describes the process through which HRM systems influence the principal intermediate variables that ultimately affect firm performance. (Paauwe 2004: 55, emphasis added)

Whilst we agree that there is a problem with the theoretical foundations of empirical research on the HRM–P link, we do not think this is a fruitful way to frame the problem. Framing it simply as a problem of under-theorisation discourages us from seeing the depth of the problem. Let us start our investigation by considering four manifestations of the problem of under-theorisation.

The black box problem

Any empirical research on the HRM–P link that is under-theorised lacks an *explanation* of what the HRM practices under investigation actually do that may influence organisational performance. Empirical researchers on the HRM–P link run into the black box problem when they measure the inputs that go into the black box (HRM practices), and measure the outputs that come out the other end (organisational performance), *but offer no explanation of what goes on between the input and output stages*. Hence the mechanisms and processes in operation between input and output stages remain unexplained. This kind of approach fails to offer a 'persuasive story about what's in the black box. You must be able to throw back the cover of that box and reveal a plausible process of value creation from HRM to firm performance' (Becker *et al.* 2001: 111). The subtitle of Purcell *et al.* (2003), *Unlocking the Black Box*, demonstrates that some researchers in the paradigm are concerned about the problem.

Being aware of the problem, understanding the problem, and being able to resolve the problem are, however, very different things. Many empirical researchers on the HRM–P link misunderstand the problem, because they conceive of it in terms of a *lack of variables at intermediate stages between input and output*. Sels *et al.* (2006b: 85), for example, explore the black box through 'a pile of quantitative studies ... introducing variables that mediate the link between HRM and firm performance'. This sets the black box problem up as follows:

Input $W \rightarrow$ [black box] $\rightarrow$ output Z

The problem is then understood as one of missing variables at intermediate stages between W and Z, and assumed to be resolved by extending the causal chain and adding variables at intermediate stages, thus:

Input $W \rightarrow$ intermediate variable $X \rightarrow$ intermediate variable $Y \rightarrow$ output Z

Unless, however, we are offered an *explanation* of the process between W and X, X and Y, and Y and Z, and not just *measurement* of variables W, X, Y and Z, then, in effect, we have something like the following:

Input $W \rightarrow$ [black box] $\rightarrow$ intermediate variable $X \rightarrow$ [black box] $\rightarrow$ intermediate variable $Y \rightarrow$ [black box] $\rightarrow$ output Z

Simply adding more mediating variables at intervening stages in the causal chain does not solve the black box problem, rather it simply adds more black boxes. The problem is quite common, and even researchers as experienced as Youndt and Snell (2004), Katou and Budhwar (2006) and Becker and Huselid (2006) misunderstand the problem in this way. For Purcell *et al.* (2009: 9), 'Even if robust causal correlations are found between the adoption of a certain mix of practices and performance we do not know why this occurs. We have no evidence of the nature of any intermediary process that needs to occur to produce such relationships. For this reason it is referred to as the "HR black box"'. They then add that 'looking inside the black box requires specifying an HR causal chain'. If, in practice, this amounts to no more than simply adding in more variables to account for the intermediary processes, then this is not unlocking the black box, just adding another one. It is not understanding the 'nature of any intermediary process'. Really understanding how, for example, line managers might 'persuade, induce, cajole, or encourage employees to do as good a job as possible (whether more, better, or more innovatively) both individually and in working with others' (Purcell *et al.* 2009: 21) is almost certainly going to require far more sophisticated, in-depth, qualitative research techniques than Likert Scales. In discussing the black box, Becker and Huselid (2006: 902) echo Priem and Butler's observation that a more careful delineation of 'the specific mechanisms purported to generate competitive advantage is required, as are more actionable prescriptions'. We agree entirely. But instead of pursuing the line of enquiry that might result in greater understanding of the 'specific mechanisms' which would indeed lead them to address the black box, they pursue the other line of enquiry relating to 'the need to construct theories with independent variables that managers can control' (Becker and Huselid 2006) and quietly forget the first line of enquiry.

The reason why many empirical researchers understand the black box problem, and subsequently try to resolve it in this way, lies in their commitment to some form of scientism. If, however, researchers are prepared to go beyond scientism, they can start to make inroads into opening the black box and explaining what goes on inside, not just adding more black boxes in the form of intervening variables. Purcell and Hutchinson (2007) and Purcell *et al.* (2009) are examples of this.[11] Whilst they are happy to engage in the usual quantitative, statistical research techniques of scientism and deductivism to identify the intervening variables, they are also aware of the need for case studies to augment their quantitative analysis. Indeed they are amongst the few empirical researchers on the HRM–P link to carry out this kind of analysis – although it always plays 'second fiddle' to their quantitative analysis. Only data collected via sophisticated qualitative analysis, not just quantitative data collected from attitude surveys, is really capable of revealing complex employee perceptions of, and attitudes to, the HRM practices and leadership behaviour they encounter. To be sure, recognising the importance of agents' interpretations of their situation strikes a chord with interpretive and hermeneutic traditions in sociology. This might encourage other researchers on the HRM–P link to go further in this direction, opening up the possibility of explaining why intervening mechanisms and processes have a causal influence, rather than simply adding new black boxes to find correlations between.

The problem of measurement without theory

Research that is under-theorised lacks an *adequate rationale* for the choice of phenomena that will eventually become the variables. In a recent overview, Purcell and Kinnie (2007: 538) note that: 'Most researchers construct a list of practices but there is no agreement of which practices to include ... There is little debate on where lists of practices come from or what criteria to use in their construction'. As we see in a few moments, simply selecting variables for estimation on the basis that they bulk large in the literature is not an adequate theoretical rationale. Such research is, thereby, guilty of 'measurement without theory'.

The problem of (lack of) justification

Empirical research that is under-theorised ends up attempting to use (pre-existing and new) empirical evidence both to generate theory and attempt to justify that theory, that is, to prove that theory to be true or false. This is an illicit move.

Lack of explanatory power

Empirical research that is under-theorised lacks explanatory power. As we will see in Chapter 5, part of what constitutes a bona fide theory is explanatory power, the ability to answer the question: *why?* A bona fide theory of the HRM–P link might be said to possess explanatory power, if it can explain *why* the introduction of certain HRM practices influences organisational performance. This will prove to be a serious problem if, as we will demonstrate later, the criteria for assessing theory turns out not to be *predictive* power (at least not prediction based upon inductive generalisation), but *explanatory* power.

Whilst there is some recognition of the black box problem, albeit only amongst those who are aware of the general problem of under-theorisation, the other three problems go completely unrecognised in empirical research on the HRM–P link. Sadly, the problems get even worse the more we look into them.

The proposed 'solution': do more, and/or better, empirical work

Some of those empirical researchers who recognise the general problem of under-theorisation, and even the black box problem, have *hinted* at a solution: *the problem of under-theorisation will be overcome, and theoretical foundations will emerge and develop, if researchers continue doing more, and/or better, quantitative, empirical, statistical work.* The following examples support this interpretation.[12]

[W]e need to be aware of the shortcomings and in so doing, return to the issue of theory. The first key issue is the lack of theory about the nature of HRM practices ... A second concern is to improve our measures of performance ... Only when we have made progress in measuring the independent and dependent variables can we begin to give full attention to the way they are linked. (Guest 1997: 273–4)

Empirical work can be useful in testing, refining, and clarifying theoretical issues. However, a form of abstracted empiricism can sometimes serve to cloud rather than clarify issues. The reality of engaging in empirical research both highlights the value of theory to focus our work and throws us back on the need for clear guiding theory. (Guest 2001: 1092)

Although theory development is critical to the development of a discipline, a proliferation of theories and concepts can impede the accumulation of knowledge. Researchers should focus as much attention on generating a cumulative body of accurate and meaningful estimates of effect sizes as on generating new concepts and theories. (Becker and Gerhart 1996: 777)

[T]he most critical missing link is between theory/hypotheses and data. Rather than having 'theory driven' research, we observe what we would call 'data-driven research' ... Thus we see one of the most important future directions for SHRM theory building to be an increasing emphasis on theory-driven studies ... We do not believe that this precludes data-driven theoretical application-type studies; only that a greater balance between the two types of studies needs to be achieved. (McMahan *et al.* 1999: 118)

A framework for SHRM metrics should enable researchers to better articulate which processes they are choosing to measure ... Thus, as SHRM researchers consider appropriate variables to test theory, a metrics framework can assist by showing the nature of the measures necessary to support or refute the inferences ... Thus it is incumbent on those who develop and apply SHRM theory to choose appropriate measures, but it is also incumbent on measurement developers to provide a theory-based framework, not simply an ever growing list of new measures ... [W]ithout a measurement framework, it will be difficult to develop a theoretical logic or measurement rigour to support the inference that investments in human resource strategies lead to organisational success. (Boudreau and Ramstad 1999: 78)

The challenge of effectively linking human capital development to financial performance is three-fold: (1) measures must capture direct and indirect effects; (2) the measurement process must be simple, repeatable and lead to actionable conclusions; and (3) results need to be compiled so that plans and forecasts can be built from them. (Thomas *et al.* 2003: 2)

After considering this catalogue of problems and challenges, some might be tempted to abandon this line of research. This would be unfortunate since exploration of the HRM-Performance link provides one of the major current research challenges in the field of HRM. It would also be unfortunate because, despite all the methodological shortcomings and possible sources of error, the research is making progress. (Guest 2001: 1004)

Comments like these serve to demonstrate just how little researchers have actually thought about the relationship between developing theory and engaging in measurement. Even in cases where some reflection is undertaken, the results are less than convincing. Hendry *et al.*, for example, use Guest's suggestion that what is needed is (a) a theory of HRM; (b) a theory of performance; and (c) a theory of how HRM and performance are linked. They then go on to suggest that the work of Becker and Huselid meets these requirements, that is, it:

Identifies HRM with a set of (or bundle of) HR practices that constitute a high performance work system (HPWS), it *defines* performance in terms

of intermediate/accounting measures, and it argues that what characterises the impact HRM has on competitive performance is the fact that the
unique configuration of HPWS factors in the successful firm cannot be
imitated by others. (Hendry *et al.* 2000: 50, emphasis added)

It is, however, far from clear that the work of Becker and Huselid
does meet the requirements in terms of providing us with the requisite theories. In what sense does *identification* constitute a *theory* of
HRM? Whether it is true or false, to identify the bundles of HRM
practices empirically associated with organisational performance
does not constitute a theory. Similarly, *defining* performance outcomes does not constitute a *theory* of performance either. True, the
resource-based theory alluded to with the phrase 'the unique configuration of HPWS factors that cannot be imitated' has the potential to
be a theory of how HRM and performance are linked. But resource-
based theory is:

(1) rooted in neoclassical economic theory which is beset by its own
    theoretical and philosophical problems;
(2) is partial in the sense that it cannot, on its own, explain the entire
    linkage;
(3) is not the only theoretical game in town as there are literally scores
    of other theories mentioned in the literature; and
(4) has a serious problem for empirical research on the HRM–P link
    that will be discussed in Chapter 4.

This 'solution' has been far less successful than many might have
hoped. Quantitative, empirical and statistical research, some of it
exceptionally sophisticated, has multiplied in the last decade with
little or no development of the theoretical foundations of empirical
research on the HRM–P link, and we are unaware of any significant
theoretical breakthroughs derived from this research. Not everyone
appears to agree. After five pages discussing a small selection of the
potential 'theories' on offer, Becker and Huselid (1998: 61) conclude
that they: 'do not subscribe to the notion that the HRM literature
lacks a solid theoretical foundation ... There is a strong theoretical
foundation in both the strategy and organizational economics litera-
tures'. No sooner have they said this, however, than they are forced
to pull their punch, writing that the existing 'theoretical foundation
needs to be sharpened ... with a better understanding of how the

HRM system affects bottom line performance'. Moreover, they too fall back on the well trodden idea that 'we need a richer empirical literature to inform theoretical development'.

Before we leave this section, we should really make the following important point. Suppose some empirical research, employing appropriate statistical techniques, tests relevant hypotheses and claims to have identified an empirical association between 'explanatory' variables measuring some bundle of HRM practices, and an independent variable measuring organisational performance. We have to be crystal clear what such research does and does not tell us. It does tell us that there *is* an empirical association. It does not, however, tell us *why* this association holds; it does not explain this association. Whilst knowing that an empirical relationship exists is important, for us, this is merely the start of the scientific journey and the next leg must reveal *why* this is the case, and this involves explanation. Unfortunately, current empirical research on the HRM–P link starts and finishes with attempts to reveal that an empirical association exists; it never embarks upon the second leg of the journey.

Taking a cavalier approach to theory

Some empirical researchers claim that theory is fairly widely discussed and debated in the literature. Ferratt *et al.* (2005: 238), for example, claim the 'SHRM literature offers extensive theory and empirical evidence supporting the existence of configurations of HRM practices'. Whilst it is true that the term 'theory' crops up repeatedly in the literature, this does not mean a serious debate or discussion about *genuine* theory is taking place. Indeed, we suspect that theory is not treated with anything like the seriousness it deserves. The question we need to consider is this: do the references to 'theory' actually constitute something that can be said to be a solid theoretical foundation for empirical research on the HRM–P link?

Boselie *et al.* (2005) have done a major service to the paradigm by surveying 104 journal articles on research on the HRM–P link in which they:

tried to identify for each article which theory seemed to inform the research. However, this proved far from obvious in many of the articles.

Theoretical frameworks tended to be presented as part of a general rationale for the study, or they were deployed to explain the study's findings. We found very few studies that had derived from a theory an explicit set of propositions, and then tested these in the research design. (Boselie *et al.* 2005: 71)

Still no consensus has emerged on what employee management activities should be in a comprehensive 'HRM checklist', since no widely accepted theoretical rationale exists for selecting practices as definitively essential to HRM. (Boselie *et al.* 2005: 72)

Between the input (i.e. some form of HRM intervention) and output (i.e. some indicator of performance) ... lies what HRM does to improve performance, how and why ... This stage is popularly referred to as the 'black box', because we know so little of what happens at this stage, and hence its content remains mysterious ... Our analysis of the 104 articles confirms the impression that the linking mechanisms' between HRM and performance ... and the mediating effects of key variables ... are largely disregarded. Indeed, whilst we found plenty of acknowledgements of the existence of the 'black box', and some speculation as to its possible content, few studies tried to look inside it. It is surprisingly rare to find a detailed exposition of the conceptual model being used to link HRM with performance, still less a diagram. In most cases, the content of the 'black box' has to be inferred from the brief descriptions of the research design, extrapolated from the methodology, or gleaned from the reported statistical analysis. (Boselie *et al.* 2005: 77)

It is worth noting that Boselie *et al.* are being rather charitable in their interpretation of whether theory informs research: 'rather than confine [their] analysis to the handful of articles that tested a theory, [they] counted all significant mentions of theories in the text' (71). It is clear that Boselie *et al.*'s survey strongly suggests that references to 'theory' often found in empirical research on the HRM–P link *do not* actually constitute something that can be said to be a solid theoretical foundation.

Sutton and Staw (1995) are so concerned at what we have called the cavalier treatment of 'theory' in organisational and management literature in general, that they produced a paper entitled: 'What Theory is *Not*'. Their five-fold account of what theory is not is useful in highlighting concepts that are often mistakenly conflated in the HRM–P literature with theory.

(1) References are not theory

Listing references to existing theories and mentioning the names of such theories is not the same as explicating the causal logic they contain ... References are often used like a smokescreen to hide the absence of theory. (Sutton and Staw 1995: 372–3)

(2) Data are not theory

Authors try to develop a theoretical foundation by describing empirical findings from past research and then quickly move from this to a discussion of the current results ... There is no attempt ... to explain the logical reasons why particular findings occurred in the past, or why certain empirical relationships are anticipated in the future. We only learn ... that others had reported certain findings ... This is a result of brute empiricism. (Sutton and Staw 1995: 374)

(3) Lists of variables or constructs are not theory

Papers ... often are written as if well defined variables or constructs, by themselves, are enough to make a theory. A theory must also explain why variables or constructs come about or why they are connected. (Sutton and Staw 1995: 375)

Many researchers appear to select the variables for their empirical analysis solely on the grounds that they bulk large in the wider literature. Batt (2001: 10) includes 'five types of supportive HR practice' because they are suggested by 'prior literature' and Galbreath (2005: 980) uses the constructs he does largely 'because they have been tested in previous literature'. Not only is this practice not theory, it is also an inadequate rationale for including variables in the analysis. This is what we referred to above as 'measurement without theory'.

(4) Diagrams are not theory

Regardless of their merits, diagrams and figures should be considered as stage props rather than the performance itself ... [W]hile boxes and arrows can add order to a conception, they rarely explain *why* the proposed will be observed. (Sutton and Staw 1995: 376)

(5) Hypotheses (or predictions) are not theory

Hypotheses do not (and should not) contain logical arguments about why empirical relationships are expected to occur. (Sutton and Staw 1995: 377)

It must be said that it is quite difficult to spot these mistakes in the empirical research on the HRM–P link precisely because of the ambiguous way theory is dealt with. The mistakes tend not to appear as clearly distinguishable and identifiable, but often tend to run into one another. Lists of references often come as part of the descriptions of empirical findings from past and wider research that then suggest certain variables which are subsequently presented in the form of hypotheses, and sometimes discussions of findings refer to 'theory'. At the end of many articles, the reader is left with only a vague idea of how 'theory' informs the empirical research. This may well be what prompted Boselie *et al.* (2005) to suggest that 'theoretical frameworks tend to be presented as part of a general rationale for the study or they were deployed to explain the study's findings'.

In what follows, we take ten examples of empirical research on the HRM–P link and, keeping Sutton and Staw's five-fold account of what a theory is *not* firmly in mind, we ask the question: *do the references to existing literature and/or theory actually constitute something that can be said to be a solid theoretical foundation?*

First, Sila (2006) explicitly claims to use 'organisational theory', especially institutional and contingency theories, to formulate propositions regarding the effects of Total Quality Management (TQM) on performance. The article opens with a brief mention of the two theories before shifting to discuss the empirical findings of several previous articles. A section entitled 'Model and hypotheses' claims that the TQM construct can be measured by seven general categories of practice. The TQM variables, along with the performance variables, are described (in one sentence) along with references to the relevant supporting literature in a table. Another table shows that the TQM variables used by Sila have been used in previous studies. A caveat is then added to the effect that although the major dependent and independent variables have been included 'no claim is made that they are exhaustive, if indeed such a claim is possible' (Sila 2006: 5). Whilst this is an understandable caveat, our concern is that Sila does not use this insight to raise fundamental questions about methodology. If not all the variables can be included, what consequence does this have for our theory and understanding of the HRM and organisational phenomena under scrutiny? Can issues like this simply be put off forever? Who is going to deal with them? The next nine sections of the paper are characterised by a couple of paragraphs on each of the nine effects that TQM and/or HRM is alleged to have on the nine outcomes of interest, generating nine hypotheses. Each paragraph offers a very brief explanation about why the particular TQM or HR practice has the hypothesised effect, with some supporting references and a mention of past research that found (or in the odd case, failed to find) positive statistical associations between TQM/HRM, and the hypothesised effect. Unfortunately, these sections remain theoretically emaciated. Describing empirical findings from past research does not constitute a theoretical foundation. The 'explanations' offered are so brief that they often border on the banal – e.g. a 'company's success in the long run depends on how effectively it satisfies its customers' needs' and making teamworking, employee empowerment and involvement in decision-making part of TQM 'contributes positively to employee results such as employee satisfaction' (Sila 2006: 5). Statements of this kind are not actually explanations at all, as they offer no account of *why*, for example, teamworking causes employee satisfaction. The nine hypotheses are not actually tests of any particular theory or theories, but seem to follow, vaguely, from the passing mentions to theory and previous empirical evidence, or perhaps from the diagram showing the structural equation model of the nine hypotheses 'developed using literature support' (Sila 2006: 5). The diagram adds nothing more to the 'theory' mentioned in the text. The paper then moves on to discuss contextual factors. Whilst a charitable reading might concede that there is slightly more theory contained in this section, because this is where institutional and contingency theory are mentioned, it seems to us that virtually the same approach is adopted as in the last section and there is little utility to be gained from analysing it further.

In the second example, Sels *et al.* (2006a) offer a two-sectioned literature review before getting on with the statistical analysis.

Reviewing the value-creating effects of HPWP (High Performance Work Practices) involves a discussion of the universalistic and configurational perspectives and the contingency approach, before going on to mention 'an additional theoretical perspective' – thereby, implying that the literature review contains a discussion of 'theory'. The discussion, however, does little more than re-state empirical relationships found in the literature. For example, 'the universalistic perspective states that a fixed set of best practices can create surplus value in various business contexts' (Sels *et al.* 2006: 322). The 'additional theoretical perspective' turns out to be a similar relational statement: 'groups of employees possess skills and perform activities that vary in importance to a firm's competitiveness'. They go on to cite two references to this perspective before adding a paragraph observing that 'the majority of empirical studies on the HRM-Performance link report a positive story'. The review of the cost-increasing effects of HPWP does carry a little more theoretical detail, but really does not go much beyond citing the empirical findings of several relevant studies. A diagram is offered (Sels *et al.* 2006: 324) which, admittedly, does make the connections between the variables easier to identify, but adds nothing more to the 'theory' mentioned in the text. A section entitled 'Conceptual framework and hypotheses' then follows. After a brief discussion of the chosen measures they caution the reader that they will 'discuss some examples (without being exhaustive) on how they [HPWP's] can be conceptually linked with productivity' (Sels *et al.* 2006: 324). Again, the problem of what to include is fudged, something that is all the more worrying since it appears in a section devoted to 'conceptual frameworks' where we might expect issues of this kind to be raised. If not here, then where? The ensuing discussion is brief, again to the point of being banal: 'Offering high wages and benefits can improve productivity by facilitating both the attraction and retention of a superior workforce' (Sels *et al.* 2006: 325). This emaciated discussion of 'theory' eventually results in hypothesis 1: 'HRM intensity has a direct positive effect on productivity'. This hypothesis is not, however, a test of any theory in particular. Indeed, it seems to be a vague kind of 'test' to see if the (arbitrarily) chosen six HRM variables are associated with productivity. The paper proceeds through the next few sections in much the same manner, so we will not discuss them.

Third, Lau and Ngo offer a 'conceptual framework' in their study to 'explain how HR is related to innovation performance, as a response to the call for more theoretical development in HR research' (2004: 686). The first two sections review some of the past studies and cite so many other studies, it can be accused of playing a kind of 'name dropping' game – their reference list contains seventy-seven references, most of them made in passing. Section three starts with the claim that: 'Three sets of HR practices have been highlighted in the literature that would support an innovation-orientated HR system. They are: (1) training focused ... (2) performance based rewards ... and (3) team development' (Lau and Ngo 2004: 688). This is followed by a couple of pages that appear to offer an explanation of why each of the three HRM practices affect performance. A close reading reveals this not to be the case. These pages offer little more than a very brief explanation about why each of the HR practices affect organisational performance and, again, are so brief that they often border on the banal – e.g. 'Training can enhance employees' knowledge and skills that are critical to new product development' and 'In order to sustain competitiveness, learning behaviours have to be rewarded' (Lau and Ngo 2004: 689). The main thrust of these sections, however, seems to be the identification of past research that found positive statistical associations between the three HRM practices and innovation performance. This section ends with hypothesis 1: 'HR practices that emphasize extensive training, performance-based reward, and team development, when configured as an HR system, have positive effects on a firm's innovation performance' (Lau and Ngo 2004: 691). This hypothesis is not, however, a test of any theory in particular. Indeed, it seems to be a vague kind of 'test' of three propositions 'highlighted in the literature' to the effect that training focus, performance-based rewards and team development might be associated with innovative performance. Section four introduces organisational culture, where more of the same is offered, and ends with a hypothesis that, again, does not test any particular theory, so we will not elaborate further. Despite claiming to offer a 'conceptual framework' to explain how HR is related to innovation performance, Lau and Ngo offer little by way of serious theoretical grounding.

In the fourth example, Ahmad and Schroeder (2003: 20–1) list Pfeffer's 'seven HRM practices that are expected to enhance organizational performance', adding that several other researchers 'have argued why these practices are expected to enhance organizational performance'. Unfortunately, Ahman and Schroeder offer no explanation for why it is just these seven variables, and not (say) the thirteen proposed by Huselid (1995). They also claim that their study will be 'testing the theory of HRM' without actually specifying which 'theory' they mean. Indeed, in the section entitled 'Theoretical background and hypotheses', several 'theories' are mentioned: internalisation and externalisation of employment, transaction cost theory, human capital theory, the behavioural psychology perspective and the resource-based view.

Fifth, Huselid's (1995) enormously influential paper carries a one-page section entitled 'Theoretical background' where there is brief mention of resource-based theory and human capital theory, coupled with comments on the need for employees to be motivated, rewarded, and to be allowed to participate. In sum, this hardly constitutes a theoretical discussion at all. Moreover, the hypotheses Huselid tests are not really tests of any theory in particular.

Sixth, Wan *et al.* (2002: 34) 'decided to test six strategic HRM variables that have been consistently identified in the literature as proactive HRM practices', seemingly oblivious to the fact that the process of 'testing variables' is meaningless.

Seventh, Combs *et al.* (2006: 515) claim to 'develop a theory explaining why HPWSs should have stronger effects among manufacturers than service organizations'. Their 'theory' turns out to be four 'reasons' why this may be the case. Whilst the reasons are plausible, it is not clear to us why they can be said to constitute a theory.

Eighth, Zheng *et al.* (2006: 1772–3) make reference to the usual oft-cited HRM–P studies suggesting that they offer 'theoretical discussions of HRM' and 'theoretical models' that 'address key ideas about HRM and effectively offer a comprehensive map of the field'. They classify HRM practices, outcomes and performance. What makes a model 'theoretical' is, however, never specified. Phrases like 'addressing key issues' and 'mapping the field' avoid having to state exactly what purpose these theoretical models serve.

In the ninth example, Katou and Budhwar (2006) are aware of the under-theorised nature of empirical research on the HRM–P link, and they consider their paper as a contribution to theory development. They claim that their paper 'supports *the theory* that HRM systems have a positive impact upon organizational performance' (2006: 1223, emphasis added). Unfortunately, this is not a theory: it is a statement about an empirical relation. Furthermore, it is not clear what 'theory' their hypotheses are actually testing. This can be seen by considering their first hypothesis: 'A positive relationship exists between HRM outcomes and organizational performance' (2006: 1227). There are, clearly, a great number of theories compatible with this hypothesis, but Katou and Budhwar do not say which one they have in mind. Furthermore, and related to the discussion a few pages ago, Katou and Budhwar also misunderstand the nature of the black box problem. For them, the black box problem arises from attempts to proceed directly from a set of HR *practices*, or an HR system, directly to business performance, thereby neglecting the intervening or mediating HR *outcomes*. The HR *outcomes*, then, constitute a black box. Framed this way, the solution to the problem is to 'specify the mediators' and 'collect measures of these constructs' and they go on to identify a series of 'mediating variables' or 'intervening variables' (2006: 124). This, they suggest, will lead to 'theoretical development'. What they miss, however, is that the black box problem is not a problem of missing mediating or intervening variables or constructs, but of *missing explanation*. What is missing is an explanation of exactly what the HR mechanisms (HR practices and HR outcomes) do to influence organisational performance. They are clearly aware that some problem lurks here because they claim their paper 'explains the mechanisms through which HRM systems improve organizational performance' (2006: 1248). Identifying a set of mediating variables, however, is not the same as explaining the operation of the mechanisms these variables are supposedly expressing.

The final example comes from Kepes and Delery (2007: 386) who note that previous researchers have 'outlined three theoretical frameworks that were being used to describe the relationship between HRM practices and performance' and then go on to outline the universalistic, the contingency and configurational approaches and perspectives. A great deal of research in the paradigm (e.g. the second example) uses these three perspectives or approaches as the theories explaining the empirical link between HRM and performance. At best, however, these approaches or perspectives might be considered proto-theories; early attempts at theorising. At worst, they are little more than statements about empirical relations, and are themselves in need of theory to explain them. Unfortunately, they are almost always treated as if they are not only, self-evidently, theories, but good theories to boot. To be fair, Kepes and Delery go on to develop a rather sophisticated model of the HRM architecture and offer a neat diagram that reveals the 'overall HRM architecture with various HRM systems and different HRM activities and components or levels of abstraction is a complex system composed of multiple elements which are likely to interact in complex ways' (2007: 392). They recognise that whilst they have sketched out some of the key sets of relations, their sketch will require others to carry out more theoretical work, perhaps along the lines they have started. If we consider their sketch to be a good start, then where does this leave the theoretical status of the universalistic, the contingency and configurational approaches that have nowhere near this level of theoretical elaboration?

What, then, can we conclude from these examples? According to Brewster (1999: 215), who in all fairness is probably being charitable to the scientistic approach: 'The strength of this approach is that good research based upon it tends to have a clear potential for theoretical development, it can lead to carefully drawn research questions.' This, however, is aspirational: it is a statement of what *should* happen. Yet as the examples above show, empirical research tends *not* to be carefully drawn from existing theory. These examples cited above (with the exception of Kepes and Delery), and there are many others,[13] strongly encourage the conclusion that in much of the empirical research on the HRM–P link where 'theory' is discussed, the discussion is often *arbitrary, ambiguous, vague, brief and unsophisticated*. We will refer to this simply as a '*cavalier*' approach to theory. Discussion of 'theory' very often turns out to be little more than a trawl through past research, 'cherry picking' theories and empirical evidence that sustains the hypotheses the particular author is keen to test – theories and evidence that would undermine the hypothesis are often ignored. Whilst some of the theory that is mentioned might well provide theoretical foundations for the empirical findings, there are usually several other unmentioned theories equally compatible with the data and hypotheses, and that could equally provide theoretical foundations for the findings. '*Theory' is repeatedly discussed, without being developed*. This is hardly unsurprising since, without philosophical reflection on what a bona fide theory might look like, it is most unlikely that empirical researchers are going to generate and/or develop a specific theory of HRM.

It is, therefore, difficult not to conclude that theory is treated in this *cavalier* manner, because empirical research on the HRM–P link is being driven, not by a commitment to bolster theory, but by a commitment to scientism, the deductive method and the quantitative, statistical and empirical techniques scientism sponsors. Wan *et al.* (2002: 35) make no bones about it: 'The prime objective' of their study is to 'ascertain the relationships between strategic HRM and firm performance', and they do not even bother to discuss theory, implying that the passing references to existing literature and theory constitute something that can be said to be a solid theoretical foundation. All too often, passing references to theory turn out to be little more than a fig-leaf exercise to hide theoretical nakedness, before getting on with what is presumed to be the task of doing the real 'science', namely, statistical analysis.

Before we leave this section, we would like to add three important caveats to head off any possible misunderstanding. First, the truth or falsity of the claims cited in the above examples is not an issue. Our objections are not based on our disagreement with this or that empirical claim, or this or that theory. The nature of theory itself and its cavalier treatment in the literature is the issue. Second, we have not singled out these particular authors in order to simply rubbish their work. Indeed, in many respects these articles are good examples of the paradigm. The point is we happen to think *the entire paradigm itself is misconceived* and these authors are simply doing what everyone else does. Third, none of the foregoing arguments and objections mean that we are asking every piece of empirical research on the HRM–P link to 'revue every nuance of every theory cited' as Sutton and Staw (1995: 373) aptly put it. We are, however, asking that enough of the previous theoretical work be included in any empirical research on the HRM–P link so that the reader can grasp the author's underlying theoretical foundations. This is, of course, a matter of judgment: and in our opinion, much of the judgment is mistaken, as the following examples illustrate. According to Sila (2006: 10) structural contingency theory 'suggests that organizations that can establish a fit between organizational structure and environmental uncertainty will achieve a higher organisational performance result'. On this definition, structural contingency theory is not a theory at all, it is a statement expressing some kind of regular or law-like relationship between an action and a consequence. Yao-Sheng (2005: 294–5) makes use of the popular 'theoretical model' referred to as the 'behavioural perspective'. According to this perspective, 'different strategies require different behaviours and different HRM practices to elicit and reinforce those behaviours. This view of the link between strategy and HRM *provides a clear explanation* for why management should be linked to strategy' (emphasis added). Sila and Yao-Sheng would have to offer a more nuanced account of structural contingency theory and the behavioural perspective to convince us that they are acting with solid theoretical foundations in their empirical work.

Theory: too little or too much?

There is a final twist to the story of under-theorisation. Claiming, as we do, that empirical research on the HRM–P link is under-theorised, does not mean that there are actually too few theories. Indeed, far from there being too few theories there are, actually, an embarrassment of riches. Scattered throughout the literature are references to a bewildering array of approaches, perspectives, frameworks, typologies, studies, theories, models, maps and accounts, all at various levels of abstraction, generality, universality, particularity, concreteness and micro or macro orientation. For brevity, and in the absence of any other suitable term, we will simply refer to them as 'theories' with the scare quotes implying our concern about calling them theories at all. In no particular order, the fifty-two 'theories' we are aware of (and there are probably others we have missed) are as follows:

- the normative model
- the descriptive-functional model
- the descriptive-behavioural model
- the critical-evaluative model
- the Michigan, Harvard, Guest's and Warwick models
- HRM as a map
- the universalistic, internal fit, best practice or one size fits all approach
- the bundling or internal fit approach

- the contingency or external fit approach
- contingency theory
- structural contingency theory
- the configurational approach
- individual-organisational performance linkages
- General Systems Theory
- the personnel systems and staff alignment perspective
- the partnership or stakeholder perspective
- the New Economics of Personnel
- the strategic contingency approach
- strategic, descriptive and normative theories of HRM
- expectancy theory
- action theory
- strategic reference points theory
- systematic agreement theory
- discretion theory
- dynamic capabilities theory
- ability, motivation and opportunity (AMO) theory
- control theory
- balanced scorecard approach
- the job characteristics model
- social exchange theory
- leader-member exchange theory
- labour process theory
- the behavioural perspective
- the role behaviour perspective
- population ecology
- cybernetic models
- agency theory
- transaction cost economics
- the resource-based theory/view
- power/resource dependence theory
- human capital theory
- organisational learning theory
- information processing theory
- Institutional theory
- New Institutional theory
- evolutionary theory
- co-evolutionary theory

- absorptive capacity theory
- real options theory
- critical theory
- Marxist theory
- Foucauldian theory

For overviews of at least some of these 'theories', see Boselie *et al.* (2005, especially the website mentioned on p. 71); Cakar and Bititci (2002); Ferris *et al.* (2004); Hiltrop (1996); Jackson and Schuler (1995) and McMahan *et al.* (1999).[14]

Jackson and Schuler's double-edged comment half grasps the problem: 'Although imperfect, potentially useful theories are relatively plentiful' (1995: 256). Whereas they see the relative plentitude making up for the imperfect nature of the theories on offer, we do not. A thousand imperfect theories may not generate a perfect, or even a good, theory. Moreover, the fact that there are so many theories, and that they exist in a kind of 'theoretical jumble', strongly suggests that they are not being taken seriously by empirical researchers: indeed it reinforces our view that theory is treated in a cavalier manner. According to Becker and Gerhart (1996: 777): 'Although theory development is critical to the development of a discipline, *a proliferation of theories and concepts can impede the accumulation of knowledge.*' And unfortunately, a proliferation of 'theories' is precisely what empirical research on the HRM–P link has at present. In an exceptionally revealing, throwaway comment, Wright *et al.* (2001: 706) mention how many empirical studies 'at least pay lip service' to the theoretical perspective known as the Resource Based View (RBV). What is true for RBV is, arguably, true for many other theories: they are mentioned in empirical research on the HRM–P link, but often by way of a fig-leaf to cover theoretical nakedness.

None of this means the fifty-two 'theories' noted above are inappropriate: some are, some are not; some might be worth pursuing and elaborating, others might not. The problem is that without theoretical and philosophical reflection on what constitutes a bona fide theory, it is going to be an uphill struggle to make any headway in sorting the wheat from the chaff. Whilst it is likely to cause frustration, and even refutation, we interpret this embarrassment of riches to mean that the empirical research on the HRM–P link is currently miles away from developing solid theoretical foundations. A paradigm that has fifty 'theories' all contributing to the explanation of (roughly) the same phenomena is not a healthy one.

It would, of course, require a book to evaluate this bewildering array of accounts, not to mention seriously taxing our multidisciplinary knowledge. We proceed, therefore, by using the work of Jackson and Schuler (1995), Schuler and Jackson (2005), Guest (1997, 1999, 2001), and Way and Johnson (2005), because they are amongst the very few writers who have recognised the problem of under-theorisation enough to actually write about it. Our aim is to show that even researchers such as these, who appear committed to some form of scientism, are sceptical of the theories that come within their orbit.

Guest

More than any other researcher in the field, Guest has sought to identify various theories, models, approaches and perspectives that might, conceivably, underpin research on the HRM–P link. In an early paper he identified three broad categories of general-level theory (i.e. strategic, descriptive and normative) and a 'host of more specific and concrete theories about particular areas of policy and practice' (1997: 264). By 1999 he identified 'eight theoretical perspectives, representing five broader, though sometimes overlapping conceptual perspectives' (Guest 1999: 7). The five broad perspectives are individual–organisational performance linkages; strategic fit; personnel systems and staff alignment; partnership or stakeholder perspective; and new economics of personnel. In 2001 he identifies the new economics of personnel; human capital theory; the strategic contingency approach; developments in theory and performance related to refinements in metrics to measure the impact of HRM on business performance; and developments that lay greater focus on outcomes of relevance to individual employees.

Guest is clearly not enamoured with many of the theories, models, approaches and perspectives he identifies. In the following section we use a combination of Guest's own comments, and some of our own observations, to demonstrate that many of these theories, models, approaches and perspectives are most unlikely to provide the much-needed theoretical underpinnings. We will attempt this by reference to the different themes within the HRM–P literature that Guest identifies.

Strategic and *descriptive theories of HRM* are dismissed because they fail to 'provide much insight into how HRM policy and practice translates into performance' (Guest 1997: 267). *Normative theories of HRM* have their roots in organisational psychology and lower-range, more specific behavioural theories, specifically *expectancy theory* – which he describes as a 'theory about the link between HRM and performance' (Guest 1997: 267). Guest is a little unsure of what to make of expectancy theory. In 1997 and 2001 it passes with no critical comment, but in 1999 he is troubled by the 'problems with the rationality assumptions underpinning Expectancy Theory' and 'the residual problem of aggregating individual responses' (1999: 8 and 11). For reasons discussed above, and related to the use of knowingly false assumptions (in this case, specifically the rationality assumption), expectancy theory cannot provide the missing theory.

Guest damns the *new economics of personnel* with faint praise. 'One of the great virtues of economics is that it is very theory driven. A drawback is that the theory, at least in this context, can be narrow and simplistic' (2001: 1093). Being 'theory driven' is, however, not a virtue when that theory is narrow and simplistic. It is even less of a virtue when it relies, necessarily, upon extensive use of knowingly false assumptions. As will become clear in the following section, this approach is not a suitable theoretical basis for empirical research on the HRM–P link. The same goes for human capital theory – we do not elaborate here because Guest does not.

Guest criticises the *strategic fit* approach because it does not 'address the black box' (1999: 11), which would seem to invalidate it immediately as a potentially useful theory. This is in contrast to the new world of metrics identified by Guest. Modest developments in theory and performance have occurred, according to Guest, in relation to 'a *refinement in the metrics* that can be used to measure the impact of HRM on business performance' (emphasis added) and he cites the work of Huselid. No matter how refined, however, a metric is not a theory. We do find it a little worrying that Guest can discuss 'refinements in metrics' in a section entitled 'Theoretical development' (2001: 1093).

Under the heading *individual–organisational performance linkages*, Guest locates expectancy theory (which we have dealt with) and *action theory*. Whilst we have no particular objection to action theory (much would depend on the specific version under examination), and would not rule out its use in investigating the psycho-dynamics of individual action, even Guest realises 'the residual problem of aggregating individual responses' (1999: 11). The best we could say is that action theory might assist in explaining some aspects of individual behaviour in the HR theatre.

Another area where Guest sees modest theoretical development comes from work focusing on outcomes that are of relevance to *individual employees* and investigates their reactions to HRM (2001: 1093). Whilst experience of the 'inside story' (Mabey *et al.* 1998) is clearly important, this issue relates to methodology rather than theory: it is a comment on how to investigate any HR related issue. Furthermore, apart from the Mabey *et al.* collection, Guest musters support for the development of this approach with references to large-scale surveys, thereby conflating the development of theory with the development of empirical evidence.

Guest explains the *strategic contingency approach* as follows: 'In manufacturing, a high performance/high commitment approach may always be preferable since labour costs are a small proportion of total costs and high-quality labour can facilitate fuller exploitation of other more costly resources. But in services, there is still a strategic choice between the high road of investment in a numerically flexible, low wage, highly controlled workforce' (2001: 1093). Whilst these may indeed be sound observations, we are not convinced this approach amounts to a theory.

The *partnership or stakeholder perspective* is rooted in industrial relations and centres around the need for some form of joint governance system to maintain employee involvement, facilitate meaningful two-way communication and minimise exploitation (Guest 1999: 13). Again, whilst these may indeed be sound observations, this perspective does not amount to a theory.

Finally, when Guest refers to *personnel systems and staff alignment*, he has in mind *resource-based theory* (1999: 12). The essence of resource-based theory (RBT) revolves around the claim that a firm's competitive advantage is generated by possession of a unique configuration of HPWS factors that cannot be imitated by others. Whilst we accept that some version of RBT may be the way forward, as it stands it is often (but arguably need not be[15]) rooted in neoclassical economic theory which, as we will see shortly, is beset by its own theoretical problems. Moreover, the very uniqueness and inimitability of the HR practices presumed to generate competitive advantage, especially when dynamic factors like entrepreneurial insights and tacit knowledge are included, would very likely make the discovery of a stable empirical link between some bundle of HR practices and organisational performance most unlikely. Whilst RBT may indeed be a fruitful way to proceed, a great deal more work will have to be done on the 'theory' aspect of RBT. We agree with Boxall and Purcell's (2000: 199) observation that 'the RBV of the firm, does not provide a sufficient basis for the theory of strategic HRM but does offer some useful signals on how to carry forward research on HR strategy'.

The fact that Guest can run through some of the most commonly mentioned 'theories' and still be extremely disappointed with them, does not bode well for current empirical research on the HRM–P link.[16]

Jackson and Schuler

Jackson and Schuler's work is useful in a different way to that of Guest. Whilst they too provide a selection of 'theories' we use their commentaries on these 'theories' for two reasons. First, because they allow us to highlight some of the difficulties and ambiguities surrounding the theoretical concepts on offer. This is not really a criticism of Jackson and Schuler, but more a criticism of the paradigm that generates the concepts Jackson and Schuler are trying to make sense of. Second, their commentaries allow us to highlight a general tension that pervades the philosophy underpinning these 'theories'.

Let us consider Jackson and Schuler's (1995: 239–43) list of 'theories' drawn from sociology, economics, management and psychology that might potentially be relevant for theorising HRM.

- In *general systems theory* (GST) skills and abilities are inputs from the external environment, employee behaviour is the cellular mechanism, and organisational performance is the output. Systems theory is a 'broad church'. Scott (1992) notes four generic categories of system: closed-rational models, closed-natural models, open-rational models and open-natural models. Putting matters simplistically, closed-system models lend themselves to scientism, whereas open-system models, especially open-system natural models, do not. GST is also criticised for its functionalism.

- *Role behaviour perspective* is a micro social-psychological, interpretive approach to studying the expectations of role holders in organisations. It has recently been used by Stone-Romero *et al.* (2003) to consider how cultural and sub-cultural phenomena affect the work-related 'scripts' that a worker is willing and able to use. As with all approaches that explicitly focus upon qualitative phenomena like interactions, this perspective does not lend itself to scientism.[17]

- *Institutional theory* focuses upon explaining the processes through which internal and external pressures on an organisation lead it to (a) resist change and (b) evolve and converge. Institutional theory is also a broad church with some of its advocates adopting scientistic philosophy and others rejecting it.

- *Resource dependence theory* focuses upon issues of control of valued resources, and hence power. Whilst it is usually considered to be a micro sociological-psychological, interactionist perspective, any form of theorising that treats power as central cannot ignore extensive work stemming from Marxist, or more fashionably, postmodern and Foucauldian approaches. Scientism, with its emphasis on quantification and measurement, would find it exceptionally difficult, if not impossible, to make sense of these concepts.

- *Human capital theory*. If the expected benefits exceed the costs, rational agents choose to invest in their (or perhaps their offspring's) human capital, that is, skills and knowledge, and this makes their human capital valuable. Rational firms then hire this human capital as they would any other capital asset because it enables these firms to generate value. Because human capital cannot be separated from the human, all those costs associated with training, motivating, monitoring and retaining are human capital investments made by the firm. Human capital theory is explicitly rooted in scientism.

- *Transaction cost theory* argues that rational firms choose governance structures that economise costs associated with establishing, monitoring and enforcing explicit exchanges. It is predicated upon the two basic ideas: that agents are rational, but are limited (bounded) in their ability to process information. Transaction cost theory is explicitly rooted in scientism.

- *Agency theory (or principle-agent theory)* deals with contractual situations where one party (the principal) delegates a task to another party (the agent). In these situations, the agent and the principle might have conflicting goals, and the principle cannot be sure the agent will act in the principle's best interest. Principles seek efficient contracts which align the goals of both parties at minimal transaction costs. Agency theory is also explicitly rooted in scientism.

- *Resource-based theory* has been used to explain why coherent HRM systems lead to sustained competitive advantage. Advantage is gained by implementing a value-creating strategy that competitors cannot easily copy or sustain. The firm's HRM system is arguably the most difficult to copy or sustain. In the hands of neoclassical economists, where it has tended to be located, resource-based theory is explicitly rooted in scientism – but see the comments above in the section on Guest.

A decade later, Schuler and Jackson (2005) return to theory. This time round resource dependence theory is not mentioned, and whilst systems theory and institutional theory get no explicit mention, they are probably subsumed within what they refer to as their integrative framework. Retained are the behavioural perspective, (previously called role behaviour perspective); human capital theory; and the resource-based *view* (previously called resource-based *theory view*). The new addition is the following:

- *An integrative framework: contextualised and dynamic.* Their own words are worth quoting at length:

Because *the internal and external environments are dynamic,* the process of managing human resources must also be dynamic. Success requires meeting the present demands of multiple stakeholders while also anticipating their demands ... Looking ahead, it seems likely that the focus of academic work ... will evolve away from its current search for effective HRM system designs and towards understanding their dynamic content. Gradually, *the rather mechanistic view of HRM systems* that prevails currently may be replaced by a perspective that recognizes the social aspects of human resource management and the processes through which organizational *members create meaning from a complex array of signals.* (Schuler and Jackson 2005: 14, emphasis added)

Given that scientism makes use of an extremely mechanical notion of causality (see below, chapters 4 and 6) and has no plausible way of dealing with the meaning actors ascribe to their situation, it is extremely difficult to see how this 'theory' could be dealt with legitimately using scientistic philosophy of science.

These three 'theories' are considered in a section designated 'Theoretical Frameworks' which they appear to consider useful for developing a 'logic for predicting' and 'explaining' which HR practices are most effective (Schuler and Jackson 2005: 12). It is interesting to note, however, that in this section they do *not* discuss 'High Performance Work Systems, best practices and HR bundles', 'Strategic contingencies', or the 'Configurational Perspective', approaches and perspectives often referred to elsewhere as providing the 'theoretical' foundations for empirical research on the HRM–P link. It is hard to know if they do or do not consider these approaches and perspectives to be theories; whether their necessary brevity denies them the space to spell out the difference between what they do and do not consider to be theoretical frameworks; or whether they too are a little confused. The latter interpretation is not unreasonable, for the following reasons. They refer, without clarification, to 'several streams of theory', 'conceptual frameworks', 'streams of research', 'logics for predicting' and 'logics for explaining' without making the differences between prediction and explanation clear. Moreover, when discussing strategic contingencies (*not* in the 'Theoretical Frameworks' section) they make reference to two 'well known typologies' namely, 'defender -reactor-analyzer-prospector theory' and 'competitive strategies'. It is hard to know if 'competitive strategies' refers to a theory, a typology, a perspective or something else. Indeed, it is hard to know how they differentiate the various 'theoretical' concepts they mention.

What is most important to note from these two papers, however, is a general tension that pervades the philosophy underpinning these 'theories' – a tension unrecognised by Schuler and Jackson. On the one hand, transactions cost theory, agency theory, human capital theory, and some versions of systems theory and resource-based theory, are rooted in scientism. This interpretation is also encouraged by their reference to 'logics for predicting' and the 'mechanistic view' currently prevailing. On the other hand some of the 'theories' are rooted in non-scientistic philosophies. This interpretation is encouraged by several references that are effectively summed up in the comment about the need to consider the 'social aspects of human resource management and the processes through which organizational members create meaning from a complex array of signals'. Non-scientistic philosophy underpins resource dependence theory, the behavioural perspective, some versions of systems theory, some versions of resource-based theory and their integrative framework.

Rather than compare and contrast all these different 'theories', we focus upon just two to give some examples of the tension. *Resource dependence theory* uses the concepts of power, interpretation, meaning and culture. Phenomena like power, interpretation meaning and culture can, often with great difficulty, be *understood* both by the lay actors and social scientists. That is, as human beings, lay actors know (although often fallibly) what it means to wield, or to lack, power, to interpret a situation, to infer meaning, or to spot a culture-laden activity. Social scientists can often (although often fallibly) come to understand how lay actors understand these phenomena. Importantly, our ability to understand these phenomena does not rest upon our ability to measure them. These phenomena, and a great many others besides, are non-quantitative, inherently qualitative, complex and multidimensional phenomena that cannot be *meaningfully* (see Chapter 4) measured.

These phenomena do not lend themselves to prediction either. *Human capital theory*, by contrast, is predicated upon measurement and predictability. In order to maintain both quantifiability and a strict 'logic for prediction', theories like human capital theory have no option but to eliminate unquantifiable concepts like power, interpretation, meaning and culture. One of the ways they do this, apart from just ignoring them, is by assuming that humans are rational, that is, assuming *homo-economicus*. It is hard to get a more 'mechanistic view' than this notion of the rational maximising human as bargain hunter. Another way of putting this is to say that intrinsically qualitative, complex and multidimensional phenomena like power, interpretation, meaning and culture are not open to analysis using regression, analysis of variance, correlation, structural equation modelling factor analysis and so on. In short, any theories that make use of phenomena such as these (and there are many other non-quantifiable phenomena that are very important to the study of HRM in general) are out of bounds for scientism.

In sum, then, Schuler and Jackson seem not to spot the fact that the 'theories' they cite as potentially underpinning empirical research on the HRM–P link are in conflict with one another. Moreover, even if we tried to create a synthesis by bundling several of them, their contradictory philosophical natures mean they would be incompatible, thereby failing to provide an overarching theoretical base.

Way and Johnson

Way and Johnson (2005) are amongst the few that not only recognise the problem of under-theorisation, but make a serious attempt to overcome it, not by doing more empirical work, but by trying to develop solid theoretical foundations. Whilst their contribution to the debate is most welcome, Way and Johnson cannot deal with the problem thoroughly because they try to address it at the level of theory and not philosophy. Because their contribution is, arguably, the best available we analyse it in some depth in order to show how even work as sophisticated as theirs cannot deal with the problem without going beyond theory. It should be noted at the outset that our disagreement with Way and Johnson is not about the substance of their claims (some of their claims we agree with, and some we do not) but with their general approach to the development of solid theoretical foundations for the paradigm. Let us start our analysis by establishing that Way and Johnson are motivated by a desire to tackle the problem of under-theorisation.

Scholars are still searching for a strong integrated theory of strategic human resource management. (2005: 1)

To date, SHRM has primarily focused on evaluating the linkages among organizational strategies, SHRM (e.g. human resource management (HRM) policies, practices, systems etc) and organizational effectiveness. (2005: 2)

in the absence of a theoretical framework which explicates these primary linkage ... we have little insight into the process by which SHRM creates value and enhances organizational effectiveness. (2005: 2) the development of a sound, theoretically integrated framework for examining the impact of SHRM ... will provide scholars with the tools necessary to generate prescriptive models that accurately explicate and evaluate organizational effectiveness and the elusive primary linkages of SHRM (i.e. the process by which SHRM enhances organizational effectiveness. (2005: 2)

We summarise Way and Johnson's comments thus: *empirical research on the HRM–P link, including research in the SHRM tradition, lacks theoretical foundations and hence lacks the ability to accurately explain and understand the process by which HRM policies, practices, systems etc., enhance organisational effectiveness* – or performance in our terminology.

Their attempt to 'review, integrate and extend several strong theoretical perspectives' (2005: 2) in an effort to offer firmer theoretical underpinnings to empirical research, starts with the resource-based *view*, the multiple stakeholder *perspective*, and the *concepts* of vertical and horizontal linkage. This starting point immediately runs into three problems. First, no rationale is offered for why these three particular 'theories' are selected from the scores available, making their choice arbitrary – which does not mean the insights these 'theories' contain are not useful. Second, despite being discussed in a section entitled 'Theoretical foundations' the term 'theory' is replaced by the terms 'view', 'perspective' and 'concept'. We are not told what allows the multiple stakeholder *perspective*, and the *concepts* of vertical and horizontal linkage to be labelled 'theories'. Is there, once again, a lesson in the terminology?

Be that as it may, their important contribution is to introduce *Systematic Agreement Theory (SAT)* and *Strategic Reference Points Theory (SRPT)*. SAT employs the notion of organisational alignment which they define as follows: 'the degree to which an organization's design, strategies and culture are co-operating to achieve the same desired goals' (2005: 6). An organisation might be in some kind of overall alignment when it achieves (vertical and horizontal) alignment in four senses: structural, cultural, performance and environmental. Way and Johnson then go on to define the outcomes that, if they were met, would allow us to say the organisation is in structural, cultural, performance and environmental alignment. Whilst we have no real quarrel with the entirely plausible idea that organisations should attempt such alignment, two problems arise. They write:

While SAT provides a broad framework for understanding the import-ance of alignment in explicating organizational effectiveness, it does not explain how an organization's leaders should approach these decisions. SRPT offers a more cognitive perspective that helps explain the decision making steps that are necessary to achieve horizontal and vertical linkage. (Way and Johnson 2005: 8)

The first problem is that Systematic Agreement *Theory* is not actu-ally a *theory*: it consists of a set of statements that define a set of desir-able organisational outcomes. A set of statements defining outcomes, however, does not constitute a theory. The second problem is far more subtle. True, being unable to explain how an organisation's leaders should make the decisions, or indeed explain the decision-making steps that would lead to alignment, may well be a problem, but it is not quite the same problem that they set out to resolve. We have to be careful here. Reference to the need for an explanation of the decision-making steps necessary to achieve some desirable outcome could be another way of referring to the need for an explanation and under-standing the process by which HRM policies, practices, systems, etc. might generate some desirable outcome. In this case, the decision-making steps are intelligible because they are anchored in explanation and understanding of why certain HRM policies, practices, systems, etc. do what they do. We suspend judgment on this until we see what Way and Johnson offer in the next section in which they introduce SRPT, which we consider next.

According to Way and Johnson, SRPT is an amalgam of theoret-ical perspectives like motivation theory, strategic intent and resource dependence. These perspectives provide a 'broad range of reference points ... from which an organization creates benchmarks' (2005: 9) which decision-makers can use to evaluate choices, make strategic decisions and signal their intent to other key personnel. Way and Johnson make use of two concepts: 'fit' and 'consensus'.

Internal fit represents the degree to which SRPs (Strategic Reference Points) of the HRM process compliment the organization's overall SRP. *External fit* represents the degree of congruency between the SRPs of the HRM process. Overall, then, 'SRPT posits that low levels of fit will have a negative impact on organizational effectiveness' (Way and Johnson 2005: 9). *External consensus* represents the degree to which functional top managers are in agreement with the strategic ends and means of functions other than their own. *Internal consensus* represents the degree of agreement between top managers. Overall, then, 'SRPT posits that low levels of consensus will have a negative impact on organizational effectiveness' (2005: 9). Unfortunately, the addition of SRPT adds to the previous problems.

The first problem is the same one we noted with SAT: Strategic Reference Points *Theory* is not, actually, a *theory*. As far as we can tell, SRPT consists of two components. First, it consists of a set of statements that define a set of desirable organisational outcomes, in this case, complementarities, congruencies and agreements. Second, it consists of a set of statements that are very similar to hypotheses, statements defining a (possible) relation between variables – e.g. 'low levels of fit, and low levels of consensus, will have a negative impact on organizational effectiveness'. Statements defining outcomes, and statements defining possible relations between variables, do not constitute theories. It is not, therefore, true to conclude that: 'When linked with SAT ... SRPT provides a better explanation of how organizations can achieve structural, cultural and environmental alignment' (Way and Johnson 2005: 9). It is more accurate to conclude that: when linked with SAT ... SRPT provides a better description of what organisations would have to do to achieve structural, cultural and environmental alignment.

The second problem derives from the previous section on SAT where we suspended judgment on whether or not reference to the need for an explanation of the decision-making steps could be another way of referring to the need for an explanation and understanding the process by which HRM policies, practices, systems, etc. operate. We can now make this judgment: the answer is no. Because the section on SRPT did not provide any theoretical development, we are still left without an explanation of the processes by which HRM policies, practices, systems, etc. might generate some desirable outcome.

Way and Johnson then offer their own extended 'theoretical framework' which is adapted from a general model of cybernetic, open, systems. Maybe here we can find the theoretical development that they seek, but that seems to allude them. They augment the resource-based view, the multiple stakeholder perspective, and the concepts of vertical and horizontal linkage with SAT and SRPT, then integrate this with claims about organisational goals and objectives and organisational strategies. Briefly stated, their theoretical framework (sketched in their Figure 1, p. 10) amounts to a map showing the links between the various components that comprise the overall system – e.g. organisational goals, objectives, culture, climate, strategies and outcomes; HR strategies, systems (SHRM) and outcomes; a pool of applicants and the human resources; external stakeholders; other functional resources and inputs, and financial outcomes. A commentary supports this sketch, carefully explaining the terms and the links before we eventually get down to the real business: putting the theoretical framework to use to 'address how SHRM can explicate and evaluate organizational effectiveness' (Way and Johnson 2005: 10). Unfortunately, instead of providing an accurate explanation and understanding of the process by which HRM policies, practices, systems, etc. enhance organisational performance, all this theoretical framework provides is a series of extremely general, platitudinous, and in many cases highly contestable, claims about what this or that HRM practice should do to promote organisational effectiveness. We cite three examples, followed by a brief note explaining why the claims offered do not provide any advancement vis-à-vis theoretical underpinnings.

Through the employment of HRM practices such as staffing, socialization, pay, benefits, job design, performance management, and training, SHRM communicates to the workforce which behaviours (outcomes) the organization expects and values. (2005: 13)

It may well be the case that through the employment of a series of HRM practices, SHRM communicates to the workforce which behaviours the organisation expects and values. What is required from a theory, however, is an explanation of why these practices communicate this message to the workforce, not to mention an explanation of why the workforce might accept the content of such communications, if indeed they do.

[T]he planned impact of SHRM on human resources is mediated by organizational climate ... SAT indicates that for SHRM to elicit the desired behaviour from the organization's human resources, the organizational climate must be congruent with the organization's culture. (2005: 13)

It may well be the case that for SHRM to elicit the desired behaviour from the organisation's human resources, the organisational climate must be congruent with the organisation's culture. What is required from a theory, however, is an explanation of why this congruence can be created and sustained, if indeed it can.

[A]s suggested by SAT as well as SRPT, the top level management of an organization must establish benchmarks that are congruent with the organization's overall SRPs as well as its HRM process across all divisions and departments. In turn, these benchmarks are used to create HRM strategies and systems that accurately communicate the organizations priorities and expectations to all the organization's human resources. (Way and Johnson 2005: 13)

It may well be the case that SRP may provide appropriate benchmarks to assist in creating HRM strategies and systems that accurately communicate the organisation's priorities and expectations to the organisation's human resources. What is required from a theory, however, is an explanation of why some HRM practices are able, when they are, to communicate the organisation's priorities and expectations, so that an appropriate HRM system might be designed.

Despite being, arguably, the best contribution seeking to develop theoretical foundations for the paradigm, even Way and Johnson fail to deliver on their promise of providing an accurate explanation and understanding of the process by which HRM policies, practices, systems, etc. enhance organisational performance. If we were to try and put our finger on the reason their attempt to provide theoretical foundations seems to miss the target, it would be related to their tendency to conflate and/or confuse statements defining outcomes and statements defining possible relations between variables, with statements that sustain explanations. The former, unlike the latter, do not constitute theories. In the end, they see the role of theory as little more than a set of statements providing researchers with a 'theoretical foundation from which they can generate predictive SHRM models' (2005: 16). As we will demonstrate in Chapter 4, scientism ends up treating theory as little more than a vehicle for delivering predictions: Way and Johnson seem unable to break free completely from this perspective.

Whilst we applaud attempts by Guest, Jackson and Schuler, and Way and Johnson to identify potential theories that might underpin research on the HRM–P link, and we recognise that they offer some theoretical insight, if other empirical researchers on the HRM–P link remain unwilling, or unable, to engage in serious theoretical and philosophical reflection, and remain committed to the idea that under-theorisation and missing theory will emerge and develop via more, and/or better, empirical work, then they are unlikely to make little theoretical headway. Indeed, we see the following problems remaining.

First, as shown above, empirical research on the HRM–P link is characterised by a bewildering array of 'theories', that is, approaches, perspectives, frameworks, typologies, studies, models, maps and accounts, all at various levels of abstraction, generality, universality, particularity, concreteness and micro or macro orientation. Writers often slide from using terms like 'approach' or 'perspective' to 'theory' or even imply that they are substitutes for one another. The fact that this kind of linguistic and conceptual confusion, ambiguity and slippage characterises the paradigm, strongly implies that we are not making theoretical headway.

Second, it is unclear what it is about the bewildering array of 'theories' that allows us to meaningfully call them 'theories'. What, for example, allows us to label expectancy theory and the partnership or stakeholder perspective as 'theories' when these two concepts involve completely different sets of ideas – the former, for example, relying on some version of *homo economicus*, and the latter relying on some quasi-ethico-political claims. As far as we can see, there is no such common feature.

Third, even if we were able to identify an adequate theoretical foundation upon which to base empirical research on the HRM–P link, it seems likely that this foundation would consist of a combination of several 'theories' operating at various levels of generality, specificity, concreteness or abstraction, with some rooted in scientistic philosophy and others rejecting this philosophy, and all 'bolted' together in some way. Yet it is unclear how any attempt to 'bolt' all this together to form a coherent framework could be done on anything other than an ad hoc basis. Indeed, this is what we have at present and is precisely what motivates the very idea that the research is under-theorised.

Fourth, empirical researchers are unlikely to just accidentally gain a clear insight into what constitutes a (bona fide) theory. And without knowing what a theory is, these researchers are most unlikely to be able to identify potential theories, never mind generate and/or develop new theories that might underpin research on the HRM–P link. Moreover, they are most unlikely to develop such an insight, precisely because they remain committed to the idea that theory (whatever it is) will emerge and develop via more, and/or better, empirical work.

Finally, it is unclear how more and/or better empirical work can overcome the perennial problem that arises when theory (if it is such) suggests the existence of a relation that cannot subsequently be found via empirical work or, conversely, when empirical work suggests the existence of a relation that cannot subsequently be accounted for theoretically. Huselid (1995: 670) for example, runs into the first version of this problem:

But despite the compelling theoretical argument that better internal and external fit will increase firm performance, I found only modest evidence of such an effect for internal fit and little evidence for external fit ... However, the theoretical arguments for internal and external fit remain compelling, and research based on refined theoretical and psychometric development ... is clearly required before such a conclusion can be accepted with any confidence ... The very large theoretical literature in the fields of human resource management based on the premise that fit makes a difference cries out for more work in this area.

To argue, as we have done in this chapter, that under-theorisation will not be overcome, and theory will *not* emerge and develop via more and/or better empirical work, is *not* to argue that empirical work has no role to play in theory development. It does mean that extricating ourselves from this sorry state of affairs will require more *explicitly theoretical*, as opposed to yet more empirical, investigation or, for that matter, different methods of collecting quantitative data. We have, therefore, to disagree with Khilji and Wang (2006: 1187), for example, who seem to think 'theoretical rigour' will improve by overcoming certain methodological issues relating to the use of multiple methods and respondents.

Under-theorisation and practice

The final manifestation of the problems of under-theorisation can be grasped not by starting from theory, but starting at the 'other end' as it were, with practice. Empirical research that is under-theorised is also under-explained, and lacks explanatory power. In this context, to lack explanatory power is to lack an understanding of the way HRM practices actually operate in the workplace and, therefore, to lack knowledge of exactly which HR practices to implement, and how to implement them 'on Monday morning'. Other stakeholders such as trade union negotiators are also left without any understanding of how any HR practices that are implemented will affect their members. And yet empirical researchers on the HRM–P link appear not to have recognised this. According to Panayotoupoulou and Papalexandris (2004: 510):

This research can provide useful data to HRM practitioners in general, as it measures the orientation of the HRM function and not specific practices based on the new trends that arise in the field. The conclusions drawn will help managers and HRM practitioners develop an effective HRM orientation that will maximise the aspects of the firm performance on which the organisation focuses.

Their empirical research demonstrates *that* (but does not explain *why*) organisations with high orientation in human relations, open system, internal process and rational goal models enjoy better overall performance compared to those with low orientation. This information may be useful for HR professionals in the sense that it provides evidence that the HR function adds value. It might also be useful for trade union negotiators to push for more HR practices to improve the quality of the working environment and, therefore, improve the bottom line. We cannot, however, see how it would help HR managers and/or trade union negotiators in ascertaining exactly which practices should be adopted, and how they should be adopted, to enhance performance. It is not really a guide to practice.

In an article examining the effects of TQM and HRM on performance, Sila (2006: 20) concludes with a section entitled 'Managerial implications':

By implementing these practices effectively (i.e. leadership, strategic planning, customer focus, information and analysis, HRM, process management and supplier management) managers can expect to realize improvements in all of the four performance areas (i.e. HRM, customer, financial and market results and organizational effectiveness) ... The results suggest that similar performance outcomes can be achieved by either taking quality initiatives or simply establishing organizational systems that incorporate these TQM practices.

To illustrate what is wrong with this claim, let us consider just *one* of the practices Sila offers to managers. The TQM practice he refers to as 'HRM' is described as: 'employee involvement, employee empowerment, teamwork, rewards, recognition and performance appraisal and employee training' (Sila 2006: 3). Suggesting to an HR manager that s/he implement (say) teamwork, would almost certainly be met with either incredulity or derision, followed by questions such as: exactly what composition should the team have? Exactly how would the team work? Exactly what techniques should I use to empower my employees? Answers to questions like these are not available in empirical research on the HRM–P link, because the preoccupation with, and domination by, quantitative, statistical and empirical analysis, rooted as it is in scientism, results in this research being under-theorised, lacking explanatory power, leaving our under-standing wanting. Guest (2001: 101) summed up the general problem recently, noting that: 'even if an association between human resource management and performance can be demonstrated, it is unclear how to apply this knowledge. More specifically, which human resource management practices matter most and if a firm wants to take action, where should it start'.

This failure of empirical research on the HRM–P link to inform practice has important theoretical and philosophical lessons about the social world. It teaches us that the social world is far more com-plex than scientism presupposes. If this were not the case, then HR managers would be able to proceed as follows. They could take any one of the scores of studies claiming to have established the 'predict-ors' of organisational performance, that is, established an empirical association between (a) an HRM practice or practices, often when the practices are appropriately bundled, often when they are aligned with corporate strategy and often when they are operating in an appropri-ate context; and (b) organisational performance. They could, then, introduce one of the specific bundles, perhaps drawn from an appro-priate context such as a similar industry, align it with their corporate

strategy, and expect a similar increase in performance. To suggest
that HR managers make such use of empirical research, and should
proceed in this manner would, we are convinced, be met with a mixture of derision and incredulity. And to be fair, empirical researchers
would probably counsel against taking their empirical work too literally. But consider the question this throws up: *if HR managers cannot proceed in this manner, why not?* Is it because the place where
HRM practices are in operation, the workplace, is not the kind of
place where we can predict which HR practices will increase organisational performance? Is it because the social world is not the kind of
place where we can find empirical relationship between phenomena
like HRM practices, and increase in performance? We believe the
answer to both questions is: yes. Further elaboration will, however,
have to await a discussion in Chapters 4, 5 and 6 on open and closed
systems.

Conclusion

In this chapter we have argued not only that empirical research on
the HRM–P link is under-theorised, but also that 'theory' is often
treated in an arbitrary, ambiguous, vague, brief, unsophisticated
or cavalier fashion, without any of the seriousness that it deserves.
Our explanation of this state of affairs is two-fold. First, empirical
researchers on the HRM–P link (not to mention empirical researchers in HRM, and organisation and management studies more generally) appear committed to the idea that being 'rigorous' and doing
'real' science is synonymous with employing scientism and/or using
quantitative, statistical and empirical techniques. Second, empirical
research on the HRM–P link is being driven, not by theory, but by a
commitment to scientism, the deductive method and the quantitative,
statistical and empirical techniques scientism sponsors. These commitments make it extremely difficult for empirical researchers to seriously consider alternative approaches. Sutton and Staw (1995: 378)
seem to have spotted this, with their rather sarcastic observation
that: 'Everyone agrees that our theories should be stronger, so long
as it does not require us to do anything differently'. Unfortunately, if
researchers on the HRM–P link are to make headway, then they will
almost certainly have to do some things differently. Guest is partly

aware of this. Indeed, he even suggests that maybe it is 'time to go back to the drawing board and take another hard look at the *theory*' (2001: 1105, emphasis added). We think it is necessary to go a step further. We suggest that maybe it is time to go back to the drawing board and take another hard look at meta-theory, or the philosophy of science as we have referred to it thus far. This is precisely what we will do in the next chapter.

4 | *Scientism: the meta-theory underlying empirical research on the HRM–P link*

Introduction and terminology

Chapter 3 suggested that the blame for under-theorisation in empirical research on the HRM–P link lay with scientistic philosophy, the deductive method and the quantitative, statistical and empirical research techniques scientism sponsors. The twin aims of this chapter are to outline what scientism actually involves, before demonstrating its shortcomings. In place of the term 'philosophy' which we used throughout the last chapter, we will now use the term 'meta-theory' which we will define in a few moments, as part of an opening discussion dealing with some terminology.

Any discussion of philosophy of science requires some familiarity with new, specialist, terminology which is always likely to be a little off-putting at first. That said, the basic terms we introduce below should be within the reach of anyone with a reasonable education, and are certainly no more difficult to understand than many of the technical statistical terms that proliferate in the literature. We will start by introducing and defining some key concepts and then introduce and define others as the chapter unfolds.

Philosophy of science is a branch of philosophy more generally concerned with how science (natural and social) is, and perhaps ought to be, conducted. From the early twentieth century it has been concerned primarily with epistemology and methodology, asking questions like: 'how is knowledge obtained', 'how can we test knowledge claims' and 'how can we judge between competing theories'?

Ontology refers to the investigation of being or existence; to what kinds of things exist, and their mode of existence. In the social world, we are often faced with ontological questions such as: 'does the workforce consist simply of an aggregate of atomistic individuals, rather like billiard balls colliding with one another' and 'does the workplace display law-like regularities like those we observe in some natural sciences'?

Epistemology refers to the investigation of how knowledge is obtained. To ask: 'how do we know *x*?' is to ask an epistemological question. This is different from the ontological question 'what is *x*?'. Realists are committed to the idea that things can and do exist independently of our knowledge of them, something that non-realist philosophers deny.

Methodology refers to investigation of the methods we use to gain knowledge. We make a distinction between method (of which there are a small number) and research technique (of which there are many). In particular, we will be concerned with the deductive method of scientism, and the causal-explanatory method of critical realism.

Aetiology refers to the investigation of causes. We make a distinction between two types of causality. Research on the HRM–P link presupposes causality as event regularity, whereby the cause of increased organisational performance is presumed to be HRM practice that regularly precedes it. Critical realism uses a notion of causality as the exercise of a power.

Meta-theory is a portmanteau term to refer, generally, to philosophy of science, ontology, epistemology, methodology, aetiology, research techniques, prediction, explanation and the way all this relates to theory. We prefer the term 'meta-theory' to 'philosophy of science' because it allows us to specify exactly what we mean by it. We focus here on two meta-theoretical approaches: critical realism and positivism, or 'scientism' as we prefer to call it.[1]

Scientism is the term we use to refer to the meta-theory presupposed in empirical research on the HRM–P link. It is important that we grasp this fully, to allow us to elaborate at length. We saw in the last chapter that empirical research on the HRM–P link is often said to be 'scientific', and most of these researchers would quite readily accept that what they do is 'scientific'. Critics like us, however, argue that this research is spurious science, and more accurately defined by terms like 'scientistic' and 'scientism'. Whilst the more obvious term to use to describe this meta-theory is 'positivism' we decline to use it for the following reason.

In the hands of its initial advocates in the Vienna Circle, positivism was a carefully worked out, sophisticated meta-theory – and we say this despite the fact we reject it. During the last fifty years, however, sophisticated meta-theoretical discussion and reflection by those who operate in the shadow of positivism has almost disappeared.[2] Most universities have now replaced philosophy of science courses with courses on research methods, consisting largely of how to collect data and process it with a heavy, and sometimes exclusive, emphasis on statistical techniques. Most contemporary empirical researchers end up just applying the statistical techniques they have learned with little or no understanding of the meta-theory underpinning what they do. The result is that what passes for contemporary positivism has evolved over half a century into a rather ill-conceived and ad hoc jumble of quasi-positivist ideas. Because the meta-theory practiced by researchers on the HRM–P link is highly ambiguous, we think the deliberately ambiguous term 'scientism' captures the practice.

The *Collins Dictionary of Sociology* (1995) defines scientism as 'any doctrine or approach held to involve oversimplified conceptions and unreal expectations of science, and to misapply "natural science" methods to the social sciences'. Hughes and Sharrock (1997: 208) define scientism as 'those philosophies such as positivism, which seek to present themselves as having a close affiliation with the sciences and to speak in their name, and which then go on to fetishize the so called scientific standpoint'. One contemporary advocate of positivism writes:

Positivist social science aims for theoretical generalizations of broad scope that explain social affairs as being determined by causes of an objective kind that lie in the minds of people … This science is inspired by, and loosely modelled on, the natural sciences. (Donaldson 2003: 116–17)

Scientism, then, refers to the employment of methods and research techniques that look similar to (some branches of) natural science, without actually specifying what these methods and techniques are. Scientism and its deductive method are grounded in empirical observation, quantification and measurement. It generates predictions and hypotheses which can be tested via mathematical and statistical techniques to ascertain whether or not they are false. The findings are presumed to be objective, generalisable, and can be replicated by other researchers. By closely resembling some under-elaborated notion of 'science' and by using scientific language and concepts (e.g. prediction, replication, quantification, hypothesis testing, mathematics and statistics) that is, by engaging a scientific discourse, scientism gains a veneer of *scientificity*. Importantly, this veneer of scientificity can easily seduce many HRM stakeholders. The following passage not only 'looks' highly scientific, it is not open to contestation by anyone who is not an expert econometrician – which is not, of course, a criticism of Katou and Budhwar.

> In order to test the indirect effect, we used Preacher and Leonardelli's interactive programme to calculate the critical z ratio. The values used in this interactive programme are taken from table 7 where the non-significant variables are withdrawn from the relationships through backward regression, in order to get better estimates. The values used are $b = 1.046$, $s_b = 0.060$, $b_2 = 0.335$ and $s_{b2} = 0.066$. The z values obtained are $z_{Sobel} = 4.873$ (p=01000), $z_{Goodman(I)} = 4.866$ (p = 0.000) and $z_{Goodman(II)} = 4.881$ (p = 0.000). These z values indicate that the indirect effect of HRM systems on organizational performance is significantly different from zero. (Katou and Budhwar 2006: 1243)

In recognising the influential role of scientistic discourse, we agree with various postmodern and poststructural approaches that emphasise the socially constructed nature of scientific knowledge. The discourse of scientism generates a misplaced veneer of scientificity. It is difficult to underestimate the semiotic power of claims like these that have a convincing gloss of scientificity about them. We consider scientism to be inappropriate not only for social science, but also for natural science – although we cannot elaborate here and point the interested reader to Bhaskar (1978).

Critical realism[3] is a relatively new meta-theory, one that takes a decidedly ontological (re)turn. Although scientism dominates research on the HRM–P link, indeed, it dominates management studies more generally, critical realism firmly rejects scientism and holds out the possibility of being a more fruitful alternative to scientism.

Presupposition refers to the act of taking some concepts, ideas, beliefs and such like for granted, whilst making claims or engaging in actions based upon them. To say, for example, 'I see it is raining outside, so I will take my umbrella', presupposes the idea that rain is the kind of thing that can be seen, that there is an inside and an outside, that an umbrella is the kind of thing that will repel rain and that the wind is not so strong as to render an umbrella useless. Many of our presuppositions are made implicitly and without reflection, but they remain presuppositions nonetheless. Because a great deal of the meta-theory that underpins empirical research on the HRM–P link is unstated, and made implicitly and without reflection, we have no choice but to 'tease out', as it were, these presuppositions.

In this and the next two chapters, we specifically use critical realism to tease out the meta-theoretical presuppositions underlying empirical research on the HRM–P link. In carrying out this task we run into two difficulties. First, there are no obvious sources or seminal texts to consult wherein the scientistic meta-theory underlying empirical research on the HRM–P link is stated clearly. Second, there is serious conceptual and terminological confusion: terms and concepts, such as 'theory', 'explanation' and 'prediction', are used inconsistently, their meaning varies from study to study and sometimes they are mistakenly treated as interchangeable. These difficulties mean that when, as we have to, we try to tease out the meta-theory from snippets of commentary and from the actual practices empirical researchers employ, we risk making two mistakes. First, we may misrepresent the meta-theoretical commitments of these researchers. If so, we are more than happy to be corrected. In any case, subsequent correction might make for more meta-theoretical clarity, so even our possible misrepresentation would have to be of considerable use. Second, we may actually give this paradigm far more meta-theoretical consistency and clarity than it actually has. If so, then at least we avoid the charge of setting up a 'straw researcher'.

The first part of this chapter steadily works its way through scientism's meta-theoretical presuppositions, touching primarily upon: the deductivist method, the nature of events and their alleged regularities, closed systems, prediction, hypotheses and aetiology in order to build up a clear idea of the meta-theory underpinning empirical research on the HRM–P link. The second part engages in a critical realist critique of this meta-theory. Whilst those who are keen to just 'get on' with doing research may find this tedious, it is precisely because this kind of thorough interrogation has been avoided that research on the HRM–P link finds itself saddled with the problem of under-theorisation mentioned in Chapter 3, not to mention a range of shortcomings we will identify in the following chapters.

Scientistic meta-theory: a critical realist interpretation

Whilst this section offers a critical realist interpretation of scientism, the claims we make on its behalf, are claims we think advocates of scientism make. We note this simply to ensure the reader is aware that we reject many of these claims. Occasionally, we will use the phrase 'from the perspective of scientism' to remind the reader that this is not a claim we would defend.

The deductive method

Brewster is one of the few who have at least tried to sketch the rudiments of the method (although not the other meta-theoretical components) underlying empirical research on the HRM–P link:

> The universalist paradigm ... is essentially a nomothetic social sciences approach: using evidence to test generalizations of an abstract and law-like nature ... Methodologically, the mechanism generally used to research this form of SHRM is deductive: to generate carefully designed questions which can lead to proof or disproof, the elements of which can be measured in such a way that the question itself can be subjected to the mechanism of testing and prediction. Built in to this paradigm is the assumption that research is not 'rigorous' unless it is drawn from existing literature and theory, focused around a tightly designed question and contains a structure of testing that can lead to prediction. (Brewster 1999: 214–15)

We accept Brewster's sketch here, with two exceptions: first, as we saw in Chapter 3, research tends not to be drawn, at least not drawn with any precision, from existing theory; and second, this methodological approach is not restricted to the universalist paradigm, but applies to almost all of the empirical research on the HRM–P link of whichever hue. Whilst the method in use is never specified in empirical research on the HRM–P link, it appears to be some variant or combination of the deductive nomological, hypothetico-deductive, inductive-statistical, and/or covering law model. Following Lawson (1997, 2003) we refer to this variant as the *deductive method* or simply *deductivism*. From the perspective of *deductivism*, to 'explain' something appears to be to predict a claim about that something as a deduction from a set of initial conditions, assumptions, axioms and law(s), or some other regular pattern of events. Chalmers (1999: 54) represents this schematically (see Figure 4.1).

Facts are acquired through observing events which are measured, quantified and transposed into variables. Regular association between these observed events (variables) allows researchers to inductively generate laws. It is, however, unclear how theories are

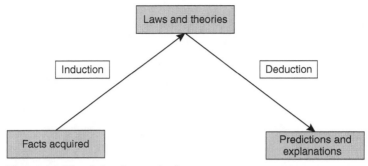

Figure 4.1 The deductive method

arrived at – something we return to in a moment. The combination of theories and laws (or some form of event regularity) allows researchers to deduce predictions and explanations about the phenomena under investigation. Deductivism, then, appears to involve the following steps:

(a) Laws or theories about a phenomenon
(b) Statements about initial conditions
(c) The phenomenon is explained and predicted as a deduction from (a) and (b)
(d) Theories or laws are often tested via their predictions.

And in the context of the HRM–P link, we might say something like:

(a) Bundles of HRM practices are regularly conjoined and statistically associated with increased organisational performance (laws or theories)
(b) The HRM bundle consists of work teams and a performance related pay scheme
(c) Increased organisational performance is explained and predicted as a deduction from (a) and (b)
(d) Theories or laws are often tested via their predictions.

This last point (d) is important. Empirical research on the HRM–P link is preoccupied with what is referred to variously, and ambiguously, as testing the prediction, testing the hypothesis, testing the theory, testing propositions, testing findings, testing the model, testing the model's predictions, finding the predictors of their dependent variable and so on. We will refer (where possible) to *testing the hypotheses* because, according to the positivist canon, this is actually what should really be tested.

Buried within the deductive method, or perhaps scientism more generally, is the idea of a cyclical research process which moves in phases. Researchers (somehow) start with a theory. The theory generates hypotheses. The hypotheses are tested via empirical data. The initial theory is re-visited, and strengthened, abandoned or modified depending upon the results of the empirical tests. As we saw in the previous chapter, however, there simply is no theory (or too many poorly elaborated ones) for empirical research on the HRM–P link to start the initial phase of the research cycle. This problem is exacerbated by the fact that scientism's idea of what constitutes a theory is mistaken – as we will see in Chapter 5.

Despite the fact that the method is rather ill-conceived, we still need to understand what it entails if we are to pinpoint its shortcomings. Let us make our way through some key meta-theoretical concepts, beginning with events, ontology, epistemology and event regularities, gradually making our way to closed and open systems and aetiology.

Events, ontology, epistemology and event regularities[4]

From the perspective of scientism, *events* are the building blocks of empirical research: they are the things of interest that happen in the social world and about which researchers collect their data. An event might, for example, be: the introduction of team working; the existence of a union; the duration of a training programme; the strength of employee commitment to organisational culture; a change in the sophistication of HR architecture; an increase in productivity, sales, return of investment and so on. If and when these events are observed, recorded, counted or measured (or approximated by proxy measures) in terms of some quantity or degree they become constructs or variables. As Whetten (1989: 491) puts it: 'The primary difference between propositions and hypotheses is that propositions involve concepts whereas hypotheses require measures'. We understand variables to be quantified events.

Although scientism has traditionally been, and still remains, preoccupied with epistemology, an ontology is always presupposed – explicitly or implicitly. In this case, the ontology consists of what can be observed and is, therefore, of observed *events*. Because these objects are confined to experience, the ontology is *empirical*; and because these objects are thought to exist independently of their identification by lay agents of social scientists, it is *realist*. The ontology is, therefore, *empirical realist*.

What are experienced are unique, unconnected, *atomistic* events. These events cannot be other than atomistic, since any connection or relation between them is impervious to experience, otherwise the nature of the connections or relations would require prior explanation, thus undermining the centrality of the observable. The presupposed ontology, then, is not only of observable events, it is also of *atomistic* observable events. Now that we know what we are dealing with, we will drop the terms 'observable' and 'atomistic' where appropriate, and refer simply to 'events'.

The social world, or at least that part of it that is amenable to scientism is, therefore, presumed exhausted by, or reducible to, that which is experienced or observed.[5] And that which is experienced is, furthermore, presumed fused with the events and actions that underlie, and give rise to, experience. This might sound a little pedantic, but it amounts to no more than a commitment to observation as a reliable, indeed as the *only*, pathway to knowledge. This ontology (schematised in Table 4.1) is referred to as 'flat', partly because of the fusion of the empirical and actual domains and partly because it lacks 'depth'. The importance of this will become clearer when, later in the chapter, we see that critical realists operate with a deeper, or *layered*, ontology, adding a domain of the 'deep'. To put it crudely, from this perspective: 'what we see is what there is'.

This ontology of events is consistent with an epistemology rooted in the observation of events. Whilst knowledge is gained from observing events, a little more than this is required for the kind of knowledge scientism requires. What we might call particular knowledge is gained through observing events, but more *general* (some might say scientific) knowledge is gained only if these events manifest themselves in some kind of pattern: a flux of totally arbitrary events would not result in knowledge. Even here, not just any old pattern will do, these events must manifest themselves as *event regularities*, or *constant conjunctions of events* – we use these phrases interchangeably. The kind of knowledge required by scientism is, therefore, completely reliant upon the existence and ubiquity of *event regularities*. This is an important claim, so let us spend some time unpacking it.

Table 4.1. *A 'flat' ontology*

Domain	Entity
Empirical	Experiences and observations
Actual	Events and actions

To observe two (or more) events simply occurring is not very illuminating, whereas to observe two events occurring in *regular succession*, such that whenever one event, call it *x*, occurs, another event *y* regularly succeeds it. To observe a firm introducing an HRM practice whilst also observing increases in productivity is not very illuminating, whereas to observe that the introduction of an HRM practice and increases in productivity occur in regular succession, such that whenever this HRM practice is introduced, productivity regularly increases, is illuminating. Moreover, the more often we observe the introduction of HRM practices and increased productivity regularly succeeding one another (either in the same firm, or in many firms), the more illuminating the observation is said to be. This is, in part, why empirical researchers seek to observe as many cases of some event regularity as possible (or practicable). If we only observed in one firm, at one time, HRM practices being constantly conjoined with increased productivity, we would perhaps claim to know a little. But if we observed in more than one firm, and at more than one time, HRM practices being constantly conjoined with increased productivity, we would claim to know far more; we might claim to have more general knowledge. This is, of course, why so many papers on the HRM–P link start off by noting that many studies have found a relationship between some HR practices and firm performance and, in part, why they seek large samples – more examples of event regularity appears to suggest more secure knowledge.

The very possibility of formulating and testing predictions and hypotheses lies with event regularities. A prediction is a statement about what will happen to one event when another event(s) is introduced, or changes. A prediction is generated *inductively*, that is to say, is based on the fact that researchers have observed event *x* being regularly succeeded by event *y*. On this basis they predict that the next time *x* occurs, *y* will follow. A prediction, then, is a statement derived from, and dependent upon, some event regularity. Hypotheses, especially the kind of hypotheses typical of empirical research on the HRM–P link, are a class of predictions whereby the events in question are expressed in quantitative form, that is, as variables. Researchers predict or hypothesise what will happen to the magnitude of the dependent variable when a new dependent variable(s) is introduced, or the magnitude of an existing independent variable(s) changes. The key point to note is that predictions and hypotheses are derived from, and dependent upon, event regularities. In one of the defining, and now widely cited, papers in the field, Huselid's (1995: 670) first hypothesis states that: 'Systems of High Performance Work Practices will diminish employee turnover and increase productivity and corporate financial performance'. His hypothesis is derived from, and dependent upon, the existence of one event (high-performance work practices) being regularly associated with a set of events (diminished employee turnover and increased productivity and corporate financial performance).

Henceforth, we will generalise and style event regularities or constant conjunctions of events as 'whenever event x then event y' or 'whenever event x_1....x_n then event y'. The fact that others come extremely close to using this terminology is highly indicative that we are not pursuing a straw person. According to Becker *et al.* (2001: 110):

Ideally, you will develop a measurement system that lets you answer questions such as, how much will we have to change x in order to achieve our target in y? To illustrate, if you increase training by 20 percent, how much will that change employee performance and, ultimately, unit performance?

The same appears to be true for the wider management literature. Mitchell and James (2001: 532) conclude a survey of articles in the 1999 volume of the *Academy of Management Journal*, by noting that: 'without reservation we can say that most theory involves fairly simple relationships of the X causes Y variety'. See also Langley (1999: 692–3).

Regularities between events are more often expressed as functional relations such as $y = f(x)$ or $y = f(x_1....x_n)$. Gerhart (2007: 533) suggests that: 'The typical approach in HRM and performance is to use a model like the following:

$$Perf = \beta_0 + \beta_{perfhr} \, hr + \varepsilon$$

where population parameters are β_0 the intercept, β_{perfhr} hr, an unstandardized regression coefficient representing the performance-HR relationship, and ε the error or disturbance term'. Whilst this is indeed a generic functional relation in empirical research on the HRM–P link, it appears in more specific forms such as the following. Katou and Budhwar (2006: 1235) use a function to explain their procedure as follows: 'Conduct a regression analysis with X predicting Y to test if there is an effect that may be mediated, $Y = a + bX + e$'. Functions can also be expressed in English without altering the sentiment of the claim. 'This model implies that employees trust in their managers is a function of organisational communication, procedural justice, empowerment, and employee development' (Tzafrir *et al.* 2004: 639). It is very important to note that it is events and their regularities that form the basis upon which any mathematical or econometric specification is derived. Consider the absurdity of trying to write something like $y = sometimes\ f(x_1....x_n)$ or Perf = sometimes $\beta_0 + \beta_{perfhr}$ hr ε. The absurdity is removed at a stroke when the *irregularity* associated with the term 'sometimes' is removed.

The foregoing discussion contains two important points. First, *events* (usually expressed quantitatively as variables) and their *regularities* are crucial to scientism, the deductive method and the empirical, quantitative and statistical research techniques sponsored by scientism. Where there are no event regularities, there is no knowledge to be had. Second, from the scientistic perspective, verifying knowledge claims is a relatively straightforward affair. Measure and quantify observable events and translate them into variables, formulate and test a hypothesis, if the hypothesis is not falsified, the knowledge is presumed to be objectively true. The only epistemological and methodological problems scientism recognises are what we referred to in Chapter 3 as 'technical' problems.

Closed systems

Where, we might ask, do we find such event regularities? The answer, according to critical realists is: only in *closed systems*. Systems are defined as closed when they are characterised by event regularities; and by extension, open systems are those characterised by a lack of such regularity. In a closed system, events are constantly conjoined in the sense that for every event y, there exists an event, or a set of events

x_1, x_2...x_n, such that y and x_1, x_2...x_n are constantly or regularly conjoined. A hi-fi system is an example of a closed system because a change in the volume control (event x) is constantly conjoined with a change in volume (event y).[6] If we find event regularities only in closed systems, the obvious question to ask is: where do we find closed systems? We will come to this later in the chapter, but for the moment it is best to concentrate on ascertaining what closed systems involve.

Some of those who might be tempted to accept the above definition of a closed system, nevertheless, argue that this is a *deterministic* conception which ignores the possibility of expressing a closed system *probabilistically* or *stochastically*. If a deterministically closed system is expressed *stochastically*, the strict condition that *every single* occurrence of event x is constantly conjoined with every single occurrence of event y can be abandoned. Instead it might be suggested that *most* occurrences of event x are constantly conjoined with most occurrences of event y. Remembering that variables are quantified events, we might write something like the mean (or expected value) of variable x (measuring event x) is constantly conjoined with the mean (or expected value) of variable y (measuring y); or the mean (or expected value) of variables x_1, x_2...x_n are constantly conjoined with the mean (or expected value) of variable y. This, of course, means that some of the observed values of x_1, x_2...x_n will *not* be constantly conjoined with variable y.

And so we arrive at a slight tension. Side-by-side we have both stochastic regularity and stochastic irregularity. Should we define the system in terms of its regularity, or its irregularity? There are two reasons to plump for the former. First, most empirical researchers, such as those researching the HRM–P link, are searching for stochastic regularity between HRM practices and organisational performance. Indeed, stochastic regularity is at the heart of concepts like correlation and regression. Second, given that closed systems are defined in terms of event regularities, it follows that stochastically closed systems should be defined in terms of stochastic event regularities. What really matters, however, is not what we call this system, but the causes and consequences of researchers on the HRM–P link presupposing that the workplace is characterised by event regularities and, therefore, closed systems – be it deterministic or stochastic. We will return to consider stochastically closed systems later in the chapter but, at this point, it seems advisable to look at a concrete example of how deterministic and stochastic closed systems manifest themselves in empirical research on the HRM–P link.

Laursen's work on the relationship between HRM practices and organisational performance in terms of innovation work offers a good example, not only because it is clear, but also because he specifies both deterministic and stochastic equations, and this illuminates the difference between deterministic and stochastic systems. The following equation expresses the system *deterministically*:

$$a = f(b_1z, b_2x)_s$$

where a is the ability to produce innovations, b_1z, b_2 are parameter vectors, and z is a set of (exogenous) determinants of innovation related to the application of HRM practices, while x is a set of other variables explaining innovative performance across business firms. The variables included in the variable x are arguably standard variables in explaining innovative performance (Laursen 2002: 145).

Laursen then operationalises this in the following regression equation which expresses the system *stochastically*:

$$A_i = a_s \, \text{SECT}_i + d_s \, \text{SIZE}_i + u_s \, \text{LINK}_i + h_s \, \text{HRMS}_i + e_{ij}$$

Control variables SECT, SIZE and LINK denote the industrial sector, firm size and degree of vertical integration respectively. Dependent variable A_i denotes the firms' ability to innovate. HRMS_i is one combined independent variable expressing the HRM practices associated with performance related pay (PPAY), delegation of decision rights (DRESP), and team work (TEAM). HRMS_i actually measures the variable denoting how large a share of the firm's workforce is engaged in:

- Interdisciplinary working groups [TEAM 1]
- Quality circles [TEAM 2]
- Planned job rotation [TEAM 3]
- Integration of functions (e.g. sales, production/services, finance) [TEAM 4]
- Delegation of responsibility [DRESP]
- Performance-related pay [PPAY]

Laursen's model describes a stochastically closed system in the sense that (after controlling for firm size and vertical integration) the firm's ability to innovate is still constantly conjoined with performance-related pay, delegation of decision rights and team work, albeit expressed stochastically. In the language we employed above, this is tantamount to saying: 'the mean values of variables TEAM 1, TEAM 2, TEAM 3, TEAM 4, DRESP and PPAY are constantly conjoined with the mean values of variable *A*'.[7]

Notice that Laursen is treating the entire firm, and not just the HRM practices, as a system. He includes the independent and dependent variables, that is, the HRM practices *and* the changes in the ability to innovate as part of the system. We believe this is the most appropriate way to approach matters, since almost all notions of systems, including those of critical realism and systems theory, include both the inputs and outputs as part of the overall system. This is, however, a little different to the way the term 'system' is often used in empirical research on the HRM–P link, where it is usually used to refer to a particular bundle of HRM practices that are consistently, and systematically, related to one another. This is a common-sense use of the term 'system' and we have no real problem with it, provided it is not misunderstood to refer to a system in the way we are using it.

Aetiology

Here we need to consider what conception of causality scientism presupposes, and ascertain whether or not it is valid. If ontology is one of observed atomistic events, then causality cannot be conceived of in terms of anything other than a conjunction between them. The cause of event x must be some prior event y. And if epistemology is one whereby knowledge is reliant upon identifying event regularities, then knowing the cause of something requires knowledge to the effect that the events are regularly conjoined. To know the cause of event x requires knowledge that event x is regularly conjoined with event y. Causality, then, is dependent not just upon event regularities, but upon knowledge derived from the observation of event regularities. On this conception, the cause of event y is the event x, or the set of events $x_1, x_2 \ldots x_n$ that regularly precede it. The cause of the lamp's illumination, for example, is the finger that flicked the light switch. *From the scientistic perspective, causality is synonymous with event regularity. Where one observes constant conjunctions of atomistic events, one may conclude causality is present; where one does not observe such conjunctions, one must conclude causality is not present.* This conception of causality is referred to as 'Humean' because it derives from the work of the eighteenth-century Scottish empiricist philosopher David Hume, although we refer to it here as 'thin' for reasons made clear in Chapter 5. There are other conceptions, and one in particular will be explored in Chapter 5, but for the moment let us delve a little deeper into Humean or thin causality.

It is useful to start with Hume himself, partly because of his clarity and sophistication. He writes: 'When I cast my eye on the *known qualities* of objects, I immediately discover that the relation of cause and effect depends not in the least on *them*. When I consider their *relations*, I can find none but those of contiguity and succession' (Hume 1888 and 1978: 77). And 'We have no other notion of cause and effect, but that of certain objects, which have been *always conjoin'd* together ... We cannot penetrate into the reason for the conjunction' (1888 and 1978: 93). Before the reader objects that things have moved on since Hume, consider the following recent comments on the subject:

I am a Humean in that I believe we cannot perceive necessary connections in reality. All we can do is set up a theoretical model in which we define the word 'causality' precisely as economists do with the $y=f(x)$. What they mean by that in their theory is that if we change x [then] y will change. And the way y will change is mapped by f, so we have a causal theory. (Leamer, in Hendry *et al.* 1990: 187)

A recent book entitled *Causal Models* (Sloman 2005) shows that Humean thinking on causality is alive and well:

As the 18th century Scottish philosopher David Hume put it, causality is about 'an object followed by another ... where, if the first had not existed, the second had never existed'. This is precisely the kind of knowledge required to predict the effect of action, how behavior changes the world. What do we really understand when we think we understand a mechanism? Presumably, at minimum, we have some idea about which inputs produce which outputs. We understand how the choice of inputs determines the outputs and that the reverse does not hold. The choice of outputs does not determine the value of inputs. This special and structured kind of knowledge requires that we understand that (1) changing X is likely to end up with a change in Y; (2) causes and effects are asymmetric: changing Y won't budge X; (3) causes and effects go together over time; and (4) Y does not occur before X. Believing that heat causes expansion requires believing that (1) changing the temperature will change the volume (of a gas, say); (2) changing the volume won't change the temperature; (3) certain temperatures are associated with certain volumes; and (4) new volumes aren't observed before new temperatures. (Sloman 2005: 5)[8]

Similar comments demonstrating the implicit use made of Humean causality can be found in empirical research on the HRM–P link.

Mediation is a hypothesised causal chain in which one variable (X) affects a second variable (M) that, in turn, affects a third variable (Y). The first step in the chain (and the only one we need mention) is styled as follows: 'Conduct a regression analysis with x predicting Y to test if there is an effect that may be mediated, $Y = a + bX + e$'. (Katou and Budhwar 2006: 1235)

Blalock ... defines causation as: 'X is a direct cause of Y if and only if a change in X produces a change in the mean value of Y'. (Becker and Huselid 1998: 69)[9]

One key part of the 'theory' of HRM ... is that it is possible to 'predict' a set of outcomes from a set of HR practices. In other words, this is the heartland of the theoretical modelling of the cause-and-effect variety. (Storey 1992: 40)

Although we have managed to find some quotations from the literature that appear to show that the conception of causality underpinning research on the HRM–P link rests on event regularities, and is, therefore, thin, the truth is, causality is almost never discussed.[10] The one exception to this is where the problem of potential *reverse causality* or *simultaneity* is concerned. Many articles make comments like the following:

[I]t is impossible to know for certain about the direction of causality. Although it is nice to believe that more HR practices leads to higher economic return, it is just as possible to argue that it is successful firms that can afford more extensive (and expensive) HRM practices. (Purcell *et al.* 2003: 2)

[I]t is also possible that firms experiencing higher productivity are better positioned to invest in high performance practices. (Datta *et al.* 2005: 143)

Unfortunately, correlation is not the same as causation. That is, it is not clear whether strategic HR management drives superior financial performance, or whether superior financial performance makes it possible to take a more strategic approach to HR management. (Thomas *et al.* 2003: 1)

Whilst the problem is recognised, it is often treated rather disingenuously. Consider Huselid's widely cited example – similar statements are found in many pieces of empirical research on the HRM–P link.[11]

To estimate the practical significance of the impact of High Performance Work Practices on productivity, I next calculated the impact of a one-standard deviation increase in each practice scale on ... net sales ... The findings indicate that each one-standard-deviation increase raises sales an average of $27,044 per employee. (Huselid 1995: 658)

Let us proceed carefully here. It is true that Huselid does not really claim anything specific about causality here, thin or otherwise. He does not actually state that the introduction of certain HRMP *caused* the increase in sales. And Huselid is not alone. To the best of our knowledge, none of the research on the HRM–P link makes any specific claims about causality – all empirical researchers know that causality cannot be inferred from statistical association. Yet if (thin) causality is *not* an implicit presupposition in this research, if researchers are not suggesting that their findings demonstrate that the introduction of HRM practices *cause* improved organisational performance, then the findings of these studies begin to lose any practical significance. As it happens, Huselid adds the comment that his measures 'suggest that firms *can indeed obtain* substantial financial *benefits* from investing in the practices studied here' (1995: 667, emphasis added) which comes pretty close to making a causal claim.[12]

Mazzanti *et al.* (2006: 132) provide a more recent example. They make the usual comment about their data being cross-sectional and, therefore, not able to 'test cause-effect relationships', noting that the 'causality links between variables are intended to be "weak linkages"'. They prefer the term 'association linkage rather than causal ones' (137) in their quest to 'assess the relationship between variables' and 'assess the significance of the intensity of relationships between those variables'. They conclude that 'although the direction of the causal effect is not detected here, the analysis highlights that ... firm performance is a significant *driving factor* of innovation' (139, emphasis added). To be fair, Mazzanti *et al.* are attempting to say something about how they deal with a problem that is recognised, but glossed over by most others. Yet in our opinion, they do not resolve the problem, instead they retreat to ambiguity. It is unclear why a statistical association between variables can be referred to as a *'weak* link' when the statistical techniques provide no grounds for a causal link of any kind. The nature of the 'assessment' being undertaken of the relationship between variables is unclear. Assessing the intensity of relationships between variables appears to be an entirely statistical endeavour, and the measures of significance are statistical artefacts, measures appertaining to the variables, not appertaining to the relationship between the phenomena the variables are intended to represent. Phraseology like 'weak association linkages' and 'significant driving factors' is an attempt to have one's cake and eat it. Claiming *de jure* that causality is *not* being investigated, whilst *de facto* investigating causality embroils Mazzanti *et al.* in a *performative contradiction*. Mazzanti *et al.* are not the only ones engaged in this performative contradiction. All research into the empirical relationship between HRM and organisational performance is predicated upon, and only relevant if, it presupposes that the introduction of some HRM practices *cause* an increase in organisational performance. If causality is not presupposed, then the practical value of the empirical research is cast into doubt.[13]

Echambadi *et al.* (2006: 1804) are quite correct advising researchers to 'first theoretically motivate the causal relationships between variables and then look for evidence of the causal relationship. The presence of non-zero effects in the absence of strong theory does not demonstrate causality'. Unfortunately, as we saw in Chapter 3, there is little evidence that empirical research into the HRM–P link is serious about developing the kind of theory that would 'motivate causality'. Instead, study after study does little more than look for statistical associations between HRM and organisational performance, leaving the understanding of causality impoverished.

The fundamental problem, however, is not reverse causality itself. The problem of reverse causality is itself a manifestation of problems that lie beyond the aetiological problems associated with thin causality. Reverse causality only raises its head when researchers have little or no theory, and hence little or no explanation, of the operation of the causal mechanisms and processes they are measuring. When asked for his advice about how to move from association to causation, the eminent statistician Fisher suggested: 'Make your theories more elaborate' (Becker and Huselid 2006: 19). Unfortunately this is a path not currently available to empirical researchers on the HRM–P link.

The functional relation

To understand why many empirical researchers on the HRM–P link get embroiled in this performative contradiction, let us take a closer look at the functional relation, which forms the basis of any regression analysis – and this is the case even if the regression equations are not made explicit in an article, which tends to be common practice.[14]

A functional relation is a specific kind of relation between phenomena that have only a quantitative dimension – i.e. variables. A function maps the magnitudes taken by one variable (x) or set of variables ($x_1...x_n$) onto the magnitudes taken by another variable (y) or set of variables ($y_1...y_n$) such as:

(1) $y = f(x_1...x_n)$

In mathematics an expression like (1) is *acausal*, purely formal and (quite legitimately) need have no content, meaning or relevance to something outside the process of mathematising. In social science, however, pure formalism without causality, content or meaning leads to irrelevance. An expression like (1) becomes (let us say) *practically* relevant when, and only when, extra-mathematical, or let us say, *social* content and meaning is imputed to the mathematical expression. Recall Laursen's functional relation:

(2) $A_i = f (SECT_i + SIZE_i + LINK_i + HRMS_i)$

Giving social content and meaning to what would otherwise be a purely formal mathematical function like (2) delivers something like the following:

(3)   Controlling for the effect of industrial sector firm size and degree of vertical integration, when a specified share of the workforce is engaged in interdisciplinary working groups; quality circles; planned job rotation; integration of functions; is responsible for delegation; and receives performance related pay, then the firm is enabled to engage in a specified amount of innovation.

The intended consequence of the translation process from mathematical to ordinary language means (2) now has social content and meaning. But an unintended consequence of the translation process is that a presupposition about causality is 'smuggled' into an *a*causal mathematical expression. The functional relation (2) now implies that a change in the magnitude of the independent variable will *cause* a predictable change in the magnitude of the dependent variable. It implies, for example, an increase in the share of the workforce engaged in performance-related pay from (say) one quartile to another, will cause a positive increase in firms' innovative performance by some predictable (discrete) value. Notice that *without* the presupposition of causality, equation (2) would, for *practical* reasons, be irrelevant. When used in social science (as opposed to pure mathematics) a functional relation either implies causality or it is irrelevant. Yet, as every first-year student with a basic knowledge of statistics knows, regressions and correlations do not imply causality.[15] This, we suspect, is why many researchers feel it necessary to remind the reader that statistical association does not imply causality, despite that fact that the way their hypotheses are set out and tested cannot do other than imply causality.

What drives the preoccupation with quantitative, statistical and empirical analysis

Before we leave this section, it is instructive to pause and consider exactly what encourages empirical research on the HRM–P link, rooted as it is in scientism, along with its ontology of events, epistemology of event regularities, and aetiology of thin causality, to be preoccupied with, and dominated by, quantitative, statistical and empirical analysis.

Bearing in mind that the commitments of empirical researchers are probably to some under-elaborated notion of scientism in general, rather than any particular conception, there does seem to be a (probably unconscious) rationale at work. The kind of knowledge sought by advocates of scientism comes via observed events and their regularities. Events are the building blocks of scientism, and events are fused with observations – such that 'what we see is what is'. If we observe an event, and we want to know something more about it, perhaps to seek its cause, or test theory about it, then all we have available to us is another observed event or events. We are 'thrown' as it were, from one observed event to another observed event(s). The movement is, metaphorically speaking, 'horizontal' – from observed event to observed event(s).

The simple movement from event to event(s) would not, however, reveal knowledge unless a pattern, indeed a regularity, was observed in the flux of events. From this event regularity, causality can be inferred: the more often event x is observed to be succeeded by event y, then the more grounds researchers allegedly have for thinking x causes y. If events manifest themselves as regularities, and the more regular the more 'causal' then it makes perfect sense to count them. We might use a Lickert Scale of 1–5, for example, to measure the degree of worker satisfaction with teamwork, and our data will reveal something like: one worker reporting some degree of satisfaction with teamwork (an event); two workers reporting some degree of satisfaction with teamwork (an event); n workers reporting some degree of satisfaction with teamwork (an event); and so on. At the other end of the process, we might measure sales and our data will reveal something like: one increase in productivity (an event); two increases in productivity (an event); n increases in productivity (an event); and so on. Once the data on these events are quantified they become variables, and it is a simple matter to perform all kinds of mathematical and statistical operations on them. We can, for example, formulate this in terms of a functional relation, specify this as a regression equation, and test for a statistical relation between the average value our empirical data reveal for the degree of worker satisfaction with teamwork, and the average value for the level of sales. The downside of this, of course, as we will see below, is that phenomena that do not take the form of observable events and their regularities, and cannot (meaningfully) be quantified, expressed in terms of functional relations and transposed into the variables of a regression equation, cannot be included in the research. And if this happens to include large swathes of phenomena that impact on the HRM–P link, then so much the worse for scientism.

Scientism: a critical realist critique[16]

Now that we have a fair idea of what scientism, the deductive method and its meta-theoretical presuppositions entail, we can turn to considerations of its shortcomings. We start by sketching critical realism's alternative conceptions of ontology, epistemology and methodology.

This will be further elaborated in the following chapter, but by having a rough idea of the critical realist alternative, we are better placed to understand scientism's shortcomings. After a brief discussion of ontology, epistemology and methodology, we will continue in more depth to discuss closed and open systems.

Ontology, epistemology, events

Critical realists are keen to make two important points; first, that there is another dimension to what we might call the 'ontological spectrum'; and second, event regularities, of the kind presupposed by closed systems, are extremely rare in the social world. Let us consider these two points in turn.

Contra to the empirical realist ontology noted above, and underpinning scientism, for critical realists, the social world is not 'flat' and so another part of the 'ontological spectrum' reveals itself for investigation. The social world is ontologically *layered*, that is, the social world is irreducible to that which is observed or experienced; and that which is experienced is not fused with events and actions. Furthermore, events and actions are themselves thought to be governed by 'deep' causal phenomena that may actually be unobservable – e.g. we cannot observe workers' capacities or powers for creative actions. This amounts to no more than a commitment to investigate domains of the world beyond the empirical and the actual, referred to metaphorically, and generally, as the domain of the 'deep'. In this domain are 'deep' social structures such as mechanisms, institutions, rules, conventions, resources, (non-human) powers, and so on. This far richer ontology is schematised in Table 4.2 – we suggest the reader flick back to Table 4.1 above. *This has one important consequence for epistemology: knowledge is not restricted to observed events.*

These causally efficacious social structures are located at deeper levels than the HRM structures typically identified as being correlated with high-performing organisations.[17]

The second point critical realists are keen to make is that event regularities, of the kind presupposed by advocates of scientism, are extremely rare in the social world. We assert this here, and develop it below when we consider open and closed systems. This has another important consequence for epistemology: knowledge is not restricted to (observed) event regularities. If knowledge is available not only via

Table 4.2. *A 'layered' ontology*

Domain	Entity
Empirical	Experiences and observations
Actual	Events and actions
'Deep'	Structures, mechanisms, rules, conventions, resources, (non-human) powers, etc.

events and their regularities, if the ontological spectrum is now deeper, critical realists are free to move, metaphorically speaking, from the 'horizontal' (from event to event) to the 'vertical' (from the event to the deep structures). They are free to turn their attention away from attempting to find regularities in the flux of observed events towards the social structures and mechanisms that govern them, even where no event regularities exist. Event regularities may not, after all, be necessary for generalised knowledge to be possible.

This has an important consequence for methodology: methods are not restricted to deductivism. With the recognition that events do not manifest as regularities, combined with the further recognition that *something must govern these events* (they are not uncaused), then the method, if it is to bear fruit, must switch. The emphasis of investigation must switch from the domains of the empirical and actual, to the domain of the deep and to the social structures and mechanisms that causally govern these events. Investigation must switch from the *consequences*, that is, from the *outcomes or results* (in the form of event regularities) of some particular human action, to the conditions that make that action possible. Because of the lack of event regularities, events cannot be *inductively* predicted, or predicted as *deductions* from axioms, assumptions and laws, as in the deductive method. But the structures and mechanisms that causally govern this human action *can* be identified and, very often, *explained*. And because to explain is to offer a (non-thin, or 'thick') causal account, we refer to the method as the *causal-explanatory method*.

Let us leave a more elaborated account of critical realism's alternative meta-theory until Chapter 5, and press on now with consideration of event regularities, open and closed systems and the conundrums and problems closed system analysis generates, quantification of qualities and qualitative change.

Event regularities, closed and open systems

Whilst it is fairly un-contentious to conceive of the organisation, firm, plant, workplace or department wherein HRM practices are put into practice, *and* changes in performance occur as a system, the important question is: what kind of system is it? Is it closed, as empirical research on the HRM–P link presupposes; or is it open as we argue?

Whilst event regularities and, therefore, closed systems, are fundamental to scientism and the deductive method, they are exceptionally rare phenomena.[18] There appear to be very few spontaneously occurring systems wherein constant conjunctions of events occur in the natural world, and virtually none in the social world. The paradigm case where closed systems are found is the bench experiment carried out in some (but by no means all) natural sciences. The point of such experiments is to close the system by engineering a particular set of conditions that will isolate the one interesting mechanism. This mechanism is then allowed to operate unimpeded and the results, the constant conjunctions, recorded. You might recall high school physics where a vacuum jar isolates objects from aerodynamic and thermal forces so that objects falling in the jar fall regularly at 9.6 ms^2. The case of the vacuum jar is a case of scientists engineering a closed system. In social science, however, constant conjunctions only occur where they are engineered in the form of theoretically closed systems.

To many, the claim that there are no event regularities and, therefore, no closed systems in the social world appears to be either false or an exaggeration. The following examples all *appear* to involve some kind of event regularities and, therefore, closed systems:

- people work for an employer and then get paid
- in hot weather ice cream prices rise
- schools close at the same time each day
- post boxes are found in high streets
- petrol prices rise in Lancaster and petrol prices rise in Bristol
- car drivers drive on the left in the UK

Let us unpack these different examples. Even in several of the above examples where event regularity appears to be obvious, a strictly accurate reading shows this not to be true. In cases where the employer goes bankrupt before meeting its wage commitments, some people do not get paid. Price wars between rival ice cream sellers, or wrongly sited ice cream vendors, mean prices do not always rise in hot weather. Heating system breakdowns cause schools to close at different times. Critical realists' argument that there are very few event regularities in the social world does not preclude the possibility that there is some stability and even a degree of regularity to many social systems, at least over some restricted space and time. Such rough and ready regularities as do exist are referred to by critical realists as 'demi-regularities' or 'demi-regs' (Lawson 2003: 79 *passim*). The existence of demi-regularities is one of the reasons why some researchers invoke stochastic closure, and/or the notion of tendency – but more of this later. It might be worth pointing out at this juncture, that when critical realists suspect the existence of a demi-regularity, their instinct is not to try and transform it into a hypothesis to be tested, but to treat it as the starting point of a scientific voyage to find the structures and agents responsible for generating the demi-regularity.

Demi-regularities, for example, occur when schools tend to close at the same time each day and post boxes do tend to be found in high streets. Whilst there is a sense of event regularity here, it is what we might call unsurprising or *trivial*. It is the kind of regularity where the cause is obvious. Policy-makers made a decision to close schools at pre-arranged times and locate post boxes in high streets. We would not expect to find, and indeed do not find, social scientists running regressions to test the hypothesis that post boxes are found in high streets. Indeed, the fact that we know the cause or causes of regularities of this kind, makes it unnecessary to engage in empirical research to find a statistical association. *Trivial* event regularities, then, are not the kind of regularities social science is concerned with.

Suppose it is true that when petrol prices rise in Lancaster, petrol prices also rise in Bristol. This is an event regularity and a form of closure, but is it a specific kind of closure. The price rise in Bristol is not caused by the price rise in Lancaster. Rather both price rises are caused by, or *concomitant* with, let us say a rise in the price of North Sea crude oil. The example of car drivers driving on the left in the UK is also a concomitant closure, with the rules of the highway code causing UK drivers to drive on the left. Lawson refers to this as *closure of concomitance*. Put more formally, this is *not* a case where event x regularly causes event y, but a case where both event x and event y are caused by event z. If the cause, event z, is known, there is little point seeking a statistical association between event x and event y. Neither is there any point seeking a statistical association between event x and event z, as we already know what caused event x. Empirical research, such as that on the HRM–P link, does not address closures of concomitance. As Bigo (2006: 509) puts it: 'In economic modeling ... when two events are correlated it is typically supposed that one stands in a causal history of the other (rather than sharing the same causal history)'. We will have more to say on this in later chapters.

Ultimately, event regularity and, therefore, the existence of closed systems is an empirical, not a meta-theoretical matter – although we are sceptics. Despite our doubts, it might well turn out that in hot weather ice cream prices do rise, at least in some geographical locations, in some time periods. The increase in ice cream price is caused by the hot weather, and not by some other concomitant cause. Lawson refers to this kind of closure as *closure of causal sequence*. This is (or would be) the paradigm case of closure, and the kind of closure styled above as 'whenever event x then event y' or in its functional form $y = f(x)$. This kind of event regularity, and closure of causal sequence, are the kinds of regularities and closure presupposed by empirical researchers on the HRM–P link – although presupposing their existence does not guarantee their existence. The use of quantitative, empirical and statistical techniques, designed to test the hypothesis that HRM practices are (stochastically) associated with increased organisational performance, presupposes an event regularity of the kind 'whenever event $x_1...x_n$ then event y' or its functional form, $f(x_1...x_n)$, and, therefore, presupposes closed systems.

Apart, then, from trivial event regularities and trivial closed systems, event regularities generating concomitant closures, and demi-regularities which do not constitute closed systems, there appear to be virtually no event regularities, and closed systems, in the social world. This includes stochastic closures as we will see later. Now as it happens, we think there are extremely plausible reasons to reject the presupposition that the social world is a closed system, and instead consider it to be an open system. We aim to establish the plausibility of this view by considering three forms of evidence, empirical and practical evidence, mentioned in Chapter 3. We will ask two questions. First, *why are social systems open*? Second: *what are the consequences of modelling open systems as if they were closed*? It is difficult to present these two questions sequentially, so each one will be discussed when it is appropriate to do so.[19]

A priori evidence

By a priori evidence we mean social ontology: knowledge of the way the social world is that we bring with us to the analysis of any concrete social system. The system of interest to us is the place wherein HRM practices are enacted and organisations perform, namely, the workplace. It will come as no surprise to anyone with practical familiarity with the workplace, or anyone familiar with theoretical and qualitative research in the sociology of work, organisation and management studies, HRM and industrial or employee relations, that the system we are dealing with is *multiply caused, complex, evolving* and subject to the *exercise of human agency*. These phenomena are not mutually exclusive, which complicates the system even more. Moreover, we strongly suspect our claim that the social world is characterised by multiple causality, complexity, evolution and human agency is not even controversial and, if spelled out clearly, may be accepted even by researchers in the HRM-P paradigm. Unfortunately, however, matters are simply never put in this (clear) way.

The system is *multiply caused* in the sense that there are, typically, scores or even hundreds of factors with some kind of causal impact on organisational performance. We are not talking here of the usual synergies (or dis-synergies) deriving from the vertical and horizontal alignment of the bundle of HRM practices. Rather, we are talking about causal factors originating outside the workplace, perhaps outside the industry and perhaps even outside the national economy. The kind of things we have in mind here are, of course, many and varied, but examples might be of political and ideological forces operating at the national level and affecting trade unions, European Union legislation or maybe even global macro-economic conditions. The impact of these causal factors can be *direct* in the sense that some causal factor influences an individual HRM practice, or directly effects organisational performance. The impact can also be *indirect* in the sense that some causal factor interacts with several

HRM practices in the bundle, the bundle generates synergy or dis-synergy, and this overall effect affects performance. Recognising multi-causality requires more than simply trying to add more control variables, trying to disaggregate variables or trying to add in as many variables as it is possible to obtain data on, or trying to find what are euphemistically referred to as 'missing variables'. The reasons for this are many and varied, but probably include the following. Many of the causal factors may lie outside of the researcher's field of enquiry, or area of competence. Researchers focusing their attention on the internal workings of organisations, for example, tend not to be familiar with what goes on external to organisations. Many causal factors may be unobservable. Think of the enormous impact 'Thatcherism' had on the UK trade union movement, and its effects on people management. Not only are these factors unobservable, they are impossible to (meaningfully) quantify and reduce to variables, so are simply left out (literally) of the equation. It is also, in part, because of complexity and evolution.

The system is *complex* in the sense that it generates its own internal changes which feed back to alter the nature of the HRM practices, and this changes the effects these HRM practices (directly and indirectly) have on performance. Complexity introduces difficulties in reducing something to a variable if that something is undergoing a change in its nature.

The system *evolves* in the sense that it is always creating and responding to changes in the external environment and, once again, these changes alter the nature of the HRM practices, and this changes the effects these HRM practices (directly and indirectly) have on performance. This often leads to causal effects being intermittent in the sense that HRM practices operating a certain way today, may 'switch off' as it were, or start to operate in slightly different ways tomorrow, only to 'switch on' again or revert back to their old mode of operating at some later date. Evolution also introduces difficulties in reducing something to a variable if that something is undergoing a change in its nature – we will return to this below.

The system is *subject to human agency* in the sense that human beings can, and do, change their minds. This should not be taken to mean that humans are entirely capricious or act whimsically. Rather, it means their actions are not entirely predictable and they retain the ability to always have done otherwise. To deny this is to deny human subjectivity, creativity, imagination, ingenuity and entrepreneurial activity. HRM practices that were accepted as legitimate by workers in one period can become unacceptable in another period and vice versa, and it is often difficult to attribute causes to this other than to say workers changed their minds.

We do not have to uncritically swallow the management discourse wherein 'the only constant is change', and we are 'surfing on chaos' or whatever, to realise that many of these management commentators make ontological presuppositions that are far more in tune with the way the world is than many empirical researchers. In *Competing on the Edge*, for example, Brown and Eisenhardt (1998) make plausible claims about much contemporary business being *unpredictable and uncontrolled*. 'The future is too uncertain for such pin-point accuracy'; 'there is simply too much going on in rapidly changing industries for a single group to orchestrate every move' (1998). A recent study notes that:

the relationship between historic trends and future performance is not always well understood, in part, because people (all stakeholders, not just employees) behave in different, sometimes unpredictable ways ... therefore, the diverse effects of people policies on business value may be both complex and, in some cases unexpected. (PricewaterhouseCoopers 2003: 9)[20]

In a seminal paper in HRM–P literature, Ichniowski *et al.* (1997: 302) consider production lines that 'switch' practices during the period of their analysis. It would be remarkable indeed if these lines ceased switching after the period of investigation. Whilst Ichniowski *et al.* are able to identify discrete changes in HRM practices, their meta-theoretical approach leaves them unable to identify subtle, qualitative changes in these practices that occur over time, even perhaps over the time of their study. The way a team operates when it is first set up is different from the way it operates when it is mature, and even then it does not continue to operate in this way for ever, it undergoes continual evolution. To suggest, as Godard (2001: 28) does, that there is 'evidence that even the most successful programmes may have a limited half-life, either fading over time or failing altogether' is merely to recognise that HRM practices change and evolve: something no one would deny. Another way of putting all this is to say that the workplace is an open system.

Empirical evidence

As we saw in the previous chapter, some studies provide evidence of a quantifiable, measurable, statistical association between various bundles of HRM practices, when variously aligned with strategy and in various contexts, and organisational performance, and other studies do not. We also cautioned against arriving, prematurely, at the conclusion that there is no connection between various bundles of HRM practices, when variously aligned with strategy and in various contexts, and organisational performance. This could simply mean that the workplace is a system of such complexity and dynamism that the connection is unlikely to manifest itself in an empirical relation of the kind captured by, say, a regression analysis. Another way of putting all this is to say that the workplace is an open system.

Practical evidence

We saw in the last chapter that the failure of empirical research on the HRM–P link to inform practice teaches us that the social world is a complex place. If HR managers cannot simply take a study identifying an empirical relationship between a specific bundle of HRM practices, perhaps when appropriately aligned with corporate strategy, and, in an appropriate context, introduce this bundle, align it with their own corporate strategy and expect a similar increase in performance, then the key question is: why not? We are now able to answer this in terms of meta-theory: managers cannot operate like this because the workplace is an open system.

What, then, can we conclude from the empirical and practical evidence? Our critical realist meta-theory allows us to re-state this evidence in terms of open systems. In an open system such as the workplace we would expect to find multiple determination, complexity, evolution and the exercise of human agency. We would expect to find that when bundles of HRM practices are introduced, aligned with strategy and in various contexts, sometimes organisational performance improves (a little or a lot), sometimes it remains unchanged and sometimes it deteriorates (a little or a lot). Moreover, we would not expect to be able to predict which of these outcomes will prevail, meaning that we would not expect managers to simply apply the results of empirical research to their own organisations. In sum, then, we have not only strong grounds to believe that event regularities are most unlikely to occur within the workplace, the mixed empirical and practical evidence supports this conclusion. We conclude that the workplace is almost certainly an open, not a closed, system.

Modelling open systems as closed systems

We have argued that because the workplace is characterised by a lack of event regularities, it should be recognised as, and treated theoretically and meta-theoretically as, an open system. Unfortunately, however, scientist meta-theory in general, and the deductive method in particular, cannot deal with open systems, so in the HRM–P paradigm the workplace is modelled as if it was a closed system. Two generic assumptions are necessary to close the system, referred to as intrinsic and extrinsic closure conditions.

Intrinsic closure conditions

The individuals that inhabit the workplace, arguably, have some kind of *internal* or *intrinsic* state or (psychological and neurological) structure that grounds their human agency and facilitates their ability to reflect, think, change their minds and so on. To deny this is to deny human agency, creativity, imagination, ingenuity or any kind of entrepreneurial activity. How an individual responds to a causal influence depends, in part, upon this intrinsic state. To accept this is to accept that the response by a workforce, vis-à-vis levels of output, to the introduction of (say) performance-related pay (PRP) is likely to depend upon factors like their *expectations* or other interpretations of their situation. Whilst they might respond to the lure of increased pay by sometimes increasing effort, they might also respond by decreasing effort, or may remain unaffected by it. Moreover, whilst they may be happy with a particular PRP system in one period, they may not be satisfied with it at some later period. In reality, workers really do behave like this; as human beings, they engage in non-regular and often unpredictable behaviour – which does not, of course, mean that their actions are characterised by total chaos or whim.

This lack of regularity is, however, a serious problem for empirical researchers who presuppose event regularities and, therefore, closed system modelling. To stick with the example, the nature of workers, as human beings who often change their minds, destroys the regularity between the introduction of a PRP scheme and increased effort. To maintain closure, researchers have (in theory only, of course) to re-engineer the nature of the human beings presupposed (implicitly) in the model so that they *always* respond in the same, regular and a priori predictable way. This is done by specifying the *internal state* of the individuals in such a way that when acted upon by causal factors x_1, x_2...x_n, the individual *always* responds in the same, a priori predictable way, by initiating action y. When PRP is introduced (and other conditions are met, such as the bonus is considered to be sufficiently high, or that the employer will actually pay and so on) rational individuals *always* respond by increasing effort. We refer to this as specifying the individual as a kind of *quasi-atom*, that is, not *totally* devoid of intrinsic structure, but almost so. In essence, what happens is that the individual is (theoretically) emptied of all intrinsic structure and re-programmed with a new, very simple programme, so that when acted upon by a causal influence, the individual will initiate a predictable and constant course of action. The intrinsic closure condition is satisfied, then, when the individual is specified *quasi-atomistically* and the most common way of doing this is by treating them as *homo economicus* or rational economic man.

Consider Laursen's functional relation as expressing a closed system.

(1) $A_i = f (\text{SECT}_i + \text{SIZE}_i + \text{LINK}_i + \text{HRMS}_i)$

The workers that populate Laursen's model are assumed to always respond to the possibility of increased pay (via the introduction of performance-related pay) by increasing their effort. He rationalises this as follows: 'rewarding shop-floor employees for minor process improvements is likely to increase such incremental innovation activity'. This is another way of saying whenever event x (introduction of a PRP scheme), then event y (increase in performance). Although he does not explicitly state this, he has (theoretically) re-engineered these workers as *homo economicus*. Laursen has to presuppose this strong version of rationality because anything less would allow workers to engage in non-regular, unpredictable behaviour. This is easier to see if we consider how Laursen *did not* rationalise PRP. He *did not* say 'rewarding shop-floor employees for minor process improvements sometimes increases incremental innovation activity, sometimes it decreases it and sometimes has no effect'.

Now, as it happens, Laursen finds empirical evidence to support the observation that PRP is linked to innovative performance. But this is not our concern here – although many other empirical studies cast doubt on such findings. How might a researcher proceed if they had hypothesised, but had *not* discovered, an empirical link between PRP and performance? A first option would be to simply admit that the link does not exist to be discovered empirically, because workers are not instrumentally rational, and abandon attempts at closed system modelling – which is the course of action we advocate. Second, the lack of an empirical link might encourage the researcher to believe that the activities of the workers had not been specified with sufficient precision. Assumptions would have to be added, such as workers will respond to the introduction of a PRP scheme by improving their productivity if (a_1) they believe that incentive targets can be met and (b_1) they believe the incentive is sufficient. And so on. Assumptions could be added, variables could be split into sub-variables, which in turn could be split into sub-sub-variables and this process could go on ad infinitum. Without a terminal point the researcher would be engaged in an infinite regress, forced to specify each variable with more and more precision. The fact that this would lose degrees of freedom is actually a minor (technical) problem compared to the meta-theoretical problems such an infinite regress would cause. In an attempt to obtain regularity and maintain intrinsic closure, the empirical researcher would be driven to disaggregate workers' actions and to measure ever 'smaller' activities.

Now, it is possible to fall back on the *a*theoretical and overtly empirical nature of research on the HRM–P link, in an attempt to turn a problem into an advantage and deflect our criticism. We know research on the HRM–P link is *empirical* in the sense that it deals with aggregate measures of HRM practices and organisational performance. We know too that it is under-theorised, and this extends to theory of human agency. If ideas about human individuals never get mentioned in empirical research on the HRM–P link, then our claim that empirical researchers presuppose *homo economicus* appears misplaced. Apart from the fact that this would be an attempt to use ignorance as a deflection, we defend our criticism by reminding the reader of the importance of presuppositions defined in the introduction. The fact that an empirical researcher does not actually state the conception of human agency they operate with does not mean they are not operating with one. The moment a researcher suggests that some HRM practice regularly causes an increase in organisational performance, they have already presupposed things about the workers who actually engage with this HRM practice, and who make organisational performance (at any level) a reality. They have already presupposed that the intrinsic (psychological and neurological) state of these workers is such that they regularly respond in the same predictable way, so that the HRM practices they engage with always increase organisational performance.

The extrinsic closure condition

The extrinsic closure condition ensures that the system is completely isolated from any *external* influences that might be causally influential. This occurs when: (1) all relevant causal factors are internalised within the system, or, if there remain relevant influences extrinsic to the system, either (2) these factors are specified such that they exercise a perpetually constant influence, or (3) the elements within the system are isolated from their effects. There are numerous context specific ways to satisfy these conditions.

Consider Laursen's work again. Laursen ensures that the system is completely isolated from any *external* influences by the use of control variables such as SECT (sector to which each firm belongs), SIZE (firm size) and LINK (firm has/has not increased its vertical integration). But these are only *some* external influences: there are a myriad of others that could easily influence (say) the operation of work teams, such as: fear of redundancy or fear of losing valued characteristics of the job after a period of redundancies, or perhaps even in anticipation of re-engineering or downsizing; adverse change in exchange rates, interest rates, or currency regimes; general mistrust of management following the introduction of some other new working practices elsewhere; changes in government or political ideology that cause changes in industrial relations climate, and so on.

If changes in external factors such as these occurred, we would consider it highly likely that the influence HRM practices have on performance would alter. Should the researcher recognise the importance of the external environment, s/he may choose to extend the number of control variables to take into account changes. Once again, the researcher runs the risk of an infinite regress, steadily including more and more control variables into the model.[21]

In sum, if the social world in general, and the workplace in particular, are open systems, then modelling them as if they are closed systems, and ensuring that the intrinsic and extrinsic conditions are met, is going to be a never-ending task.[22]

Stochastic closure

In the first part of this chapter, we defined stochastically closed systems as those wherein 'the mean (or expected value) of variables x_1, $x_2...x_n$ is constantly conjoined with the mean (or expected value) of variable y'. We also noted that what really mattered was not what we called such a system, but what event regularities and closed systems (deterministic or stochastic) require empirical researchers on the HRM–P link to presuppose about the social world in general, and the workplace in particular. So, what is presupposed, and what does it matter?

Critical realists did not 'invent' event regularities and closed systems – although they did explicitly define and name them. Critical realists maintain that event regularities and, therefore, closed systems are presuppositions necessary in order for scientism in general, and the deductive method in particular, to 'work'. At the same time critical realists' ontological investigations suggest (as we will see later) that the social world is *multiply caused, complex, evolving* and subject to the *exercise of human agency*, all of which lead them to suspect that event regularities are most unlikely to occur in social systems. A tension now stands revealed. Scientism presupposes event regularities and closed systems, which in turn presuppose that social structures, and the agents that engage with them, have what we might call a *relatively high degree of stability* to them. After all, the very fact that (social) events of any kind occur is due to agents routinely engaging with social structures. If these structures were unstable in the sense that they could simply come and go, change their nature or whatever, and agents could do likewise, then society would probably not display anything like the level of event regularity it does. It is no contradiction to reject event regularities and at the same time accept the relative stability of social structures, and the agents that engage with them.

What critical realists doubt is the degree of stability necessary to generate event regularities and, therefore, closed systems. Whilst doubt clearly involves deterministic closures, it also extends to stochastic closures. This is because the mean value of variables $x_1, x_2 \ldots x_n$ could *only* be constantly conjoined with the mean value of variable y *if* a relatively high degree of stability existed in the structures, and the agents who engage with them. To see what is at stake here, consider the following question: what would the social world have to look like in order for this relatively high degree of stability to exist? It is easier to address this question by considering social structures and human agents in turn.

For a high degree of structural stability to exist, social structures would have to be characterised as follows:

- Social structures cannot undergo changes in their internal development/evolution.
- Social structures cannot be subject to changes in external forces that would cause them to change.
- Social structures deemed to be influential at some past time period cannot cease being influential at some later period.
- Social structures not influential at some past time period cannot start being influential at some later period.
- Alternately, should any of the above changes occur, these changes must be insufficient to alter the mean values of the variables.

Now consider agency. For a high degree of agential stability to exist, humans and their actions would have to be characterised as follows:

- Human agents cannot be subject to changes in their internal development/evolution.
- Human agents cannot be subject to changes in external forces.
- Human actions influential at some past time period cannot cease being influential at some later period.
- Human actions not influential at some past time period cannot start being influential at some later period.
- Alternately, should any of the above changes occur, these changes must be insufficient to alter the mean values of the variables.

If these conditions (and there are likely to be many others) hold, then social structures and human agents are unlikely to change, or change sufficiently to alter the mean values of the variables, making it likely that the mean values of variables x_1, $x_2...x_n$ will be constantly conjoined with the mean value of variable y. This regularity would be stochastic, and the stochastic nature of the regularity would be caused by the way the social world is, and by the way human beings are. Moreover, if and when we know what the mean values of variables x_1, $x_2...x_n$ are, we can (inductively) predict that variable y, with a mean value, will follow. If these conditions *do not* hold, by contrast, then social structures and human agents are likely to change and alter the mean values of the variables, making it most unlikely that the mean value of variables x_1, $x_2...x_n$ would be constantly conjoined with the mean value of variable y. In this case, even if and when we do know the mean values of variables x_1, $x_2...x_n$, we will not be able to (inductively) predict that variable y, with a mean value, will follow.

And now we come to the nub of the problem that affects stochastic closure as much as deterministic closure. The moment empirical researchers engage in scientism, the deductive method and the empirical, quantitative techniques scientism encourages, they necessarily presuppose that stability conditions like those suggested above exist. They have little or no choice in the matter, because scientism and the deductive method do not 'work' without them. If, however, these conditions do not exist, and we argue below that they do not, then to presuppose stochastic regularity and, therefore, stochastic closure, is to presuppose a social world that is at odds with the way the social world really is. This is a serious error in the sense that ontology and epistemology have no connection with each other. Claims about the way the social world is, bear no resemblance to the way the social world actually is – although some of those who make such presuppositions are aware of this, and defend their endeavours on grounds of mathematical tractability or some such.

Systems theory, open and closed systems

Whilst many readers of this book will be new to critical realism, they will be familiar with General Systems Theory (GST) and, via GST, open and closed systems. Whilst there are some similarities between critical realism and GST vis-à-vis systems, there are also important differences that need to be addressed to avoid any confusion. Let us try to explain how two sophisticated commentators on the HRM–P link can advocate an open systems approach whilst also advocating structural equation modelling, which from our point of view involves a contradiction. Way and Johnson (2005: 15) write:

Our framework is an open system and thus allows us to consider the numerous factors that are simultaneously .in play in a complex organization. Although systems theory does not easily lend itself to empirical testing, structural equation modelling (SEM) is a statistical methodology that may enable scholars to empirically test complex SHRM models ... Although the inclusion of interactions and other non-linear effects is problematic ... we encourage future SHRM research to use this statistical methodology.

Parts of this quotation make them sound like critical realists, and parts of it make them sound like advocates of scientism. To understand what is going on, it is important to realise that what systems theorists mean by systems, closed systems and open systems is not quite the same thing as what critical realists mean. Some versions of systems theory, however, get extremely close to critical realism, and we suspect more in-depth enquiry would reveal more similarities than differences. A good example of this is Harney and Dundon (2006) and Scott's (1992) 'open-natural system models'. Way and Johnson's recognition (a) that systems theory does not easily lend itself to empirical testing and (b) of the problems arising from the inclusion of interactions and other non-linear effects, is strongly suggestive of open-natural system models. Open-natural systems (ONS) are those that most resemble the open systems of critical realism in that they have characteristics like the following – all these comments and quotations are from Scott (1992: 88–100).

ONS are characterised by morphogenesis, that is processes that elaborate or change the system. 'To survive is to adapt, and to adapt is to change'. ONS are structured. The 'normative structure of an organization is only loosely coupled to its structure. Rules do not always govern actions: a rule may change without affecting the behaviour, or *vice versa*'. ONS are best conceived of as a 'loosely linked coalition of shifting interest groups'. ONS are not conducive to methodological individualism, nor to theories that place the rational individual, *homo economicus*, at the centre of analysis – as many economic and psychological theories do. 'Enhancements in the productivity of individual workers does not quickly or easily translate into gains in productivity at the departmental or firm level'. ONS are characterised by complexity, in the sense of giving rise to unpredictable outcomes. ONS are characterised by normal accidents, that is, unexpected and unpredictable ways in which the system can change or fail. ONS exist in environments that are themselves complex and uncertain. Finally, ONS require the active involvement of human beings who engage in a process of enactment, that is, a process of making sense of their world, and selecting a set of rules which allow them to organise. Here Scott not only cites Weick, but also Giddens, whose structuration process is very similar to the critical realist notion of a transformational ontology (Scott 1992: 100).

Before we get carried away with the similarities, however, it is worth mentioning one significant difference between Scott's open-natural systems and critical realism's notion of open systems. Systems theorists often define *closed* systems as 'simple and deterministic' and *open* systems as 'complex and probabilistic' – whereby the latter can 'generally be described and predicted with statistical procedures'. Unfortunately Scott goes on to add that 'exceedingly complex probabilistic systems ... currently defy mathematical modelling' (1992: 93) which does make it hard to know whether he thinks complex and probabilistic systems are open to statistical analysis or not. Be that as it may, understanding open systems as probabilistic and capable of being predicted with statistical procedures is tantamount to conceiving open systems in terms of what we would *not* call open at all, but stochastically closed. This difference arises because systems theorists, of whatever hue, define open systems in terms of interactions between the system and its environment, whereas critical realists define open systems in terms of (the absence of) event regularities. Hence for critical realists, a probabilistic event regularity is still an event regularity, denoting a (probabilistically) closed system. Note that we are not arguing that the critical realist definition of open and closed systems is better than that offered by systems theory, we are simply pointing out that they are different.

We can now see how Way and Johnson, who appear cognisant of open-natural systems, can end up advocating structural equation modelling (SEM). For them, because open systems are complex and probabilistic, complex SHRM models can be dealt with via appropriate statistical methods. That said, we cannot help feeling that Way and Johnson can advocate SEM only by turning a blind eye to: their own recognition that systems theory does not easily lend itself to empirical testing and the problems that arise from the inclusion of interactions and other non-linear effects; their own insights about the effects of multiple stakeholders which are bound to create effects on the organisation of an unpredictable nature; and the characteristics of open-natural systems listed above which they must be familiar with.

We could make similar comments about the work of Schuler and Jackson (2005). Not only do we accept their sketch of the stakeholders, and the need for stakeholders' concerns to feature as part of the causal account of the influence of HRM on organisational performance, we recognise much of our social ontology in their phraseology, despite the fact that we and they use different terminology. The following comment (reproduced from the last chapter) presupposes many of Scott's ideas about open-natural systems and is perfectly acceptable to us as critical realists.

Because the internal and external environments are dynamic, the process of managing human resources must also be dynamic. Success requires meeting the present demands of multiple stakeholders while also anticipating their demands … [T]he focus of academic work … will evolve away from its current search for effective HRM system designs and towards understanding their dynamic content. Gradually, *the rather mechanistic view of HRM systems* that prevails currently may be replaced by a perspective that recognizes the social aspects of human resource management and the processes through which organizational members create meaning from a complex array of signals. (Schuler and Jackson 2005: 14)

Unfortunately, as we noted in Chapter 3, when we first cited this quotation, Schuler and Jackson manage to combine a kind of implicit critical realism with what we consider to be the vestiges of scientism – Way and Johnson do something similar.[23] Is their commitment to scientism thoroughgoing, or is it due to them not being aware of alternatives like critical realism? Whilst only they can answer this question, the reader will be in a better position to consider his or her own position after we have a more in-depth understanding of critical realism in Chapter 6.

Conundrums

Modelling an open system as if it were closed brings with it a series of conundrums – i.e. problematic and counter-intuitive implications.

The mere existence of conundrums of this kind tells us immediately that something is not quite right.

(1) Outside closed systems, that is, in the open systems that appear to constitute the social world in general and the workplace in particular, and where constant conjunctions of events are *not* ubiquitous, we would have to conclude that nothing governs, and hence nothing explains, the (non-constant) flux of events. With no constant conjunctions, with no possibility of identifying causal mechanisms, and with no possibility of explanation, on this account, science would become a fruitless endeavour.

(2) It may be the case that, in open systems, HRM practices do cause changes in organisational performance. Yet because causality is reduced to event regularities, and because the latter are not ubiquitous, then the causal connection simply cannot be understood, in fact, it will (or should, on pain of inconsistency) be denied. The particular notion of causality (i.e. thin) presupposed, stands in the way of understanding the nature of the connection between HRMS and performance.

(3) It is often the case that conclusions derived from experimental situations (i.e. in closed systems) are successfully applied outside experimental situations (i.e. in open systems). Because of (1) above, this state of affairs would have no valid explanation.

(4) The obvious problem of how one may, justifiably, claim anything about a reality that constitutes an open system from an analysis of a closed system has never been *seriously* addressed by scientistic/scientistic orientated social scientists. In fact, deducing statements about the action of agents operating in a closed system, and transferring them to the action of agents in the open system, commits the fallacy called *ignoratio elenchi*. This entails 'assuming that one has demonstrated something to be true of X when the argument or evidence really applies to Y which is not the same as X in some respect' (Gordon 1991: 108). What is 'not the same' is the existence and ubiquity of constant conjunctions of events.

(5) The mathematical precision that analysis in terms of closed systems usually entails is *spurious precision*. We often see incredible mathematical precision used to model social systems that are incredibly messy, naturally qualitative, inherently complex,

multidimensional, subjective and evolving. Claims to the effect that precisely because the social world is like this, we need to simplify it in order to model it, are dealt with, and rejected, in Chapter 5.

Despite these problems and conundrums, closed system modelling remains a kind of 'best practice' in empirical research on the HRM–P link.[24] How much of this is down to the fact that most of these researchers are unaware of the meta-theoretical presuppositions they make every time they run a regression is unknown.

Qualitative change

Since constant conjunctions of events only occur in closed systems, the theoretical components that comprise the system must be framed in such a way that constancy is never threatened by qualitative changes in the phenomena under investigation, the observed events. And for this, (at least) two requirements must be sought after:

(1) The events that are expressed in a variable must be identical, that is, episodes of the same kind. 'Whenever event x', implies that a number of episodes of the same kind (x) have occurred.[25] Event x could, for example, be a change in the number of oranges or apples, or the share of the workforce engaged in interdisciplinary working groups. Whatever event x refers to, all episodes of it have to be identical. The requirement of identity implies a *common* dimension.

(2) These events must be susceptible to quantification and measurement in space and time. This imperative to quantify and measure implies an *unchanging* dimension. If one is counting apples in a barrel, and the timespan is so long that by the time one gets to the end of the barrel, the apples have rotted, and are no longer apples, then the dimension will have changed and (meaningful) addition will become impossible. If one is adding numbers to the workforce engaged in interdisciplinary working groups, then the qualitative nature of the workgroup cannot be allowed to change in response to the addition of new workers. Whether 1 per cent or 50 per cent of the workforce join the working group, the dimension (share of the workforce interdisciplinary working groups) must be presumed to be unchanging.

The requirements of a *common* and *unchanging* dimension are presumed to be met by re-conceptualising, re-defining or reducing events to *variables*, whence changes in their magnitude can be recorded. A variable, in turn, must retain two important features:

(1) It must possess one, and only one, common and unchanging dimension – i.e. number, quantity or magnitude. The only change a variable is permitted to experience is change in this number, quantity or magnitude; larger or smaller.

(2) It must maintain a stable reference to some real object or feature of reality.

Problems arise, however, if the real object to which the variable refers undergoes a process of *qualitative* change in its nature. If, for example, one is measuring ice cubes with the variable 'width' and during the process the temperature rises sufficiently, the qualitative nature of the ice cubes will change. The variable 'width' of ice cube and the object 'ice cube' will in a sense come adrift. The variable, unable to maintain a stable reference to its object, becomes an *inadequate conceptualisation of reality*.

What is true for ice cubes is also true for almost all of the naturally qualitative, inherently complex, multidimensional, subjective and evolving phenomena involved in HRM. These phenomena undergo qualitative change, not simply quantitative change where their magnitude changes. And this poses a problem for empirical research on the HRM–P link. Consider the following statement: 'whenever the new HRM practices are adopted, then the extent of innovation increases'. Here we are measuring a HRM system (which is a qualitative phenomenon) with a variable (which is a quantitative phenomenon). Laursen (2002) measures actual team working with the following variables:

- Interdisciplinary working groups [TEAM 1]
- Quality circles [TEAM 2]
- Planned job rotation [TEAM 3]
- Integration of functions (e.g. sales, production/services, finance) [TEAM 4]

But something like a team, as a naturally qualitative, inherently complex, multidimensional, subjective and evolving phenomenon, can and usually does change. To put matters simply for ease of exposition, a 'good quality' team can become a 'poor quality' team and vice versa.

Laursen's variables clearly do not capture the inherent qualitative nature, multidimensionality and richness of team working, and hence run into the following problem. Suppose planned rotation gradually evolves into task enlargement (something for which there is ample evidence) and this causes friction in the team. The quality of team-work may change, but the variable that measures teamwork, TEAM, remains unchanged. Actual teamwork and the variable TEAM will have come adrift. The variable, unable to maintain a stable reference to its object, becomes an *inadequate conceptualisation of reality*. The theorist is then forced onto the horns of a dilemma. S/he must choose between (a) embracing the qualitative change, violating an import-ant feature of their variable and, therefore, having to re-conceptual-ise team working; or (b) continuing with their variable, ignoring the qualitative change, and proceeding with an *inadequate* conceptual-isation of employment. Let us elaborate this important point.

(a) If researchers wish to embrace qualitative change in teamwork, and if the variable 'TEAM' is to continue to maintain stable ref-erence to its object, then the variable will have to undergo a quali-tative change. Some other way will, then, have to be found for adequately conceptualising employment. But as noted in (1) above, this will violate one of the important features of a variable because a variable can undergo quantitative but not qualitative change.

(b) If researchers wish to continue with the variable 'TEAM', they will have to ignore qualitative change in the actuality of team-working and hence proceed with an *inadequate* conceptualisation of the latter.

It is important to note that it is the scientistic meta-theory and the deductive method that is setting the agenda here, restricting the choice to one of embracing or ignoring qualitative change. Typically, those committed to scientism and deductivism have no option but to opt for the latter. The result is a set of theoretical concepts, variables, that cannot capture the properties of naturally qualitative, inherently complex, multidimensional, subjective and evolving phenomena.

Quantification of qualities

Whilst empirical research on the HRM–P link is rooted firmly in quantification and measurement, so that the usual statistical, empirical research techniques can be applied, the appropriateness of measuring and quantifying the social world remains unquestioned.[26] Measuring and quantifying *might* be appropriate in those cases where we simply want to *count* phenomena that have (or maybe just appear to have) a quantitative dimension, like counting the number of workers in an organisation or the number of hours of training undergone. Even here, however, problems with the qualitative nature of social phenomena creep in; not all workers are of the same quality and not all training hours are the same, or have the same effect on all workers. If problems of quality creep into phenomena that appear to be straightforward to quantify, then how much worse are these problems going to be when researchers turn their attention to counting phenomena that do not have a quantitative dimension such as corporate culture, justice, effectiveness, organisational philosophy, expectations, interpretations, perceptions and so on. Phenomena like these are inherently complex, evolving, multidimensional qualities, often with a subjective dimension to them. And whilst phenomena of this kind can, often with difficulty, be *understood*, this does not mean they can be measured, or at least *meaningfully* measured.

This term 'meaningful' is important here, so let us pursue it a little. In one sense, anything and everything can be measured given various assumptions, proxies and indices, but the key question is: would the resulting variable mean anything? Would the resulting variable meaningfully capture, reflect or express the phenomenon under investigation? Empirical researchers Wright *et al.* (2003: 32) clearly seek meaningful measures because they suggest that 'using employees as a source of the HR practice measures ensures that *the measure represents the actual practices* rather than the espoused policies of the business' (emphasis added). Whilst we agree that it is useful, indeed, it is crucial, to investigate employees as well as managers, it does not follow that simply using employees as a source of the HR practice measures ensures that the measure represents the actual practices.

We might, to take a rather extreme example to make the point, try to 'measure' whether Da Vinci's *Mona Lisa* is a 'happier' painting than Constable's *The Hay Wain* on the assumption that a predominantly light coloured painting expresses happiness. We could divide each painting into small squares, ask respondents to identify the predominant colour of the square and assign a number to the coloured squares ranging from one for dark squares to five for light squares.

Adding the scores would then provide a 'happiness' index, which we could use to compare the paintings. Although (we hope!) social scientists would reject this as preposterous, the interesting question is: why? This would probably be rejected on the grounds that phenomena like 'happiness expressed in paintings' is a wholly qualitative phenomena, and whilst it can be understood, or perhaps 'felt', it cannot be *meaningfully* measured. Although this is a preposterous example, it is not clear to us that attempts to measure corporate culture, justice, entrepreneurship, social identity, effectiveness, organisational philosophy, expectations, interpretations, perceptions and so on are actually less preposterous. The fact that measuring phenomena like these is a very common practice in empirical research on the HRM–P link, and is done with little or no critical reflection, does not mean it is unproblematic. Consider the following examples.

Lau and Ngo (2004: 700) measure 'developmental culture' with a four-item scale, where data is collected via responses to the following questions:

- Our firm is a very dynamic and entrepreneurial place.
- The head of our firm is generally considered to be an entrepreneur, an innovator or a risk taker.
- The glue that holds our firm together is commitment to innovation and development.
- Our firm emphasises growth and acquiring new resources.

Den Hartog and Verburg (2004: 64) attempt to measure the extent to which an organisation has an 'overarching philosophy' via a questionnaire enquiring into whether the organisation has a mission statement and whether the organisation has a written HRM strategy.

Leaving aside the problems of measuring 'procedural justice' on a four-item scale, Tzafrir *et al.* (2004) measure 'organisational communication' with a four-item scale, requiring respondents to state how much they agree with the following statements: 'there is a frank communication among all members of the organization' and 'there is a free flow of information between managers and employees'. They also measure 'employee development' on a two-item scale, requiring respondents to 'indicate the degree they received systematic and formal training in the past year'.

In their attempt to explain the statistically non-significant effect of information-sharing association on organisational performance,

Combs *et al.* (2006: 518) are forced to come to terms with the fact that the way employees handle information is incredibly complex. Some types of information, they suggest: 'are more critical than others for empowering employees. A machinist might consider knowing raw-material inventory levels for different orders more essential than the organization's quarterly financial performance'. They call for more research into the 'specific practices as well as conditions under which implementation effectiveness' of information-sharing processes is most critical. We completely agree.

We accept that employees have perceptions, employees develop, and that organisations have culture, philosophy, communication flows and so on. We also accept that these phenomena are extremely important for the way HRM practices are operationalised and should be investigated thoroughly. What we do not accept, however, is that phenomena like these that are naturally qualitative, inherently complex, evolving, multidimensional and subjective can be *meaningfully* captured by the kind of blunt research instruments sponsored by scientism and the deductive method.[27]

Fully elaborating upon our claim that naturally qualitative, inherently complex, evolving, multidimensional and subjective phenomena can be *meaningfully* captured by scientism, the deductive method and the quantitative, empirical and statistical research techniques scientism sponsors, would require us to write another chapter. Because space restrictions rule this out we opt for a different strategy. We place the onus on empirical researchers on the HRM–P link by asking the following question: why have these researchers chosen to ignore all the lessons about the dangers and limitations of quantification, measurement and mathematisation, penned by generations of ethnomethodologists, phenomenologists, interpretivists and hermeneuticists, not to mention postmodernists, poststructuralists, social constructionists, critical realists and others operating with an explicitly non-scientistic perspective? There are library shelves full of plausible arguments detailing the dangers and limitations of the quantification, measurement and mathematisation of naturally qualitative, inherently complex, evolving, multidimensional and subjective phenomena. It appears that these lessons have not been learned, and empirical research on the HRM–P link is so much the worse for it.[28]

Experience tells us that criticisms of the kind we are making here are likely to be met, *not* with a robust defence of quantification and measurement but with responses like: 'OK since you guys are so smart, how would *you* measure naturally qualitative, inherently complex, evolving, multi-dimensional and subjective phenomena of the kind involved in the HRM–P link?'. Our reply would be simple: 'phenomena like these cannot be measured, not because we (and you) are intellectually feeble, but because this is the way the world is'. An entirely different approach is required for phenomena of this kind. Unfortunately, however, few are looking for alternatives.

Conclusion

The first part of this chapter steadily works its way through scientism's presuppositions, thereby building up a clear idea of the meta-theory underpinning empirical research on the HRM–P link. The second part then engages in a critical realist critique of this meta-theory to reveal serious shortcomings. We offered a priori, empirical and practical evidence to suggest that event regularities are most unlikely to occur within the workplace, and concluded that the workplace is almost certainly an open, not a closed, system. Unfortunately, however, scientistic meta-theory in general, and the deductive method in particular, cannot deal with open systems, so in the HRM–P paradigm, the workplace is modelled as if it were a closed system. Modelling an open system as if it were closed, however, brings with it a series of conundrums, the mere existence of which tells us immediately that something is not quite right. Moreover, scientism, deductivism and the quantitative, empirical and statistical techniques sponsored by scientism, encourage empirical researchers to quantify and measure their subject matter, ignoring the possibility that naturally qualitative, inherently complex, evolving, multidimensional and subjective phenomena cannot be *meaningfully* measured and quantified. As if this were not bad enough Chapter 5 reveals even more shortcomings.

5 | Prediction, explanation and theory

Introduction

This chapter will demonstrate that empirical research on the HRM–Performance link is characterised by: a preoccupation with prediction to the neglect of explanation; serious confusion surrounding, and between, the concepts of prediction and explanation; and a lack of clarity vis-à-vis the nature and purpose of theory. It will also demonstrate that these problems cannot be resolved by retaining scientistic meta-theory and 'bolting on', as it were, a theory or theories drawn from other disciplines.

The first part of the chapter considers prediction and the following contradiction. Whilst prediction is central to scientism's (alleged) scientificity, scientism actually *lacks predictive power* and, therefore, fails to meet its own criteria for scientificity. This is not commonly recognised because of the ambiguity that surrounds the use of the term 'prediction'. The second part considers explanation by considering what explanation is *not* (Chapter 6 will deal with what it is, or should be) and highlights serious confusion between the concepts of prediction and explanation. The third part of the chapter considers the possibility that under-theorisation of empirical research on the HRM–P link could be reduced by borrowing theories from other disciplines, especially psychology and economics. We will use the latter to show that raiding other disciplines for theories, especially for a paradigm that lacks sophisticated meta-theoretical insight, coupled with a limited understanding of the nature and purpose of theory, introduces more problems than it solves. The final part of the chapter takes us back to why empirical research on the HRM–P link is under-theorised in the first place. We show that from the scientistic perspective, a theory is merely a vehicle for delivering predictions and hypotheses in terms of regularities between events, so we should not be at all surprised when it fails to deliver explanation.

Predictive power

Half a century ago the economist Milton Friedman (1988) famously (mis)used the power of prediction to make the 'Instrumentalist' argument that realisticness does not matter when formulating theory because prediction, not realisticness, is the sole test for evaluating theory. A theory that predicts well, he argued, irrespective of its realisticness, is preferred to one that does not predict well. Whilst this kind of Instrumentalism is not evident in research on the HRM–P link (although this may be due to the lack of meta-theoretical discussion, not because some version of it is no longer accepted) prediction remains a kind of (unelaborated) scientistic touchstone. Noon (not an advocate of the scientistic perspective) articulates what appears to be conventional wisdom:

As a model or theory, HRM is elevated to a position of scholarly and practical importance in terms of its analytical and *predictive powers*, whilst as a map it only lays claim to being a diagnostic tool aimed mainly at practising managers. (Noon 1994: 17, emphasis added)

References to prediction, predictive, predictors and various derivatives litter the literature. For Wright *et al.* (2003: 32) the 'results of the study reveal a detailed predictive model of HRM's impact on profitability'. For Panayotoupoulou and Papalexandris (2004: 507) 'some combinations of the three models seem to be better predictors of market performance'. For Schuler and Jackson (2005: 11) strategic HRM places 'emphasis on predicting firm financial performance'. For Way and Johnson (2005: 16) 'our framework provides scholars with an integrated theoretical foundation from which they can generate predictive SHRM models'.

There appear to be at least six reasons for the centrality of prediction in scientistic meta-theory.

(1) In the previous chapter we saw that scientism gains a misplaced veneer of scientificity by closely resembling science, by (mis)using some of its concepts. One such concept is 'prediction'. Although it is almost never stated, conventional wisdom holds that one of the most powerful arguments for the alleged superiority of scientism over other perspectives is that *it alone makes use of the power of prediction*. Only empirical research stemming from

scientism makes, and tests, predictions in the form of hypotheses. Perspectives that do not, or cannot, harness the power of prediction and aim instead for things like the recovery of actors' meaning (interpretivists, hermeneuticists, ethnomethodologists), the deconstruction of the organisation as text (postmodernists or poststructuralists), the analysis of discourse (critical discourse analysts) and/or explanation and description of the causal mechanisms that actors interact with (critical realists), are presumed to be un-scientific and, in this sense, inferior.

(2) Theories that generate hypotheses that are successfully tested via their predictions appear to provide a basis for policy prescription. If we can use a theory to test the hypothesis that when event X occurs, event Y follows, then our policy is to generate event X so that event Y, some desired outcome, occurs.

(3) In some natural sciences (typically those whereby the system under investigation is spontaneously closed or can be closed easily), successful predictions can be made. This success encourages the belief that, if social scientists continue to follow the example of these 'mature' sciences, one day, social sciences like HRM will be able to make successful predictions. In the meantime, we should continue our efforts to generate successful predictions.

(4) The ability to predict appears to support the ability to generalise the results of empirical research.

(5) Drawing on the work of Tsang and Kwan (1999: 769), we might say that prediction is superior to its close relative *accommodation*. A researcher who constructs theory to fit the data, *accommodates* the data. Another researcher may use this theory to make and test a prediction. Accommodation can be fudged, that is, the researcher knows the result the theory should generate and fudges the theory to make the theory fit the data. In the case of prediction, however, the theory comes into existence before the data and cannot be fudged (see Lipton 1993: Chapter 8).

(6) The particular notion of prediction used by scientism presupposes a mode of inference called *induction*. Induction involves a move *from the particular to the general*, that is, from claims about many particular instances of P to claims about Q. To use the well worn example, we might move from claims that 'all ravens thus far observed are black', to the claim that 'all ravens are black'. Researchers on the HRM–P link seek a statistical

association between changes in the magnitude of HRM practices X_1, X_2,...X_n, and changes in the magnitude of organisational performance Y. The empirical association is then used to *induce* the conclusion that firms who introduce practices X_1, X_2,...X_n, experience an increase in Y. Whilst conclusions are never stated with such boldness in the literature, and are always hedged with qualifiers, this does not avoid the fact that induction is the mode of inference at work – however ambiguously it is used. Three things must, however, be noted. First, induction as a mode of inference is recognised by almost all philosophers to be mistaken on the grounds that no amount of confirming particular instances can prove a general claim. Second, as we saw in the previous chapter, if the social world is an open system wherein event regularities do not occur, then there is no basis to establish statistical associations between HRM practices and organisational performance and no basis, therefore, for *inductively based* prediction. Third, critical realists advocate a completely different concept of prediction – although elaboration will have to wait until the following chapter. Henceforth, then, whenever we use the term 'prediction' in the scientistic lexicon, we mean inductive prediction. We will use the term '(inductive) prediction' occasionally to remind the reader.

From a scientistic perspective, predictive power is the criterion by which a body of knowledge may be adjudged to be scientistic or not and is the mark of a good theory. Empirical research on the HRM–P link seeks to provide theories with predictive power. Unfortunately, however, there is a snag. The scientistic approach suffers from a fundamental, if unacknowledged, limitation: despite the fact that it flirts with prediction, it actually *lacks predictive power* and, therefore, *fails to meet its own criteria for scientificity*. It does not actually allow us to successfully predict the future, judge between competing theories and formulate policy. Rather, it *appears* to allow us to do these things. This misleading appearance is not commonly recognised, largely because of the ambiguity that surrounds the use of the term 'prediction'. Let us consider this ambiguity with some examples from the HRM–P literature.

Some researchers are prepared to state quite boldly that their findings have predictive uses:

The results indicate that ... the direct effect on the sales volume is $19.30 for each dollar invested in customer services, and $25.50 for each dollar spent in sales training ... *The approach may also be used for forecasting* future training ROI [returns on investment]. (Wang *et al.* 2002: 217, emphasis added)

Wang *et al.* do not, however, do this or state how it can be done. Ahmad and Schroeder (2003: 27–8) claim that whilst canonical correlation analysis 'is primarily descriptive ... it can be used for predictive purposes' – ignoring the fact that statistical association such as correlation does not imply causality and, without the latter, it seems difficult to know how predictions could be made.

For Becker *et al.* measurement is closely connected to prediction because:

it improves HR decision making by helping you focus on those aspects of the organization that create value. In the process, it provides you with feedback that you can use ... to predict the impact of future decisions. (Becker *et al.* 2001: 110)

A good measurement system will let you predict *how much* improvement in firm performance you can expect if you boost your HRM system to a higher target-percentile level. Or, let's say you find your firm is already in the nineteenth percentile on the HPWS index. You can then calculate how much of the company's shareholder value is attributable to your outstanding HRM system, compared to the value created by a HR system at the fiftieth percentile. (Becker *et al.* 2001: 111, original emphasis)

Huselid (1995) appears to use his measures to facilitate prediction:

To estimate the practical significance of the impact of High Performance Work Practices on productivity, I next calculated the impact of a one-standard deviation increase in each practice scale on ... net sales ... The findings indicate that each one-standard-deviation increase *raises* sales an average of $27,044 per employee. (1995: 658, emphasis added)

A one-standard deviation increase in such practices is associated with a relative 7.05 percent decrease in turnover and ... $27,044 more in sales and $18, 641 and $3,813 more in market value and profits respectively. (1995: 667)

These ... values suggest that firms *can indeed obtain* substantial financial *benefits* from investing in the practices studied here. (1995: 667, emphasis added)

This study also provides one of the first *tests of the prediction* that the impact of High Performance Work Practices on firm performance is contingent. (636, emphasis added)

Careful reading reveals two notions of prediction are buried within research on the HRM–P link and, unfortunately, they are not always carefully disentangled.[1]

Untangling two notions of prediction

The first, and most *discursively powerful*, notion uses prediction in the sense of *predicting a future* event or state of affairs. Most empirical research, such as that on the HRM–P link, is littered with phraseology like 'predicting the impact of future decisions'; 'practical significance'; 'an increase in HRM raises sales'; and 'firms can indeed obtain benefits', which suggest the use of prediction in this sense. Let us refer to this as prediction$_f$ – with the subscript denoting 'future' or possibly 'forecast'. Note well that this kind of prediction$_f$ is what really carries the discursive weight of scientism's alleged scientificity and superiority and is why we refer to it as 'discursively powerful'. If a social theory predicts that X will occur at a stated future time, and X does occur at this stated time, this theory may be considered a good theory. And this reflects well on the scientistic meta-theory that allowed this prediction to be formulated and tested. This does not, of course, mean that this is a valid argument for establishing what a good theory is, it is simply a recognition of what is accepted as a valid argument within scientistic discourse.

The second, and less discursively powerful, notion uses prediction in the sense of *testing hypotheses* via events or states of affairs that have already occurred and are now in the past. This is variously described as ascertaining data consistency or fitting a model. From past data, on phenomena that occurred in the past, we deduce or 'predict' an outcome that has already occurred. While this outcome has already occurred it could have been predicted from the data had we done so at an earlier time. Let us refer to this as prediction$_p$ – with the subscript denoting 'past'. Prediction$_p$ might be less discursively powerful than prediction$_f$, but it still carries connotations of being scientistic and, therefore, retains a degree of discursive power.

Now, the problem is that research on the HRM–P link never quite specifies which notion of prediction is being used at any moment. Huselid's work, for example, displays elements of both.

Consider the case for prediction$_p$. Amongst others, Huselid tests the hypothesis that High Performance Work Systems (HPWS) will increase sales and profits. He obtains data by recording *past* instances where HPWS were in use and *past* instances where sales and profits changed. If a (significant and positive) statistical association is found in the data between these events of the past, he suggests that the data confirms (or does not falsify) the hypothesis. The data are consistent with events from which they are drawn.

Consider the case for prediction$_f$. Huselid does not go as far as saying: 'my findings allow me to predict$_f$ that if your firm introduces these practices, then your firm will enjoy decreases in turnover and increases in sales and profits of something like these magnitudes'. Yet something like prediction$_f$ is not only implied, it follows quite naturally from the hypotheses his research tests. If prediction$_f$ is not implied, then his findings have no practical significance, and one of the key features of his paper is lost. This is similar to the way causality is implied, something we discussed in the previous chapter.

Huselid uses the more discursively powerful notion of prediction$_f$ whilst actually *practicing* the less discursively powerful notion of prediction$_p$. As far as we are aware, Huselid has not actually made any kind of predictions$_p$, despite the odd phrase to the contrary. But, then again, neither has anyone else in the literature. *Our point here is not to criticise Huselid (and others) for not engaging in prediction$_p$, but to illuminate the ambiguity surrounding the term 'prediction'.* This ambiguity allows advocates of the scientistic perspective to harness the discursive power of prediction$_f$ whilst actually practicing prediction$_p$, which is less discursively powerful. In this way, the scientistic credentials of deductivism are enhanced and mythologised.

So, whilst research on the HRM–P link often appears to make predictions$_f$, in reality it almost always makes predictions$_p$. This might take some of the shine off scientism's (alleged) scientificity, but it still leaves this prediction$_p$. Whist prediction$_p$ might not be as discursively powerful as prediction$_f$, it still appears to harness the power of prediction, and this gives the impression that scientism is superior to alternatives that do not, or cannot, predict. Clearly we need to know a little more about prediction$_p$.

Imagine a social scientist has conducted a typical piece of research and predicted$_p$ that the existence of teamwork and incentive pay will be associated with increased productivity. Suppose this prediction$_p$

turns out to be data consistent, allowing us to say teamwork and incentive pay are good predictors$_p$ of increased productivity. What we have is a consistent prediction$_p$ from a set of data about a firm or a sample of firms. And this is, typically, where most empirical research (on the HRM–P link or otherwise) ends. Now, imagine a natural scientist has conducted a typical piece of research on cold fusion. Imagine she predicted$_p$ that the existence of substance S_1 and substance S_2 (in a test tube) are associated with cold fusion. Suppose this prediction$_p$ turns out to be data consistent. What we have is a consistent prediction$_p$ from a set of data about a single experiment. Unlike the previous case, however, research would *not* end here. Other researchers from within this natural scientific community would almost certainly seek to *replicate* these findings – indeed this is exactly what happened in the case of alleged cold fusion a few years ago. And if in subsequent experiments the prediction$_p$ turns out to be data consistent, then the theory that led us to combine substances S_1 and S_2 would be confirmed, or not-falsified.

Notice that the process of *replication* is crucial here. Until and unless prediction$_p$ is replicated it would not be accepted in the kinds of natural sciences for which experiments are possible, and from which scientism gets its discursive veneer of scientificity. If research on the HRM–P link does not, or cannot, engage in replication, then what is left of the scientism's shine of scientificity will disappear. Let us consider this in more depth.

Replication

Replication is not a straightforward notion. Tsang and Kwan (1999) identify six types of replication, and we add a strange kind of seventh:

- *Checking of analysis.* Subsequent researchers employ exactly the same measurement, analysis and data set.
- *Reanalysis of the data.* Subsequent researchers employ different measurement and analysis but exactly the same data set.
- *Exact replication.* Subsequent researchers employ exactly the same measurement and analysis, on the same population, but a different sample and hence different data set. This is done to assess whether the findings are reproducible.

- *Conceptual extension.* Subsequent researchers employ different measurement and analysis on the same population, but a different sample and hence different data set. Subsequent models are extended to include different causal mechanisms, or different variables.
- *Empirical generalisation.* Subsequent researchers employ exactly the same measurement and analysis on a different population, different sample and hence different data set. This is done to assess whether the findings are generalisable to another population.
- *Generalisation and extension.* Subsequent researchers employ different measurement and analysis but on a different population, different sample and hence different data set.
- *Confusion.* In empirical research on the HRM–P link, most researchers appear to be confused about exactly what they are doing when carrying out new empirical research based, in some sense, on earlier theoretical and empirical studies. Most of the time they appear to have some vague notion of replication in mind where they test aspects of earlier research with new models that vaguely resemble them. Hence we find comments about testing earlier findings, claims, concepts, theories, models, predictions, hypotheses, but there is little meta-theoretical reflection on what they are really doing and why they are doing it. For example, Gant *et al.* (2002: 290) hit the nail on the head, writing that: 'The existing studies on HRM practices and HRM performance implicitly try to mimic an experiment that compares the performance of identical production processes, some of which are managed under innovative HRM practices and others under more traditional HRM practices'. Unfortunately, the phrase 'mimicking an experiment' obfuscates rather than clarifies exactly what the process involves. Guthrie (2001: 180) 'offers a test of whether Arthur's (1994) results generalize beyond his small, U.S., single-industry sample'.

It should be noted here that Tsang and Kwan are discussing replication in epistemological, rather than ontological, terms. Although subsequent researchers might employ different measures, estimation techniques, population, sample and data sets, there is no suggestion that the actual phenomena under investigation are fundamentally different. They are discussing different ways of gaining knowledge (epistemology) of the same relatively unchanging phenomena (ontology).

To see why this matters, think of the way a classical physics experiment is replicated. If some high-school students failed to replicate Ohm's Law,[2] it would not be because the nature of the physical world had changed, but maybe because the experiment was conducted incorrectly. In cases where the material under investigation does *not* change, replication makes perfect sense; we can replicate, find that results are non-falsified and have some warrant for generalising the findings.[3] Matters are very different, however, when we are dealing with social science where the nature of the social world can and does change. This will become important below.

What about replication of empirical research on the HRM–P link? As far as we are aware, none of the scores of studies on the HRM–P link have been replicated, at least not in the way replication is usually understood (i.e. in natural science) and few are even attempted.[4] In what follows, we will show not only that replication is not carried out, but that it would actually not be sensible to try *if* the social world in general, and the workplace in particular, is an open system. Let us start by considering one of the clearest *attempts* at replication in the HRM–P paradigm.

Alleyne *et al.* (2006: 624) claim their 'research replicates Hoque's (1999) study of HRM and performance in the United Kingdom's (UK's) hotel industry', by considering the case of the Barbados hotel industry. When we compare the two studies closely, however, whilst we do find similarities, there are also significant differences. We noted differences between the way Hoque, and Alleyne *et al.*: constructed some of the questionnaires; who the questionnaires were administered to; some of the rating scales used; some of the categories into which the hotels were allocated; the sizes of the hotels; and the categories of hotels that were actually used in the statistical analysis. What this really means is that Alleyne *et al.* do not actually replicate Hoque's analysis, but conduct a slightly different study.[5]

Alleyne *et al.* have, quite understandably, made these changes due to the kind of practical problems that would face any social scientist attempting to replicate someone else's findings. If Alleyne *et al.* find problems in the way Hoque collected the data, for example, it would make sense to correct these problems, not simply ignore them and hence reproduce them in order to remain true to some idea of perfect replication. Moreover, because no two social situations are likely to be identical, changes like the ones they engage in are almost inevitable. This would be a little like attempting to replicate Ohm's Law, but instead of experimentally testing the hypothesis that $I = V / R$, we substituted the variable V (Volts) for the variable J (Joules) and tested the hypothesis that $I = J / R$ because, in the new context, we had difficulty measuring voltage, but could measure energy. The analogy is not perfect but the point, we hope, will be taken.

Whilst problems of this nature appear to be epistemological, we have to consider the possibility that some of this appearance is misleading. That is to say, whilst there may always be some problems that are epistemological in their own right, other problems that appear to be epistemological might have ontological roots. And this raises a very different set of problems.

Alleyne *et al.* note that: 'one must acknowledge that the data on the UK against which Barbados is being compared were collected in 1995. The situation in the UK may well have moved on since then' (Alleyne *et al.* 2006: 643). Recognising that the situation may well have moved on, however, is tantamount to recognising that the social world in general, and operation of hotels in particular, may well have changed. And this is an ontological matter. This would be a little like attempting to replicate Ohm's Law, but instead of experimentally testing the hypothesis that $I = V / R$, we substituted the variable V for the variable J, not this time because we had (epistemic) difficulty measuring voltage, but because we suspected something in the physical world (ontic) had changed significantly. Indeed, this would not be an experiment to replicate Ohm's Law, but an experiment to test a new hypothesis and evaluate some new (bizarre!) law.

What this means is that in situations where the social world changes, or at least changes significantly, ontological problems cast doubt on the very point of attempting to replicate findings in the social world. Let us take Alleyne *et al.*'s entirely sensible insight that the social world in general, and workplace in particular, may well change, and generalise the problems this would raise for attempts at replication. We proceed by considering a hypothetical scenario of what would occur if one researcher ever attempted to replicate the findings of another researcher (or indeed attempted to replicate her own findings) in a changing social world.

Let us assume, for argument's sake, that there is a theory explaining why three HRM practices (teamwork, performance-related pay and flexible working practices) cause an increase in productivity.

From theory T, Smith constructs the following model[6] with the HRM practices as independent (or 'explanatory') variables and productivity as the dependent variable:

$$Y = \alpha + \beta_1 X_1 + \beta_2 X_2 + \beta_3 X_3 + \varepsilon \tag{1}$$

This is used to test the hypothesis$_1$ (or the prediction$_1$) that changes in teamwork, performance-related pay and flexible working practices (X_1, X_2 and X_3 respectively) are associated with changes in productivity (Y). He collects data on the practices and productivity levels in a large UK organisation and estimates the coefficients. The usual diagnostic tests are run, the coefficients have the appropriate sign and are all significant. Smith concludes that the hypothesis$_1$ is not rejected by the data, and theory T gains support.

Two years later new data on HRM practices and productivity levels become available for the same large UK organisation that Smith investigated. Jones decides to use this new data to replicate the findings of Smith. This is what Tsang and Kwan referred to as 'exact replication'. She takes the same theory T that Smith used along with the same model and same hypothesis$_1$, and re-estimates the coefficients. It would, of course, be most unlikely if no changes had occurred in the organisation and its environment in the ensuing two years, so it is not unreasonable to suppose there have been some changes. Jones finds that the previous model no longer fits the new data. Suppose X_2 is now insignificant and has the wrong sign. Jones faces two problems.

First, Jones has to deal with the thorny problem of what to do when theory T suggests the variable X_2 *should* be included, but the data suggests the variable *should not* be included. Does she stick with theory T and include a now insignificant and incorrectly signed variable X_2; or does she drop the variable? Dropping the variable implies there is something wrong with theory T and, moreover, damages the theory that suggested it should be included in the first place. Jones is now in an awkward position because she has no theory to guide her choice of what else to measure and estimate. Incidentally, whilst this dilemma raises its head every day for empirical researchers (in the HRM–P paradigm and elsewhere) to the best of our knowledge, it is never recognised or addressed.[7]

Second, let us suppose Jones proceeds by dropping X_2 from her new model. She then decides to include data on a new HRM practice, employee communication, (denoted X_4) that has recently been introduced to the organisation. She re-specifies the model thus:

$$Y = \alpha + \beta_1 X_1 + \beta_3 X_3 + \beta_4 X_4 + \varepsilon \qquad (2)$$

Jones now re-estimates these coefficients. The usual diagnostic tests are run, the coefficients have the appropriate signs and are all significant. Jones concludes that the hypothesis$_2$ is not rejected by the data. Before concluding that Jones has successfully replicated Smith's findings, however, we need to probe a little deeper.

It is now unclear what this new evidence says about theory. The new research is not a test of theory T. Moreover, because no theory guided the introduction of employee communication (X_4) there is no theory of why X_1, X_3 and (now) X_4 might be related to Y. This appears not to be a test of any theory whatsoever.

Although Smith started out to perform an 'exact replication', she ended up performing something more akin to 'generalisation and extension'. Tsang and Kwan question whether this is a replication or *a test of a different conceptual model.*

- Hypothesis$_1$ and model (1) suggest that productivity increases are associated with teamwork, *performance-related pay* and flexible working practices, but not employee communication.
- Hypothesis$_2$ and model (2) suggest that productivity increases are associated with teamwork, flexible working practices and *employee communication*, but not flexible working practices.

Hypothesis$_2$ is no longer the same hypothesis that was initially modelled. Whilst this may only be a small change, only affecting two variables, the number of variables involved is irrelevant; it is the principle that matters. In order to properly test a hypothesis, both Smith and Jones must specify the set of variables that constitute the model with absolute clarity; only one particular set of named variables is associated with one particular hypothesis. If Jones changed one or more of the variables in the model, then she is, to be strictly accurate, specifying a *different* model. *Jones would not have replicated Smith's initial study, she would, effectively have carried out another, different, study.*[8]

This hypothetical example helps us to tease out a crucial presupposition underlying the idea and practice of replication in social science. *For the attempt to replicate earlier findings to make sense and to be worthwhile, nothing (of significance) would have had to change in the HRM–P system under investigation.* The HRM practices in place in a later period would have to be virtually identical to those in place in a previous period, would have to operate in a virtually identical manner, and the environment in which they occur would have to remain unchanged. This is not only an ontological presupposition, it is almost certainly a mistaken presupposition – that is, of course, if the system is open. To paraphrase Heraclitus, 'we cannot put our foot twice in the same (open) system'. In open systems, where the social world changes, or at least changes significantly, empirical researchers would never be able to replicate earlier findings. In open systems, replication loses the force it has in (some versions of) natural science. And by extension, scientism loses a little more of its veneer of scientificity.

Now, we are well aware that a hypothetical case does not prove that researchers on the HRM–P link *cannot* replicate earlier studies, theories, predictions, hypotheses, findings or whatever. Moreover, if someone actually did succeed in exactly replicating someone else's study, or even replicating their own study at a later date, then our argument would be weakened. After all, the claim that the workplace is an open system, a system not characterised by event regularities, is ultimately an empirical claim even if we have strong a priori empirical and practical grounds to believe it.

What can we conclude, then, about prediction and replication? First, we find no cases of the more discursively powerful notion of prediction$_f$ in empirical research on the HRM–P link, only cases of prediction$_p$ used as the basis of hypothesis testing. This takes some of the shine off scientism's scientificity. If the workplace is an open system, where change is highly likely, then previous predictions$_p$ are unlikely to be replicated. The open systemic nature of the workplace means that empirical research on the HRM–P link is unlikely to ever succeed in replicating others' studies. Yet more of scientism's scientificity shine is rubbed off. The scientistic perspective's claim to be superior to other perspectives on the grounds that *it alone can formulate empirically testable predictions* is unsustainable. *The scientistic perspective fails, therefore, to meet one of its own criteria for scientificity.* What about explanation?

Explanation

Following Lipton (1993: 33) we argue that to 'explain a phenomenon is to give information on the phenomenon's causal history'.[9] The following section offers several reasons why scientism lacks explanatory power, by demonstrating that things that, from the scientistic perspective, are often confused with explanation are not really explanation at all when looked at closely.

Explanation is not an 'explanation' of variance

In the lexicon of statistics, to 'explain' is to use the independent, often (misleadingly) referred to as *explanatory*, variables to account for some proportion of the variance in the dependent variable. Gould-Williams and Davies (2005: 15–16) claim that in their study:

the independent variables explained a significant degree of variance in the dependent variable, with the explanatory variables explaining 58 percent of the variance in commitment, 53 percent of the variance in worker motivation, and 41 percent of the variation in respondent's desire to remain with the organization.

Whilst empirical researchers and statisticians are at liberty to use the term 'explanation' in this very specific, or *technical*, sense, it will not satisfy the rest of us because it offers such an emaciated kind of explanation – if indeed, it can be considered an explanation at all. Such an 'explanation' does not explain *why* the independent variables account for some proportion of the variance in the dependent variable. That is, it does not provide an account of the operation of the causal mechanisms that the explanatory variables are assumed to reflect. However useful it might be to know that X_1, X_2 and X_3 'explain' 75 per cent of the variance in Y, neither the regression equation itself, or the empirical data that constitute the variables, give us any idea *why* this is the case. A bona fide explanation would have to provide detail about the causal mechanisms that the variables X_1, X_2 and X_3 are assumed to reflect. A bona fide explanation, then, is not simply a matter of 'explaining' some proportion of the variance in a dependent variable.

This distinction is implicitly recognised by many empirical researchers, and often reflected in two very different uses of the term 'explanation'. Consider one example. In the 'theoretical' section of their article, Horgan and Muhlau (2003) provide a fairly detailed account of how five HR practices interact in complex ways that reinforce, flank and/or compensate one another to generate an overall effect on employee performance. Without using the term 'explain' they, in effect, offer a non-technical or traditional explanation in the form of an account of the operation of the causal mechanisms (the five HR practices) that their explanatory variables are assumed to reflect. In the 'results' section of their article, and when discussing the results of their regression analysis, however, Horgan and Muhlau (2003: 434) use the term 'explain' in its technical meaning, writing: 'The effects of the single HR dimensions *explain* about half of the performance difference between the non-adopters and the high performance HR management systems' (emphasis added). Finally, in the 'summary and discussion' section, when discussing a puzzling empirical effect, they use the term 'explain' once again in its more traditional meaning. They ask: 'is there an explanation for the negative systems effect in the Netherlands' compared to Ireland? Their answer uses non-statistical reasoning and refers to differences in the complex institutional arrangements in the two countries. The point of this example is simply to note that different conceptions of explanation can occur without the researchers even being aware that they are using them. Moreover, being unaware of what actually constitutes an explanation, and perhaps (mistakenly) assuming that to explain is to explain the variation in the dependent variable, many empirical researchers provide very little, or sometimes nothing, that can be considered a bona fide explanation.

Explanation is not statistical association

Reflecting on the contribution of their study, Allen *et al.* (2003: 114) note that 'perceptions of supportive HR practices ... were consistently positively related to POS' (i.e. perceived organisational support), before stating that this adds 'to our understanding of the factors leading to the development of POS'. In one sense, of course, the generation of a correlation or some other empirical relation, in itself, can be said to have added to our understanding. But this is not the sense in which Allen *et al.* suggest their empirical work has added to our understanding. Their language strongly suggests that the various statistical relations they have established add something like an explanation. POS, they write: 'may be valuable in explaining relationships between supportive organizational practices and turnover' (2003). At best, a statistical association describes a state of affairs which then demands an explanation which, if forthcoming, may be said to have added to our understanding.

A recent paper by Combs *et al.* (2006: 502) seems to conflate 'understanding', which we take to be part of explanation, with measures of 'how much' HPWS affect organisational performance. Knowing that the overall effects of the HPWS on organisational performance is 20 per cent does not explain, nor improve our understanding of, why this might be the case.

Gelade and Ivery observe that:

> the influence of HRM on DMU [decision making units] performance cannot be explained without the identification of intervening variables, and understanding the joint and interacting roles of HRM and climate is therefore a vital element in furthering our understanding of performance at the DMU level of analysis. Our purpose in this paper is thus to clarify the processes by which HRM and climate relate to each other and to DMU performance, and in this way to evaluate the climate-performance relationship. (2003: 387)

By the end of the paper, it becomes clear that, for them, explaining, furthering our understanding, clarifying and evaluating the various relationships they identify is a matter of testing for correlations. They may have demonstrated that, for example, the role of work climate is 'a partial mediator between HRM practices and DMU performance' (2003: 398) but their analysis does not explain why this is the case.

It is a mistake, then, to suggest as Ramsay *et al.* (2000: 510) do that the 'set of regressions in the analysis examined *the processes* through which HPWS practices result in commitment and job strain' (emphasis added). Regression treats the actual processes, the real things that are 'going on' as it were, as black boxes and such like cannot explain them. As Purcell and Kinnie (2007: 539–40) observe: 'Even if robust causal correlations are found between the adoption of a certain mix of practices and performance, we do not know why this occurs'.

Explanation is not regularity

We do not explain why the bus is late today by stating that it is always, or regularly, late (Sayer 1994: Chapter 3). Neither do we explain why some bundle of HRM practices causes an increase in organisational performance by stating that this bundle of HRM practices always, or regularly, causes an increase in organisational performance. Furthermore, it is possible to provide an explanation of something that only happens once and hence does not display regularity. What may be happening here is a confusion between explanation and *verification*, where the latter refers to a process (the basis of hypothesis testing) of demonstrating that the relationship between two or more variables is due to more than pure chance.

Explanation is not prediction

Explanation is often confused with prediction. Schuler and Jackson (2005) write of 'logics of explanation' and 'logics of prediction' without ever clarifying their meanings or even hinting that they are different things. In the first sentence in a section entitled 'Predictors of Commitment', Gould-Williams and Davies (2005: 16) write: 'the explanatory variables explained 58 percent of the variance in commitment'. They then add: 'The most significant predictors of commitment were trust in management ($\beta.32$) and teamworking ($\beta.24$).' This is not only widespread, it is also encouraged by scientistic metatheory. Conflating explanation with prediction and, then, citing the Beta coefficient as an indication of the significance of the prediction of commitment were trust in management ($\beta.32$) and teamworking ($\beta.24$) is tantamount to using the Beta coefficients as an indication of the significance of the explanation!

From the scientistic perspective, and deriving from the deductive method, prediction and explanation are often conflated in the 'symmetry thesis' (Caldwell 1991: 54). This thesis, deriving from the deductive-nomothetic model, conflates prediction and explanation so that the only difference between explanation and prediction relates to the direction of time. Explanation entails the deduction of an event after it has (or is known to have) occurred. Prediction entails the deduction of an event prior to (knowledge of) its occurrence. If, for example, we can successfully predict that the introduction of a bundle of HRM practices, when appropriately aligned with corporate strategy, will be followed by an increase in ROI, then we can explain the increase in profitability by the introduction of the HRM practices. This is not to say that empirical researchers on the HRM–P link consciously adopt the symmetry thesis. On the contrary, most researchers seem unaware that there is a problem and more often than not confusion reigns, as the following comment from Youndt and Snell (2004: 356) illustrates: 'the HR configurations explained only twenty-eight percent of the variance in social capital, the most important predictor of organizational performance'.

Prediction does not, however, constitute explanation. Even in those cases where successful prediction can be made (almost never in the social world), it is often possible to predict *without explaining anything at all*. Whilst doctors can predict the onset of measles following the emergence of Koplik spots, the latter does not explain measles. An adequate explanation of measles would involve an account of underlying causal mechanisms such as the virus that causes both spots and the illness. Similarly even if we could predict that organisational performance would increase following the introduction of some bundle of HRM practices, the regression equation used to make the prediction would not contain the explanation and we would simply be left asking: why? In fact, such a prediction would not rule out the possibility that the cause of increased organisational performance was not something else completely, something not contained in the model.

Suppose we use regression analysis to demonstrate that teamwork and incentive pay are good predictors$_p$ of increased productivity. The regression equation might be grounded in no theory whatsoever. This was precisely what we pointed out in Chapter 4 when we referred to the related problems of black box theorising. With no theory to draw upon we would be left trying to explain increased productivity by simply pointing to the introduction of teamwork and incentive pay that preceded it. But this simply begs a question: why? The answer to this question cannot be derived from the regression equation, and there is nowhere else to go.

Or is there? What if the regression equation was grounded in theory, but that theory was rooted in another discipline?

The turn to multidisciplinarity

Some researchers attempt to address the lack of theory or theories, and hence the lack of explanatory power, by shifting their gaze outside the discipline of HRM. Taking such a multidisciplinary approach is not only a perfectly valid way to proceed, it is one we enthusiastically endorse, and agree with Boxall and Purcell who observe that: 'Greater progress will be made only when organizations are studied in much more *interdisciplinary* or systematic way' (2000: 183, emphasis added). What worries us, however, is the way it is carried out. As we argued in Chapter 4, empirical researchers on the HRM–P link appear not only to lack sophisticated meta-theoretical insights, they also appear committed to scientism and the deductive method. Without meta-theoretical sophistication, however, raiding other disciplines for a theory or theories that can then be 'bolted on' to the existing scientistic meta-theory, simply introduces any problems that happen to afflict these other disciplines.

We saw in Chapter 4 that scattered throughout the literature are references to a bewildering array of approaches, perspectives, frameworks, typologies, studies, theories, models, maps and accounts, all at various levels of abstraction, generality, universality, particularity, concreteness and micro or macro orientation. For brevity, and in the absence of any other suitable term, we will simply refer to them as 'theories'. These 'theories' come from a variety of disciplines. Whilst 'theory' or 'theories' from other disciplines abound, it is actually very difficult to take any one of these 'theories' and 'bolt it on' to the existing scientistic meta-theory. This is difficult because not every theory can be dealt with in terms of scientism.

Recall problems mentioned in Chapter 4 relating to the measurement and quantification of naturally qualitative, inherently complex, multidimensional, subjective and evolving phenomena. We would not, for example, anticipate insights on power by Foucauldian scholars to be amenable to regression analysis. If somehow an empirical researcher attempted such a feat, this could only be undertaken by losing the sophisticated insights from Foucauldian theory in the search to quantify power. If a glance at other disciplines reveals theories that entertain phenomena like power, that are impossible to quantify in a meaningful way, it is highly likely that there may be other non-quantifiable phenomena that are also incompatible with scientistic meta-theory. What are empirical researchers on the HRM–P link, committed as they appear to be to scientism, to do when faced with this state of affairs? In our opinion, they would either attempt to derive (meaningless) proxies or simply ignore the theories that entertain these problematic phenomena. The point is not lost on Pfeffer, one of the more sceptical writers in the HRM–P paradigm, who writes: 'Unfortunately, in almost all aspects of organizational operations, what is most easily measurable and what is important are only loosely related' (Pfeffer 1997: 360) .

A similar problem arises when specific theory or theories are attached to specific disciplines and schools within disciplines. When, for example, the discipline of economics is raided for theoretical insight, only mainstream economics is drawn upon, especially schools such as New Institutionalism and sub-branches such as human capital theory and the economics of personnel management. Non-mainstream schools of economics such as Austrian, (Old) Institutional, Feminist, Marxist, Post-Keynesian and Social economics are, typically, overlooked because the meta-theoretical perspective upon which a great deal (although not all) of the theoretical insights emanating from these schools is incompatible with scientism. We cannot, therefore, agree with HRM–P researchers Wang *et al.* (2002: 205) who claim that: 'For more than forty years, economists have brought to research on training ROI [i.e. returns on investment] *a full spectrum of theories, approaches and techniques*' (emphasis added). On the contrary, a very narrow spectrum of theories has been considered. Henceforth, when we refer to economic theory, we have mainstream economics in mind, not non-mainstream versions. Grimshaw and Rubery (2007) have recently made the case that HRM researchers need to consider heterodox approaches to economic theory.

Furthermore, many other disciplines are dogged by theoretical and meta-theoretical problems at least as bad as those facing researchers on the HRM–P link. This is easily overlooked for the simple reason that we tend not to be as well versed in other disciplines as we are in our 'own' – assuming that 'we' have a clearly defined discipline, which may not be the case, especially with disciplines like HRM. Problems within the disciplines of economics and psychology with, for example, the concept of *rationality*, do not cease to be problems when they are imported from economics or psychology into HRM. Huselid (1995: 653), for example, uses 'traditional economic theory' to alert us to the possibility that 'the gains associated with the adoption of High Performance Work Practices cannot survive into perpetuity because the returns on these investments will be driven towards equilibrium as more and more firms make them'. Yet many non-mainstream economists either reject the entire notion of equilibrium altogether, or reject the very idea of a convergence to equilibrium (Fleetwood 1995).

Let us pursue the problems in more depth with an example. Ichniowski *et al.* (1997) attempt to provide a rationale for the selection of HR and performance variables and an explanation of the causal mechanisms and processes in operation, by drawing their 'theory' from *labour economics*. Ichniowski *et al.* seem to take pride, not only in the fact that they personally visited each of thirty-six work sites, toured each line with an experienced engineer, area operations manager or superintendent, but also that they:

gathered HRM data by conducting standardized interviews with HR managers, labour relations managers, operations managers of the finishing lines, superintendents, line workers, and union representatives in organized lines. [They] collected supporting information from personnel files, personnel manuals, collective bargaining agreements and other primary source documents. We used this information ... to answer survey-type questions about HRM practices and then to construct a detailed set of HRM dummy variables. (1997: 293)

The HRM variables are: incentive pay; recruiting and selection; teamwork; employment security; flexible job assignment; communication; and labour relations. We elaborate upon two of these variables to get a flavour of how Ichniowski *et al.* proceed.

- *Incentive pay* consists of two variables: (a) profit sharing, defined as: 'is there a company profit-sharing scheme covering the line workers?'; and (b) line incentives defined as: 'are operators covered by a "non-traditional" incentive pay plan which applies across shifts of workers and which is sensitive to quality as well as quantity aspects of output?'.
- *Flexible job assignment* consists of one variable 'job rotation' defined as: 'do operators rotate across jobs or tasks on the line?'.

Even if these site visits were very comprehensive indeed, they would still be superficial relative to the kind of in-depth studies necessary to generate what we described in the previous chapter as a *thick* explanation of phenomena like incentive pay or flexible working, because such a study of each site would take weeks, if not months. This is, of course, inevitable and is a key difference between quantitative and qualitative techniques. The key question, however, is this: whilst Ichniowski *et al.*'s paper does attempt to provide a rationale for the selection of HR and performance variables, and does attempt to explain the causal mechanisms and processes in operation, is the rationale and the explanation *adequate*?[10]

The rationale for selecting their particular twenty-six variables is that they are 'the most common combinations of HRM practices in these production lines'. However, they also note that their seven main HRM variables just happen to be found in several economic theories (1997: 295, n. 1). We leave it to the reader to judge whether this constitutes an *adequate* rationale. As a theory and explanation of the causal mechanisms and processes in operation, however, it is clearly inadequate because they offer no more than a mere description of the most common practices. *Why* these practices are linked to performance does not derive from the data they gathered on their site visits, and there is no recourse to theory to provide an explanation.

There is, furthermore, a more pressing problem. Recall the discussion in the previous chapter about problems arising from measuring and quantifying the kind of naturally qualitative, inherently complex, multidimensional, subjective and evolving phenomena involved in HRM practices. Practices such as incentive pay and flexible working practices are phenomena of this kind, characterised by a host of tricky psychological, sociological, political, ideological, gendered and cultural factors. To think that something as naturally qualitative, inherently complex, multidimensional, subjective and evolving as the practices involved with 'flexible job assignment' can be grasped by instruments as blunt as a variable called 'job rotation', obtained from a questionnaire asking 'do operators rotate across jobs or tasks on the line?' is spectacularly naïve. Even if operators can be observed to rotate across jobs, this mode of enquiry provides no explanation whatsoever about why they do it, how they do it, under what conditions they are prepared to do it, under what conditions they might stop doing it or oppose it, their attitudes and understandings of it, the consequences arising from it, and so on. Even if it is statistically associated with increased performance, we have no explanation for this association. What if the increase in performance comes not from job rotation itself, but from the consequences of job rotation such as multi-tasking, multi-skilling, de-skilling, job enlargement, increased work intensity and so on? Nor does it explain how this practice might complement or negate other HR practices such as incentive pay.

Scientism and the deductive method discourage researchers to learn the lessons about the dangers and limitations of quantification, measurement and mathematisation, penned by generations of ethnomethodologists, phenomenologists, interpretivists and hermeneuticists, not to mention postmodernists, poststructuralists, social constructionists, critical realists and others operating with an explicitly non-scientistic perspective.

An 'escape' to labour economic theory?

There is, however, a possible 'escape route' for Ichniowski *et al.* and, of course, other empirical researchers on the HRM–P link, when faced with the charge that they lack plausible theoretical underpinnings for their empirical research. They can invoke some theory from another discipline. Indeed, none other than Pfeffer (1995: 615) suggests that research on HRM could usefully learn from the discipline of economics. Perhaps labour economic theory can come to their rescue and provide the theory and explanation for the kinds of empirical relationships they estimate. Let us consider this possibility.[11]

It is important to notice that shifting from empirical research on the HRM–P link to the *particular* kind of labour economics research they cite involves a *significant meta-theoretical shift*. Ichniowski *et al.* seem to pride themselves on the quality, and perhaps the realisticness, of the data they obtained from their site visits. Moreover, they are archetypical empirical researchers in the sense that they are extremely concerned to test their predictions against the empirical data obtained from site visits. The meta-theoretical approach used in the particular labour economics studies they cite, however, is from an *entirely different tradition*, and they end up trying to mix oil and water. Let us unpack some of the meta-theory underlying this other tradition. Borrowing a term from eminent mainstream economist Robert Lucas, Cartwright (2007: 217) refers to the models developed by these labour economists as 'analogue economies':

[T]he important point about analogue economies is that everything is known about them ... and within them the propositions we are interested in can be formulated rigorously and shown to be valid ... The method of verification is deduction: we know what does happen in one of these economies because we know what must happen given our general principles and the characteristics of the economy. (Cartwright 2007: 218)

There is, however, an unfortunate side-effect with the term 'economy' in the compound term 'analogue economy', namely, that it glosses over the distinction between a model (of an economy) and a real economy. Notice how even Cartwright, a critic of this approach, ends up using phraseology like 'we know what does happen in *one of these economies*' (emphasis added) and even refers to 'economies that are not real' (2007: 218). Put simply, economies that are not real, i.e. models, are not 'economies' of any sort, and glossing this fact lends legitimacy to what we consider to be an illegitimate move. Indeed, we prefer to borrow the term 'toy' from empirical economist Pencavel (1994) who, pejoratively, although in our opinion, accurately, refers to '*toy*' theories. 'Toy' theories and models are purely algebraic theories and models not designed to be confronted with empirical data, but are kind of pure thought experiments. They also rely on a deductive, as opposed to an inductive (or, as we will see in the next chapter, a retroductive), mode of inference. There is only a semantic difference between what we call toy models and what Cartwright calls analogue economies. The main point, however, is that these models are populated by fictitious agents, inhabiting a fictitious environment, undertaking fictitious forms of behaviour, and doing so for fictitious reasons. It is only by stripping these models down to the bone, removing any potential frictions or imperfections, that mainstream economists can be 100 per cent certain that their deductions will go through. Cartwright puts her finger on the problem with these toy models: 'We are, however, faced with a trade off: we can have totally verifiable results but only about economies that are not real' (Cartwright 2007: 218).

There are, as you might expect, several ways in which the practice of toy theorising is defended. Unfortunately, because meta-theoretical discussion is almost as absent in economics as it is in HRM, these defences are virtually never clearly articulated, and often take the form of passing comments.[12] Let us consider some of the typical defences. For a critical look at these ideas, see Lawson (1997: Chapter 8) and Cartwright (2007: Chapter 15).

- All theory has to abstract from reality otherwise the 'theory' would simply be a one-to-one description of reality. Whilst this is perfectly true, we will have a little more to say about it in a moment.

- Toy theorising allows consistent behaviour to be deduced or predicted from antecedents.
- Toy theorising allows our thoughts to be presented systematically, with clarity and with the precision of mathematics.
- Because it presents an idealised version of reality, toy theorising allows the relationships between certain important variables to be expressed simply and free from the 'clutter' of other, less important variables.
- Toy theorising allows one to understand pathological states (i.e. disequilibrium) by comparing them to hypothetical non-pathological states (i.e. equilibrium).
- Proving the existence of a unique solution or an equilibrium, under idealised conditions (somehow) gives economists a reason to believe that they are 'on the right track' as Hausman (1992: 100–1) puts it.
- Some, but not all, mainstream economists who employ toy theories, advocate subsequent empirical testing of hypotheses via predictive power. This is likely to be Ichniowski *et al.*'s position.

A recent book by Nurmi, entitled *Models of Political Economy* (2006) advocates toy theorising, although he does not use this term and would probably reject it. The point of mentioning it, however, is that it demonstrates that even when contemporary mainstream economists *do* reflect upon their meta-theoretical commitments, they refuse to break from scientism. Nurmi not only ignores a range of non-scientistic and non-deductivist methods, he also ignores many well-known objections to this kind of toy theorising. Indeed, it is as if almost half a century of developments in philosophy of science and methodology had simply never happened. His book can be considered a contemporary defence of scientism in economics, and toy theorising in particular.

Generally speaking, then, and for reasons that are almost never clearly spelled out, economists appear to believe they have demonstrated something important about the real world when they have constructed a toy model in which they can consistently deduce a set of conclusions from a set of initial premises. The following comments from Kandel and Lazear (1992: 803–14) are designed to give a flavour of this kind of mode of theorising:

Suppose that output from a group of identical workers is some function of each worker's effort ... To motivate the analysis we introduce a 'peer pressure' function

peer pressure = $P (e_i ; e_j. ..., e_N, a_i, a_j. ..., a_N)$

The peer pressure that worker I feels depends generally on his own effort, e_i ; on the effort of his peers $e_j. ...,$ e_N and on the actions that he and his peers may take $a_j, ..., a_N$ ...The peer pressure function is an attempt to formalize the discussion of tastes. By making explicit assumptions about $P ( )$, we clarify the exact nature of the tastes required to explain a particular behavior.

Suppose that the world consisted of two types of workers: the social for whom P1 < 0, and the independent from whom P = 0 ... If one's type is known by the individual himself, does a separating equilibrium exist in which each type of worker prefers firms of his own kind?

Kandel and Lazear also ask us to: 'Suppose that, in addition to exerting effort, workers can monitor each other at a cost. Workers who are caught shirking can be penalized by their partners [by] mental or physical harassment'. They then define 'the expected penalty associated with being caught shirking' in functional terms and assuming that 'since all workers are *ex ante* identical, the choice of monitoring level k will be identical'. Each worker chooses a 'monitoring level' and 'puts forth monitoring effort because he believes that other workers will increase their effort as a response'.

Let us be crystal clear. Many of these claims and assumptions are not simply unrealistic, they are also false. More importantly, however, they are very often *known to be false* by the economists who employ them. Using a known falsehood is not, of course, the same as simply being mistaken. Employing a falsehood by mistake, that is, employing an assumption believed to be true, which then turns out to be false, is a possibility all theorists confront, and *not* what we are discussing here. Toy models are populated by agents *known* to be fictitious, inhabiting environments *known* to be fictitious, undertaking forms of behaviour *known* to be fictitious, and doing so for reasons *known* to be fictitious. We will not waste time demonstrating that real workers undertaking real tasks, for real reasons in real workplaces are not like this, because this is freely admitted by most advocates of toy models. Writing of 'analogue economies' Lucas writes: 'Any model that is well enough articulated to give clear answers to the questions we put to it will necessarily be artificial, abstract, patently "unreal'" (Lucas, cited in Cartwright 2007: 218). Hahn, a leading exponent of 'toy' theorisation makes this clear:

> When a mathematic economist assumes that there is a three good economy lasting two periods, or that agents are infinitely lived ... everyone can see that we are not dealing with any actual economy. The assumptions are there to enable certain results to emerge and not because they are taken descriptively. (cited in Lawson 1997: 110)

Mainstream economists have two counter-arguments against criticism of this sort – although we only rehearse one here.[13] If it was explicitly articulated, which it never is, the counter-argument would run as follows: all theory has to leave out the inessential, has to abstract from reality, has to make unrealistic assumptions. All theory, if it is not simply to be a one-to-one description of reality is, inevitably and knowingly, *false in the strict sense of the word*. All theory is an abstraction.[14] Now, we fully accept that the process of abstraction, that is, the process of leaving out the inessential, at least where this can be done without doing violence to the analysis, is a perfectly legitimate process. Abstraction does make all theory *false in the strict sense of the word*. Abstraction is also necessary in any kind of theoretical analysis, at least in any analysis that does not merely seek to describe reality. We also accept that there may be cases where the difference between the legitimate use of abstraction, and the illegitimate use of what we call *fictionalisation*, may be difficult to discern. Most of the time, however, mainstream toy theorising is not operating anywhere near this margin. The labour economic theories which are often referred to by empirical researchers on the HRM–P link, and exemplified by Kandel and Lazear, are replete with such obvious falsehoods that to suggest they are really legitimate abstractions is merely a rhetorical ploy to avoid meta-theoretical discussion. Most of the time we can usually spot the difference between: (a) constructing categories by reflecting carefully upon the nature of the phenomena under investigation, leaving out phenomena considered to be inessential, focusing on the essential without fictionalising the remaining categories and, in the process, generating legitimate abstractions; and (b) constructing categories driven by the desire to apply the deductive method, leaving out phenomena that are unquantifiable and/or mathematically intractable (whether essential or not) and/or translating phenomena into a form that facilitates deductive modelling, and in the process, creating fictional categories. In other words, we can usually spot the difference between abstraction and fictionalisation: much mainstream labour economic theory, driven by scientism and deductivism, opts for the latter. We seriously doubt, to return to the previous examples, that Kandel and Lazear (1992: 803) construct their category 'group of identical workers' by reflecting carefully upon the nature of real workforces and then choosing to leave out inessential differences. Rather, they make this assumption for methodological convenience; it facilitates deductive theorising and/or is mathematically tractable.

Nurmi's (2006: 12–20) defence of scientism and deductivism only serves to confirm this conclusion. Mainstream economists are committed to the use of models and assumptions driven by a combination of mathematical tractability, or 'amenability to formal manipulations' and predictability. He distinguishes between 'theoretical' and 'imaginary models'. The former consist of simplified, but we assume, still true, descriptions of the objects of study; the latter 'make assumptions that are known to be false' and are 'tools of thought experiments'. Both are 'constructed with manipulability in mind'. The necessity of guaranteeing mathematical tractability, coupled with the necessity of making deductions or predictions, discourages economists from building models with reality in mind, and encourages them to build models that are convenient. Indeed, Nurmi accepts that 'much work in political economy is focused on the study of models rather than the part of the world they are models of'. He refers to the use of 'heuristic assumptions' which are 'done in order to simplify the manipulation of theories, e.g. by assuming certain parameter values in mathematical formulae in order to make the derivation of solutions possible', adding that these assumptions have 'instrumental value in deriving predictions' (2006: 20).

Occasionally, the tension between toy theorising and more explicitly empirical research surfaces. Whilst Becker and Huselid (1998: 61) advocate the use of organisational economics, they are forced to distance themselves from some commonly held views in economics, such as: the assumption that work is a disutility, that 'it's the employees job to shirk and employer's job to catch them'. Quite correctly, in our view, they claim that: this is 'not a useful foundation for a HPWS'. Unfortunately, however, this view of human agents, as *homo economicus*, is not something that can simply be jettisoned from the corpus of mainstream labour economic theory. Without it, the deductive machinery fails and conclusions cannot be deduced or predicted from initial conditions. Put another way, the assumption of *homo economicus* is one of the assumptions that ensures the intrinsic closure condition is met and the system remains (in theory of course) closed.[15]

There is, however, a price to pay for engaging in fictionalisation. Toy modellers, prepared to use known falsehoods, face three possibilities:

(1) They may know their theories contain known falsehoods and defend the use of them on grounds of mathematical tractability or some other meta-theoretical convenience. In this case, the meta-theoretical critique we employ in a moment (failing to offer bona fide explanations) comes into effect.

(2) They may reject the suggestion that their theories contain *known* falsehoods on the grounds that they believe the assumptions they make are not false. This would involve a defence of the assumption that, for example, all workers in the group are identical, or all workers in the model are instrumentally rational, on the grounds that all workers in the group are believed to be identical or instrumentally rational. Whilst this would avoid the meta-theoretical critique we employ in a moment, it would immediately lead to an empirical critique on the grounds that these assumptions are *empirically* incorrect, and those who use them are simply mistaken. In other words, our critique would move from meta-theory to theory.

(3) They may reject the suggestion that their theories contain falsehoods on the grounds that they believe the assumptions they make are legitimate abstractions; hence their assumptions are not knowingly false. In this case we would have to scrutinise the assumptions to try and ascertain whether they are fictions or abstractions. We are confident that, as the example just noted from Kandel and Lazear shows, most of these assumptions would turn out to be fictions.

In scenarios (2) and (3) the onus would be on labour economists to demonstrate either that their assumptions are not false, or that they are legitimate abstractions. Whilst we have to keep these possibilities open (we do not really know how they will respond because they never discuss matters like this) we suspect the first scenario reflects widespread mainstream economic practice. And in this case, the following critique bites.

Explanation does not allow known falsehoods

Known falsehoods are commonly employed in mainstream economic theory for purposes of mathematical tractability, that is, because they are useful in making the analysis amenable to mathematical modelling. Popularity does not, however, make this procedure right. We noted above that a theory consists, in part, of statements that deliver *explanation*. The moment *known* falsehoods enter a theory, however, that theory immediately ceases to fulfil the requirement of explanation, because bona fide explanations cannot include *known* falsehoods. It does not require a sophisticated philosophical argument to demonstrate this, so a simple example will suffice.

Suppose my colleagues heard me trying to explain to my boss how I arrived at the office by claiming that I flew here by magic carpet. Suppose they asked me if I really believed this to be true and I replied that it was not true, adding that I merely said it for an instrumental reason, namely to impress them with my bravado in dealing with the boss. Whilst my colleagues might fully accept the reason why I adopted such a posture, they would immediately reject my explanation on the grounds that, whatever my reasons for making this false claim, even I did not believe I arrived by this mode of transport. The use of a known falsehood would immediately discount the explanation as a bona fide explanation. We suggest this conclusion is self-evidently correct: if known falsehoods are allowed to constitute 'explanations', imagine the bizarre 'explanations' that could be advanced. We could, for example, explain a firm's productivity increases on the grounds that the introduction of teamworking has magical properties! This would, of course, be ridiculous, but the reason why we would object to it is instructive. We would reject it because we *know* workers cannot perform magic. The assumption is a *known* falsehood and, as such, it invalidates the explanation.

Notice that scientism and deductivism is driving this. The overriding necessity of (theoretically) closing an open system makes it necessary to leave out of the theory all phenomena that might violate the (intrinsic and extrinsic) closure conditions. Whilst Ulrich is correct in claiming that '[t]heory explains why things happen the way they do' (1997: 140), what if this requires an analysis of phenomena like power, or actors' understandings? From the scientistic perspective, these phenomena are inadmissible because they are unobservable, unquantifiable, and cannot be reduced to events and variables. But here is the rub: once removed from the theory (for meta-theoretical reasons) these phenomena cannot subsequently be recalled and offered as part of an explanation. Phenomena like powers and actors' understandings are either included in the theory, in which case they *can* contribute to the causal explanation, or they are excluded, in which case they *cannot*.[16] Let us be clear about what our argument is *not*. We are not suggesting that toy theorists are insufficiently intelligent to construct models that do not contain falsehoods. We are suggesting that if they tried to do this, whilst adhering to scientism and the deductivist method, they would be setting themselves an impossible task because economic systems are open systems. In closing the system they are forced to meet intrinsic and extrinsic closure conditions that are virtually guaranteed to require the use of known falsehoods. Their mistake is simply to keep faith with a meta-theoretical perspective that presupposes that the social world is other than it is.

Irrespective, then, of any merits 'toy' theorising might have, it should be crystal clear that the meta-theoretical tradition at work here is, *or should be*, antithetical to that used by empirical researchers on the HRM–P link. It is worth stating, for the record, that our criticism of the labour economic models and theories exemplified above is not just because we happen to dislike these particular ones. Rather, we consider that all models that make use of known falsehoods are devoid of explanatory power. Ichniowski *et al.* cannot, therefore, legitimately find the theoretical underpinnings for their empirical research in this kind of labour economics – and the same lesson applies to other empirical researchers on the HRM–P link who have illusions in this kind of labour economics.[17] This 'escape route' is not available.

From lack of theory to lack of explanation

The last three chapters have armed us with a reasonable grasp of scientistic meta-theory, leaving us in a position not simply to bemoan the lack of theory and explanation, but indeed to *explain* the lack of theory and explanatory power that bedevils research on the HRM–P link. Sutton and Staw's (1995) excellent paper entitled 'What Theory is *Not*' hints at several reasons why much of the work in organisation and management studies in general (and we see no reason why this cannot be applied to the field of HRM) is theoretically underdeveloped. Their hints (1995: 372 and 380–2) are grounded in what is, essentially, a *sociology of science* perspective. That is to say, they note the way various institutional structures, mechanisms and processes, such as those involved in the journal refereeing process, operate to maintain the status quo. Whilst we do not disagree with this, we go further and consider something that they overlook, namely, the possibility that the problem of under-theorisation lies not (just) in the *sociology* of science, but rather in the *philosophy* of science, or meta-theory more generally.

In order to identify the root cause of the problem of under-theorisation, it seems entirely sensible to us to start with a question that no empirical researchers on the HRM–P link, not even those who are aware of the problem of under-theorisation, have asked: what is the nature and purpose of a theory or, simply put, what is a theory?

What is a theory?

This simple question remains unsettled within philosophy of science; is not widely discussed in social science (Hughes and Sharrock 1997: Chapter 3); is discussed even less in management studies and organisation analysis (Johnson and Duberley 2000: Chapter 3);[18] and not discussed at all in research on the HRM–P link. This lack of discussion is one reason for the embarrassment of riches we saw in Chapter 2. To get some ideas of how theories are conceived of in management studies in general, consider the following comments.[19]

[A] theory consists of units whose interaction allows us to forward propositions about their relationships. These units are ... represented by variables. Likewise propositions can be operationalised as hypotheses, stating a relationship between variables. (Noon 1994: 18)

One key part of the 'theory' of HRM ... is that it is possible to 'predict' a set of outcomes from a set of HR practices. In other words, this is the heartland of the theoretical modelling of the cause-and-effect variety. (Storey 1992: 40)

Theories consist of causal explanations of the occurrence of phenomena or the relationships between phenomena or between characteristics thereof ... A theory is dominant if it can account for all of the successful predictions made by competing theories and can make at least one more successful prediction than any competing theories ... A theory must be corroboratable in the sense of being amenable to the deduction of predictions which can be subjected to empirical evaluation ... Evaluation refers to the empirical assessment of predictions deduced from the conjectured theory ... Conjecture consists of the positing of causes of phenomena or of the causes of the relationships between phenomena. (Kane 2001: 247)

Theories, if accurate, fulfil the objectives of prediction (knowledge of the outcome) and understanding (knowledge of the process) regarding the relationships among the variables of interest. Thus, a good theory enables one to both predict what will happen given a set of values for certain variables, and to understand why this predicted value should result. (Wright and McMahan 1992: 296)

[T]heory is the answer to queries of why. Theory is about the connections among phenomena, a story about why acts, events, structure, and thoughts occur. Theory emphasizes the nature of causal relationships, identifying what comes first as well as the timing of such events. Strong theory, in our view, delves into underlying processes so as to understand the systematic reasons for a particular occurrence or non-occurrence. It often burrows deeply into micro processes, laterally into neighbouring concepts, or in an upward direction, tying itself to broader social phenomena. It usually is laced with a set of convincing and logically interconnected arguments ... [A] good theory explains, predicts, and delights. (Sutton and Staw 1995: 376)

[A] complete theory must contain [the following] essential elements ... (i) *What*. Which factors (variables, constructs, concepts) logically should be considered as part of the explanation ... (ii) *How*. Having identified a set of factors, the researchers next question is, How are they related ... (iii) *Why*. What are the underlying psychological, economic or social dynamics that justify the selection of factors and the proposed causal relationships? ... To summarize thus far: What and How describe; only Why explains. What and How provide a framework for interpreting patterns ... in our empirical observations. This is an important distinction because data, whether quantitative of qualitative, characterize; theory supplies the explanation for the characteristics. (Whetten 1989: 490–1, numbers added)[20]

The first thing to note is the complete lack of anything like a consistent vocabulary, with different writers using different terms to mean similar things, and using similar terms to mean different things. The second thing to note is the blurring of prediction and explanation. Whilst some of this stems from lack of careful exposition, the cause of clarity is not helped by the existence of the 'symmetry thesis' which is often found lurking within the scientistic perspective – as we saw above. The third thing to note is the lack of clarity vis-à-vis normative and positive statements; it is unclear if these commentators are suggesting what theory *is*, or what theory *should* be. To avoid this, we use 'ought' where we can, but will use 'is' in places where it becomes necessary to differentiate. The final thing to note is the suggestion that theory should explain *and* predict. This commitment to prediction gives the game away here, and reveals that all these comments, to a greater or lesser extent, accept one of the basic presuppositions of scientism. Despite ambiguity, however, it is possible to identify a commitment to the idea that a viable theory consists of a set of statements that facilitate prediction and another set that facilitate explanation. In other words, a viable theory should have *two* dimensions: *predictive* and *explanatory*.

First, the *predictive dimension of theory* should consist of statements that deliver predictions in terms of relations between events. When theory predicts, it does so by asking 'what' and 'how' questions. As Whetten (1989: 491) puts it: 'Combining Hows and Whats produces the typical model, from which testable propositions can be derived.' This is almost certainly what Brewster has in mind when he describes the scientistic approach in the following way – although in all fairness he is probably being over-charitable:

The strength of this approach is that good research based upon it tends to have a clear potential for theoretical development, it can lead to carefully drawn research questions, the research tends to be easily replicable and research methodologies sophisticated, and there is a coherence of criteria for judging the research. (Brewster 1999: 215)

Second, the *explanatory dimension of theory* should consist of statements that deliver explanation. When theory explains, it does so by asking 'why' questions and answering them by delving into the underlying processes and causal mechanisms at work. Remember, just because something is called an 'explanation' in the HRM–P literature does not mean it is a bona fide explanation.

Combining the predictive and explanatory dimensions allows us to see that from the scientistic perspective a theory should consist (minimally)[21] of statements that deliver predictions in terms of relations between events, and statements that deliver explanations – although what constitutes such statements is never really specified in the HRM literature. It is one thing, however, to claim that theory *should* predict and explain, it is another matter entirely to suggest that it *can* predict and explain. Let us consider (inductive) prediction and explanation in turn.

We saw in the last chapter that the ability to make (inductive) predictions rests on the existence of event regularities, that is, on the system being (stochastically) closed. To say, as empirical researchers often do, that HRM practices X_1, X_2 and X_3 are good *predictors* of increased organisational performance Y, presupposes that whenever HRM practices X_1, X_2 and X_3 have occurred in the past, they have been accompanied by increases in organisational performance Y. Unfortunately for advocates of scientism, the social world in general, and the workplace in particular, appear to be open systems wherein event regularities of the sought-after kind do not exist. Without event regularities, however, there is no basis to establish statistical associations between HRM practices and organisational performance, and hence no basis to expect accurate (inductive) predictions. In open systems, making accurate (inductive) predictions appears to us to be impossible. This is why social science has such a poor track record of making accurate predictions and why the empirical evidence on the existence of an empirical relation between HRM practices and organisational performance is inconclusive. The idea that a theory should have a predictive dimension might be acceptable for *some* kinds of natural scientific theory, typically, those theories involving bench experiments where system closure is practicable and legitimate. The idea that a social scientific theory should have an (inductively) predictive dimension is a serious misconception.[22] The scientistic perspective is mistaken about the role of prediction in theory: a social scientific theory, one that refuses to turn a blind eye to the open systemic nature of the social world, cannot consist (and hence the idea that it *should* is moot), in part, *of* statements that deliver predictions in terms of relations between events.

What about explanation? If the ontology presupposed by scientism is one of observed atomistic events, then causality cannot be conceived of in terms of anything other than a conjunction of some kind between these events; the cause of event *y* must be sought in terms of some prior event *x*. We referred to this conception of causality as *Humean*, suggesting that 'explanations' like this are emaciated, if indeed they can be considered explanations at all. The scientistic perspective is partly correct about the role of explanation in theory: a social scientific theory *can* and *should* consist, in part, of statements that deliver explanations. Unfortunately for scientism, it lacks the meta-theoretical apparatus to deliver anything other than emaciated explanation. In fact, matters are worse than this. Scientism's understanding of ontology, aetiology, epistemology, methodology and commitment to quantitative, empirical and statistical research techniques work together in such a way that the sum of their effects actually discourages the generation of bona fide theory. Let us see this by tracing the links in the meta-theoretical chain from ontology to the nature and purpose of theory.

If the social world is reduced to observed atomistic events (ontology), then causality is reduced to Humean causality (aetiology), knowledge is reduced to identifying event regularities (epistemology), and methodology is reduced to engineering closed systems so that event regularities can be presented in the form of functional relations (or derivatives such as regression equations) and predictions or hypotheses tested (research technique). There is no place in this meta-theoretical chain for explanation. From the scientistic perspective, then, a *theory is merely a vehicle for delivering predictions and hypotheses in terms of regularities between events expressed as variables*. If the nature and purpose of theory is (explicitly or implicitly) solely to deliver predictions and hypotheses, then we should not be surprised when it fails to deliver something different, namely a (bona fide) explanation.

The idea that explanation matters is not a new idea and, moreover, is known outside critical realist circles. Indeed, almost thirty years ago, management guru Henry Mintzberg wrote:

Theory-building seems to require rich description, the richness that comes from anecdote. We uncover all kinds of relationships in our 'hard' data, but it is only through the use of this 'soft' data that we are able to 'explain' them and explanation is, of course, the purpose of research. (cited in Shah and Corley 2006: 11)

Lacking the meta-theoretical concepts to deliver anything other than emaciated explanations, and maybe even thinking that to predict is to explain, empirical researchers on the HRM–P link end up pursuing prediction and predictive power, whilst often implying (and maybe thinking) they are pursuing explanation. The fact that predictions cannot be delivered, nor that there is confusion surrounding the meaning of prediction, does not mean prediction is not the de facto objective.

It has taken a long time, and involved some fairly difficult meta-theoretical concepts and arguments, but we are finally in a position to fully understand why empirical research on the HRM–P link is generically under-theorised, that is, why what passes for theory is treated in such a cavalier manner, why it lacks practical import, and why we seem to have an embarrassment of riches. Moreover, we are also in a position to understand why, as long as empirical research on the HRM–P link remains committed to scientism, it will never develop theories with explanatory power, and hence will remain under-theorised.

Unsuccessful tests of predictions

The inconclusive nature of empirical evidence on the HRM–P link means that some studies successfully, whilst other studies unsuccessfully, test earlier findings, claims, theories, models, predictions and hypotheses. What happens in cases where tests are unsuccessful? We consider this question via the work of Ramsay *et al.* (2000) because it is an example of empirical researchers who, whilst using scientism, the deductive method and empirical, qualitative and statistical techniques, are aware of some very serious limitations of this approach. The tension between their meta-theoretical commitment and their recognition of its limitations surfaces in their conclusion, so let us unpack it. Ramsay *et al.* (2000: 501) seek to 'test the competing claims of theories advocating and criticizing so-called high performance work systems (HPWS)'. They proceed by testing the predictions of three models: the High-Commitment Model; the High-Involvement Model and the Labour Process Model. After using the standard range of statistical techniques they arrive at the conclusion that their analysis provides little support for the theory underlying the models. What is most interesting, however, is the way they deal with their own conclusions. 'How', they ask, 'can we explain the fact that none of the three models tested provides an adequate account of the outcomes of HPWS's?' (2000: 521).

They reject the possibility that the data are problematic, because they are based on the respected WERS 98 data. They reject the possibility that the statistical models are problematic, because they encapsulate established measures that have been tested previously. This is important, because it shows there is nothing odd or untoward in the data or the basic statistical models. They then consider two further avenues.

They consider the problems raised by attempts to measure and quantify the kind of inherently complex, evolving, multidimensional and subjective phenomena that constitute HPWS. They write: 'even if the variables covered the appropriate range of factors, they may have been unable to capture, in a sufficiently detailed, subtle and nuanced way, employee responses to HPWS' (2000: 521). These problems lead to two conclusions. First, empirical researchers on the HRM–P link should work harder to obtain more 'detailed, subtle and nuanced' variables.[23] Second, empirical research, driven by attempts to measure and quantify the kind of inherently complex, evolving, multidimensional and subjective phenomena that constitute HPWS will never be able to capture, in a sufficiently detailed, subtle and nuanced way, the employees' perceptions and attitudes, nor the processes and mechanisms with which employees interact. The second conclusion, and the serious possibility that some things just cannot be meaningfully measured, does not appear on their radar screen. Given the arguments we have deployed in this chapter, we think the second is the most consistent, albeit the most uncomfortable conclusion – at least it is uncomfortable for empirical researchers on the HRM–P link.

They also consider the possibility of 'limitations inherent in the theorization of HPWS's that underlie the analysis' (2000: 522). They cite three possibilities – and we can think of many more: (1) managers may be incompetent at managing innovative practices, so the latter fail to positively influence organisational performance; (2) there may be limitations to the kind of innovative approaches that can be implemented; (3) the indeterminancy of labour, with its capacity to resist, passively or actively, leads us to 'expect an unevenness of outcomes disruptive for hypotheses based on simplistic ... accounts' (2000).

[T]he statistical models of the relationships between employees responses to HPWS practices, employee response and organizational outcome used in the analysis are perhaps too simplistic to capture the complex reality of the implementation of the operation of HPWS ... It is quite plausible that outcomes flowing from managerial innovation are much less determinate than our models apprehend. (2000: 520–1)

What exactly do phrases like 'unevenness of outcomes', 'simplistic models' and 'outcomes are much less determinate than our models apprehend' really boil down to, and why would they be 'disruptive for hypotheses'? Recall that predictions or hypotheses, typically, state what will happen to the magnitude of the dependent variable when a new dependent variable(s) is introduced, or the magnitude of an existing independent variable(s) changes. Recall too the key point that predictions and hypotheses are derived from, and are dependent upon, event regularities and, therefore, closed systems. In closed system models, even and determinate outcomes that do not disrupt hypotheses occur – because we make them occur. If, however, the workplace is an open system, event regularities are unlikely, and closed system models are inappropriate, because the relationship between management practices and performance outcomes is likely to be indeterminate or uneven and hypotheses will be disrupted. When, for example, practices such as performance-related pay (one of Ramsay *et al.*'s independent variables) are introduced, sometimes performance improves, sometimes it deteriorates, and sometimes it remains unchanged. Closed system models predicting and testing hypotheses to the effect that the introduction of performance-related pay will increase organisational performance are inappropriate for open systems.

We are now in a position to offer an answer to Ramsay *et al.*'s concluding question: 'How can we explain the fact that none of the three models tested provides an adequate account of the outcomes of HPWS's?' (2000: 521). For critical realists like ourselves, the answer is: 'because if the workplace is an open system, we would not expect to find statistical associations between HPWS's and organisational performance', so we would not expect the models to provide such an account.[24]

Conclusion

The last chapter highlighted several shortcomings stemming from the scientism that underlies empirical research on the HRM–P link. Whilst the workplace is an open system, modelling it as if it were closed brings with it a series of conundrums and problems. Moreover, the preoccupation with quantifying and measuring HRM practices encourages researchers to turn a blind eye to the possibility that because they are naturally qualitative, inherently complex, evolving, multidimensional and subjective, practices cannot be *meaningfully* measured. This chapter revealed more shortcomings. Not only is there confusion surrounding the concepts of replication, prediction and explanation, (inductive) prediction is impossible in open systems, and scientism leads to the generation of theories lacking explanatory power. Scientism, the deductive method and the quantitative, empirical and statistical research techniques scientism sponsors, appear to be generating extremely serious shortcomings. Moreover, it appears to us that the tail is wagging the dog; scientism, the deductive method and quantitative, empirical and statistical research techniques are driving research, and much of what passes for theory, on the HRM–P link.

What worries us even more than these shortcomings, however, is the fact that empirical researchers on the HRM–P link are totally unaware of them. Indeed, in a very recent stocktaking exercise, two of the leading empirical researchers in the field (Becker and Huselid 2006: 910) identify the 'three key methodological challenges' facing the paradigm as: 'omitted variable bias, measurement error, and mutual causation or simultaneity'.[25] Whilst they are problematic, they are as nothing compared to the real meta-theoretical challenges we have highlighted in the last two chapters.

6 | *Critical realism: a meta-theory for analysing HRM and performance*

Introduction

Would you choose a pneumatic drill to clean a window? Probably not, but the important question is: why not? You would not choose a pneumatic drill to clean a window because you would almost certainly, if implicitly, consider the nature of glass and conclude that a pneumatic drill would be an inappropriate tool to be applied to this material. In other words you would start with an enquiry into the nature of the phenomena under investigation. That is, you would start with *ontology*. You would then choose a tool appropriate for dealing with the phenomena in question; to clean a window you might choose a damp cloth. This simple example suggests that we should start with ontology and then choose or design a 'toolkit' appropriate to the phenomena under investigation. The term 'toolkit' is, of course, metaphoric, and whilst it can refer to the physical world, we are more concerned with the social world, and so our 'toolkit' will be conceptual, in this context, meta-theoretical.

Empirical researchers working on the HRM–P link do *not*, however, start with ontology. Instead, they start with an 'off the shelf toolkit' in the guise of scientism, the deductive method, and its quantitative, empirical and statistical research techniques and apply this 'toolkit', without questioning its appropriateness.[1] Purcell and Kinnie, whilst perhaps not being as thoroughgoing in their critique as us, nonetheless notice something similar:

Thus, the usual steps in research, of theory determining the research questions and hence the choice of method, have been reversed. Methodological considerations have determined what questions can be asked while factors beyond the reach of the chosen method, however important, have been ignored. (2007: 540)

Unfortunately, as we have demonstrated in previous chapters, the multifarious shortcomings of scientism, the deductive method and these research techniques make it singularly inappropriate for investigating the influence of HRM practices on organisational performance. Commitment to this inappropriate meta-theory leads these researchers to do the equivalent of using a pneumatic drill to clean a window. Critical realists, by contrast, *do* start with ontology and choose or design a meta-theoretical 'toolkit' appropriate for dealing with the phenomena in question. Critical realists like us, concerned with the influence of HRM practices on organisational performance, choose and design a meta-theoretical 'toolkit' with the workplace, workers and managers in mind.

The aim of this chapter, then, is to consider the meta-theoretical 'toolkit' offered by critical realism – although we will drop the 'toolkit' analogy as it has done its job, and we do not want to give the impression that we are advocating the rather mechanistic application of a set of procedures. In summary, and contra scientism, critical realist meta-theory provides the following:

- A social ontology wherein the world is taken to be open, layered, transformational, and consisting not only of human agents, but also structures, institutions, mechanisms, resources, rules, conventions, (non-human) powers, as opposed to a 'flat' ontology of events and experiences.
- A 'thick' notion of causality as the exercise of a capacity, disposition or *power*, as opposed to the Humean or 'thin' notion of causality as event regularity.
- A notion of tendency as opposed to the notion of law-like event regularity.
- An agency and structure framework, with the associated notion of positioned-practice.
- A sophisticated notion of the human being, the agent, as opposed to the atomistic conception *of homo economicus* presupposed by scientism.
- A 'thick' form of explanation, as opposed to a 'thin' form.
- A distinction between theoretical and applied explanation, utilising retroduction and retrodiction as modes of inference, as opposed to deduction and induction.

- A clear objective for social science in the form of explanation, as opposed to prediction based on induction, and hence a plausible method which we call causal-explanatory.
- A notion of tendential prediction as opposed to inductive prediction.
- A clear idea of what constitutes a theory, namely, a causal-explanatory account, as opposed to the vague idea of theory as a vehicle for delivering hypotheses and predictions.

The rest of this chapter will elaborate and expand upon all these points to demonstrate why critical realism appears to be a superior meta-theory for the task in hand.

Social ontology

Not only is the social ontology subscribed to by critical realists open and layered, it is also *transformational*. Whilst traditionally most commentators recognise that society consists of, on the one hand, agents, and on the other hand social structures and/or institutions, the debate centres upon the way they interact. Agents do not create or produce structures and/or institutions *ab initio*, rather they *recreate, reproduce* or *transform* a set of pre-existing structures and/or institutions. Society continues to exist only because agents reproduce and/or transform those structures and/or institutions that they encounter in their social actions. Every action performed requires the pre–existence of some social structures and/or institutions which agents draw upon in order to initiate that action, and in doing so reproduce or transform them. For example, communicating requires a medium (e.g. language), and the operation of the market requires the rules of private property. This ensemble of social structures and/or institutions simply *is* society. The transformational principle, then, centres upon the structures and/or institutions that are the *ever-present condition, and the continually reproduced and/or transformed outcome, of* human agency. Agents, acting purposefully or consciously, unconsciously draw upon, and thereby reproduce, the structures and/or institutions that facilitate their actions in daily life. To understand this transformation process in more depth, however, we need to have a closer look at the notion of agency, and then of structures and/or institutions. Let us start with agency.

Agents

People, real people, human beings, actors, agents or whatever we choose to call those we study, have not been well treated by social science – with notable exceptions. Social sciences dominated by scientism (e.g. contemporary economics) operate with a modernist conception of the human being as rational economic man, or *homo economicus*. Social sciences dominated by what is variously referred to as poststructuralism, postmodernism, social constructionism, continental philosophy or the linguistic turn (e.g. contemporary sociology) have abandoned this modernist conception, only to have deconstructed and decentred the self to the point where there is no self, and in the process reduced human beings to bloodless entities that simply internalise linguistic or discursive scripts. The now unfashionable ideas of structuralism morphed into *post*structuralism, whilst retaining the idea that genuine human agency is a myth – the structuralist anthropologist Levi-Strauss famously referred to the individual as the 'spoilt brat of history' and endeavoured to remove it from analysis.

Whilst poststructuralism replaces structuralism's determining effect of social structures, it only does so by introducing a different determining force: language or discourse. In so doing, however, genuine human agency effectively disappears, reduced to a mere mirror, reflecting the power–knowledge discourses of the agent's environment. Instead of exercising genuine agency, genuine choice, being able to have done otherwise, agents are assumed to act according to scripts written in societies' discourses. In the HRM literature, the work of Townley (1994) and Hancock (1999) are examples of this notion of agency. There are, of course, several versions of this notion, some more strongly determinist than others, and we cannot elaborate upon them all here. In (correctly) rejecting *homo economicus*, however, poststructuralists and postmodernists have transformed their conception of human beings (incorrectly) into empty vessels lacking any intrinsic capacities, dispositions or powers.

Unhappy with this 'Hobson's choice', some theorists (e.g. Archer 2000, 2003; Davis 2003 and Layder 2004) have attempted to recover a more plausible sense of human beings. In opposition to scientistic claims, critical realists like us consider human beings to be more than rational bargain hunters, and although there may occasionally be times when human behaviour starts to resemble something like this kind of rationality, it is certainly not often enough to make a general case for it. In opposition to many postmodernist and poststructuralist claims we consider human beings to be more than just the effects of discourse – or some other linguistic or semiotic determining factor. Whilst human beings are rooted in a world consisting of discursive and extra-discursive phenomena, and both have a role to play in shaping the human being, the human is irreducible to these phenomena. That is to say, genuine human agency exists, defined as *the ability to have done otherwise*, although it is always constrained and enabled by a range of discursive and extra-discursive phenomena.

It is fair to say that, hitherto, critical realist work on agency-structure has tended to focus on structures to the neglect of agency. This not only leaves our understanding of agency relatively weak, it also prevents us getting to grips with the question of how structure (and institution) really does impact upon agency. The ever-present danger here is that we slip into some kind of structural determinism where structure, metaphorically speaking, reaches inside our heads, throws a mental switch, and causes a change in our ideas and, subsequently, actions. Archer's more recent work (2000 and especially 2003) focuses specifically on agency.

Whilst the following section considers structures and institutions in depth, it does so without ever losing sight of the centrality of agency in the reproduction or transformation of structures and institutions.

Structures and institutions

Whilst the terms 'institutions' and 'social structures'[2] feature extensively in many social scientific disciplines, there is more than a little ambiguity about what each term means and how they relate to one another.[3] Let us consider some of the ambiguities we have in mind – see Fleetwood (2008a and 2008b) for further elaboration.

Perhaps the most common way of (mis)treating the *relationship* between institutions and social structures is to use them interchangeably. This may be done without thinking, or it may be rooted in the common idea that institutions are kinds of social structures. For Hodgson (2006a: 2 *passim*): 'Institutions are the kind of structures that matter most in the social realm: they make up the stuff of social life'. For Wells (1970: 3): 'Social institutions form an element in a more general concept known as social structure'. Risman (2004: 431) simply 'prefers' to define gender as a social structure rather than defining 'gender as an institution', but she sees the difference as largely linguistic.

Another common approach to institutions and social structures, noted by Jessop and Nielsen (2003: 1), is to (mis)treat them as patterned social practices, in particular regularities in the flux of events. This confuses the *conditions* that make action possible with the action itself. This is remarkable given that Giddens' (1979, 1984) *Structuration* theory, Bhaskar's (1989) *Transformational Model of Social Action* (TMSA) and Archer's (1995, 1998) *Morphogenetic* approach, all of which reject the idea that institutions and social structures are patterns, have been available for decades.

The term 'institution' is often used to refer to things like: gender, money, the family, religion, property, markets, the state, education, sport and medicine, language, law, systems of weights and measures and table manners. This ignores important differences in the nature of these things. The institution of money, for example, does *not* contain human beings, whereas the institution of the family clearly *does*. Are money and families different kinds of institution, or is one of them not really an institution at all? For Schmid (1994: 3–5) 'early retirement, further education, retraining and regulation of working hours, trade unions, labour and social security laws, labour market programs, codetermination and collective bargaining' are all institutions. The problem here is that the term 'institution' becomes a 'catch all' term to refer to all kinds of social phenomena. Portes (2006) refers to this as the 'institutions are everything approach'.

The term 'social structure' is also used in many ways and, as Porpora (2007: 195) notes: 'there continues to be a certain blurriness in the way we speak of social structure'. The term can be used negatively, to refer to phenomena like 'rules, relations, positions, processes, systems, values, meanings and the like that *do not* reduce to human behaviour' (Lawson 2003: 181, emphasis added). But because there are many things that *do not* reduce to human behaviour, this meaning is impractically broad. Moreover, even if social structures and institutions are irreducible to human behaviour, this tells us nothing of the differences between them. In a similar vein, and by emphasising the first word of the pair, '*social* structure' can be used to refer to anything that is the result of human action, as opposed to some naturally occurring phenomenon, once again making the meaning impractically broad. The term 'social structure' can be used in an 'architectural' sense where we refer to the structure of a bridge, market, industry or organisation; or to the way a bridge, market, industry or organisation is structured. It can be used to refer to society as a whole, or perhaps in a general sense to mean anything that is external to an organisation or an individual which, once again, makes the meaning impractically broad. It can be used to refer to *specific* phenomenon like the structure of social class or gender. And last, but not least, it can be used to refer to *general* phenomena, where it acts as a place-holder for a series of un-named, non-agential, phenomena. It is this general sense that we have used throughout this book, often referring to things like the structures and mechanisms drawn upon by agents.

Finally, discussion of social structures and institutions often involves the use of terms like habits, *habitus*, rules, conventions, norms, values, roles, customs, laws, regulations, practices, routines, procedures and precedents, not to mention less commonly used terms like mores, scripts, obligations, rituals, codes and agreements. Once again, there is often confusion about what each of these terms mean, how they relate to one another, and how they relate to social structures and institutions. Consider two examples. In considering 'habits, routines, social conventions, social norms' as types of rules, Rogers (1994: 92) conflates properties that should be associated with human agency (i.e. habits) with properties that should be associated with institutions (i.e. conventions and norms). He also makes the common mistake of confusing the conditions that make action possible (i.e. conventions and norms) with subsequent actions (i.e. routines).

In order to reduce some of the ambiguity surrounding the terms 'structure' and 'institution', thereby being able to understand the morphogenetic or transformation process in more depth, we need to understand the differences and similarities between social structures and institutions. Let us start by considering the similarities.

The similarities between social structures and institutions vis-à-vis agents

We open this section (based upon Hodgson 2004: 179–81) by stating the social ontology that forms the basis of our analysis, because this: allows the reader to identify fundamental points of agreement or disagreement, without having to guess our position; obviates the need to repeat arguments that, if not widely known, are readily available; and highlights those issues and arguments that, whilst important, are beyond the scope of this book.

(1) *Ontic differentiation between agents, and social structures and institutions.* Agents on the one hand, and social structures and institutions on the other, are fundamentally different kinds of things. Social structures and institutions are non-agential phenomena; and agents are non-structural, non-institutional, phenomena.

(2) *Ontic differentiation between agential properties and social structures and institutions.* Habits are embodied or internalised dispositions, capacities or powers and, as such, are *properties of agents*. The causal influences that generate habits might well lie (directly or indirectly) in phenomena like social structures and institutions that are external to agents, but once they are embodied or internalised, they become the emergent properties of agents.[4]

(3) *The dependence of social structures and institutions on agents.* Social structures and institutions exist only via the intentional and unintentional actions of human agents.

(4) *The dependence of agents on social structures and institutions.* For their socialisation, survival and interaction, human agents depend upon social structures and institutions that influence their behaviour. Taking the previous three points together, we might say that agency, and social structures and institutions, whilst independent in the sense of different, are nevertheless mutually dependent: no agency, no structure or institution; and no structure or institution, no agency. This meaning of *dependence* should be borne in mind later, when we refer to social structures and institutions *existing independently* of agents.

(5) *The rejection of methodological and ontological individualism.* Social structures and institutions are irreducible, in an ontological and/or an explanatory sense, to individuals, to the subjectivity of individuals, and to inter-subjectivity. This is a rejection of what Archer (1995: 84 *passim*) calls 'upwards conflation'.

(6) *The rejection of methodological and ontological collectivism.* Individual actions are irreducible, in an ontological and explanatory sense, to social structures. This erroneous doctrine results precisely from reducing individual actions and intentions to social

structures. This is a rejection of what Archer (1995: 81 *passim*) calls 'central conflation'.

(7) *The temporal priority of social structures and institutions over any one agent.* Social structures and institutions pre-date any particular episode of human action. Social structures and institutions can be changed, but the starting point is not of our choosing. This is a rejection of what Archer (1995: 87 *passim*) calls 'downwards conflation'.

(8) The foregoing points, encapsulated in Bhaskar's TMSA and Archer's *Morphogenetic* approach, constitute an updated and more sophisticated version not only of Giddens's *Structuration* theory, but of the 'agency-structure' framework more generally – although it is more accurate, if more cumbersome, to refer to the 'agency-structure/*institution*' framework. The basis of these two critical realist approaches is this: in order to undertake (even the most insignificant) social action, agents have no choice but to (consciously and/or unconsciously) engage with the social structures and institutions that pre-exist them. To hold a conversation, agents have to engage with the institutional rules of grammar, and the convention of how far to stand from the interlocutor. To enter paid employment, and thereby sell their labour power to those who own capital, agents have to engage with the social structure of class. By engaging with these institutions and structures, agents *reproduce* or transform these structures and/or institutions, and are themselves reproduced or transformed in the process. Social structures and institutions are the *conditions* of human action, they make human action possible; but they are not outcomes or actions and so cannot be *patterns* of actions. To put matter bluntly, there is more going on here than agents interacting (intersubjectively) with other agents; agents can only interact with other agents because they can interact with non-agential phenomena.

(9) Everything that has been said above for social structures and institutions holds also for rules conventions, norms, values, customs. It does *not*, however, hold for laws, regulations practices, routines and precedents, or roles, and we want to eliminate the latter group from the analysis in three steps. First, we eliminate practices, routines and precedents on the grounds that they are not conditions of action; they *are* actions. They are probably what

we have in mind when we say things like: 'John routinely treats his female employees as if they were idiots'; 'the practice around here is to buy cakes on your birthday' or 'Sue set the precedent of leaving early on Friday'. Second, I eliminate roles on the grounds that they are properties of organisations, not institutions. Agents are obliged to undertake a particular set of practices when they take up positions within an organisation. Finally, we eliminate laws and regulations on the grounds that, whilst they are a kind of rules they are: (a) explicitly and consciously specified and identified; (b) often backed by formal sanctions; and (c), in virtue of (a) and (b) are, once again, properties of organisations, not institutions. By a process of elimination, then, we are left with *rules, conventions, norms, values*[5] *and customs*, and these will form the basis of my analysis of institutions. Whilst it might be possible to identify distinctions between these terms, we will not do so in this book.[6] Henceforth, and where appropriate, we will place the terms 'rules', 'conventions', 'norms', 'values' and 'customs' in brackets after the term 'institution'.

(10) *Ontic similarity between social structures and institutions.* What makes social structures and institutions (and for reasons that will become clear below, rules conventions, norms, values and customs) similar is that they are drawn upon, reproduced and transformed by human agents.

Now that we know how social structures and institutions are similar, we need to consider how they differ. Let us start with institutions.

Institutions, agency and habits

For Hodgson, 'Institutions are systems of established and embedded social rules that structure social interactions' (Hodgson 2006a: 18). Our initial definition, then, is that institutions are: *systems of established rules; put another way, institutions consist of, or are constituted by, rules.* We will augment this below. Hodgson (2006a: 18) describes rules as: 'socially transmitted and customary normative injunctions or immanently normative dispositions, that in circumstances X do Y'. This is an unfortunate turn of phrase because, despite his best efforts to repudiate this interpretation, it encourages the (mis)interpretation that rules are *rational decision* rules, rather like rules economists (and game theorists) invent for *homo economicus* to follow; and follow to the letter. The rules Hodgson has in mind, however, are not of this ilk. Indeed, they ought to be thought of as 'rules of thumb' that guide, but do not determine, action. Students and lecturers, for example, know that in lectures, there is a tacit, unwritten rule that (effectively) states: 'when in the lecture theatre, do not interrupt the lecturer unless invited'. Because this rule is adhered to, by most students, most of the time, the lecture can 'go on'. Yet as is well known, not all students observe this rule. Rules can be broken, and they guide to varying degrees, but this is often sufficient for them to work (MacCormick 1998).

We noted above (point 9) that everything we said about social structures and institutions holds also for rules, conventions, norms, values and customs. Whilst there have been various attempts to define (some of) these terms, and a few attempts to identify differences between them, there is a sense in which differences tend to disappear when these terms are actually put to use. Many writers use rules, conventions, norms, values and customs interchangeably.[7] Recognition that (a) rules are similar to conventions, norms, values and customs, and (b) institutions consist of rules, allows us to augment our initial definition thus: *institutions are systems of established rules, conventions, norms, values and customs; institutions consist of, or are constituted by, established rules, conventions, norms, values and customs.*

What, then, is the link between institutions and human action? The short answer is this: external institutions (rules, conventions, norms, values and customs) become internalised or embodied within agents as habits via a process of habituation, whereupon the habits dispose agents to think and act in certain ways, without having to deliberate. The long answer is to explain this more fully, and involves habit, *habitus* and habituation, which we now deal with in turn.

Habit and *habitus*

According to Camic (1986: 1044) 'the term "habit" generally denominates a more or less self acting disposition or tendency to engage in a previously adopted or acquired form of action'. Furthermore, Camic (1986: 1046) and Burkitt (2002: 225) suggest that the term 'habit' has become associated with a rather mechanistic, deterministic and unchanging response to stimuli. To avoid this interpretation Marcel Mauss substituted the term 'habit' with the Latin term '*habitus*'.

Because I am not convinced that simply substituting *habitus* for habit makes matters clearer, I will continue to use them interchangeably, using whichever of the terms is more appropriate in context. Whilst Bourdieu's works are littered with various definitions of *habitus*, the following seems the least ambiguous:

Habitus, understood as a system of lasting, transposable dispositions which, integrating past experiences, functions at every moment as a matrix of perceptions, apperceptions, and actions and makes possible the achievement of infinitely diversified tasks, thanks to analogical transfers of schemes permitting the solution of similarly shaped problems. (Bourdieu 1998: 82)

Whilst we cannot go into great detail on *habitus*, it is probably wise to state the following key points. First, *habitus* is not an observable behaviour, pattern, routine or action but a *disposition, capacity or power* that generates a *tendency*. Kleptomaniacs, for example, might possess the *habit* of stealing, but this does not mean they steal all the time: sometimes they do and sometimes they do not, and there may be no pattern to their behaviour. *Habitus* is, however, always present in the form of a disposition generating a tendency to steal. A *habitus*, then, is an *agential disposition* that generates a *tendency* for the agent to do *x* – on tendencies see Fleetwood (2001) and (2009a 2009b and 2010b).

Second, *habitus* is a largely unconscious disposition to engage in an action. The 'feel for the game' is something that allows us to play 'the game' (a metaphor encapsulating living and acting in society) without stopping to deliberate about every move – although it might be possible to do this in some circumstances by stopping to reflect upon our actions (Noble and Watkins 2003).

Third, despite the fears of many, *habitus* is not (necessarily) a mechanistic, deterministic and unchanging conception implying determinism. Indeed, once *habitus* is understood as a tendency in the manner noted above, then many of these fears disappear.[8]

Fourth, *habitus* governs the physiological or biological aspects of actions like holding a cup and playing golf, *and* the social-psychological aspects of actions like holding the cup with an extended 'pinkie' and deferring to the golf club captain – in certain social environments. *Habitus*, then, is a psychophysical concept; it is 'in' the mind/brain (embrained) and in the body (embodied).

Fifth, it is often implied, if perhaps not intended, that *habitus* is something external to human agency, often via terminology like 'institutional *habitus*', 'family *habitus*', 'class *habitus*', 'gender *habitus*' and so on. We think this is a mistake.

Sixth, and in contrast to the last point, many writers conflate agency and structure/institution, as in the following example – which we also think is a mistake:

Any conception of institutional *habitus* would similarly constitute a complex amalgam of agency and structure and could be understood as the impact of a cultural group or social class on an individual's behaviour as it is mediated through an organisation. Institutional *habitus*es, no less than individual *habitus*es, have a history and have been established over time. (Reay *et al.* 2001: para 1.3)

Seventh, *habitus* is not (somehow) in two places at once. It is not internal *and* external; not a property of agency *and* structure; not a property of the human mind/body *and* the social world. Let us be clear. Institutions (and social structures) are always and everywhere *external* to human agents. *Habitus* is always and everywhere *internal* to human agents. In appropriate circumstances, *habitus* emerges within the nervous system of our mind/brains and bodies. The institutions (rules, conventions, norms, values and customs) remain precisely where they were, namely, external to us, and another phenomena, *habitus*, emerges, internal to us.

Habituation

Building upon Hodgson (2006a: 18), we define habituation as the process through which institutions (rules, conventions, norms, values and customs) become internalised and embodied within agents, generating the dispositions we call habits or *habitus*. It seems to us that the process of habituation involves the following three (main) processes:

(1) Repetition, regularity, routinisation and continuity. The (let us say) rule-guided agent finds herself repeating the same action over some extended period. As Hodgson (1988: 127) puts it: 'repeated acts tend to congeal into habits'.
(2) Reinforcement, or incentive and disincentive. There are positive and negative reinforcements to engaging in rule-guided action,

such as approval or disapproval by members of the appropriate community – although this should not be interpreted to mean that agents necessarily deliberate about whether or not to be guided by the rule. See Hodgson (2003).

(3) Intimacy, familiarity or close proximity. To internalise or embody institutions (rules conventions, norms, values and customs) the agent has to engage with them, live with them and use them, until agents feel 'like a fish in water', as it is commonly put.

It is via these three (main) processes of habituation that institutions and agents are linked. Metaphorically speaking, through these processes, institutions (rules, conventions, norms, values and customs) 'touch' agents. This is very often recognised, even if implicitly – as the following example shows. In an article investigating the way a 'masculine *habitus*' is internalised within young boys in UK schools, Connolly (2006: 144) writes of the 'importance of wider social relations and structures'. He then goes on to define these wider social relations and structures in terms of 'the local housing estate, the boy's immediate family, their peer group, the school, the classroom'. In his empirical findings, Connolly goes into detail on what, in our terminology, would be the rules, conventions, norms, values and customs drawn upon by teachers when dealing with pupils of different ethnic backgrounds and gender. Moreover, it is not just teachers that are so guided. Black boys, for example, are guided by the rule, convention, norm, value or custom that: 'Asian boys cannot run fast' (2006: 150).[9]

It is worth noting that habituation does not *necessarily* require one agent (or agents) to *instruct* another agent (or agents) on which rules, conventions, norms, values or customs are appropriate in which context, or how to be guided by them. The degree of consciousness involved in the process of habituation is an empirical matter, but for the purposes of this book, it does not change matters.

Reconstitutive downward causation

Hodgson has recently identified one vitally important property of institutions, and I would extend this to rules, conventions, norms, values and customs: they have the capacity for *reconstitutive downward causation*. Whilst there may be something of a consensus (at least between those that accept points 1 to 9 above) on the claim that *social structures* enable and constrain agents' intentions and actions, it is also believed, although less commonly, that social structures *cannot* directly affect agents' intentions and actions. *Institutions, but not social structures, can cause reconstitutive downward causation.*

This important difference between social structures and institutions gets lost, or at least is confused, in the writing of Bourdieu and his followers, because it is extremely common to read of structures generating the *habitus*. Metaphorically speaking, social structures are not 'magical forces' that penetrate agents' minds and bodies, throwing a kind of mental switch and causing them to change their intentions. And yet institutions (rules, conventions, norms, values and customs) do have something like this ability – although we do not want to push this metaphor any further. What prevents this explanation from being 'magical' is the fact that the process of habituation explains how institutions affect agents' intentions and actions. The following comments from Hodgson incorporate the points made thus far, and then extend them to the idea of reconstitutive downward causation:

What have to be examined are the social and psychological mechanisms leading to such changes of preference, disposition, or mentality. What does happen, is the framing, shifting and constraining capacities of social institutions give rise to new perceptions and dispositions within individuals. Upon new habits of thought and behaviour, new preferences and intentions emerge ... [R]econstitutive downward causation works by creating and moulding habits. (Hodgson 2002: 170–1)

Whilst Hodgson plays down the role of deliberation, he has to admit there are times when deliberation, not habit, is the cause of agents' intentions. In one place he writes: 'deliberation and reason are deployed to make a choice when habits conflict, or are insufficient to deal with the complex situation' (2004: 172). If the cause of agents' intentions is not just habit, but deliberation also, then both habit *and* deliberation can cause agents' intentions. Furthermore, the agential capacity to deliberate, including the capacity to deliberate on habits, strongly suggests the existence of a genuine interior, a domain of mental privacy.

In sum, then, institutions: (a) consist of systems of established rules, conventions, norms, values and customs; (b) are sometimes consciously, at least at first, but more often unconsciously, internalised or embodied as habits or *habitus*, via a process of habituation, itself rooted in, but irreducible to, the nervous system; (c) assist in making the intentions and actions of other agents relatively predictable; (d) exist independently of the agents who draw upon, reproduce or transform them, and in so doing, reproduce or transform themselves; and (e) may, via a process of reconstitutive downward causation involving habituation, *habitus* and habit, transform the intentions and actions of these agents. The foregoing arguments suggest that:

An institution is a system of established rules, conventions, norms, values and customs that become embodied or internalised within agents as habits or habitus, via a process of habituation rooted in the nervous system, to assist in rendering (relatively) predictable, the intentions and actions of agents who draw upon, reproduce or transform these phenomena, whilst simultaneously reproducing and transforming themselves and who may, via a process of reconstitutive downward causation, have their intentions and actions transformed.

Social structures, agency and reflexive deliberation

Lopez and Scott (2000) identify three broad approaches to social structures which they refer to as *institutional, embodied* and *relational structures*. Of these three approaches, one of us has argued (Fleetwood 2008a) that only the latter are bona fide social structures; the former are both *very similar, if not identical to, what many would just call institutions*. Lopez and Scott define *relational structure* as:

the social relations themselves, understood as patterns of causal interconnection and interdependence among agents and their actions, as well as the positions that they occupy. (Lopez and Scott 2000: 3)

Based upon this definition, we offer the following definition of social structure:

A social structure is a latticework of internal relations between entities that may enable and constrain (but cannot transform) the intentions and actions of agents who draw upon, reproduce and/or transform these relations.[10]

In comparison to institutions, the relation between agency and social structures is far more straightforward, largely because nothing like habits and habituation intervenes. Whereas institutions are linked to agency via *habit, social structures are linked to agency via reflexive deliberation, via the internal conversation.* For Archer (2003), being in the world necessarily brings agents into contact with (1) structures that constrain and enable their intentions and (2) the natural, practical and social orders, which give rise to concerns about physical well-being, performative achievement and self-worth respectively. Agents, knowing their own minds, take these factors into consideration when they reflexively deliberate upon the course of action they feel they ought to take. This reflexive deliberation occurs via the *internal conversation* whereby agents literally talk to themselves (and sometimes others) about their needs, concerns and the things that might constrain or enable them. They then formulate (fallible) courses of action, or agential projects, they think might result in these needs being met and concerns being addressed. Archer is also keen to establish the existence of a genuine interior, a domain of mental privacy where this process happens. In short, *reflexive deliberation, via the internal conversation then, is the mechanism linking structure to agency.*[11] This will be picked up again in Chapter 7.

Positioned-practices

If social structures exist, and are relational, then *relata* must also exist. That is, agents relate to one social structure and to each other. Whilst it does depend upon the level of abstraction at which any analysis takes place, at relatively high levels of abstraction such as that demanded when engaging in theory and especially meta-theory, we tend not to try and explain the actions of *each named individual.* This feature obviates the need to investigate every single individual in the workplace because it is, typically, the practices we are often interested in, rather than the named person who carries them out. That is, we are, usually, more concerned with the actions of classes of persons. We are more likely to be concerned to know how call centre operatives, as a group, respond to certain HR practices – although research might well involve interviewing or observing named individuals. Individual, unique, named agents enter into specific social relations by taking up certain slots or social positions such as landlord and tenant, teacher and pupil, manager and worker, HR business partner and internal customer. Attached to any position is a set of practices such as overseeing production processes, turning up for work on time or ensuring that customers' expectations are met. This combination is referred to as a *positioned-practice*.

The positioned-practices of an HR manager entail practices such as recruiting, training, measuring the performance, motivating and occasionally disciplining those in the position of worker. Notice, however, that whilst the particular agent (managers or worker) could be replaced, the position would still remain, and the practices would still be carried out. This should not be misunderstood to imply the 'death of the subject' or the absence of agency, or some other (post)structuralist position. Subject to certain structural constraints, the HR manager is free to engage in these practices in various ways and, clearly, to invent new practices – e.g. to implement flexible working practices, performance-related pay systems or internal shared services.

At the level of abstraction we are operating at, then, it is more appropriate to think in terms of positioned-practices rather than individual named persons. This is what we refer to most of the time when referring to 'agents'.

Causal powers

Most things have capacities, dispositions, liabilities, potentials or causal powers. Causal powers, or just powers for short, enable certain outcomes, but not others. Water has the power to slake thirst but not prevent sunburn. Humans have the power to hold a conversation and plant crops, but not read people's minds or levitate. Bureaucratic organisations have the power to handle downward information flows, but not upward flows. Patriarchal structures and mechanisms have the power to produce gendered discrimination in the workplace, but not class- or race-based discrimination. For critical realists, the powers possessed by phenomena make them causally efficacious. Causal powers (not event regularities) are the basic components of causality. Something like this is recognised in versions of the resource-based view of the firm, or competence theories of the firm. In these cases, some bundle of phenomena is assumed to possess competencies or powers.

Phenomena have the powers they do in virtue of their internal structure, in virtue of their internal make-up. Whilst many phenomena have causal powers, we are particularly interested in the powers of human beings, and the powers of HR practices. In virtue of the biological, neurological, physiological and psychological structures that constitute us as human beings, we have certain powers – although it is important to note that these levels are irreducible to one another so we cannot, for example, reduce social behaviour to psychology, as some psychologists do, or to biology as socio-biologists often do. Although human powers are many and varied, in terms of HRM we are concerned specifically with human powers that we will refer to generally as powers of creativity, imagination, ingeniousness, self-motivation and self-direction. These powers might have an interpretive dimension to them, in the sense that people who possess certain powers have to interpret them, and make decisions about how to use them (Purcell and Hutchinson 2007; Sandberg 2000). Although we are not used to using this language, we can say that HR practices too have powers. Shopfloor based work-teams have the power to generate cooperative working practices, but not to take strategic corporate decisions. HRM practices involving information and consultation have the power to improve employee relations, but not prevent macro-economic recessions. And, of course, HR practices might act to trigger human powers.

Now it is important to note that powers can be in (at least) two 'states' as it were. They can be *exercised* and they can, in addition, be *actualised*. Powers that are only exercised exist without manifesting themselves in some observable outcome. There is no mysticism here, people with the (exercised) power to speak French have this power irrespective of whether or not they actually speak it (it is actualised). Powers may be exercised with or without being actualised. Let us consider these points in turn.

A power is *exercised* by an entity in virtue of its internal make-up, and this power endures whether or not it is actualised and, therefore, endures irrespective of any outcomes it generates. When a power endures in this sense, it can be said to act *transfactually*. A bicycle has the exercised power to transport a rider from A to B, but this does not mean the power will be actualised. A punctured tyre, for example, will prevent the actualisation of the power, but will not eradicate the power itself. An employee has the exercised power to work effectively in the sense that she may be highly productive or highly value-adding. Or she may not. Poor management, for example, may prevent the actualisation of this power. Appropriate HRM practices *may* actualise the power, generating high value-adding behaviours. Or they may not. The point is the power acts transfactually: it is exercised even if it remains unactualised. A power *actualised* is an exercised power that is generating effects in an open system. Due to interference from the effects of other actualised powers in the system, however, we can never know a priori what the outcome of any particular power will be.

Consequently, it is not the existence of key HR practices in the HRM–P literature that *cause* enhanced performance. Rather, the actualisation of the powers of HRM practices is itself contingent on the coming together of them with underlying human powers that may, or may not, be actualised at any particular time and/or place. Understanding the mechanisms and processes through which certain HR practices or strategies enable certain powers represents the Achilles heel of current HRM–P literature and, in many ways, represents the starting point in our empirical analysis of HRM's role in explaining the performance of people, their teams and the organisations to which they belong.

Consider the positioned-practice of a 'worker' and his or her powers.[12] Unlike most animals, humans do not just execute genetically pre-programmed tasks; they conceive these tasks first – although there may be a complex and recursive process between conception and execution. The power of conception is of crucial importance here, and we will return to this below, because it consists of the powers of *imagination, ingenuity* and *creativity* that conceived of the pyramids, the Guggenheim, the cart, the MIR space station, surgical tools – although sadly, they also conceived of nuclear weapons. These same powers of imagination, ingenuity and creativity are also exercised in the conception of less grandiose endeavours such as creating the HR business partner, finding better ways of producing a rivet, writing a programme or engaging in a telephone conversation. HRM practices such as performance management, retention, job design, and especially engagement along with schemes to increase employee participation and empowered employees, are designed to unleash and harness the powers of imagination, ingenuity and creativity that workers bring with them to the workplace. Understood in this way, working is the key, or at least one of the key activities that differentiates humans from other animals and becomes the key activity that defines us as human beings, makes us what we are, expresses our human essence.

Working, understood in this way, is not an activity that we necessarily have to be cajoled, bribed, coerced or 'measured' into doing: it is something that we just do because it is part of what we are. If this is true, then human beings not only possess powers for imaginative, ingenious and creative work, they also possess powers for self-motivated, self-directed and high-performance work.

There are, of course, solid theoretical foundations to support claims that workers possess powers of creativity, imagination, ingeniousness, self-motivation, self-direction and high-performance working, to be found in perspectives as far apart as Marxism and Human Relations. Moreover, the very existence of HRM is predicated upon the existence of powers such as these. If workers did not have these powers there would be no point whatsoever in even contemplating the introduction of HRM practices: we cannot *empower* a workforce that lacks the potentiality, that lacks the powers to be 'switched on' as it were, or actualised. The subtitle of Pfeffer's (1994) book, *Unleashing the Power of the Workforce*, captures the point beautifully.

Claims like this run into the obvious problem of counter-factuality. If workers really do possess powers of creativity, imagination, ingeniousness, self-motivation, self-direction and high-performance working, then how come we so rarely see them exercised? Rather than HRM providing evidence of the existence of these powers, surely the very need for HRM provides evidence to the contrary: workers really do not possess these powers. As we see it, if there is actually a problem here, then it is a self-inflicted one, arising because of a commitment to scientism.

Recall that for scientism, what cannot be observed, cannot be allowed into the investigation; what we see is, effectively, what there is. Powers such as those under discussion are, of course, unobservable. Upon being rarely able to witness the actualisation of these powers, the consistent advocate of scientism must conclude that these powers do not exist. We will come back to this in a few moments, but for now, let us simply note that critical realists take a very different tack. There are plausible theories explaining the existence of these powers, allowing us to use a retroductive mode of inference and an applied explanation. Moreover, most readers of this book probably accept the existence of these powers, or they would not be interested in HRM. The fact, and it probably is a fact, that these HRM practices have not succeeded in unlocking these powers does not mean they do not exist. Conceiving powers as acting tendentially (which will be elaborated upon below), critical realist meta-theory encourages us to enquire into possible countervailing tendencies that might be in operation, counteracting these tendencies. We do not intend to proceed any further with this line of argument, as we would quickly pass from meta-theory into theory and beyond, which is not within the remit of this book, so let us simply accept the existence of workers' powers.[13]

Causal configurations

It is almost always the case that social entities such as organisations, orchestras, unions, workplaces, HRM practices, high-performance work systems, or whatever, exist as clusters of components that endow them with powers. An organisation consists of a cluster of social structures and mechanisms – the terms 'structures' and 'mechanisms' are used here in a general sense, as a placeholder for more specific things. Because the entity usually does whatever it does in virtue of the *interaction* of these causal components, we need a term to refer to them as a whole. The term we use is a *generative ensemble*. This insight is, of course, recognised in the concept of synergy.[14] In the social world, it is most unlikely that any two configurations will ever be the same (although they can be very similar) because they have different clusters of components that constitute them. Thus, one part of an organisation may differ from another part because they each consist of different structures and mechanisms.

We can think of the firm as a causal configuration that enables the production of goods and services. Or we can think of the workplace, the shop floor, the work-system or the team as a complex web of interlocking causal configurations, sub-configurations, sub-subconfigurations and so on. Much depends upon the questions we are asking, and the level of abstraction we are using. Some empirical researchers would, we suspect, be in agreement with the notion of causal configurations. Take, for example, the idea of 'horizontal integration'. HRM practices are said to be horizontally integrated if and when they 'fit together to mutually support a defined set of employee behaviours, competencies and motivations' (Schuler and Jackson 2005: 12). If HRM practices are appropriately (or inappropriately) horizontally integrated, the ensuing bundle can create synergies (or dis-synergies). This is an implicit recognition of causal configurations in the shape of horizontally integrated HR systems. Unfortunately, however, because empirical research remains committed to scientism and its quantitative, empirical and statistical analysis, the best it can do is test to establish that the bundle is horizontally integrated. These techniques cannot provide an explanation of *why* some bundles are better integrated than others, nor can they explore the nature of the integration. This is why empirical researchers committed to scientism treat the HRM system as a black box.

Tendencies

The term 'tendency' hardly crops up in empirical research on the HRM–P link; indeed, the term is not part of the lexicon of scientism. If, however, we proceed from this critical observation, directly to critical realism where the term does form part of the lexicon, we would miss a trick because it is possible that the term might be used implicitly by empirical researchers, even if it never makes it into print. Let us, then, be charitable. We know from our experience of discussing and debating the term 'tendency' in workshops and conferences that many empirical researchers would be perfectly happy claiming to be empirically investigating something called the *tendency* for HRM practices to increase organisational performance. If so, what would they mean by the term? We feel certain they would have in mind some kind of rough and ready event regularity, rough pattern of events, quasi-law or stochastic regularity. To say, in this context, that there is a *tendency* for HRM practices to increase organisational performance, is to say something like, 'well not exactly all the time, but much of the time, HRM practices increase organisational performance'. The wording would be ambiguous, because the conception of tendency would be ambiguous. But ambiguity aside, we are out to make a different point here; an ontological point.

In this context, *the tendency is not causal, it is caused*. Metaphorically speaking, we might say the tendency is 'attached' to the *events*. These events and, therefore, these ambiguous interpretations of tendency, refer to the *outcomes* of something, not to *a something* itself. It is easier to understand this by recalling (from Chapter 4) the diagram illustrating a 'flat' (empirical realist) ontology, but adding the concept of tendency (see Table 6.1).

Table 6.1. *A 'flat' ontology with tendencies*

Domain	Entity	
Empirical	Experiences and observations	Tendency is an outcome vis-à-vis events
Actual	Events and actions	

Whilst anyone is free to use a term like 'tendency' any way they want, it is crucial to understand that critical realists use the term to mean something very different. Since it is virtually impossible to over-state the importance of this, allow us to state the point a little bluntly. On this interpretation, the existence of a tendency has *nothing* to do with empirical observation; it has *nothing* to do with events; it has nothing to do with probabilistic of stochastic law/tendency. There is, however, one important caveat that our bluntness should not be allowed to obscure. Whilst we use the term 'nothing to do', there is in fact one way in which tendency has *something* to do with events. This is raised via the possibility that a tendency might be causally implicated in the occurrence of an event or events – albeit, typically, in conjunction with other tendencies. Indeed, it is often because we see some kind of (non-regular) pattern in the flux of events that we are alerted to the possibility that a tendency might be at work, and this prompts us to investigate further. But the fact that the tendency might be causally implicated in an event or events, means the tendency and the events are radically different things.

This interpretation of tendency does not refer to the outcomes of something, but to the something itself. To continue with the meta-phor, we might say that the tendency is 'attached' not to the events, but to the structures, institutions, mechanisms, rules, conventions, resources, (non-human) powers, etc. that constitute the domain crit-ical realists refer to as the 'deep'. For critical realists, the term 'ten-dency' refers to the *force* that caused the outcome or result and most definitely not to the outcome or result itself. Metaphorically speaking, a force drives, propels, pushes, thrusts, asserts pressure and so on. This can be sketched by adding 'depth' to the previous diagram, illus-trating the 'layered' (critical realist) ontology (see Table 6.2).

Now that we have a grasp of the critical realist interpretation of tendency, let us consider how tendencies manifest themselves in open

Table 6.2. *A 'layered' ontology with tendencies*

Domain	Entity	
Empirical	Experiences and observations	
Actual	Events and actions	
'Deep'	Structures, institutions, mechanisms, rules, conventions, resources, (non-human) powers, etc.	Law as tendency, where tendency is a power

systems. To write that some causal phenomenon has a tendency to *x*, does not mean that it will *x*. In an open system, one phenomenon does not exist in isolation from other phenomena, rather there is usually a multiplicity of phenomena each with their own tendencies. And these tendencies converge in some space-time location. The relation between a causal phenomenon and its tendency might be characterised as follows. The phenomenon does not always bring about certain effects, but it tends to. Hence it acts transfactually. Phenomena continue to causally govern the flux of events, irrespective of the conditions under which they are said to operate. We do not say of a transfactually acting causal phenomenon that it would bring about certain events if certain conditions prevail, or it would bring about certain events *ceteris paribus*. Rather, we would say that the causal phenomenon tends to bring about certain events, period. Causal phenomena continue to govern the flux of events irrespective of any events that ensue. A transfactually acting causal phenomenon does not depend for its causal powers upon the patterns of events that it generates: it continues to govern events, whether the ensuing events are constantly or non-constantly conjoined.

We can, of course, think of causal phenomena as configurations (and sub-configurations) that generate tendencies and these tendencies can counteract, and augment, one another in complex ways. The sub-configuration that constitutes a workforce with the tendency to resist control, co-exists simultaneously with the sub-configuration that constitutes a management team with the tendency to assert control. The outcome, however, depends upon the relative strengths of the tendencies. Notice, then, that it is *the causal configuration as a totality, and not any of its individual components that generates the powers and, therefore, the tendencies the causal configuration has.*

Let us consider this in more depth by imagining that we wanted to investigate a series of activities that are highly inter-related, such as: how the causal configuration like a workforce creates value; how skill levels are established; or how the workforce is controlled. Each of these processes is governed by different sub-configurations with their own tendencies. We could, in all probability, identify various sub-configurations that generate tendencies: to de-skill and up-skill the workforce; decrease and increase value creation; increase and decrease levels of direct employment; increase control of the workforce; and for the workforce to resist control. These tendencies can counteract, and augment, one another in complex ways. A few examples should suffice.

Tendencies to *de-skill* the workforce counteract tendencies to *up-skill* the workforce, yet both can be going on simultaneously within the same organisation. Tendencies to up-skill the workforce may augment tendencies to increase value creation, yet value creation could still decline because of the negative influence of other tendencies such as those arising from outsourcing. Tendencies to increase value creation may be counteracted by tendencies to decrease the workforce via downsizing. Tendencies to increase control of the workforce may augment tendencies to increase value creation, or may counteract the latter if, for example, the chosen mechanisms of control lead to dissatisfaction and even increased resistance.

Because in open systems like this there are so many possible permutations, (and in reality there are, of course, many, many more), predicting (inductively) what event or events will follow from a change in another event or events will be difficult, if not impossible. This is, however, not a council for despair. What is difficult, but *not* impossible, is identifying the tendencies and counter-tendencies, and explaining and making judgments as to which we think are likely to be dominant over some relatively restricted spatio-temporal space. It is, then, an empirical (not a meta-theoretical) question to discover which of these tendencies are actualised at any point in time. Indeed, we suggest that HR managers and trade union negotiators have little option but to do this all the time (which does not mean they get it right all the time) and something like this probably motivates many researchers on the HRM–P link – although their commitment to scientism prevents them from framing matters in this way.

Let us bring the concepts of structures, institutions, mechanisms, agencies, powers, tendencies and generative ensemble together. The workplace can be gainfully re-described as a causal configuration, that is, a complex entity where a totality of structures, institutions, mechanisms, human and non-human powers generate tendencies and counter-tendencies. Workers interact with other workers and managers (agent–agent interactions) and with a range of social structures (agent–structure interactions) – and, of course, with the material world (agent–material interactions). This is indeed a complex web of interactions. In agent–agent interaction workers and their powers interact with other workers and their powers. Managers and their powers interact with other managers and their powers. Workers and their powers interact with managers and their powers. Depending upon the nature of the interaction with other agents these powers may remain unaffected, remain unexercised, become actualised, become modified in the sense that the power is enhanced, or retarded. Powers in this sense might refer to the people–people relationships that generate a tendency towards improved (or otherwise) performance. In the agent–structure interactions workers and their powers interact with social structures and mechanisms such as HRM practices. Managers and their powers interact with (slightly or very) different social structures and mechanisms. Depending upon the nature of the interaction with social structures and mechanisms these human powers may remain unaffected, remain unexercised, become actualised, become modified in the sense that the power is enhanced, or retarded. Powers in this sense might refer to the people–organisation relationships that generate a tendency towards improved (or otherwise) performance. This complex configuration of structures and mechanisms, human and non-human powers, generates tendencies to increase organisational performance, and counter-tendencies to decrease performance.

We will end up treating this complex configuration as a black box, until and unless we arrive at an explanation of how its various components work and interact. It is time to see what we mean by explanation, and its close relative, causality.

Causality and explanation

We share with Lipton (1993: 33, emphasis added) the thesis that to 'explain a phenomenon is to *give information on the phenomenon's causal history*', but must stress that what is meant by 'causal history', what is meant by 'explanation' and how causality and explanation articulate with one another need some extremely careful unpacking.

It is possible to identify two conceptions of causality, which we call *thin* and *thick causality*.[15] It is also possible to identify two conceptions of explanation which, to keep the terminology consistent, we call *thin* and *thick explanation*. It is, furthermore, possible to 'map', as it were, the two conceptions of explanation to the two conceptions of causality. *Thin causality* maps onto *thin* explanation and *thick causality* maps onto *thick explanation*. Diagrammatically:

Thin causality $\longleftrightarrow$ Thin explanation
Thick causality $\longleftrightarrow$ Thick explanation

For ease of exposition, we explicate this with examples from the physical world first, and then introduce examples from HRM.

Thin causality refers to a situation where the cause of an event is assumed to be the event(s) that preceded it. The cause of the lamp's illumination, for example, is a flicking of the light switch.

Thick causality refers to a situation where the cause of an event is not assumed to be the event(s) that preceded it, but rather is the wider conflux of interacting causal phenomena. The cause of the lamp's illumination, for example, is the nature of the glass, the gas, the filament, the wire, the switch, the plug, the electricity, as well as the finger that flicked the switch.

It is extremely important to note that thin causality does not become thick causality simply by adding more causal factors into the analysis, which would, for example, mean simply extending the regression equation by adding more independent variables. Now let us map these two conceptions of causality to two types of explanation.

Thin causality and thin explanation. Giving a causal history, or account, of a phenomenon, and hence explaining it, could be interpreted to mean giving information about the event(s) that preceded the phenomena. That is, explanation could be based upon thin causality. If and when causality is reduced to thin causality, then explanation is reduced merely to giving information about a succession of events and becomes, thereby, thin. The explanation of the lamp's illumination simply requires information to the effect that 'a finger flicked a switch'. Any further information about the finger, the switch, or anything else, adds no more information than is necessary and is, therefore, superfluous. If this information can be said to constitute an explanation at all, then it is a very *thin* one: indeed most of us would not even recognise this as a bona fide explanation, as it would simply leave us asking: Why? It would be a curious 'explanation' indeed that left us with little or no *understanding* of the phenomena it purported to explain. Interestingly, many practising HR professionals tell us they are inclined to agree with us – as we will see in the final chapters.

Thick causality and thick explanation. Giving a causal history of a phenomenon, and hence explaining it, could be interpreted to mean giving information about the underlying mechanisms and structures, along with (if we are dealing with social phenomena) the human agency that reproduces and transforms these mechanisms and structures. That is, explanation could be based upon thick causality.[16] If and when causality is thick, then explanation cannot be reduced merely to giving information about a succession of events but rather requires information about the wider conflux of interacting causal phenomena beyond that captured even by sophisticated techniques utilised in the multiple analysis of variance (MANOVA). Information about the nature of the glass, the gas, the filament, the wire, the switch, the plug, the electricity, as well as the finger that flicked the switch, all add to the richness of the explanation and are, therefore, not superfluous but absolutely necessary. There is little doubt that most of us would recognise this information immediately as constituting a very rich, or thick, explanation as it would (at the very least) go some way to answering the question: why? This explanation would deliver some *understanding* of the phenomena it is purported to explain. To 'thickly' explain is to provide an understanding. Once again, as we will see in the final chapters, many practising HR professionals tell us they are inclined to agree with us.

Let us now turn to the social world, and consider thin and thick explanations, and thin and thick conceptions of causality, via the example of an increase in productivity following the introduction of a typical HRM practice: team working.

If and when causality is presumed to be the thin version, then explanation is thin because it is reduced merely to giving information about a succession of events. The explanation of the increase in productivity requires no more than information about the prior event, namely that '*team working was introduced*'. Any further information adds no more information than is necessary to establish thin causality, and is, therefore, superfluous. Thick explanation might be nice, in some sense, but it is no more than window dressing. If this information can be said to constitute an explanation at all, then it is a very thin one.

Notice that thin explanation lacks practical impact. An HR manager or trade union negotiator, offered as an explanation of an increase in productivity the statement 'team working was introduced', would not be in a position to act upon this information. Indeed, they would require an awful lot more information about team working before introducing, or accepting the introduction of, this practice in their company. Notice too that thin explanation and thin causality are presupposed in functional relations or regression equation. Recall Laursen's regression equation:

$$A_i = a_s \text{ SECT}_i + {}_s \text{SIZE}_i + u_s \text{ LINK}_i + h_s \text{ HRMS}_i + e_{ij}$$

Ignoring the control variables, A_i denotes the firms' ability to innovate and HRMS_i is one combined independent variable expressing the HRM practices associated with: interdisciplinary working groups [TEAM 1]; quality circles [TEAM 2]; planned job rotation [TEAM 3]; integration of functions (e.g. sales, production/services, finance) [TEAM 4]; delegation of responsibility [DRESP]; performance-related pay [PPAY]. As we saw in Chapter 4, when a functional relation is used in social science, it either implies causality or it is otiose. The conception of causality implied here is, of course, thin because the functional relation can be interpreted to read: 'Whenever TEAM 1, TEAM 2, TEAM 3, TEAM 4, DRESP and PPAY, then A'. Moreover, if we asked: 'What explains the firm's ability to innovate?', the only answer available would be an 'explanation' that ran: 'because interdisciplinary working groups, quality circles, planned job rotation, integration of functions, delegation of responsibility and performance related pay were introduced'.

If and when causality is *thick*, by contrast, then explanation is irreducible merely to giving information about a succession of events. A thick explanation of the increase in productivity requires two kinds of information. First, a thick explanation requires what we might call *hermeneutic* information. That is, information relating to a range of human cognitive activities such as understanding, intention, purpose, meaning, interpretation, reasons and so on – which we refer to under the umbrella-term understanding – borrowed from the *verstehen* tradition in sociology. Hermeneutics is the discipline concerned with phenomena like these. Human actions are, typically, the result of human intention, and so intentions are causes – actually, they are, in the Aristotelian lexicon, *final* causes. An action is not merely a behaviourist or mechanical response to an emotional or mental state, as it is in the case of Pavlov's dog; nor indeed is it the equally mechanical utility maximising response as in the case of *homo economicus*. An action is a response to an intention and an intention is a final cause. We do not, however, know what the cause of the action is, we do not understand it, until we know the intention that underlies it, that is, until we know *why* the actor did what s/he did. If, to explain an action is to give causal account of it, and to give a causal account is to give (amongst other things) a final causal account, then to explain an action is to give an account of *why* the actor did what s/he did. If and when we can do this, we can understand the action. Notice that gaining access to this kind of hermeneutic information is impossible via the quantitative, empirical and statistical techniques used in empirical research on the HRM–P link. As a consequence, this research cannot provide the hermeneutic information necessary for a thick explanation.

Second, a thick explanation requires information about a significant (but not infinite) set of interacting causal phenomena through which agents initiate this action. This might, for example, include information on: the social, political, economic and spatial environment of the industry and/or the firm; the industrial relations system; the composition of the team; the experiences and wishes of individuals comprising the team; the nature of the new jobs, tasks and skills (if any); the relationship between team members, the line managers and corporate strategy; the nature of control in the firm; the nature of any synergies (or dis-synergies) created by the interaction of these causal phenomena and so on.[17]

Clearly, this list is not exhaustive and, furthermore, each of these causal factors could be broken down into their component parts, as we try to provide more detailed information.[18] All this hermeneutic and other information adds to our understanding, adds to the richness of the explanation and is, therefore, not superfluous but absolutely necessary. There is little doubt that most of us would recognise this information immediately as constituting a thick explanation because it would (at least to some degree) answer the question: why?

Moreover, thick explanation has practical impact, but we will return to this below.

Causality, explanation and scientism: a digression

The damage done to scientism's aetiology by the thin conception of causality is almost impossible to overstate. Now that we have a better grasp of aetiology, taking some time to unpack this thin conception will deepen the criticism we discussed in previous chapters.

Thin causality can, but thick causality *cannot*, be accommodated within scientism, nor within the statistical techniques such as regression analysis, partly because the inherently qualitative, complex, multidimensional and often hermeneutic nature of the phenomena in operation in the workplace cannot be (meaningfully) quantified. There are, however, even more fundamental reasons for this, related to the ontology of powers and capacities.

Whilst we may (or may not) see the effects of powers, the powers themselves are impossible to observe directly. This is not usually a problem. Although we cannot directly observe a bicycle's causal power to transport its rider, we can, and do, infer this power from a knowledge of the components that constitute the bicycle as a causal configuration. Moreover, this power may exist unactualised, as in the case when the bicycle lies in the garden shed. Most people would probably reject the idea that the bicycle does not have this causal power simply because we could not observe it being actualised.

As we have already noted, a work-team, for example, may be usefully conceived of as a causal configuration with capacities of powers, and in open systems this almost certainly generates event *irregularity*. A work-team may possess capacities or powers for things like creative, imaginative, ingenious, self-motivated and self-directed action. Any such powers a work-team possesses are impossible to observe directly. This need not be a problem: although we cannot directly observe the work-team's causal powers, we consider it entirely possible for us, as social scientists, to infer these powers from a knowledge of the components that constitute the work-team as a causal configuration. Indeed, this is what many researchers come close to doing when they engage in in-depth ethnographic research, despite the fact that they do not make use of the critical realist terminology – as Ackroyd and Fleetwood (2000) point out, many social scientists appear to have been operating with something like a critical realist meta-theory for well over a century, despite the fact they do not use its terminology.

Moreover, work-teams' powers can exist unexercised for example, if the work-team is engaged in some kind of industrial action such as a go-slow. Furthermore, even if these work-teams' powers are exercised, other powers generated by other causal mechanisms and structures, may intervene, possibly even cancelling out the initial work-teams' powers. An exercised power with its effects being cancelled out would never manifest itself empirically, and so could not become part of the data, nor find its way into a regression analysis.

The root cause of this problem lies in the ontology of powers. Let us once again consider Hume for his clarity and sophistication: 'The distinction, which we often make betwixt *power* and the *exercise* of it, is equally without foundation' (Hume 1888 and 1978: 171). Meikle elaborates upon the point, writing that for the Humean: 'There is no distinction to be drawn between a capacity [or power] and its exercise ... To say that something can do something – that is, that it has a capacity [or power] to do it – is just to say that it does do it' (Meikle 1985: 114). For the Humean, then, if something does not do what it allegedly has the power to do, then we have no grounds for the allegation, and should withdraw it. Once causality is presumed based upon, and exhausted by, event regularities, the consistent (as opposed to the inconsistent) advocate of scientism faces a dilemma: s/he must either reject the notion of powers; or reject the notion of thin causality. Whilst we doubt that empirical researchers *would* dismiss a work-team's powers of creative, imaginative, ingenious, self-motivated and self-directed action because they could not observe them being exercised, they *should* dismiss them if they wanted to be consistent with their meta-theoretical roots.

Notice also that adopting a thin notion of causality invites the well-known problem of reverse causality or simultaneity (see Chapter 4) because the information required is limited to events and their regularities. Even if we succeed in demonstrating, statistically, that event X did precede Y in time, the victory would be pyrrhic as we would then run into the 'after, therefore, because of' fallacy. Indeed, we strongly suspect that the problem of reverse causality is never going to be resolved as long as empirical researchers remain committed to thin causality which, as we have been at pains to point out, is a key component in the meta-theory of scientism. Seeking thick causality, by contrast, minimises problems of reverse causality, in part because it demands that we uncover and explain the causal mechanisms, structures and processes in operation, and the tendencies they generate – which does not mean this is easy. If and when we come to know this, we will know which direction causality is running.

From ontology to the causal-explanatory method[19]

As we saw above, when concerned with investigating aspects of the social world, such as HRM practices and organisational performance, critical realists *do not* start with an 'off the shelf toolbox', such as that available from scientism – i.e. atomistic ontology of observed events, epistemology of event regularities, thin causality, deductive method, closed systems and the usual quantitative, empirical and statistical research techniques. Instead, they start with social ontology and then design meta-theoretical tools appropriate to dealing with the way the world is. If it transpires that the social world, or important parts of it at least, is or are inherently qualitative, incapable of being (meaningfully) measured and, therefore, not amenable to the usual empirical, statistical research techniques, then so be it: critical realists advocate using other research techniques, not ploughing on regardless because this or that set of techniques are commonly used, or because they just happen to be the ones we learned in graduate school. Critical realists end up, then, with a set of meta-theoretical concepts and research techniques that, because they were designed with the phenomena in mind, at the very least hold out the possibility of uncovering and explaining the tendencies generated by the phenomena under investigation: in this case the workplace HRM practices.

The *method* advocated by critical realists[20] is referred to as *causal-explanatory* because its objective is to *explain* and it explains in terms of providing a *causal* account. On this account, explanation means *thick explanation* (as we will see in a moment); explanation not prediction is central; explanatory power not predictive power is the criteria used to evaluate theory; and explanation is not confused or conflated with prediction. Harney and Dundon (2006: 53) appear to have arrived at a similar conclusion without explicitly mentioning critical realism. They write: 'Given that causality cannot be attributed in a linear fashion within such a complex system, the focus on operationalising the framework was not prediction, but rather understanding what is contextually unique and why it is so'. The causal-explanatory method can be used with a particular research technique, known as 'contrastive explanation' (Lawson 2003: Chapter 4). Let us consider what this entails.

Contrastive explanation

Contrastive explanation turns on the existence of rough and ready, but not law-like, event regularities. We referred to them in Chapter 4 as 'demi-regularities'. The existence of demi-regularities reflects the fact that, although the social world is open, and strict event regularities are rare, there are occasions where a particular mechanism exerts a sufficiently powerful impact on the system that its operation results in demi-regularities. It might, for example, be the case that a demi-regularity exists in the form of the association between HRM practices and organisational performance; the evidence does not support the existence of a law-like regularity, but it might suggest there is some regularity, at least enough to encourage researchers to probe a little deeper and try to explain the association. *Contrastive* demi-regularities can arise in situations where two similar states of affairs exist that provide a useful contrast. We sometimes come across two (or more) phenomena with similar characteristics and histories and, moreover, we know that they both tend to generate similar outcomes. Sometimes, however, we are surprised to find that the outcomes differ. The existence of contrastive demi-regularities provides prima facie evidence that there is an unidentified causal mechanism(s) at work, whose influence accounts for the unexpected contrast between the two outcomes under investigation. Demi-regularities assist researchers both by alerting them to the existence of situations where there is something to be explained and by directing their activities in a fruitful way. What critical realists call contrast explanations, then, are explanations of contrastive demi-regularities.

Like all bona fide explanations, contrast explanations seek answers to 'Why?' questions, but the questions asked in contrast explanations have a particular twist. Instead of asking 'Why this', contrastive explanations ask 'Why *this* rather than *that*' or, more formally, 'Why p rather than q?'. In this case, p is the fact to be explained, and q is the foil, the alternative. Posing questions in this way sets us off in the direction of seeking the particular causal mechanism(s) responsible for the differential outcomes. Our efforts are made easier by the fact the two situations are similar, and this should help us to spot the mechanism that is causing the surprising difference. Let us see how this might be useful for research on the HRM–P link.

Suppose we find evidence of demi-regularities suggesting that many (but not all) firms introducing certain bundles of HRM practices experience improved organisational performance. What we need is to *explain* why some firms use bundles of HRM practices and experience improved performance whilst others do not. To do this, we might proceed as follows.

When designing the initial stages of the research, we seek out 'similar' firms. By 'similar' we mean, for example, firms of a similar size, producing a similar product, producing for a similar market, similarly financed, interacting with similar labour markets and so on. This is by no means easy, and it requires judgment about just what is and is not 'similar'. But in principal, there is no reason why this cannot be done. Even where we have reason to believe there may be differences in important areas, we can always 'keep an eye on them', as it were, and return to them later in the analysis when we might be in a better position to see how important the differences are, and whether they are so serious as to invalidate the rest of the analysis.

Suppose we manage to find (let us say) two similar firms. We then need to consider their relative performance, and the HRM systems they have in place. The HRM systems can be understood as being completely different, identical or somewhere in between. At this stage, we are only interested in broad similarities as we will return to the HRM systems in the next phase of the analysis. Relative performance might be easiest to grasp when it refers to outputs that are proximal to the HRM system because the 'farther away', as it were, the effect is from the cause, the more other causal influences are likely to be at work – and bear in mind we are always operating in open systems. Relative performance might be *measured* using descriptive statistics such as productivity levels, absence rates and so on; or it might be *understood* using more qualitative research techniques. This might sound strange given that we have argued against the quantification of inherently qualitative, complex, multidimensional and hermeneutic phenomena. We have three responses. First, being anti-empiricist (which we are) is not the same as being anti-empirical data (which we are not). There is no necessary problem with counting what can *legitimately* be counted, as long as we are aware of the dangers we face in quantification and simply desist when our measures start to become meaningless. Counting the number of days staff have off due to sickness, for example, can *suggest* (although closer analysis might actually show this 'suggestion' is mistaken) that something is going on, even if it does not *explain* what is going on. Second, there is no need to restrict the analysis of performance to that which can be measured. Our suspicion is that performance is rather like the proverbial baby elephant: difficult to describe, but you know one when you see one. We might simply have to invent more sophisticated, non-quantitative ways of finding out whether performance is good, bad or indifferent. Bear in mind, the aim of ascertaining relative performance is not the end of the analysis; it is the starting point of the explanation; it provides the phenomenon to be explained. All that we may need is an ordinal measure, that is, a ranking so we can say one firm performs better than another. Third, once we are aware of the problems involved in the quantification of inherently qualitative, complex, multidimensional and hermeneutic phenomena, the usual box of quantitative, empirical and statistical tools should no longer blind us into rejecting other non-quantitative ways of ascertaining relative performance.

Suppose we manage to satisfy ourselves that firm X performs better than firm Y. The question now is: why? Here we have to 'open the black box' and scrutinise the HRM systems. This is not just a matter of counting the number of HRM practices in place; it is also a question of considering the quality of the practices. As Purcell and Hutchinson (2007) observe, much empirical research merely counts whether a firm has (or does not have), say, teamworking, but does not enquire into whether or not the work-teams in place are any good. Research using contrastive explanation *must* consider qualitative aspects to HRM systems, despite the fact that this will almost certainly require judgment. This is where the genuine social science (as opposed to mere scientism) gets going.

The attempt to seek contrastive explanation, then, has encouraged us to pose a fine-tuned, and manageable research question: why does firm X's HRM system perform better than firm Y's? We say it is 'fine tuned and manageable' in the sense that it has kept the causal history within manageable proportions; we are not trying to find every single cause of organisational performance. Researchers are encouraged to concentrate their attention upon the narrowed-down set of HRM practices that might account for the observed contrast in performance. Answering the above question is clearly not straightforward and will necessarily involve a whole range of qualitative research techniques. But there is no a priori reason why researchers should not be able to compare and contrast different aspects of two HRM systems to ascertain which one works better than the other and then explain why. Indeed, this should be the real task of research into the influence of HRM systems on performance.

Two types of (thick) explanation and two modes of inference

What we seek to explain often depends upon the knowledge we currently have and, therefore, the knowledge we seek. This creates a need for two types of explanation: *theoretical* and *applied*. There are also *two modes of inference: retroduction* and *retrodiction*. It is possible to 'map', as it were, the two notions of explanation onto the two modes of inference. Diagrammatically:

theoretical explanation ⟷ retroduction
   applied explanation ⟷ retrodiction

Before we expand upon these two types of explanation, however, let us clarify the meaning of a *mode of inference*. A mode of inference refers to a procedure for deriving claims about one thing, from claims about another thing: claims about Q from claims about P. Most readers will already be aware of two commonly used modes of inference, *deduction and induction*, but are unlikely to be familiar with other modes such as *retroduction* and *retrodiction*.[21]

When we use *deduction*, we move *from the general to the particular*, that is, from claims about P in general to claims about particular instances of Q. To use the well-worn example, we might move from claims that 'all ravens are black' to the claim that 'the next raven observed will be black'. The deductive mode of inference is most readily seen in what we referred to in the last chapter as 'toy' theories. A set of axioms, typically about the behaviour of some maximising agent, are buttressed by a set of assumptions which narrow down the range of possible agential responses. A change in the initial conditions is then introduced and a conclusion is deduced in terms of how this agent will respond.

As we saw in Chapter 5, when we use *induction*, we move *from the particular to the general*, that is, from claims about many particular instances of *P* to claims about *Q*. We might move from claims that 'all ravens thus far observed are black', to the claim that 'all ravens are black'. Researchers seek a statistical association between changes in the magnitude of a set of 'explanatory' variables (quantified events) measuring HRM practices $X_1, X_2...X_n$, and changes in the magnitude of a set of variables measuring organisational performance, *Y*. The quantitative, empirical and statistical association is then used to induce the conclusion that firms who introduce practices $X_1, X_2...X_n$, experience an increase in *Y*.

Critical realists, in complete contrast, make use of a different mode of inference: *retroduction*, and close relative *retrodiction* – which does not, of course mean we abandon deductive logic, without which it would be difficult if not impossible to form coherent arguments or write coherent sentences.

Retroduction

Lawson neatly highlights the difference between modes of inference. Retroduction consists:

in the movement, on the basis of analogy and metaphor amongst other things, from a conception of some phenomenon of interest to a conception of some totally different type of thing, mechanism, structure or condition that, at least in part, is responsible for the given phenomenon. If deduction is illustrated by the move from the general claim that 'all ravens are black' to the particular inference that the next one seen will be black, and induction by the move from the particular observation of numerous black ravens to the general claim that 'all ravens are black', retroductive or abductive reasoning is indicated by a move from the observation of numerous black ravens to a theory of a mechanism intrinsic ... to ravens which disposes them to be black. (Lawson 1997: 24)[22]

We engage in retroduction when we are relatively ignorant about the mechanisms in operation that are causing the phenomena under investigation. Because retroduction usually operates with cutting-edge science, it usually involves a stage similar to Popper's hypothetical conjecture. Because there is no existing theory to act as a guide, we must take a voyage of discovery, we must make hypothetical conjectures, requiring imagination, and the use of analogy and metaphor – which we will refer to as the 'scientific imagination' (see Lewis 1999). The scientific imagination is not predicated on total ignorance, and does require knowledge, but knowledge in the form of theories, observations and other knowledge, often *drawn from other disciplines*, to inform our conjectures, analogies and metaphors. Retroduction usually involves asking a specific kind of question: 'what thing, if it existed, might account for the existence of P?'. Retroduction might result in the identification of Q as the thing in question. We would say we have retroduced from phenomenon P to phenomenon Q. This might sound complicated, but in fact, it is very straightforward: indeed, we probably make use of retroduction all the time in our daily lives. For example, when someone does not answer the doorbell, we may infer that they are not at home because this best explains the knowledge we have, about the person failing to appear at the door.[23] We would have retroduced the causal mechanism (not being at home) as the best of several explanations of the doorbell remaining unanswered.

Retrodiction

There are times, however, when we are not ignorant, but relatively knowledgeable of the mechanisms in operation that are causing the phenomena under investigation, and we do not have to make use of the scientific imagination. In this case, we use existing theories, observations, claims and other knowledge to *retrodict*, that is, make claims about the way these mechanisms tend to operate perhaps in combination with other mechanisms, and perhaps in important contexts, to bring about Q. We use what we *do* know to explain what we *do not* know. When someone does not answer the doorbell, we use what we rather playfully refer to as the established 'non-appearance at the door because not at home' theory along with the knowledge that Mrs Smith is not deaf, and that her doorbell is in working order, to retrodict the claim that Mrs Smith does not answer the doorbell because she is not at home. Notice that our retrodiction would have eliminated the possibility that she did not answer because her doorbell is broken or that she is deaf, or suchlike. We would have eliminated alternatives such as the 'non-appearance at the door because of broken doorbell' theory and the 'non-appearance at the door because deaf' theory.

Now that we understand the two modes of inference favoured by critical realists, retroduction and retrodiction, we can combine them with two types of (thick) explanation: theoretical and applied.

Theoretical explanation

We engage in *theoretical* explanation when we are relatively ignorant of the causal mechanisms underlying phenomenon *P*, and our aim is to *retroduce* these causal mechanisms, to discover what they might be. In effect, we use what we *do* know (in the form of theories, observations and knowledge, possibly from related areas or even other disciplines that inform our conjectures, analogies and metaphors) to explain what we *do not* know. We attempt to answer the following question: why does *P* tend to cause *Q*? We have a theoretical explanation when we can say: theory *T* explains why *P* tends to cause *Q*. Notice that scientism in general, and empirical research on the HRM–P link, does not have the conceptual apparatus to get anywhere near formulating statements like this.

Applied explanation

We engage in *applied* explanation when we are relatively knowledgeable about the causal mechanisms underlying phenomenon *P*. Our aim is to use existing theories, observations and other knowledge from various sources to *retrodict* the way these mechanisms will tend to operate in some new context. We use what we *do* know to explain what we *do not* know. We attempt to answer the following question. If we know that *P* tends to cause *Q*, what happens if *P* occurs in context *C*? We have an applied explanation when we can say: theory *T*, observations *O* and other knowledge *K*, explain why *P* will (or will not) tend to cause *Q* in context *C*. Applied explanation can be prescriptive: it can tell us what to do to bring about a desired outcome.

Whilst it is possible that some empirical researchers on the HRM–P link may have heard of the retroduction, retrodiction, theoretical and applied explanations, there are no references to them in the HRM–P literature. Moreover, as we have established, induction is the mode of inference underlying scientism and the qualitative, empirical and statistical techniques it sponsors. Let us, for a moment, engage in a thought experiment. Let us accept critical realist meta-theory and use its concepts to investigate the relationship between HRM practices and organisational performance, what would the endeavour look like?

Theoretical explanation and the HRM–P link

We would engage in theoretical explanation when we have some initial reason to suspect that HRM practices *tend* to cause increased performance, but are relatively ignorant of which HRM practices they might be and *why* they might have this tendency. Our aim would be to *retroduce* the HRM practices that tend to cause increased performance. If and when we successfully retroduced the right HRM practices, we would be relatively knowledgeable *that* these HRM practices tend to cause increased performance; we would have eliminated those HRM practices that *do not* have this tendency; and, crucially, we would know *why* these HRM practices have these *tendencies*.

This last point is important and distances critical realism from what we described in Chapter 3 as measurement without theory and illicit justification. That is, retroduction is not an exercise in data-mining. It does not amount to simply selecting a set of convenient or oft-cited variables, unguided by any real theory, and then trying to see if there is a statistical association between them. Nor does it involve using the ensuing results both to generate a theory and attempt to justify that theory. If, for example, we retroduced to a specific integrated bundle of HRM practices that we had reason to believe tend to cause increased organisational performance, we would have some kind of theory to explain this claim, and this theory would then be open to empirical validation. We would have a theoretical explanation, then, when we could say: theories *T*, *U* and *V* explain why, in the open system that is the workplace, this specified bundle of integrated HRM practices tends to cause increased organisational performance.

Applied explanation and the HRM–P link

We would engage in applied explanation when we are relatively knowledgeable about an identified bundle of HRM practices that tends to cause increased performance; when we know why this is the case; and when we had eliminated those practices that do not contribute to this tendency. Our aim would be to use existing theories, observations and other knowledge of the way these practices operate in *open systems*, to *retrodict* the way they will tend to operate in some new context. This means, for example, ascertaining the co-tendencies in the form of synergies arising from appropriate horizontal alignment with other HRM practices, and the counter-tendencies in the form of dis-synergies arising from inappropriate horizontal alignment. To be sure, because we would be dealing with an open system, this would also mean ascertaining the tendencies and counter-tendencies arising not only from HRM practices, but from other working and management practices and a range of other causal mechanisms that we recognise as exerting an influence on organisational performance. Which mechanisms and tendencies we would include in the analysis; what we would consider to be a tendency and a counter-tendency; and the relative strengths of these tendencies to override other counter-tendencies, would all be matters relating to the design of the research, and involve abstraction, judgment and empirical verification. We would have an applied explanation when we could say: theories T and W, observations N and O, and other knowledge K, explain why, in the open system that is the workplace, this specified bundle of integrated HRM practices will tend to cause increased organisational performance in this specific firm.

Some important observations

Do empirical researchers on the HRM–P link engage in theoretical or applied explanation? In one sense, because they do not explicitly make use of retroduction, retrodiction, theoretical and applied explanations, and because they are committed to induction, we could simply answer in the negative. But this would foreclose the discussion before some interesting conclusions could be drawn. We suspect empirical researchers on the HRM–P link have something like theoretical explanation in mind as they are, clearly, interested questions like: 'Do HRM practices X_1, X_2...X_n, tend to cause increases in organisational performance, Y'? Moreover, despite the limitations of their own meta-theory, they are also interested in knowing *why* this is the case. Yet they cannot answer questions such as: '*Why* do HRM practices X_1, X_2,...X_n, tend to cause increases in organisational performance, Y' because they do not have the sophisticated concepts of tendency and so are forced to operate with thin causality. Moreover, if empirical researchers were aware of retroduction as an alternative mode of inference, we suspect many would be happy to make use of it, and many may already believe they use something like it anyway.

Empirical researchers on the HRM–P link would like to engage in applied explanation as they would like to answer questions like the following: if we know that HRM practices X_1, X_2,...X_n, tends to cause Q, what happens if P occurs in context C? Unfortunately, the under-theorised nature of the research means that there is no appropriate theory underpinning the empirical research on the HRM–P link. Researchers are not in a position to say: theory T, observations O and other knowledge K, explain why X_1, X_2,...X_n, will (or will not) tend to cause increased performance in context C.

Anyone, critical realist or otherwise, engaging in retroduction and/or retrodiction might, of course, be mistaken. Unfortunately there is no infallible mode of inference and we might be just as mistaken using deduction and induction. We have, therefore, nothing to lose by engaging in retroduction and/or retrodiction and can only gain. The recognition of fallibility means that any claims that are retroduced and/or retrodicted, need to be verified empirically. The term 'verified empirically' is a far looser notion than the scientistic notion of hypothesis testing via quantitative techniques – but we hope to have convinced the reader by now that scientism is not a credible way to conduct social science, and so again, we have nothing to lose by abandoning such techniques, and can only gain. To verify claims empirically, simply means to check them out against reality using whatever means available. Critical realists are fairly permissive epistemologists, tending not to prescribe which research technique or techniques should be used, but favour designing the techniques to the phenomena under investigation.[24]

Even if we had an (applied) explanation of why some bundle of HRM practices tends to cause increased organisational performance in some organisations, we cannot predict that they always will have this tendency on the basis that they always have – i.e. we cannot make inductive predictions. We are, however, no worse off because empirical research on the HRM–P link cannot make accurate predictions either due to the workplace being an open system. To be sure, we are actually better off because in order to generate an applied explanation, we would have had to retrodict, we would have had to discover *why* these HRM practices generate the tendencies they do and might be in a position to engage in what we call tendential prediction – which we elaborate upon below.

Generalisability

We are aware that the causal-explanatory method raises issues of generalisability. Whilst we think generalisability is a worthwhile goal, we wish to distance ourselves from scientism where generalisability is presumed to be based upon the formulating of law-like, and perhaps universal, statements resulting (presumably) from 'replicated instances of identical events' (Sayer 2000: 139). We also wish to distance ourselves from a great deal of postmodernism and poststructuralism, where any attempt to generalise beyond the parochial is not only (mis)understood as evidence of scientism (or positivism) at work, but is also treated as doomed from the outset (Johnson and Duberley 2000: Chapter 5).

Problems of generalisability are, however, no more acute for the causal-explanatory method than for methods rooted in scientism – although this is not widely recognised. There are several reasons for this, of which we mention just two. First, as Popper taught, the deductive method relies on induction, and induction cannot establish generalisability because of the fallacy of induction. Observing a thousand white swans does not prove that all swans are white. Observing a thousand firms using some bundle of HRM practices and experiencing an increase in organisational performance does not prove these HRM practices will always lead to increases in organisational performance. The best it can do is ascertain whether or not the claim is false, hence the notion of falsifiability. Some natural scientists[25] are able to make the general claim that 'all sticks immersed in water appear bent' not because they have carried out millions of experiments and found, via induction, a pattern between the appearance of being bent and being immersed in water. Nor on the grounds of falsification we might add. The general claim is possible because natural scientists have uncovered the mechanisms involved with light refraction and the way they operate, thus they can explain the phenomena. A million regressions showing a statistical association between HRM practices and increased organisational performance cannot provide an explanation of this and, on their own, cannot establish this association as general. A general claim would be possible only if social scientists could uncover the mechanisms involved with HRM practices and the way they operate and, thereby, could explain the phenomena. Falsification makes induction more plausible, but it does not alter the point that induction cannot provide explanatory power.[26]

Second, the failure of empirical research on the HRM–P link to inform practice leads us to doubt the generalisability of empirical research. If this were not in doubt, then HR managers could take a piece of research that studied (say) one thousand firms, perhaps drawn from a similar industry, introduce the specific HRM practices that were found to be statistically significant, align it with their corporate strategy, then sit back and wait for similar increases in performance. HR managers do not do this, and empirical researchers do not actually suggest they should. Yet if empirical research like this really was generalisable, then managers could do this. We are, then, no worse off vis-à-vis generalisability employing the causal-explanatory method, as opposed to the deductive method, and may even be better off.

Problems of generalisability are no less acute for those employing the causal-explanatory method than for those employing case studies or ethnographies, because these research techniques are often compatible with critical realist meta-theory. The difference is that the meta-theoretical sophistication of critical realism allows researchers who seek, for example, to take a more hermeneutic approach to HRM, to reject the received wisdom that regression analysis can generalise, but participant observation cannot. Generalisation is difficult for all research techniques, but if we are more reflexive about the meta-theory underlying our methodology, we might begin to see hitherto unseen strengths in the latter. Why might this be the case? Sayer makes the point well, writing that for critical realism:

Theory is no longer associated with generality in the sense of repeated series of events but with determining the nature of things or structures, discovering which characteristics are necessary consequences of their being those kinds of objects. Generality, in the sense of extent of occurrence, thus depends upon how common instances of the object are, and upon the circumstances or conditions in which objects exist, these determining whether the causal powers and liabilities of objects are activated, and with what effect. (Sayer 2000: 136)

Causal-explanation uses retroduction (not induction) to seek knowledge of the nature and typical ways of acting of phenomena – which does not mean this is an easy task. If and when we come to know the typical ways of acting of some phenomenon through uncovering the key mechanisms that constitute it and give it its powers, we can express these typical ways of acting as a tendency. If and when we have a causal explanation, then we have knowledge about what the phenomenon tends to do and, moreover, why it tends to do it. We are, therefore, in a position to know the tendencies of entities in this class of phenomena; and of phenomena characterised by these same key structures and mechanisms. From knowledge of the structures and mechanisms that constitute a successful team of employees, and the powers it possesses, for example, we are able to generalise and claim that certain entities (culture, gender, social poetics, mindset, personalities, human and social capital, etc.) in this team have a tendency to facilitate its enhanced performance. Correctly analysing one team will yield this knowledge; analysing a thousand more associations between these entities and team performance will, in and of itself, yield no more knowledge, even if it does satisfy the scientistic obsession with statistical significance. Verisimilitude as opposed to proof beyond all reasonable doubt will suffice; indeed, it has to (Tsoukas 2000).

The causal-explanatory method demands far more knowledge than that obtained from quantifying a set of events, reducing them to variables, carrying out (say) a regression analysis and concluding that some hypothesis is not falsified. True, being more 'knowledge-hungry' requires researchers using the causal-explanatory method to work far harder, but if and when it results in greater explanatory power, then the effort is worth it. Again we are no worse off vis-à-vis generalisability employing the causal-explanatory method, and may even be better off.

That said, there are two difficulties. First, knowing what the causal mechanisms and structures are, and how they operate to generate their tendency, is easy to say and difficult to do, but (something like) this is simply the challenge all social scientists accept. Second, knowing if the next entity we are investigating belongs to this same class of phenomena is also difficult to do. But it is not impossible. If it was impossible, then we would not be able to differentiate between (say) a workplace and a prison.

From causal-explanation to causal-explanatory account

Social scientists employ a method or methods to help refine a theory. Whilst the causal-explanatory method is no different, and helps refine what would normally be referred to as a theory, we wish to avoid the unwanted baggage that comes with the term 'theory' and so we refer to the causal-explanatory *account* – or just 'account' for short. We need, however, to be clear what this account can and cannot do. We saw in Chapter 4 that commitment to scientism (its ontology, epistemology, methodology and aetiology) and the quantitative, empirical, statistical techniques it sponsors, the failure to recognise the open systemic nature of the social world, the lack of meta-theoretical reflection, and the confusion and conflation of prediction and explanation, generate *theory that is merely a vehicle for delivering predictions and hypotheses in terms of regularities between events expressed as variables*. Whilst we clearly do not want to end up with a theory or account along these lines, anyone seeking an alternative runs into a very serious problem. This scientistic version of what a theory is, despite being ill-conceived, has become the benchmark against which all other theories or accounts are judged. If we were to offer an account that seeks to explain why some bundle of HRM practices tends to increase organisational performance, yet did *not* use the basic scientistic approach or the deductive method, and did *not* yield predictions in the form of hypotheses that were empirically tested, we would more than likely be accused of being poor researchers, and of failing to offer a theory. To reject the entire scientistic approach, as we do, is of course to refuse to be judged according to scientism's benchmark. This means we have to make clear what our alternative account looks like.

To obtain a clear picture of what our causal-explanatory account looks like, let us consider how we would go about constructing a causal account of commuting – an example more relevant to HRM will be offered below. We select this example because the point is to illustrate the nature of the account itself, not the specifics of the account, and this way we can make the point more forcefully. Commuters make the journey from home to the workplace. Whilst we know *that* they do this, we may not know *why* they are able to do this. To explain *why*, we need to uncover the causal phenomena that make this activity possible. Some form of case study designed specifically to identify the typical causal mechanisms and structures that facilitate a typical commuter would reveal typical commuters necessarily drawing upon a variety of physical structures and mechanisms such as: various kinds of pavements, roads, cycle-ways, bridges, tunnels, traffic signals, road markings, computer-controlled crossing systems and so on. An account of these activities would have to explain

(a) the powers possessed by commuters and (b) how commuters interact with these physical structures and mechanisms, noting how these structures and mechanisms are reproduced and/or transformed by this interaction. This account would identify the tendencies possessed by the causal configuration(s) of the transport system. If and when such an explanation was forthcoming, the account would be complete. We would have explained the typical physical structures and mechanisms drawn upon by the typical commuter successfully undertaking a typical journey from home to work. It is difficult to see how statistical analysis would yield knowledge that would contribute to such a causal account. Even if a statistical association could be found (say) between successful commutes as the dependent variable, and pavements, roads, cycle-ways, bridges, tunnels, traffic signals, road markings and computer-controlled crossing systems as independent or 'explanatory' variables, this would do no more than tell us *that* successful commuting requires the existence of these phenomena: it would not tell us *why*.

Now let us consider what would be involved in applying the causal-explanatory method to generate a causal-explanatory account of action in the workplace. In order to carry out the set of tasks associated with her job, a worker necessarily draws upon a variety of social structures, mechanisms, institutions, rules, resources, (non-human) powers and so on. Whilst we know *that* she does this, we may not know *why* this is possible. To explain *why*, we need to uncover the causal phenomena that make this activity possible. Some form of case study designed specifically to identify the causal structures (etc.) would reveal typical workers necessarily drawing upon a variety of social structures such as: the explicit rules laid out in the employment contract and tacit rules that constitute the psychological contract. An account of this activity would have to explain (1) the powers possessed by workers and (2) how workers interact with these social structures, noting how these structures are reproduced and/or transformed by this interaction. This account would identify the tendencies possessed by the causal configuration(s) that is the workplace. If and when such an explanation was forthcoming, the account would be complete. We would have explained the typical social structures drawn upon by the typical worker carrying out the set of tasks associated with her job. The workplace would no longer be just a black box. Note five important things.

First, even assuming qualitative, complex and multidimensional workplace phenomena could be meaningfully measured, it is difficult to see how statistical analysis would yield knowledge that would contribute to a causal-explanatory account. Suppose we found a statistical association between some work tasks, and the explicit rules laid out in the employment contract and tacit rules that constitute the psychological contract as independent or (mis-labelled) 'explanatory' variables. This association would do no more than tell us *that* these work tasks require the existence of employment contracts and psychological contracts; it would not tell us *why*.

Second, if and when an explanation is forthcoming, then we have uncovered and explained the typical structures and mechanisms drawn upon by the typical agent successfully undertaking a typical activity and the account would be complete. Because the clear and attainable objective, to explain, has been met, then we do not need to transpose this into a prediction and test it via the usual quantitative, empirical and statistical techniques. In an open system, accurate predictions are, typically, unattainable anyway.

Third, there is no suggestion that obtaining such an explanation is easy. In fact, most explanations that are worth pursuing in social science are extremely hard to come by. Critical realism is a meta-theory, and no meta-theory can do the actual empirical work necessary for generating explanations.

Fourth, the meta-theoretical apparatus of critical realism furnishes us with a clear idea of what a theory, or in our terminology an account, can, and should, do: it can, and should, *explain*.

Fifth, and of crucial importance, we are now in a position to move beyond scientism's understanding of a theory as a mere vehicle for delivering predictions and hypotheses in terms of regularities between events expressed as variables. The meta-theoretical apparatus of critical realism allows us to offer an alternative. *For critical realists, a theory or account is (minimally) a set of statements designed to support a causal-explanation.* Whilst this appears to be rather small beer, its importance is virtually impossible to overstate because, as we have shown, empirical research on the HRM–P link not only lacks theory, it lacks a notion of what a plausible theory should look like. Now that we have some idea of what a plausible theory looks like, we at least know what it is we should be trying to generate.

Causal-explanation and tendential prediction[27]

We hope by now to have advanced a plausible argument as to why prediction based upon induction is impossible in open social systems such as workplaces. No doubt there will be some who will simply ignore our meta-theoretical arguments and press on regardless, collecting better data, devising better estimating techniques and getting more computer power, all in the quest to make more accurate inductive predictions. Others might share some of our meta-theoretical reservations, yet in the end they too will press on with the quest to make more accurate inductive predictions on the grounds that prediction is necessary if we want to make practical or policy recommendations. Whilst this course of action is intellectually indefensible (the *desire* to inductively predict, no matter how laudable, cannot be transformed into the *ability* to inductively predict if the social world is an open system) we share the desire to make practical or policy recommendations. There is, however, a way out of this seeming dilemma. We can accept the critical realist meta-theory and the social ontology developed above, including the commitment to open systems, whilst making practical or policy recommendations. The starting point is explanation.

Explanation, and by this we mean thick, not thin, explanation, can guide practice; indeed, it is probably our only guide to practice in open systems. Let us use the meta-theoretical apparatus developed above to sketch how a tendential prediction might be developed in the case of research on the influence HRM practices might have on organisational performance. Note that nothing we are about to say implies that doing any of the following is easy – hence the rider 'to the extent we can...'. Note also that whilst this sketch will remain at a very high level of abstraction, the point is to illustrate how the meta-theoretical concepts of critical realism might be used in such an endeavour.

- *To the extent that we can* retroduce (using the scientific imagination) the various structures and mechanisms governing organisational performance, we can identify (1) the HRM practices, the relevant practices of corporate strategy, and the practices of relevant stakeholders that combine to constitute the causal configuration (the HRM system) governing organisational performance and (2) the workforce that enacts all these practices.

- To the extent that we can retrodict (using existing theories, observations and other knowledge) the various HRM, corporate and stakeholder practices we have just identified, we can explain the properties each of these practices possess when acted upon by these workers.
- To the extent we can retrodict the powers possessed by human beings, we can identify the key powers they bring with them into the workplace and, furthermore, identify those that are utilised by various practices in operation in the configuration, and those that are not. We can also use hermeneutic research techniques to explain the way agents interpret, and interact with, these structures and mechanisms, to form their agential projects.
- To the extent that we can identify and explain the properties each of the various HRM, corporate and stakeholder practices possess, we can explain how workers will be enabled and constrained by them, and explain some of the key agential projects. Using positioned-practices, rather than named individuals, we can explain how and why the agents engaged in practices such as working in teams, issuing instructions, carrying out evaluations, designing strategies, associated with given positions, will tend to act when confronted by constraints and enablements.
- To the extent that we can explain the properties of each of the various HRM, corporate and stakeholder practices, when acted upon by workers in specific positioned-practices, we can explain the tendencies generated by each practice. But practices and their tendencies do not exist in isolation, and neither can they simply be added and/or subtracted mechanically.
- To the extent that we can explain the tendencies each HRM practice, each corporate practice and each stakeholder practice generates, when acted upon by workers in specific positioned-practices, with agential projects, we can explain how these tendencies interact with one another. Clearly, this constitutes a complex tendential web, so for ease of exposition, let us abstract from stakeholder practices.
- Each HRM practice generates its own tendency. If the HRM practices that constitute the bundle are horizontally aligned or integrated then the tendencies mutually support one another, creating synergy – lack of integration in the HRM bundle causes the tendencies to conflict causing dis-synergy. To keep the example simple we assume that the HRM bundle is horizontally aligned.

- Each corporate strategy practice generates its own tendency, and we will assume for ease of exposition that the corporate strategy bundle is also aligned.
- But, now we have the tendencies generated by the HRM bundle, interacting with the tendencies generated by the corporate strategy bundle. If the practices that constitute the HRM bundle are vertically aligned or integrated with the practices that constitute the corporate strategy bundle, then the tendencies will mutually support one another, creating synergy – again lack of vertical integration causes the tendencies to conflict causing dis-synergy. To keep the example simple we assume that the practices are vertically aligned.
- An evaluation of the relative strengths of the tendencies and counter-tendencies generated by HRM, corporate strategy (and stakeholder practices) that constitute the HRM bundle will, of course, require judgment. The point is we have the knowledge upon which to base this judgment, because the causal-explanatory method encourages us, indeed, requires us, to seek it.
- To the extent that we can explain the tendencies and counter-tendencies of the causal configuration, when acted upon by workers in specific positioned-practices, with their agential projects, and do so in a specific, open systemic, context, we are in a strong position to identify which tendencies are likely to predominate and may be able to make the following tendential prediction: *'the HRM system will tend to do X'*.

We hesitate to call this a prediction because it is not an *inductive* prediction of any kind, and because the term 'prediction' is soaked in ambiguity within scientistic meta-theory. Unfortunately, the (ambiguous) meaning of prediction is now so embedded in scientistic meta-theory that it is difficult to give it another meaning.[28] Nonetheless, because it is a claim about what is likely to happen in a future period, it is a prediction of some kind, albeit heavily qualified, and hence we call it *tendential prediction*. It is important to remember that a tendential prediction is a claim made in full recognition that the system under investigation is an open system. This has the following important connotations.

First, as we saw in Chapter 4, in an open system such as the workplace we would expect to find multiple determination, complexity, evolution and the exercise of human agency. We would expect to find that when bundles of HRM practices are introduced, aligned with strategy and in various contexts, sometimes organisational performance improves (a little or a lot), sometimes it remains unchanged and sometimes it deteriorates (a little or a lot). Moreover, we would not expect to be able to inductively predict which of these outcomes will prevail. The search for law-like regularities, that have been discovered in some branches of natural science, that do allow deductive prediction (think Ohm's Law, or the Gas Laws) has evaded social sciences not because social scientists are intellectually inferior to their natural science counterparts, but because the social world constitutes an open system where law-like regularities do not occur. All this means that (inductive) predictions derived from the usual quantitative, empirical and statistical analysis are likely to be inaccurate and, as such, poor guides to what is likely to happen in the future. Tendential prediction is, at the very least, no worse than this, and indeed may be much better.

Second, as we saw in Chapter 3, we would not expect managers to simply apply the inductive predictions derived from the usual quantitative, empirical and statistical analysis to their own organisations. This means inductive prediction is practically inadequate. Tendential prediction is, at the very least, no worse than this, and indeed may be much better.

Third, and related to the last point, if and when we can explain the structures, mechanisms, tendencies and counter-tendencies of the causal configuration and the actions of agents in specific positioned-practices, then we even have some leeway to allow for variations in the context and still make a tendential prediction. Clearly this is a matter of judgment. We have to judge whether any change in structures, mechanisms, tendencies, counter-tendencies or actions of agents is likely to result in the configuration tending to do X, or tending to do something else, such as Y. The point is, and this is a very important point, we have the knowledge upon which to base this judgment, because the causal-explanatory method encourages us, indeed, requires us, to seek it. This is in complete contrast to the deductive method which seeks only to make inductive predictions, based on the claim that Y is statistically associated with X_1, $X_2...X_n$. If the context in which this association was generated should change, we simply have no knowledge upon which to base a judgment about whether or not the association will remain intact, nor about what action to take.

Fourth, HR managers and trade union negotiators are constantly faced with matters of judgment like those just mentioned. Whilst they do not use critical realist terminology, they constantly have to judge whether any change in structures, mechanisms, tendencies or actions of agents is likely to result in the configuration tending to do X, or tending to do something else, and then take appropriate action. In this sense critical realism re-describes, albeit in a more nuanced way, what people tend to do in their dealings with the open systemic nature of the social world.

Fifth, Becker and Gerhart (1996: 784) refer to the 'architecture' of an HRM system and others (e.g. Hoque 1999: 421) have found the analogy useful. Whilst it is used rather cryptically, a charitable interpretation runs something like the following. Whilst buildings come in many shapes and sizes, there are certain structural properties that all buildings must have in order for them to be proper, useable, safe buildings. Architects have to engage in analysis that goes beyond the outward appearances (empirical form) of buildings, to the structural properties. They may employ retroduction and retrodiction in order to ascertain these structural properties and their powers and, thereby, explain the tendencies and counter-tendencies at work in the building. They may, therefore, be in a strong position to identify which tendencies are likely to predominate and may be able to make the following tendential prediction: 'the building will tend to stay erect in winds of force X'. Whilst the analogy between buildings and HR systems is not exact, the point is taken. The problem for Becker and Gerhart, and others who would like to delve into the 'architectural' level, is that scientism, deductivism, and the quantitative, empirical and statistical techniques they favour, simply do not allow them to do this. Their intuition founders on the rocks of their mistaken meta-theoretical commitments.

Cutting the Gordian Knot of systemic complexity

Let us take an exceptionally well-known example, Huselid's (1995) paper on High Performance Work Systems (HPWS) and re-describe it in terms of a causal configuration with powers and tendencies. The aim here is not only to show the level of complexity that characterises such a system, but to discourage researchers from being overwhelmed by it, and retreating to the safety of scientism.

Huselid considered the following practices: personnel selection, performance appraisal, incentive compensation, job design, grievance procedures, information sharing, attitude assessment, labour-management participation, intensity of recruiting efforts, training hours per employee and promotion criteria. Whilst we could re-describe all this in terms of a causal configuration with powers and tendencies, it would take up far too much space for relatively little gain, so let us simply focus attention on the practice described as 'labour-management participation'. Labour-management practices can take many forms but, in essence, they involve a set of structures, mechanisms, institutions, rules, conventions, resources and procedures designed to encourage workers to use their powers in ways that fit with the objectives of enhanced performance pursued by managers. Workers may exercise their powers of creativity, imagination and ingenuity and to do so in a self-directed and self-motivated, high-performance manner in ways that fit with the objectives pursued by managers (which we take as synonymous with the objectives of the firm). They may also exercise these same powers to frustrate all or some of management's objectives, or to pursue other objectives such as improved pay and conditions.

Labour–management forums are created and sustained by both firms and unions devoting (various) resources – other resources may come from organisations like ACAS and/or government. Successive rounds of collective bargaining may have already established a set of written and unwritten (i.e. tacit) rules, conventions and procedures that constrain and enable the actions of workers and managers in order to discourage conflict and encourage consensual behaviour. Labour-management practices generate tendencies that discourage conflict, and counter-tendencies that encourage conflict. The overall outcome depends upon the interplay of tendencies and counter-tendencies. The interplay of tendencies and counter-tendencies is complex and will depend on the wider context and a range of external structures and mechanisms that have a causal influence. External class and patriarchal structures, market mechanisms and a range of what might be called discursive or semiotic mechanisms routinely influence these (internal) structures and mechanisms. They also influence agents and, thereby, the way the (internal) structures and mechanisms are drawn upon by agents.

At the same time as (external forces and) labour-management practices are in operation, so too are many other practices. Huselid recognises eleven HRM practices in total, and whilst he does not mention them, any student of HRM would be able to point to several other causal factors likely to be in operation also. Furthermore, these other causal factors might generate tendencies that would act as co-tendencies or countervailing tendencies to the eleven HRM practices cited.

The overall effects of these eleven HRM practices on organisational performance will depend upon the interplay of a complex web of tendencies and counter-tendencies. Because the workplace is an open system, we will be unable to make definite predictions about which of the multiplicity of tendencies and counter-tendencies will 'win out' – although as we noted above, tendential predictions might be possible, and we sketch an example in a moment. Not that this has precluded authors of 'airport' books seeking to establish which HR systems represent the magic bullets or touchstones to enhanced performance. It does mean that any identification will involve in-depth research, almost certainly of a qualitative nature, and, ironically, the very approach that many business gurus and many academics suggest we avoid.

Now some empirical researchers on the HRM–P link are likely to agree with something like the complex scenario we have just described. Indeed, recognition of this complexity makes scientism even more seductive, as it promises to cut the Gordian Knot of complexity at a stroke. Scientism implies there is no need to delve into the black box to identify the structures, mechanisms, institutions, rules, conventions, resources, positioned-practices; no need to identify the agents who reflexively deliberate about these phenomena, or the agential projects they formulate; no need to identify the tendencies and counter-tendencies this causal configuration generates. All that is, allegedly, needed is to measure an arbitrary set of HRM variables, measure organisational performance and test various hypotheses about the associations between them by applying the usual quantitative, empirical and statistical techniques. Unfortunately, as we have been at pains to point out in the last four chapters, scientism has not, nor is it likely to, deliver the goods. We have little to lose and everything to gain by trying alternatives such as critical realism's causal-explanatory method.

The big question, of course, is how might we actually go about employing the causal-explanatory method and constructing a causal-explanatory account of HRM practices and their potential impact on organisational performance? And unfortunately we cannot answer this question in this book. Recall that we started the chapter by suggesting critical realism offers a bespoke meta-theory, that is, one tailored to suit the nature of the social system under investigation, as opposed to an 'off-the-shelf' meta-theory. Whilst we have made some very general claims about ontology and aetiology, we have made no practical, epistemological or methodological prescriptions. The epistemology and methodology advocated by critical realism cannot really be offered in advance of the actual research. What we can say, however, is that the kind of knowledge we seek is the kind of knowledge sought, and often obtained, via the usual range of techniques used by *qualitative* researchers in social, organisation and management science. Is it really beyond the wit of good researchers to identify the powers that workers bring with them to the workplace? Is it beyond the wit of researchers to identify the causal configuration of structures and mechanisms that workers and managers engage with? Is it beyond the wit of researchers to identify the agential projects that are the outcome of reflexive deliberation on the enabling and constraining effects of structures and mechanisms? Is it beyond the wit of researchers to identify the tendencies and counter-tendencies generated by the causal configuration? Is it beyond the wit of researchers to identify tendencies and counter-tendencies generated external to the organisation that nonetheless impact upon the operation of internally generated tendencies? The answer to questions like this is: 'Whilst it is difficult, none of this should be beyond the wit of good qualitative researchers'. The problem is not so much that we cannot identify any of these phenomena, but that we are currently not even trying!

Conclusion

We have, then, arrived at the end of the meta-theoretical journey begun in Chapter 3. We have developed the meta-theoretical 'toolkit' offered by critical realism to provide us with:

- A social ontology wherein the world is taken to be open, layered, transformational, and consisting not only of human agents, but also structures, institutions, mechanisms, resources, rules, conventions, (non-human) powers, as opposed to a 'flat' ontology of events and experiences.

- A 'thick' notion of causality as the exercise of a capacity, disposition or *power*, as opposed to the Humean or 'thin' notion of causality as event regularity.
- A notion of tendency as opposed to the notion of law-like event regularity.
- An agency and structure framework, with the associated notion of positioned-practice.
- A sophisticated notion of the human being, the agent, as opposed to the atomistic conception of *homo economicus* presupposed by scientism.
- A 'thick' form of explanation, as opposed to a 'thin' form.
- A distinction between theoretical and applied explanation, utilising retroduction and retrodiction as modes of inference, as opposed to deduction and induction.
- A clear objective for social science in the form of explanation, as opposed to prediction based on induction, and hence a plausible method which we call causal-explanatory.
- A notion of tendential prediction as opposed to inductive prediction.
- A clear idea of what constitutes a theory, namely, a causal-explanatory account, as opposed to the vague idea of theory as a vehicle for delivering hypotheses and predictions.

All this amounts to a very sophisticated toolbox, one that is far superior to anything offered by scientism. But this is as far as meta-theory can take us. From here on, empirical analysis has to take over. It is one thing to explain, in meta-theoretical terms, what a generative ensemble is, but it is quite another to state which generative ensembles are in operation in the workplace and how they influence organisational performance. This is a task befalling the next generation of researchers on the HRM–P link – once, that is, they abandon scientism.[29]

PART III

Reflexive performance

7 | *Putting critical realism to work*

In the preceding chapters we have made it clear that research based upon scientism (its ontology, epistemology, methodology and aetiology and the quantitative, empirical, statistical techniques it sponsors), has seriously misled research on the HRM–P link. The previous chapter drew upon critical realism to sketch some of the meta-theoretical building blocks on which an alternative approach to research on the HRM–P link might be undertaken in future. This leaves two possible directions for us to travel. One direction would lead us in the direction of undertaking empirical research ourselves, exploring the relation between HRM and organisational performance not via scientism, but via critical realism and the research techniques it sponsors. This direction is not, unfortunately, open to us at the moment. It would, of course, take years to fund, design, undertake and then report upon such empirical research, and we simply did not want to delay publication of the book any further. In any case, the main purpose of this book is to convince the reader that current research on the HRM–P link is flawed and alternatives need to be sought. The other direction is to make use of interviews we carried out with senior HR professionals to ascertain their views on the meta-theory underpinning research on the HRM–P link. This research led us to conclude that many senior HR professionals are not only unhappy with scientism, they are far happier with critical realism as it meshes with their own implicit modus operandi. This is the direction we took.

Most HR professionals are not, of course, experts in meta-theory so the way we approach this research is to use language that they understand. We do not, then, ask them for their 'views on the deductive method' or, for that matter, their 'views on the use of closed system modelling'. We take meta-theoretical concepts, translate them into questions using 'everyday' language, then translate the answers, often couched in metaphor, back into meta-theoretical concepts. When, in a particular context our respondents say they 'lift up the stones and have a look underneath', we are able to translate this into them saying they retroduce to a mechanism that is causing some phenomena that they seek an explanation to. With careful attention paid to how we ask questions, and the metaphors used by practitioners, our research shows that many HR practitioners are far happier operating with something like a critical realist perspective than from something like a scientistic one. Knowing this gives us more confidence to argue that something like critical realism is actually more useful to HR professionals. Incidentally, there is not reason to believe that this is something specific to senior HR professionals, this is simply who we chose to conduct research on. It could, and should, be extended to include wider stakeholders.

To gain a flavour, consider two comments from our respondents. The first is from an HR director who staunchly defends the view that HR's contribution can not only be captured, but also converted into financial or data form. The following represents one of the strongest views we heard to this end:

There is the recognition at long last that HR needs data in order to fulfil its expressed aspiration to be more strategic. I've sat round many boardroom tables and I don't think I've ever been at one board meeting in a strategy session that doesn't begin with context and data. This doesn't mean they don't have opinions. My God, they have strong opinions! Data is the basis on which businesses make decisions. If HR wants to be taken seriously in helping an organization in deriving competitive advantage you need data in order to point out when and where HR can intervene in the matter of talent. Without data all you are going to encounter is opinion. There are plenty of people with an opinion around a boardroom table and unless you have data to support your opinion, you're going to lose. Having effective administration from which one can derive data is no less important to the HR function as it is to the accounting function ... If you can create a strong people database and get your administrative systems smooth and slick to the consumers of them, the chances are that you can then derive insights around important themes to do with people: how many are we recruiting? How many are we losing? What's the segmentation of our loss? What's the cost of our training initiatives? How does career development work? What's the cover ratios for the top jobs in our organization?

Yet many HR professionals see this quantitative approach as misguided. In the words of one HR director, herself a former accountant, the veracity of what is on offer is far from accepted and yet, still, organisations and people within them are still happy to proceed with activities. Indeed, she sees a kind of 'game' being played here where all parties know, but refuse to explicitly acknowledge, that this approach is extremely unenlightening:

It's the same with all of our estimates. We walk into the budgetary process every year with our projections on costs. We go through this little ritual where we tell them that this is what we think it will cost – which is usually wrong – and what the returns to those costs will be from HR. We know it's bullshit, they know it's bullshit, and yet still the process persists. There is a certain level of give and take from the parties involved that this stuff cannot be accurately measured and that's how we get from one meeting to the next. Of course, if you were wildly off-target with your numbers the whole thing might get politically difficult, but as a rule, the margin of error is probably wider than you think, or what the shareholders might like it to be! (HR director)

The first quotation is a broad defence of something like scientism, the second quotation is a broad rejection of scientism. This final chapter, then, is not about using critical realist meta-theory to conduct empirical research into the relationship between HRM and performance; it is about demonstrating that critical realism can actually be useful.

Moving away from the quantum form

Some researchers and practitioners have sought and gained knowledge of the underlying mechanisms at work influencing the outcomes of people management in organisations. This knowledge has then been applied to ongoing management and research. In short, individual managers and researchers have explored and applied their knowledge through a process, first, of retroduction, and then, second, retrodiction – although they do not, of course, use this terminology. As we shall see below, what is striking about the working lives of many HR professionals are their daily experiences of circumnavigating the processes used to manage the metrics used to 'measure' their interventions to introduce the mechanisms their experience has taught them works, not simply in a pragmatic way, but because they have a basic understanding of why it works.[1] Incidentally, the fact that many of the mechanisms their experience has taught them works often turn out *not* to work, is not due to their stupidity, but due to the systemic openness of the workplace. Their knowledge might be fallible, but it might be the best we have, and it is certainly better than the 'knowledge' generated by the empirical studies on the HRM–P link.

This has not been a superficial process, or one without its own claim to veracity.[2] As has become clear to us during our research, the experiences of senior HR professionals leaves them in a unique, even privileged, position to understand the likely impact of HRM processes on the performance of the business units they are practised in, and those upon which they have influence. Note immediately here how we do not suggest such experiences have an impact on the 'Tier 1' or 'Top Level' financial performance of organisations represented by measures such as market capitalisation, price/earnings ratios, etc. That senior executives can foresee the likely impact of their interventions on the people they manage is not the same as the prediction of the future financial performance of their organisations. Interventions of various types are understood in a deeper, more structured way insofar as executives understand and explain initiatives as making contributions to particular organisational outcomes. Such contributions are seen to be 'nested' within other contributions, the causality of which cannot simply be deductively read-off or measured by scientistic methods. On the contrary, the contribution of many interventions can rarely be directly measured. But just because they cannot be measured does not mean the impact of such interventions cannot be measured. They have to be retroductively understood.

Nor, importantly, are we suggesting that every account offered to us by HR professionals is indubitably accurate. Paraphrasing both Bruner (1986) and Tsoukas and Hatch (2001), the accounts of performance that we have sought in our research equates more to verisimilitude as opposed to truth, and ones seeking to endow our understanding of how HR impacts upon the performance of people through experience and meaning as opposed to having an empirically tested truth. It is for this reason why we introduce the metaphor of the *alethiometer* to differentiate this, our Reflexive School of thinking, from the preceding four schools we have identified in previous chapters (see Table 7.1).

Readers familiar with the *His Dark Materials* trilogy by Philip Pullman will recognise the alethiometer's literal translation as 'truth

Table 7.1. *The different methods and schools of the HRM–P link*

School	Metaphor	Method	Seminal example
Contingency	'Russian doll'	Performance contingent on alignment of different HR processes with organisational strategy and processes	Schuler and Jackson (1987a)
Universalistic	'Black box'	A linear relationship between organisational performance and certain HR practices	Huselid (1995)
Configurational	'Rubik's Cube'	How the pattern of configuration of multiple HR processes are related to each other and to organisational performance	Delery and Doty (1996)
Contextual	'Kaleidoscope'	A complete overview of the factors influencing the shaping of HRM policies and practices	Paauwe (2004)
Reflexive	'Alethiometer'	First understanding (retroduction) then explanation from experience (retrodiction) of underlying mechanisms at work	Fleetwood and Hesketh (this volume)

measure', given to the books' heroine, Lyra. Far from reading-off truth in a deductivistic or scientistic way, Lyra has to learn how to use the alethiometer through a trial and error process of explanation, understanding and experience to accurately interpret the underlying mechanisms shaping the events she encounters.[3]

We are unaware of any HR professionals or academics in possession of an alethiometer, despite some of the claims forwarded by or on behalf of academics as well as consultants or business leaders (see Pfeffer and Sutton 2006 for a full-blown critique). Nevertheless, as we began to articulate in the previous chapter by opening up the discussion on agency, we can, through a process of reflexive deliberation, begin to understand the underlying mechanisms shaping outcomes on a daily basis at our places of work. We do not rely on statistical modelling to project answers in order to understand and deal with the complex social contexts we face. On the contrary: our perspective is one suggesting numbers can exacerbate confusion and are riddled with contradictions in their interpretation. Where numbers finish, explanation and understanding begins. Similarly, this same intersection at which we leave the clarity of numbers is where complexity increases exponentially. Whilst it is relatively easy to state whether a company is making a profit (or not), it is less straightforward to attribute causality to other causal mechanisms. Consequently, sceptics might suggest that where numbers end, narrative constructions – or performativity – begins.[4] We have some sympathy with this view. Nevertheless, how individual HR professionals construct an account of how, under appropriate conditions, people enable organisations to perform better (or not) is based more on what they believe. It turns also upon their experiences of what (they think) works, or not. How then might we see (ontology) certain activities and how might we make claims about whether they work, or not (epistemology)?

Opening up experience with the internal conversation

Actors' experiences reveal to us how the complexities, fluidities and ongoing changes to fundamental processes that make up the open social world we inhabit need to be negotiated on an ongoing, daily basis. For Tsoukas (2005: 5), this requires a *poetic praxeology* which:

sees the practitioner as an active being who, while inevitably shaped by the sociocultural practices in which he/she is rooted, necessarily shapes them in turn by undertaking action that is relatively opaque in its consequences and unclear in its motives and desires, unreflective and situated in its mode of operation, but inherently capable of self-observation and reflexivity, thus susceptible to chronic change. According to this view, a human agent is similar to a poet, who gives distinctive form to linguistic materials in often unexpected ways, but under the influence of past genres and current literary norms and the *Zeitgeist*, without being fully conscious of the process of creation and without controlling how his/her work will be interpreted by others and incorporated into further cycles of poetic creation and language change. A poetic praxeology acknowledges the complicated motives of human action, makes room for the influence of the past and its transmutation into new forms in the present, understand the relatively opaque nature of human intentionality, allows for chance events, influences, and feedback loops, and accepts the inescapable contextuality and temporality of all human action.

In order to deal with such complexities Tsoukas advocates a method in which a poetic praxeology be joined by individuals seeking organisational knowledge and understanding through an *open-world ontology* in which, 'the future is open, unknowable in principle and … always holds the possibility of surprise', together with an *enactivist epistemology* in which, 'we bring the world forward by making distinctions and giving form to an unarticulated background of understanding' (Tsoukas 2005: 5). We wholeheartedly agree. How we have dealt with these requirements in our research and new theoretical construct of *Reflexive Performance* requires us to revisit the dialogue opened up in Chapter 6 in relation to agency, and now, principally, by utilising the work of the influential critical realist, Margaret Archer.

Recall how in Chapter 6 we noted that for Archer, being in the world necessarily brings agents into contact with (i) social and cultural structures that constrain and enable their intentions and (ii) the natural, practical and social phenomena, which give rise to concerns about physical well-being, performative achievement and self-worth respectively. Crucially, these structures do not have the power of efficient causality. That is, structures can influence, but not (efficiently) cause agents to alter their ideas. Rather, agents, knowing their own minds, take these factors into consideration when they reflexively deliberate upon the course of action they ought to take. For Archer:

[A]gents have to respond to these influences; which being conditional rather than deterministic, are subject to reflexive determination over the nature of the response. In sum, no structural or cultural emergent property is constraining or enabling *tout court*. To become constraints or enablements, depends upon the nature of the relationship with the use made by personal emergent properties. *Whether or not* their causal power is to constrain or to enable is realised, and for *whom* they constitute the constraints or enablements, depends upon the nature of the relationship between them and agential projects. (Archer 2003: 8)

This does not, of course, mean that agents are free to 'think' any old enablements and constraints into being. It does mean that they are free to interpret them, and act in ways agents deem appropriate. Agents have the capacity to reflect about (say) the constraining effect of a structure, recognise that they will pay a penalty (which could be financial, political, social, social-psychological) yet ultimately decide to try and avoid its constraints – which does not mean they will succeed, merely that they try. This reflexive deliberation occurs via the 'internal conversation' which Archer defines as:

the modality through which reflexivity towards self, society and the relationship between them is exercised. In itself it entails just such things as articulating to ourselves where we are placed, ascertaining where our interests lie and adumbrating schemes of future action. (Archer 2003: 9)

To state this rather simplistically, agents literally talk to themselves (and sometimes others) about their needs, concerns and the things that might constrain or enable them. They then formulate (fallible) courses of action, or *agential projects*, that they think might result in these needs being met and concerns being addressed. This first-person subjective ontology equates to a genuine personal interior, a domain of mental privacy where this process happens. This internal domain is the space of human agency as it were, a place where the 'I' does its thing. Reflexive deliberation, via the 'internal conversation' then, links social structure to human agency in a non-deterministic way.[5] Archer sums her own ideas up succinctly:

What is advanced throughout this book is a concept of the 'internal conversation', by which agents reflexively deliberate upon the social circumstances that they confront. Because they possess personal identity, as defined by their individual configuration of concerns, they know what they care about most and what they seek to realise in society. Because they are capable of internally deliberating about themselves in relation to their social circumstances, they are the authors of projects that they (fallibly) believe will achieve something of what they want from and in society. Because pursuit of a social project generally spells out an encounter with social powers, in the form of constraints and enablements, then the ongoing 'internal conversation' will mediate agents' receptions of these structural and cultural influences. In other words, our personal powers are exercised through reflexive interior dialogue and are causally accountable for the delineation of our concerns, the definition of our projects, the diagnosis of our circumstances and, ultimately, the determination of our practices in society. Reflexive deliberations constitute the mediatory process between 'structure and agency,' they represent the subjective element which is always in interplay with the causal powers of objective social forms. (Archer 2003: 130)

There is, however, one particular kind of social phenomena that Archer does not engage with, namely, an *institution*. As an Institutionalist (and fellow traveller with critical realism) Hodgson engages extensively with the basic properties of institutions, and has identified one crucial characteristic: unlike social structures, institutions can efficiently cause agents to alter their beliefs. Hodgson steers clear of determinism, by retaining a space for genuine human agency, the possibility that agents can go against the force of institutions – even if they rarely do. Following the Institutionalist tradition, and the work of Hodgson, Fleetwood defines institutions as follows:

An institution is a system of established rules, conventions, norms, values and customs that become embodied or internalized within agents as habits or habitus, via a process of habituation rooted in the nervous system, to assist in rendering (relatively) predictable, the intentions and actions of agents who draw upon, reproduce or transform these phenomena, whilst simultaneously reproducing and transforming themselves and who may, via a process of reconstitutive downward causation, have their intentions and actions transformed. (Fleetwood 2008a)

When institutional rules and conventions are drawn upon with sufficient regularity, they can become embodied via a process of habituation resulting in the adoption of a habit. Habits reflect the wider social, cultural and economic environment agents find themselves engaging with. Hodgson's process of habituation involves a kind of tacit knowing or embodiment, reminiscent of Bourdieu's notion of *habitus*, indeed Hodgson suggests this (2004: 187).

Repeated practice triggers neurological processes, generating habits that become stored in our neural networks – which does not, of course, mean habits are reducible to neural networks, neurons, synaptic connection or some such. Habits form via this process of habituation, and intentions can change, *entirely without deliberation*. Indeed, the process of forming a habit often bypasses consciousness. Hodgson would agree with Archer that social structures may enable and constrain, and therefore influence, agents' ideas, but cannot cause them to change. But he goes further, arguing that institutions, operating via habituation and habits, do not only *influence* agents' intentions, but also have the capacity to cause intentions to change, something he refers to as *reconstitutive downward causation*. Habit, then, links agency and institution.

A melding of these two sets of ideas on human agency offers a useful alternative to treating humans as rational bargain-hunters on the one hand, and fully determined automata on the other. Sometimes agents' ideas are governed by institutional rules, working through habits; sometimes they are governed by social structure working via reflexive deliberation and the 'internal conversation'; and sometimes agents' actions are governed by both processes working simultaneously.

Introducing reflexive performance

Archer's recent work has also been useful in helping us interpret the data we obtained from interviewing senior HR professionals. A key process in our fieldwork has been the development of what Archer calls 'reflexive determination', to which we give a slight twist and refer to as 'reflexive performance'. Reflexive performance is a specific case of reflexive determination, where agents reflect specifically upon some aspect of their performance, or the performance of others. Indeed, Archer recognises this, referring to 'our performative achievement in the practical order' (2003: 120) as one of human beings' key concerns. We incorporate what are labelled 'predicates' (e.g. thinking, deliberating, believing, loving, etc.) into the reflexive processes engaged in by individuals when deliberating over some specific personal or agential project.

This reflexive determination represents the personal process by which individuals identify the enablements and constraints of social structure, and link them to *their* agency. For Archer, some social structures enable or constrain the execution of particular processes. The key to reflexive performance, therefore, is identifying the structures and mechanisms deemed to enable or constrain wider organisational performance and constructing personal emergent properties to formulate strategies and processes to use them to pursue their personal goals. Reflexive determination, or reflexive performance, affords two critical observations in examining the HRM–P link: namely, the *transfactuality* of HR practices and their impact upon wider organisational performance, and, secondly, the *contingency*, and hence *variability*, in the capacity of certain HR practices to generate the outcomes expected. Let us deal with each of these in turn.

In terms of transfactuality (defined in Chapter 4) we have already alluded to Archer's recognition of the absence of event regularity in relation to cultural or structural emergent properties. In short, some structures and mechanisms that constitute HRM practices may enable enhanced organisational performance, or they may not. This goes a long way to explaining the wide variations in the performance of organisations with similar HR structures, processes and practices. This in turn relies on the reflexive determination of those HR professionals and other employees engaged in the processes thought to be performance enhancing. To predict outcome y as the direct result of implementing HRM practice x, therefore, negates (or at least fails to consider) the role of individuals in adopting or aligning (or not) certain prescribed HR processes and practices with their, and others', agential projects.[6]

For Archer, this process of explanation is about the interplay between the subjective world of agents and the objective and independent world of social structures and mechanisms.[7] All this takes place in a process labelled 'discursive penetration'. Individuals, be they HR professionals, managers, trade union negotiators or other employees, must all diagnose their own situations, identify their own interests and align the situations in which they find themselves in some way with their own agential projects. For Archer, at all three of these points individuals are fallible in terms of misdiagnosis of their situations, the misidentification of their own interests and of course the misjudgment of what they deem appropriate action. All these processes require an internal conversation:

> The answer to this is held to be 'via the internal conversation'. This is the modality through which reflexivity towards self, society and the relationship between them is exercised. In itself it entails just such things as articulating to ourselves where we are placed, ascertaining where our interests lie and adumbrating schemes of future action. (Archer 2003: 9)

Whilst reflexive deliberation via the internal conversation facilitates agential projects, these projects are not infallible. Nevertheless, the 'internal conversation' for HR professionals, the group we focus on, reveals to us what *they* believe to be the case and it is causally efficacious, at least to a degree, because we consider they have the power to implement practices they deem appropriate. The conversation then becomes one between what might be labelled self-knowledge (what one knows and thinks), societal knowledge (knowing what others think), a stance (the adoption of a position of what one wants to achieve) and the legitimacy of this agential project underpinned by the accompanying *explanations* to justify one's project to oneself. Here at last we move away from scientistic notions of thin causality, event regularity and deductivism (and away from a naive form of social constructionism) to the genuine interplay between subjective properties (discursive penetration through the internal conversation) and objective outcomes (organisational successes, failures, 'good' performance, 'bad' performance, etc.). People and their predicates, then, are as influential and important for analysis as the structures they necessarily engage with, reproduce and occasionally transform. This is not always appreciated by those with a limited knowledge of critical realism, who confuse it with a form of structuralism and lack of human agency.

Our research

With these meta-theoretical foundation stones in place, we are now in a position to begin outlining our new lexicon for capturing reflexive performance in the workplace. Before doing so, we must first qualify the foundations on which our foundations sit. Research for *Explaining the Performance of Human Resource Management* was first initiated in 2001 with a seedcorn research grant awarded by Lancaster University to the authors to empirically examine senior HR executives' views of the meta-theoretical underpinnings to their practices and decision-making. Part of this research took place in the United States in a FTSE100 organisation then going through a major programme of change. We were fortunate to attend interviews with senior HR directors as they were put through their paces over how, amongst other challenges, they understood and explained how HRM practices contributed to organisational performance! This research continued back in the UK as the organisation concerned then initiated the same process with UK HR directors. We were granted access to the senior executives in charge of running this evaluation process. With ideas beginning to develop for an alternative ontology on performance and complex-explanation, we then widened our empirical net still further, culminating in the publication of the first report by the (then) Group for Performance-Led HR examining how HR professionals captured the impact of talent pipelines using non-financial methods (Hesketh 2004). By now we had a data set of over seventy interviews with senior HR executives across over twenty-five blue-chip organisations to draw from. The ideas first initiated in 2001 by the group, comprising the authors and Martin Hird, former HR director at BAE Systems, who were then joined by Cary Cooper, were followed by the formal launch of the Performance-Led HR Centre at Lancaster in 2006. The Centre now comprises fifteen organisations and their senior HR directors representing over half of the entire UK labour market, five of which took place in the original research in 2001.

This account of the development of the Centre not only demonstrates how our ideas have gained credence in the senior ranks of professional HR, but also to illustrate how representative of the UK's commercial activities the group of people we have researched are. Representational brevity, as we have made much of in previous chapters(!), does not equate to epistemological accuracy, however.

To this end we have sought in all of our interviews, now over 100, with the inclusion of chief executives, financial directors, commercial directors, as well as additional HR directors from other organisations drawn from the United States and Europe as well as the UK, to establish the predicates upon which their own agential projects have rested. Each interview has always tried to establish, in the respondent's own terms as opposed to the discourse of meta-theory and social theory, the meta-theoretical position, or in Archer's terms, stance, adopted in relation to how executives account for the efficaciousness on performance enabled by their practices. The authors have not defined what constitutes 'performance' during interviews unless required by the respondents. When prompted we have suggested performance equates to *an unstable equilibrium of enabling entities and mechanisms that may or may not operate and/or endure to the benefit of people and their organisation.* The conversation has then evolved from there, sometimes defining performance more in terms of financial form, sometimes defining performance more in terms of a narrative or 'performativity' but always exploring how respondents understand and explain in their own terms and daily praxis how people enable performance, or not.

The following sections run through some of the key concepts of critical realist meta-theory developed in Chapter 6, demonstrating how HR professionals make use of something like them in their day-to-day activities.

Generative ensembles

It is almost always the case that artefacts such as information technology, and social entities such as organisations, unions, high-performance work systems, or whatever, exist as clusters of components that endow them with their causal powers. An organisation consists of a cluster of social structures, institutions, mechanisms, rules, resources, conventions, procedures, etc., along with the human agents that activate them. Because the entity usually does whatever it does in virtue of the interaction of the totality of causal components, we need a term to refer to them as a whole. The term we use is a *generative ensemble.*

We can think of the firm as a generative ensemble that causes the production of goods and services. Or we can think of the workplace, the shopfloor, the work-system or the team, as a complex web of interlocking generative ensembles, sub-configurations, sub-sub-configurations and so on. Just-in-time production, for example, is possible because the sub-configuration that enables inventory interlocks with the sub-configuration that enables distribution within the plant. The sub-configuration that causes distribution within the plant interlocks with the sub-sub-configuration that consists of the maintenance of fork-lift trucks. Much depends upon the questions we are asking, and the level of abstraction we are using. Certain business processes manifest themselves as sub-configurations more readily than others. Rarely, however, do such configurations, sub-configurations and sub-sub-configurations lend themselves to measurement. This complexity is routinely overlooked by the HRM–P literature that often utilises simplistic and overarching HR structures as proxies, thereby ignoring the influential and complex underlying causal mechanisms at work in the social processes underpinning such HR work practices.

From our interviews, we found clear parallels between our notion of generative ensemble with the ways in which practitioners understood and conceptualised their day-to-day activities. One HR director exemplified our point of generative causality as the exercise of powers by referring to the individual instruments which ultimately contribute to the overall sound of an orchestra:

When I'm working on the implementation of [HR] processes I find myself thinking about the orchestra analogy. You know, like a conductor. The conductor plays no instrument and makes no sound, but without a conductor you're just going to get a cacophony of noise rather than something which conforms to a score. Your [High Performance Work Systems] are the score which describes, or denotes, what the thing should sound like in the end, and the implementation [of HR processes] is the conductor. And if you're trying to evaluate different sections of the orchestra and how well do they work, the answer is it doesn't all depend on the score. If you have a score that actually doesn't have any brass in it, you can't say the brass section is pretty crap because they're not making much noise. The score simply doesn't call for that. When one is trying to evaluate the whole impact of HR one very much has to take into consideration the whole score. *Some things are very much in the fray, and others aren't called for very much. You will bring in things in operations which can make a difference, and then afterwards the effect might be quite muted.* (HR director, blue-chip organisation, emphasis added.)

Powers

Entities (including humans and social structures) possess powers, that is, dispositions, capacities and potentials to cause certain things, but not others. Gunpowder, for example, has the power to explode, but not to speak a language: humans have this power. Now powers are rather complex things. Powers may be possessed with or without being exercised and may be exercised with or without being actualised, hence the italicised section in the above interview extract. We would add to this observation some additional points.

First, a power is possessed by an entity in virtue of its internal make-up, and this power endures whether or not it is exercised or actualised and, therefore, endures irrespective of any outcomes it generates. When a power endures in this sense, it can be said to act *transfactually*. An employee has the power to work effectively in the sense that she *may* work in a highly productive, highly value-adding manner. Or she may not. When exercised, certain HRM practices *may* have the power to foster certain high value-adding behaviours. Or they may not. The point is the power endures even if it remains unexercised and un-actualised. One CEO, this time of a major consulting house, emphatically concurred with this view:

I think the question you ask encapsulates the problem we face. If a sceptical CEO needs to be convinced about our proposition that the performance of their infrastructure can be improved, I'm frankly not interested. If they are seeking some proof of concept that is null until proven, then I'm already on my way out of the door. I really have not got the time, patience, or inclination to go through that sort of meander down to Damascus, frankly. If you're looking for a well articulated scientific model with evidence, then, unless you are prepared to listen to marketing hyperbole, you won't find it.

Second, and following on from the previous point, a power exercised is a power that has been triggered, and is generating an effect in an open system. Due to interference from the effects of other exercised powers, however, we can never know, a priori, what the outcome of any particular power will be. An exercised power may act transfactually. Consequently, it is not the existence of causal mechanisms and their powers often labelled as key HR practices in the HRM–P literature that *cause* enhanced performance. Rather, the actualisation of these powers is itself contingent on other, causal mechanisms and their powers that may, or may not, be actualised at any particular time and/or place. Understanding the processes through which certain HR practices or strategies enable certain powers – or not – represents the Achilles heel of current HRM–P literature and, in many ways, represents the defining point between scientism and our interpretation of our empirical analysis of HR's role in explaining the performance of people, their teams and the organisations to which they belong. Again, this point is wonderfully illustrated by the managing director of a multinational bank in her recognition that many underlying powers need to be triggered over time to generate the result executives might be looking for:

The team does not confuse program leadership with the ability to manage and synthesize a myriad of individual projects. It takes the long view but understands that the path of change is affected by thousands of small decisions. The smart executive embraces its role as an orchestrator of events, decisions, and solutions, and is flexible to adapt to changing conditions, always taking the long view.

Third, a power actualised *is* an exercised power generating its effect and not being deflected or counteracted by the effects of other exercised powers. An actualised power does not act transfactually but factually in the sense that the power generates its effect.

Finally, people can have '*personal powers*' – a 'reference to agents' subjective and reflexive formulation of personal projects' (Archer 2003: 5). Powers are possessed by workers in virtue of their biological, physiological, psychological and social make up – although it is important to note that these levels are irreducible to one another so we cannot simply reduce social behaviour to biology. Unlike most animals, humans do not just execute genetically pre-programmed tasks; they conceive these tasks first – although there may be a complex and recursive process between conception and execution. The power of conception is of crucial importance here because it consists of the powers of *imagination, ingenuity* and *creativity* that conceived of the pyramids, the Guggenheim, the cart, the MIR space station, surgical tools, nuclear weapons and the HR business partner. These same powers of *imagination, ingenuity* and *creativity* are also exercised in the conception of less grandiose endeavours such as finding better ways of producing a rivet, writing a programme or engaging in a telephone conversation. HRM practices such as performance management, retention, job design, and especially *engagement*, along with schemes to increase employee participation and empowered employees, are designed to unleash and harness the powers of imagination, ingenuity, customer service and creativity that workers bring with them to the workplace. If workers did not have these powers there would be no point whatsoever in even contemplating HRM practices. Indeed, the subtitle of Pfeffer's (1994) book *Unleashing the Power of the Workforce* captures the point beautifully. The fact (and it probably is a fact) that HRM has not succeeded in unlocking workers' powers does not mean they do not exist: something could be counteracting these powers. Or, alternatively, these powers may well have been unleashed: that they – or their impact – cannot be statistically captured does not preclude their existence.

Tendencies

As we saw in Chapter 6, to write that a configuration has a tendency to *x*, does not mean that it will *x*. In an open system, configurations do not exist in isolation from one another, rather there is a multiplicity of such configurations each with their own tendencies and these tendencies converge in some space-time location. Each configuration (and sub-configuration) generates tendencies and these tendencies can counteract, and augment, one another in complex ways. The sub-configuration that constitutes a workforce with the tendency to resist control co-exists simultaneously with the sub-configuration that constitutes a management team with the tendency to assert control. The outcome, however, depends upon the relative strengths of the tendencies. Notice, then, that it is *the generative ensemble as a totality, and not any of its individual components that generates the powers and, therefore, the tendencies the generative ensemble has.* Notice also that statistical analysis cannot deal with tendencies because it can only deal with phenomena that are actually manifesting their generative powers, whence they can be observed in action. We cannot statistically analyse the powers of imagination, ingenuity and creativity possessed by a workforce.[8]

In the following example, this HR director illustrates our point about the interplay between powers and tendencies, their configurations (and sub-configurations), whilst at the same time alluding to the transfactuality of HR's capacity to work only when in the right hands and minds derived from experience. In short, it is not the actual insertion of certain HR systems and structures, but understanding through experience and reflexivity how they work in light of the subtle complexities, 'and processes by which societal expectations of appropriate organizational action influence the structuring and behaviour of organizations in given ways' (Dacin 1997: 48) that is crucial:

All of this stuff about High Performance Work Systems to my mind misses the point. It's a bit like taking a Formula 1 motorcar and asking somebody with a conventional driving licence to race it round Silverstone. They know that the car has gears, a clutch, a steering wheel and brakes, but that person has no idea about the capability of the car, its nuances and what you have to do in order to get the best out of that car. That is not to say that they will not be able to drive it around the track. But you have to know what you're doing with it, have the experience, and understand the whole process of racing the car. There are all sorts of complications that you have to bring into the equation. You have a team of mechanics to support you, they need to know when you're coming in in order to prepare. You need to know when you need them, and what the other cars on the track are doing. In the same way as Schumacher has turned Formula 1 Grand Prix into a tactical art of strategy and execution, HR has to do the same. It's not just about picking up tools and then putting them down in the place you want them. If you take the drag and drop approach you'll have one almighty mess on your hands. It's about understanding the processes and how to use them ... And you use these processes in different ways. If you don't know how to use your back-up team and processes, they are just going to stand at the side of the race track and watch you eventually break down. Similarly, if you transfer from one team to another it takes time for both parties to understand how the other works. You have to learn how to leverage each other, what to use and what not to use. A lot of HR is like bad racing car driving. They've got the kit but it doesn't always work because you have to know when to use some things and not others. It's about experience, not textbooks telling you what to do. Everybody wants to isolate the 'it' and do something with 'it'. It's much more subtle and powerful at the same time. (HR director, blue-chip organisation)

Complex causality

Complex causality refers to a situation where the cause of an event is not assumed simply to be the event(s) that preceded it (which would be some kind of simple causality), but rather is the entire conflux of interacting causal phenomena. The causality of the lamp's illumination, for example, is the nature of the glass, the gas, the filament, the wire, the switch, the plug, the electricity, as well as the finger that flicked the switch. None of these events in isolation causes light.

Rather, it is their configuration in a particular form that *causes* in a complex way their aggregated powers to generate light.

Complex causality is connected to what we call *thick explanation*. Providing a history of a phenomenon, and hence explaining it, could be interpreted to mean giving information about the underlying mechanisms and structures, along with (if we are dealing with social phenomena) the human agency that reproduces and transforms these mechanisms and structures. That is, explanation could be based upon complex causality. If and when causality is complex, then explanation cannot be reduced merely to giving information about a succession of events, but rather requires information about the entire conflux of interacting causal phenomena beyond that captured even by sophisticated techniques utilised in the multiple analysis of variance (MANOVA). Information about the entire conflux of interacting causal phenomena is necessary for a thick explanation. Information about the nature of the glass, the gas, the filament, the wire, the switch, the plug, the electricity, as well as the finger that flicked the switch all add to the richness of the explanation and are therefore not superfluous but absolutely necessary. There is little doubt that most of us would recognise this information immediately as constituting a very rich, robust, or thick explanation as it would (at the very least go some way to) answer the question: why?

People and HR processes, of course, do not behave in similar ways to glass, gas, filaments, wires, switches and electricity, so let us consider what would constitute a thick explanation. If and when a particular outcome is complex in its enablement, then explanation is irreducible merely to giving information about a succession of events. A thick explanation of the increase in, for example, the performance of any given HR processes and their capacity to drive business performance requires two kinds of information. First, a robust explanation requires what we might call *hermeneutic* information. That is, information relating to the way the relevant agents (i.e. stakeholders) interpret, understand and make sense of the workplace and thereby initiate action. The following example from our interviews sets these observations into institutional context:

That thing about numbers is quite interesting because they are not a differentiator in their own right. All they are is an indicator that the sausage machine is churning out what it is supposed to be churning out. Once the numbers settle down, after the initial blips, we don't even need to see them. They don't drive the performance of HR. They're just numbers which we use occasionally to see where we are. What drives the performance of HR are things like the visibility of HR staff, ease of access to them, the nature of the relationships, the ability of HR to understand the strategy and map onto that. It's much more detailed and complicated. The numbers are just the sausage machine at the end telling us about the results. So we come to measurement from a very different perspective. (HR director)

Second, a thick explanation requires information about a significant (but not infinite) set of interacting and causal phenomena through which agents initiate this action. This might, for example, include information on: the social, political, economic and spatial environment of the industry and/or the firm; the composition of the team; the experiences and wishes of individuals comprising the team; the nature of the new jobs, tasks and skills (if any); the relationship between team members, the line managers and corporate strategy; the nature of control in the firm; the nature of any synergies (or dis-synergies) created by the interaction of these enabling causal phenomena and so on. The following provides an example of this from our interviews:

When I want to know, 'Well, what do we actually in fact "do"?' I have to lift up the stones and have a look underneath. Many in HR are almost exclusively reactive; put the structures in place and see what happens. You can't just buy-in things or people and help organizations through major change programmes. You have to work at it, to better understand what's in there in front of you. You need to spend a lot of time understanding people's specific roles in the business ... The critical part that you have to understand is who has the critical parts you need to hang on to, you know, who are the critical people or the critical fora within the business that you map onto to help you to do your job? ... If you don't understand these processes you have [internal] customers who do not really understand what the processes are and what impact they have. (HR director)

Clearly, these examples are not exhaustive but they are indicative of many of the accounts we have heard. Furthermore, all of the causal phenomena identified in the examples we provide could be broken down into their components as we try to provide more detailed information. Needless to say, a great deal of this information will be irreducibly qualitative. All this information adds to the richness of the explanation and is therefore not superfluous but absolutely necessary. There is little doubt that most of us would recognise this information immediately as constituting a thick explanation because it would (at least to some degree) answer the question: why?

Explanation and tendential prediction

Because of the openness of social systems, events cannot be *inductively* predicted, or predicted as *deductions* from axioms, assumptions and laws – as in the deductive method underpinning scientism sketched in previous chapters. But the social structures, institutions, mechanisms, rules, resources etc. that human agents draw upon in order to initiate action, *can* be *retroduced* and their operation uncovered and *explained*.

For critical realists, then, retroduction replaces induction and deduction as modes of inference, and explanation replaces prediction as the key objective of scientism. To the extent that we can successfully retroduce to the causal structures (etc.) that govern some observation (and there is no denying the difficulty of this), we have a theory that explains this observation. To the extent we have a theory and an explanation, we have an understanding of the tendencies generated by these structures (etc.). To the extent that we understand these tendencies we can make claims about how the structures (etc.) are likely to govern the actions of the human agents that draw upon them. We hesitate to call this a prediction because the term is now so entwined in scientistic discourse that it is almost impossible to untangle it and give it another meaning. Nonetheless, it is a prediction of some kind, albeit heavily qualified, and we call it *tendential prediction*.

If we can successfully retroduce to the social structures (etc.) that, when drawn upon by workers and managers, cause bundles of HR practices to (say) increase organisational performance, then we have a theory with an explanation of organisational performance. Such a theory with an explanation would allow us to understand the tendencies generated when workers and managers engage with HR practices and social structures (etc.). If we understand these tendencies we can make *tendential predictions*. We might, for example, be able to understand the tendencies generated by the exercise of human labour power to activate workers' powers for creative, imaginative, ingenious, self-motivated and self-directed action, as well as the counter-tendencies generated by the alienation, exploitation and commodification of human labour power. We might, therefore, be able to assess the efficacy of tendencies and counter-tendencies, and make a *tendential prediction* about the likelihood of specific bundles of HR practices increasing organisational performance. This process involves us being able to understand the combination by individuals of their agential projects with reflexive performance.

The 'internal conversation' of the HR directors we have presented above reveals to us what they believe to be the case and it is causally efficacious, at least to a degree, because their thinking is deemed to be efficacious – i.e. they have the power to implement practices they deem appropriate. The conversation then becomes one between what might be labelled self-knowledge (what one knows and thinks), societal knowledge (knowing what others think), a stance (the adoption of a position of what one wants to achieve) and the legitimacy of this agential project underpinned by the accompanying *explanations* to justify one's project to oneself. Here at last we move away from 'scientistic' notions of causality (as event regularity) to the genuine interplay between subjective properties (discursive penetration through the internal conversation) and objective structures (organisational successes, failures, 'good' performance, 'bad' performance, etc.). People, their diagnoses and their actions, then, are as influential and important for analysis as the structures and institutions they necessarily engage with.[9] That said, institutions and their environments play a major role in shaping how the causal role of HR is perceived and explained. Moreover, even when individuals, and in the case of the example below, very powerful individuals have one view of how the HRM–P link should be understood, institutional isomorphism takes over:

This is a financially focused world, with finance being focused on a daily, weekly basis. It is almost all consuming, and I see insufficient time to take a cold look at where [in HR] we are going to make some investments. Everything here is driven by today's financial issues. I'm alarmed at the time devoted to financials by HR. We do not have a long-term strategic view. There are measures that we are immersed in, dissecting every dollar for the CEO whose focus is on the score and on the numbers. Nothing else here appears to matter. It's just a cultural issue for us. Most of the issues we have in the business are leadership issues, talent issues or organizational and structural issues. These are probably 70 per cent of all our problems and 7 per cent of our attention! We spend all of our time focusing on how to measure the financials and not the problems we need to manage to get the financial results we're supposed to be delivering. (HR director)

In sum, then, critical realism provides us with three meta-theoretical insights. First, it provides us with a sophisticated understanding of the limitations of the 'scientistic approach' and, therefore, sound reasons to move beyond it. Second, it provides us with one possible alternative, namely, the causal-explanatory method – a method more suited to the openness of the social world in general, and one identified by institutional theorists in particular. Third, it provides us with a notion of reflexive performance where we seek to identify the enabling generative ensembles at work, through the discursive penetration of HR professionals' internal conversations. Understanding the underlying processes which enable or constrain certain processes is far more important than the adoption of some form of scientistic thinking in which outcome y is guaranteed through the implementation of x.

Playing the 'scientistic' card is a high-risk strategy. The tactic of trying to defend the use of enlightened HR, or other high-performance work systems, practices on the grounds of an *empirical association* between these practices and organisational performance will fail if the data remain, statistically speaking, inconclusive. The non-existence of an *empirical association* will undoubtedly be interpreted as the non-existence of any kind of *causal connection* between them. Trying to argue, belatedly, that a causal connection might exist, but the nature of this causality is more complex than can be captured in terms of an empirical association, will look like a rather lame excuse after two decades spent promoting the 'scientistic' approach. Moreover, our research shows many HR professionals' understanding of the role of HR in enhanced organisational performance is not in line with the 'scientistic' approach anyway, but aligned more with a critical realist approach.

Whilst the 'scientistic' approach, with its commitment to empirical research techniques, might be a useful *starting point* for understanding the HRM–P link, it is currently treated as the *end game*. We suggest that critical realism, by offering a more fruitful meta-theory, can play a significant part in developing this understanding. Indeed, our contention is one suggesting the meta-theory of critical realism offers the HR profession an alternative understanding to the causal role played by HR in determining organisational performance. But we do not live in a social vacuum; this much has been revealed to us in our ongoing work with HR directors, who may well subscribe to much of the meta-theory we propose here, but have to implement it in the real-world institutions in which our research took place. It is for this reason we leave the final word to one of our respondents, Chief Operating Officer and Vice President of HR of one of the world's largest financial houses:

HR plays, or I should say, HR *should* play a fundamental role in helping the organization achieve it's mission. I've always said, you know, I got the questions when I announced I was moving into HR, 'Carlos, wait a second, what are you doing? Have you lost your marbles going into HR?' My response to this was, 'Guys, I'm moving into the most important function of the bank,' and they all laughed. For me it's very simple, what drives business performance? It's all about people, right? And who's focused on people? HR. So, therefore, my definition, or my assumption is that I'm in the most important function. You have to get the basics right. You don't want to get into budget discussions. You don't want to get bogged down in budgets. You want to demonstrate you manage budget and drive value. We need to understand not just the direct budget we control but the budget we influence across the organization and metrics don't exist for this yet. The challenge is finding the linkage and for this you need to move to the next level of understanding what's going on.

Conclusion

Our research lends support to the idea that many senior HR professionals are not only unhappy with scientism, they are far happier with something like critical realism as it meshes with their own implicit modus operandi. What this demonstrates is that, far from being some arcane philosophical endeavour, carried out within the ivory tower of academia, critical realism can actually be useful on the ground, as it were.

If we have managed to convince the reader that there is something fundamentally mistaken with scientism, and that critical realism might be a better option, the next task is to actually undertake empirical research, exploring the relation between HRM and organisational performance, not via scientism, but via critical realism and the research techniques it sponsors. This is, however, a task that a new generation of empirical researchers must take up. We sincerely hope they do.

Notes

Preface

1 Although this link is sometimes referred to as the link between High Performance, or High Commitment, Work Practices or Work Systems and organisational performance.

1 Crisis? What crisis?

1 Of course, the proportion of costs represented by people varies from sector to sector, and from firm to firm. We also flag here, and discuss in some detail later (see Part II), the dangers associated with fetishising sectoral differences. We should also flag the additional confusion, often overlooked, between the costs of paying people and the costs of running HR systems to support them: in effect, the distinction between HR and talent (see Hesketh 2008a).
2 In what follows we will be referring to three separate groups. These are the *academy*: comprising academics and, to a lesser extent, other government-funded policy think tanks; the *advisors*: comprising the large scale and boutique consulting houses, together with individual gurus; and the *practitioners*: comprised mainly by those working inside organisations, including executives, managers and employees. The collective noun we use for all three is *stakeholders*.
3 Hesketh (2008a) draws on a number of sources to establish the typical HR function costs a FTSE 100 organisation £100 million per annum.

2 Tracking the emergence of the HRM–P link paradigm

1 Whilst there are some non-positivists, often coming from postmodern, poststructuralist, phenomenological, ethnomethodological and other perspectives, their voice is hardly heard in the literature on the HRM-P link.
2 It will probably have not escaped the experienced reader's attention that David Ulrich and his frequent writing and consulting partner, Will Brockbank, are also based at Michigan. At the time of writing, Tichy and colleagues have yet to combine forces with Ulrich and Brockbank.

3 We made these calculations based on a comparison of the Consumer Price Index in 1995 and 2007.

3 The state of contemporary research on the HRM–P link

1 Consultants Accenture make great play of their *Human Capital Development Framework*. They claim it is a measurement tool to 'help executives understand how human capital contributes to the bottom line financial results'; that it 'has established empirical links between specific human capital investments and business results'. They also claim it is based upon 'published research findings' although they do not state the sources (Cantrell *et al.* 2005: 15–16). When, however, we look to Accenture research reports (Balageur *et al.* 2006 and Brakely *et al.* 2004), where we might expect to find this research detailed, all we are offered are surveys enquiring into business leaders' perceptions of what HR (and other) practices contribute. Researchers cannot, at least not legitimately, claim to 'identify which factor has the most impact' (Balageur *et al.* 2006: 50) in terms of contributing to high performance, simply by asking respondents for their impressions. This kind of survey is not really evidence of a relationship between HR practices and organisation performance.

2 Our excitement in coming across a recent article by Mayson and Barrett (2006) entitled 'The "Science" and "Practice" of HRM in Small Firms', soon turned to disappointment, as the discussion simply asserted that the resource-based view is scientific, without specifying how the term 'science' is being defined or used. The question we are left with is: what is it about this view that makes it scientific?

3 See Boselie *et al.* (2005: 74) for a summary of the most common ways in which HRM practices are quantified.

4 The terms 'rigour' and 'rigorous' often crop up in the literature. Wright and Boswell (2002), for example, refer to the 'more rigorous methodologies and techniques' now available to researchers in the HRM–P paradigm. The term 'rigour' has now become synonymous with quantitative analysis and mathematical statistical techniques. By default, non-quantitative, non-mathematical and non-statistical techniques are presumed to lack rigour. We consider any piece of research that is carried out properly, and using research techniques appropriate to the phenomenon under investigation, to be rigorous.

5 The *Human Resource Management Review* (Steele 2003) has a symposium devoted to methodological issues in absenteeism research. Whilst this is a slightly different subject matter (there is nothing similar in the HRM–P literature) there are lessons for us here. The symposium

does not address 'genuine' methodological issues beyond problems of quantification and research design. The tenor of the symposium can be grasped from Steel's opening comment: when the editor 'invited me to serve as the guest editor on a special issue devoted to methodological issues ... I immediately decided that the issue's panellists should be drawn from amongst the ranks of the discipline's most active and prolific researchers. No keener insight into methodological issues is attainable than that won on the empirical battlefield, where our most careful and painstaking efforts are so often held hostage to the whims and vagaries of the methodological equivalent of the Greek Fates' (Steele 2003: 153). The guest editor is, we feel, operating with a rather limited view of what 'methodology' consists of.

6 As we will see later in this chapter and the next, many of the problems besetting scientism are not simply related to the crudity with which empirical researchers often attempt to measure naturally qualitative, inherently complex, evolving, multidimensional and subjective phenomena, but also due to 'the even greater crudity with which many concepts are theorized' (Johnson and Duberley 2000: 53).

7 Examples include: Becker and Gerhart 1996; Gerhart 1999, 2007; Gerhart *et al.* 2000; Huselid and Becker 1996; Khilji and Wang 2006; Purcell and Kinnie 2007; and Wright and Sherman 1999.

8 Examples include: Alleyne *et al.* (2005); Applebaum *et al.* (2000); Bhattacharya and Wright (2005); Bowen and Ostroff (2004); Bowman and Ambrosini (2000); Boxall (2003); Boxall and Purcell (2000); Danford *et al.* (2005); Delaney and Godard (2001); Doornward and Meihuizen (2000); Elias and Scarbrough (2004); Edwards and Wright (2001); Elvira and Davila (2005); Folger and Turillo (1999); Ghorpade (2004); Harney and Dundon (2006); Hendry *et al.* (2000); Knox and Walsh (2005); Lowe and Jones (2004); Murphy and Southey (2003); Paauwe and Boselie (2003 and 2005); Sparham and Sung (2007); Thompson (2007); Tomer (2001); Truss (2001). In a very interesting article, Ferris *et al.* (2004) use their own terminology, but come very close to critical realists like ourselves not only in their interpretation of the meta-theoretical problems facing research on the HRM–P link, but also on the kinds of alternatives that might be necessary. The fact that they do not use critical realist terminology is not, of course, a criticism.

9 Examples include: Evans (1999); Foley *et al.* (1999); Harley and Hardy (2004); Keenoy (1997); McGoldrick *et al.* (2001); Sandberg (2000); Watson (2004). Symon and Cassell (2006) have attempted a meta-theoretical critique in the field of organisational psychology, a discipline where research on the HRM–P link is undertaken and, moreover, a discipline dominated by scientism.

10 This is not confined to non-academic literature, many academic papers
    add to this misleading discourse. Huselid, for example, is cited by Chow
    (2005: 576); Den Hartog and Verburg (2004); Horgan and Muhlau
    (2003: 27); Rynes *et al.* (2002: 149); Tomer (2001: 65–6); Toulson and
    Dewe (2004: 3); Wright *et al.* (2003), to name but a few.

11 The work by Purcell (1999) and Purcell *et al.* (2003); Purcell and
    Hutchinson (2007); Purcell and Kinnie (2007) and Purcell *et al.* (2009)
    seems to flirt with scientism whilst recognising the need for alternatives.
    Consider the most recent offering from this 'team'. Whilst the authors
    have conducted significant qualitative work, and carried out extensive
    interviews, the overall thrust of their book is quantitative – indeed, it is
    rooted in 'scientism'. Much of the qualitative work is designed to pro-
    vide quantitative data. This is clearly exemplified in their second chap-
    ter entitled 'Culture and Values', especially their section on Selfridges
    which ends up showing correlations between HR practices and employee
    attitudes. This is also exemplified in their sixth chapter where they pre-
    sent a large regression model and conclude that: 'There is consistent evi-
    dence that the commitment of employees is positively associated with
    the social support provided by managers' (Purcell *et al.* 2009: 112). A
    similar story emerges in their eighth chapter where another regression
    model is used because 'Quantifying the links between people and per-
    formance ... requires an intergrated modeling approach' (2009: 173). All
    this is a far cry from their comments in the opening chapter where they
    repeatedly warn of the dangers of 'excessive emphasis on the quantita-
    tive analysis of data' (2009: 3) and even on the 'need to understand ...
    the links between HR and performance' (2009: 11). Taking a slightly
    different tack, let us consider the causal chain model linking HR and
    performance that is at the centre of their 'theory'. Thus, they observe,
    'the purpose of this [causal chain] model is to identify the key causal
    steps in the chain from intended HR practices to performance outcomes.
    It does not seek to show all interconnections, nor map in any accurate
    way the HRM experience of a given firm and its employees. The model
    allows attention to be focused on critical steps that have to be taken
    if HRM is to have a performance outcome' (2009: 15–16). The argu-
    ment then develops away from this causal chain model to suggest that
    'performance outcomes can be distal or proximal and can be restricted
    to short-term definitions of performance or can be expended to include
    measures of effectiveness' (2009: 17), only to then return to an 'impli-
    cit' causal chain model in which, 'the choice of performance measures
    that have meaning and significance for the companies and are close to
    the employee attitudinal data' (2009: 17). What 'close' constitutes in an
    ontological or epistemological sense is left unclear both in this section

and throughout the rest of the book until the penultimate chapter where a standard regression model is deployed to 'allow us to model some of the interactions between employee commitment, turnover, customer satisfaction and business performance' (2009: 173). Ultimately, we are informed that 'these relationships are not only significant, but they are also managerially meaningful. To illustrate this we calculated the ultimate impact of a one standard deviation increase in organisational commitment on business performance. This represents a 4.2 per cent increase in commitment' (2009: 174). The authors simply could not refrain from reverting to scientism for a way through the cloudiness between inputs and outputs they had previously acknowledged when originally publishing their findings. Our overall conclusion of this book is that their aim to 'develop a theoretical model which is underpinned by extensive empirical and previous research to analyse the people management – performance link' remains committed to scientism, despite their awareness of the need to really conduct more in-depth qualitative work to understand what is really going on in the black box. Purcell et al. want to have their cake and eat it.

12 The one exception is Wright and McMahan (1992) whom we cite below.

13 There are many other articles on the HRM–P link that, to a greater or lesser degree, appear to offer solid theoretical foundations for their empirical analysis. When looked at closely, however, these theoretical foundations turn out not to be quite as solid as they initially appeared. Some of the more recent examples are: Allen et al. (2003); Alleyne et al. (2006); Cho et al. (2006); Chow (2005); Colakoglu et al. (2006); Datta et al. (2005); Ferratt et al. (2005); Fey et al. (2000); Kim and Gray (2005); Khilji and Wang (2006); Marks and Lockyer (2005); Meyer and Smith (2000); Neal et al. (2005); Panayotoupoulou and Papalexandris (2004); Sels et al. (2006b); Tsai (2006); Tzafrir et al. (2004) and Youndt and Snell (2004).

14 Lest we be accused of ignoring some of the more dominant theories found in the literature, it is worth noting that Boselie et al. (2005) found three dominant clusters of theories: (1) strategic contingency approaches/external fit approaches; (2) AMO/high performance, involvement, commitment, systems; and (3) resource-based view.

15 See Bowman and Ambrosini (2000) for a non-neoclassical interpretation of resource based theory.

16 Guest (2007) has recently turned to the psychological contract to help explain how HRM has a positive impact upon employee attitudes and perhaps on wider employment relations. We have no particular objection to the use of this theory, and the reason we note it is that this

chapter is the kind of work that we consider necessary to overcome the problem of under-theorisation.

17 We will see in Chapter 4 that researchers committed to scientism are prepared to employ their meta-theory, and the quantitative, empirical, statistical techniques it sponsors (illegitimately) when dealing with naturally qualitative, inherently complex, evolving, multidimensional and subjective phenomena.

4 Scientism

1 In this book we do not deal with the meta-theoretical approach rooted in insights stemming from what is variously described as postmodernism, poststructuralism, social constructionism, continental philosophy and the linguistic or discursive 'turn' in social science.

2 See Donaldson (2003), Gordon (1991) and McKelvey (2003) for discussion of the way positivism has evolved over the last decades.

3 It derives mainly from the work of Bhaskar (1989) and has been developed by thinkers like Archer (1995, 2000, 2003). For an introduction to critical realism see Archer *et al.* (1998); Carter and New (2004); Danermark *et al.* (1997); Lawson (1997 and 2003); Reed (2001); Sayer (1994 and 2000). For a discussion in organisation and management studies more generally, see Ackroyd and Fleetwood (2000); Edwards (2006); Fleetwood and Ackroyd (2004); Fleetwood (2005); Godard (1993); Johnson and Duberley (2000: especially Chapters 2 and 3); Leca and Naccache (2006); Mutch (1999, 2000, 2002, 2004, 2006); Mutch *et al.* (2005); Reed (2001, 2003, 2007). For critical engagement with critical realism see Willmott (2005); and Contu and Willmott (2005).

4 Note that the following discussion is written from the 'perspective of scientism' as it were. If we write that 'events are the things observed to happen' then this is not a claim we endorse, simply one that would be endorsed by an advocate of scientism. We will occasionally state this or that is 'from the scientistic perspective' in order to remind the reader of this point.

5 This empirical realist ontology is not altered by the recognition, by researchers that some things exist, and matter, yet are unobservable. If these things are unobservable, and *cannot* be operationalised by proxy measures (i.e. proxied by things we can observe), then they are inadmissible to scientism and these unobservables are excluded from the scientistic ontology. If, however, things are unobservable but can be proxied, then the things that give rise to the proxies become part of the ontology: but the things themselves remain excluded from the ontology. In short, what matters vis-à-vis the ontological presuppositions *of*

scientism is not what this or that researcher thinks exist, but what scientism can deal with. Another way of putting this is to say that ontology (being) is reduced to epistemology (knowledge) and the epistemic fallacy is committed.

6 Systems theorists have a different notion which we will touch upon in the conclusion of this chapter.

7 Another example of stochastic closure is found in Huselid (1995: 648). Huselid concludes that 'a one standard deviation increase in High Performance Work Practices yields a $27,044 increase in sales and a $3,813 increase in profits'. This is not deterministic. Huselid is *not* suggesting that *all* firms in the sample who used these practices experienced increases in sales and profits of these magnitudes. It is stochastic because he is suggesting that some firms in the sample who used these practices experienced *average* increases in sales and profits of these magnitudes. Similarly, summarising the findings of three leading studies, Gerhart (1999: 32) observes that 'a one standard deviation increase in various HRM measures is associated with profits (return on assets) that are higher by 23, 16 and 23 percent respectively'.

8 Unfortunately, Sloman is extremely confused on the nature of mechanisms.

9 They also cite, approvingly, Blalock's comment that 'it is the regression coefficients that give us the *laws of science*' (emphasis added).

10 A recent handbook dedicated to methodology in social science encapsulates the way advocates of quantitative, statistical and empirical research techniques think about causality. Whilst the handbook contains two examples (Hayduck and Pazderka-Robinson 2007 and Freedman 2007) where the role of causality in statistical analysis is specifically discussed, the authors do not mention (1) that the concept of causality they are dealing with is of a Humean variety; (2) that there are problems with this concept; and (3) that there are other concepts available. The result is that their discussion of the limitations of statistical analysis is extremely partial. They simply do not consider the kind of meta-theoretical criticisms we raise in this book.

11 Indeed, in a recent paper, Datta *et al.* (2005: 142) proceed in the same vein, claiming to be 'Following the advice and previous practice of SHRM scholars' and citing Huselid's paper as an exemplar.

12 Consider another example. Ahmad and Schroeder (2003: 27) interpret the results of their correlation as indicating causality although they never use causal language. What else does the following imply, if not causality: 'A higher status difference in a plant is associated with lower efforts in other HRM practices. That is, it is unlikely that the HRM practices will flourish in a plant where high status differences exists'.

13 In an otherwise extremely insightful paper reflecting upon the way time is (or more accurately is not) dealt with in causal relationships in management literature, Mitchell and James (2001) fail to consider *non-*Humean forms of causality.

14 See Fleetwood (2001) for further elaboration of functional relations from a critical realist perspective.

15 Hayduck and Pazderka-Robinson (2007: 148) write: 'correlation is not causation but causal actions produce correlations'. We will see in Chapter 6 that it is quite possible for causal actions not to cause correlations, and that causality has nothing to do with patterns in the flux of events such as correlations.

16 The meta-theoretical problems discussed below are found in empirical research in wider social and managerial science and cannot, therefore, be explained away by noting that HRM and, especially, research on the HRM–P link, is relatively immature as researchers like Rogers and Wright (1999: 311) suggest. Indeed, these meta-theoretical problems are found in almost all research operating (implicitly or explicitly) from a scientistic perspective.

17 Typical examples often cited here, and discussed at length by us elsewhere, include internal career opportunities, training, result-oriented appraisals, profit sharing, employment security, etc. We are not disputing that these practices may well *tend* (although the concept of a 'tendency' is crucial and discussed in Chapter 6) to enhance performance. We do object, however, to the reduction of the complex social structures, mechanisms and powers which comprise these activities to simple headline policies and practices, thereby negating the almost infinite number of permutations of their enactment at the deeper levels of human activity and experience. We return to this observation below.

18 In a recent book on economic modelling, written from a scientistic perspective, Nurmi (2006: 8) writes: 'the first problem we encounter is that, at least intuitively, much (indeed most) of our behaviour is not subject to law-like regularities. This is, of course, not to say that there are no laws of behaviour, but, at least our present day knowledge does not include them to the extent that one could argue that many (let alone most) social science explanations were based on them. Yet, explanations abound in the social sciences, but rather than law-like universal statements they typically invoke more restricted invariances of tendencies that may include exceptions'. Nurmi's recognition that law-like regularities are rare in the social world is tantamount to recognising that the social world is an open system. Unfortunately for him, the deductive modelling he advocates would only 'work' in cases where

event regularities exist, that is, in closed systems. His retreat to the concept of 'tendency' is probably an attempt to retreat to stochastic closure, which we will elaborate upon in a few pages. We will return to the notion of tendencies in Chapter 6.

19 For discussion and debate on open and closed systems, see Bigo (2006); Chick and Dow (2005); Dow (2006); Fleetwood (2006) and Mearman (2006).

20 The PricewaterhouseCoopers (2003) study seems not to spot the contradiction it highlights. There simply may not be a 'relationship between historic trends and future performance' in part 'because people ... behave in different, sometimes unpredictable ways'. Hence, the idea that this alleged relationship is 'not always well understood' misses the point completely. The report confuses the (reasonable) desire of firms to be able to predict the future with their ability to do so. Wishing doesn't make it so!

21 The language of 'missing variables' used by statisticians is instructive. The phrase gives the impression that it is a technical problem, something that could be solved; if we just took a little more time and effort we would 'find' them. In language hides a far more serious problem. Social theory is often so poor that researchers really do not know many of the causal mechanisms at work. Because they know they do not know them, and have chosen to proceed without better theory, they simply refer to this as the problem of missing variables. Referring to the problem of missing variables, in terms of problems of maintaining intrinsic and extrinsic closure conditions, forces us to recognise that, in an open and let us not forget multiply caused, complex and evolving system, a vast number of causal mechanisms (expressed as variables) will remain 'missing' until and unless we try to look for them using more sophisticated techniques, guided by better theory.

22 Many empirical researchers on the HRM–P link actually have an intuitive grasp of the problems posed by intrinsic and extrinsic causal factors, although they do not, of course, use this terminology. Youndt and Snell (2004: 356) conclude by considering the need for future empirical studies to include extrinsic factors such as 'other boundary spanning activities, market relations, hierarchical relations, symbols and values' and intrinsic factors such as 'organizational design and R&D'. Furthermore, Youndt, this time with another colleague, Skaggs, shows that the customer can also be a causal factor in organisational performance (Skaggs and Youndt 2003). Whilst Bhattacharya and Wright (2005: 929) make no reference to critical realism, they clearly have something similar to our ideas in mind when they write: 'Human assets are valuable to the firm, but their returns may not remain stable over

time due to changes in business conditions, changes within the firm or changes in individuals that comprise human capital'.

23 Many researchers get embroiled in various contradictions that spring from the attempt to remain within, and yet go beyond, scientism. Lahteenmaki *et al.* (1998) make use of a range of statistical techniques in their search for positive relations between strategic HRM and company performance. That they identify hardly any such relations is besides the point here as they use the same kind of empirical approach as those that do claim to find positive relations, which implies they accept their usefulness. Yet they end up raising doubts about these same techniques and call for intensive case studies to reveal the complex nature of the relationships. Despite their obvious desire to go beyond the current state of affairs, Peccei and Rosenthal (2001: 883) cannot break with scientism and end up 'first modelling and then testing the core assumptions linking HR practices and management behaviours to the customer orientated behaviour of front-line workers'. Whilst much depends upon the methods adopted, many who opt for a mixed-methodology strategy (e.g. Budhwar 2000), actually end up with what amounts to scientism with some (often useful) insights bolted on.

24 Indeed, Nurmi's recent (2006) book can be read as describing the state of the art in contemporary economic modelling. He advocates closed system modelling – although he does not describe his ideas in these terms.

25 The same applies, of course, to the event *ys*.

26 Ingham (2007) raises some basic problems with measurement and quantification (and complex systems) and tends to favour understanding over measurement. Although Baron and Armstrong (2007) devote a chapter to 'Measuring Human Capital' they do not move beyond superficial warnings about 'measurement difficulties' (2007: 60), nor do they address the deeper problems arising with attempts to quantify inherently qualitative phenomena. The same goes for Hirsh *et al.* (1995). In a far more sophisticated paper, Gerhart (2007) deals with methodological issues in the HRM–P literature. His consideration of measurement errors, however, deals with the technicalities of statistical analysis, but does not think to call into question whether it is in fact possible to measure the kind of inherently complex, evolving, multidimensional, subjective qualities found in HRM.

27 Bhattacharya and Wright run into a contradiction based upon their recognition of the inherently uncertain and qualitative nature of returns generated by employees, and their commitment to some form of scientism. On the one hand they recognise that the 'sources of uncertainty of real assets may be multiple and not quantifiable' (2005: 938) and that 'the valuation of human capital is at best problematic and

at worst impossible (2005: 945). On the other hand, they have illusions in the ability to build mathematical models and make predictions (2005: 937). Many years ago John Maynard Keynes made the distinction between risk and uncertainty, and this is well known to contemporary post-Keynesian economists. Risk can (even here matters are far from straightforward) be dealt with using probability, but uncertainty cannot. Whilst we can calculate the probability of drawing a red ball from an urn of fifty red and fifty white balls, we simply have no way of calculating the probability of another Gulf War, or the probability of a workforce getting fed up with a performance-related pay scheme because these things are uncertain. And yet these things are the stuff of HRM. Incidentally, this is another reason why stochastic closure is problematic.

28 Shah and Corley (2006) make a good case for the use of qualitative analysis to overcome the limitations in quantitative data of theory construction.

5 Prediction, explanation and theory

1 There is a strange paradox to scientism's search for predictability vis-à-vis the HRM–P link. Suppose we actually found the Holy Grail, that is, suppose we actually succeeded in establishing a thick statistical link between some precise bundle of HRM practices and increased organisational performance. We would then be able to predict that if this bundle was introduced into an organisation, then that organisation's performance would increase. But notice that we would have also locked ourselves into a worrying state of determinism. If the prediction is accurate, there is nothing that intervention by human beings could do to prevent organisational performance from increasing and the future would be completely determined. If human intervention could alter the future course of events, then it could frustrate the prediction, thereby rendering it inaccurate. It seems that our ability to intervene to change the future is compatible with inaccurate predictions and incompatible with accurate predictions.

2 Ohm's Laws states: $I = V / R$, where V = voltage in volts; I = current in amps; and R = resistance in ohms.

3 It should be stressed, however, that even in natural sciences where law-like regularities are discovered, the objective of science is not to find the law. Finding the law is the first step. After that, 'why?' questions are raised. Natural scientists do not stop with the discovery that $I = V / R$, but go on to ask: 'What mechanisms are at work in the structure of matter that explain why this relationship holds?'.

4 We asked the authors of the twenty-five 'key empirical studies' mentioned in Wall and Wood's (2005) survey if their studies had been replicated. Just under half replied. From what they said, and from our reading of the literature, it appears that none of them have actually been replicated.

5 Something similar occurs when Ichniowski and Shaw (1999) extend the work of Ichniowski *et al.* (1997).

6 The point is easier to grasp if we *do not* use matrix notation and we treat every HRM practice as a single variable. What is at issue here are the meta-theoretical principles involved, not claims about how HRM practices are bundled.

7 Katou and Budhwar (2006: 1243) withdraw 'the non-significant variables' from the statistical analysis 'through backwards regression, in order to get more efficient estimates'. Withdrawing a variable from the model because it is insignificant does seem to ride roughshod over theoretical claims that suggest the variable should be included in the first place.

8 Mirowski and Sklivas (1991) observe something similar in economics, claiming that most economists do not 'replicate' the findings of others, rather they 'reproduce' them. Replication involves subjecting a theory to the same empirical tests, using the same data source and the same model to see if the original prediction: (a) can be generated again; (b) remains valid when additional data is added. Reproduction involves subjecting a theory to the same empirical tests, but with a data source and model that can be quite different from the original. Fleetwood (1999a) investigated the economics of trade unions and concluded that, in this paradigm, replication is not undertaken.

9 See also Ruben (1992).

10 In the introduction to a series of case studies, Becker and Huselid claim to provide 'an outline of the theoretical rationale and empirical literature linking HRM systems with corporate performance' (1999: 288). We see little that can be described as 'theoretical rationale'. They also claim the case studies provide 'rich detail on how leading firms use their HRM systems'. Whilst these case studies offer description, we doubt 'rich detail' can be obtained from 'a day and a half interviewing the senior HR and line leadership'.

11 Ichniowski *et al.* cite labour economists Baker *et al.* (1994); Holmstrom and Milgram (1994); Kandel and Lazear (1992) and Milgrom and Roberts (1990 and 1995).

12 This is another reason why we prefer the term 'scientism' over 'positivism'. The former expresses the unreflexive way in which meta-theorising is carried out by mainstream economists.

13 See Fleetwood (2001) for the other argument.

14 For a good discussion of the legitimate uses of abstraction, see Sayer (1998).

15 *Homo economicus* also appears in the guise of the rational maximising firm. The following comment shows Gant *et al.* (2002) unable to break with the rationality assumption. A 'firm's decision to invest in a new system of innovative HRM practices would be determined by the added revenues associated with the productivity and quality benefits due to innovative HRM systems less the costs of adopting and implementing those systems:

$$I_{it} = 1 \text{ if } EP_{it} - C_{it} > 0.$$

Adoption of innovative HRM practices by line i at time t, or I_{it}, will occur when the expected productivity gains, EP_{it}, exceed the costs of adoption' (Gant *et al.* 2002: 298–9). This kind of mechanistic, actually, closed systemic, behaviour is rejected by many non-mainstream economists such as Elvira and Davila (2005: 2273) who observe that: one 'serious limitation shared by ... SHRM theories is they rest on the assumption that firms act as economically rational actors ... This assumption is questionable'. Tomer (2001) advances a similar critique of mainstream theory.

16 They could, of course, be measured in some meaningless way, as we noted in Chapter 4, but this would lead to another line of criticism.

17 For further consideration of economic theory and its meta-theoretical problems, see Downward (2003); Fleetwood (1999b); Lawson (1997 and 2003) and Lewis (2004).

18 See also the forum in *Administrative Science Quarterly* (introduced by Sutton and Staw 1995; and the symposium in *Academy of Management Review* introduced by Van de Ven (1989).

19 Apart from Wright and McMahan (1992) we could not find any examples from within the HRM–P literature.

20 See also Bacharach (1989) and Van de Ven (1989).

21 We say 'minimally' because there are other criteria that need to be met for something to be said to be a bona fide theory, such as generalisability, verisimilitude and parsimony. We do not elaborate upon these other criteria here, because a 'theory' (of the HRM–P link or whatever) that explains nothing falls at the first hurdle as it were.

22 It is easy to see how this mistake is easily made once one has a commitment to scientism. Recall that in Chapter 4 scientism was defined as loosely referring to the employment of methods and techniques allegedly similar to (some aspects of) natural science, without actually specifying what these methods and techniques are and why they are appropriate to social science.

23 The fact that their appendix describes their variables, details the way they are measured, and there is no mention of meta-theoretical problems with empirical research on the HRM–P link, encourages this conclusion.

24 A similar conclusion might be drawn from Guest *et al.* (2003: 311) who conclude by asking a question very similar to that of Ramsay *et al.*, namely: 'We are still left with the question of why, when the stricter tests are used, the results of this study appear to be more negative than many other published studies showing little or no association between HRM and performance'. What they seem unable, or unwilling, to face is the possibility that in an open system like a workplace, associations of this kind are most unlikely to occur.

25 Gerhart (2007) engages in a similar kind of analysis, also failing to consider the kind of meta-theoretical problems we raise in this book.

6 Critical realism

1 For example, Ostroff *et al.* (2005: 592) write that: 'The functional form of these relationships is tested with polynomial regression *because this technique has been touted as a more appropriate methodology*'. This is tantamount to using a technique simply because everyone else does, totally unconcerned as to whether this technique is appropriate to the social phenomena being analysed.

2 I will not distinguish between social and cultural structures. On this see Archer (1995).

3 Others share this concern. Bateira (2006); Hodgson (2002, 2003, 2004, 2006a and 2006b); Jessop and Nielsen (2003); Lawson (2003); Nielsen (2006); Portes (2006); Rogers-Hollingsworth (2002) and Searle (2005) seek to tighten up our understanding of institutions. Archer (2000); Elder-Vass (2006, 2007a, 2007b); Jackson (2007); Lewis (2000); Lewis and Runde (2007); Lopez and Scott (2000); Lounsbury and Ventresca (2003); Porpora (1998, 2007); Risman (2004) and Scott (2001) have done something similar for social structures.

4 See Elder-Vass (2006 and 2007a) for an elaboration of emergence.

5 Rule-guided behaviour may have an ethical element to it, because rules do not just guide, they often guide us to do the 'right' thing – hence the inclusion of values. See Van Staveren (2001: Chapter 7) and MacCormick (1998).

6 Should it transpire that a convention, norm, value or custom has a property that means it should be not be associated with a rule, I

will happily disassociate it. Until such time I proceed with this more inclusive definition.

7 Burns and Carson (2002); De Cindio *et al.* (2003); Lindbladh and Lyttkens (2002); O'Mahoney (2005) and Rogers-Hollingsworth (2002) are recent examples.

8 See McLeod (2005) and Burkitt (2002) for refutations of *habitus* as a mechanistic and deterministic concept.

9 Something like these three processes is going on, even if it is not explicitly mentioned, in the following articles – selected because they are relatively recent, and they deliberately use the concept of *habitus*: Colley (2003); David *et al.* (2003); Holdsworth (2006); McDonough (2006); Nash (2003); O'Mahoney (2007); Taylor (2005).

10 This is in-keeping with Porpora (1998: 344) and (2007: 198).

11 It is important to note that Archer's notion of deliberation does *not* equate to making calculatively, rational, maximising decisions; she totally rejects *homo economicus*. It simply means that agents often think about their concerns, what they need, what will enable and constrain them, and what action might be appropriate in the circumstances. This can result in wholly inappropriate action when agents' deliberations are mistaken, sub-optimal outcomes, and can involve genuine altruism – i.e. not self-interest in disguise.

12 We could do the same for the positioned-practice of a manager, but space does not allow it and the principle point can be made by considering one set of agents.

13 Whilst powers are rarely discussed in literature on the HRM–P link, the distinction between an exercised power and its actualisation may be understood, but in different terminology. Conceiving of 'competencies and capabilities' in a similar way to which we conceive of powers, Wright *et al.* (2001: 711) write that: 'competencies and capabilities refer to organizational processes, engaged in by people, resulting in superior products'. This is a recognition of the distinction between the conditions necessary for an outcome, and the outcome itself. Committed as they are to scientism, however, it is not easy to see how Wright *et al.* can actually deal with something like an exercised power that can exist unactualised. Cardy and Selvarajan (2005: 236–8) are unclear about whether a competence is an underlying causal power (a condition for action) or a set of patterns (an action itself). If they have the former in mind, it is not clear how such things might be measured if they are unexercised.

14 Humans can be considered generative ensembles, although we insist on maintaining an ontological distinction between humans (as configurations) and social phenomena like organisations (as different kinds of

configurations). Humans and organisations may be causal configurations, but they are different kinds of causal configurations with different constitutions and properties.

15 The term 'thin' comes from Cartwright's (2007: 19) phrase 'thick causal concepts'. Her book is a recent, and extremely sophisticated, elaboration of causality that is critical of much of what passes for ideas on causality. Like us, Cartwright (a realist but not necessarily a critical realist) prefers the notion of tendency, although it is not exactly clear whether her notion of tendency, which appears to derive from J.S. Mill, is similar to the one we prefer.

16 This is Aristotelian in origin as it employs four kinds of causes – *material* (that out of which something is made), *formal* (that into which, or according to which, something is made), *efficient* (that by which something is made) and final (that for the sake of which something is made). For an elaboration see Kurki (2003) and Groff (2004).

17 Some empirical researchers on the HRM-P link are aware of the limitations. Gelade and Ivery (2003: 399) state clearly that their model: 'almost certainly represents a considerable simplification of the complex, and possibly reciprocal, system of causal relationships that characterize a sophisticated commercial DUM [decision making unit]'. They do not, however, suggest ways that their model might be made more sophisticated, probably because it cannot be, at least not without abandoning thin causality and adopting a different aetiology than that presupposed by scientism.

18 It is important to tackle the red herring here. It is true that the list of what *could, in principle*, be included in a thick explanation, could easily expand until it included, literally, everything, and go all the way back to the big bang. In practice, however, social scientists usually avoid a potential infinite regress by making use of *abstraction* (Sayer 1998). That is, they make judgments about which factors need to be included and which can safely be excluded. This is of course fallible, and sometimes investigators get it wrong – but it is, in principle, no different than deciding upon which variables to include and which to exclude (Runde 1998).

19 The term 'causal-explanation' appears in early positivist writing and in the work of Weber. Whatever the meaning attributed to it outside contemporary critical realism, it is important to note that the term 'causal' does not refer to causality as regularity, that is, causality described in this book as thin.

20 To avoid any confusion, please note that we distinguish between method and research technique – such as interviews that generate qualitative

data or questionnaires that generate quantitative data. This section unfolds in two stages.

21 For example, Echambadi *et al.*'s (2006) recent overview of best practice in quantitative research mentions induction and deduction, but does not consider other modes of inference.

22 Retroduction is often said to be a form of abduction. We need to be a little careful here as abduction is often associated with the idea of postulating a new statistical hypothesis to explain some set of facts. In this guise, it stands in opposition to critical realism and to retroduction. When it is used simply to refer to something like inference to the best explanation (Ladyman 2002: 47) it is compatible with critical realism. Retroduction is a form of transcendental inquiry and has its roots in Kant.

23 Lipton (1993) refers to this process not as retroduction, but as 'inference to the best explanation' (actually, it is the title of his book) but we consider this merely a difference in terminology.

24 For discussions of epistemology and methodology compatible with critical realism see Ackroyd (2004); Knight (2002); Johnson and Duberley (2000).

25 Much depends upon the branch of science we have in mind. It is relatively easy to generalise about (basic) optics, but difficult to generalise about meteorology or oceanography.

26 This is sometime recognised by empirical researchers. Gelade and Ivery (2003: 398), for example, note that a limitation of their study is that 'the observations are of a single organization and the extent to which they are representative of organizations in general ... can be determined only by reference to the work of other researchers'. In a social system where no two organisations are alike, and in an open system where phenomena constantly evolve and change, it is hard to know just how much work by other researchers would be necessary to make their conclusions generalisable.

27 We would like to thank Anne Fleetwood for coming up with the conception of 'tendential prediction' one day whilst walking in the UK's Lake District.

28 If it turns out that we use our explanation to generate a policy and this policy is successful, then this is not a successful *prediction*: it is a successful *practice*. We did not predict the future, we made the future happen.

29 In a paper setting out a model of labour markets, Fleetwood (2010a) puts critical realism to work in ways that we might put it to work in HRM.

7 Putting critical realism to work

1 What will also become clear below is what 'works' in the day-to-day practice of running organisations does not necessarily work when seeking scientistic 'evidence' of causality through changes in the metrics used to measure HR interventions. Again, our argument in preceding chapters has been one suggesting that this says less about the impact of the actions of the HR professionals, and more about the methodological inadequacies of the scientistic assumptions underpinning the utilisation of the metrics.

2 Of course, researchers located in the scientistic paradigm will also point to both their veracity and experience. But, as Bruner (1986: 13) succinctly puts it, 'Scientists, perhaps because they rely on familiar stories to fill in the gaps of their knowledge, have a harder time in practice. But their salvation is to wash the stories away when causes can be substituted for them'.

3 We wouldn't want to run away with ourselves in the literary exercise of drawing parallels between the alethiometer or Golden Compass and our own perspective. Nevertheless, the resonances are striking. For example, Alethia is not just the Greek word for truth, but it is also the original name of the International Association of Critical Realism's journal. Reading the alethiometer is not a deductivistic, predictive exercise. On the contrary, retroduction is very much the name of the game. When asked to explain how she reads the instrument, Lyra suggests, 'I just make my mind go clear and then it's sort of like looking down into water. You got to let your eyes find the right level, because that's the only one that's in focus. Something like that' (Pullman 1995: 173–4). The alethiometer itself has a structured ontology insofar as three needles represent three levels of analysis, together with a fourth needle for further reflection, through which the movements of the other three arrows ultimately reveal the answer to the questions of 'why?' posed by the reader of the alethiometer. We will refrain from drawing further parallels between *Northern Lights* and our meta-theoretical framework as the metaphor has now served its illustrative and comparative purpose.

4 We have in mind here Butler's (1990: 173) definition of performativity, which she defines as, 'acts, gestures, enactments, generally constructed [and are] *performative* in the sense that the essence or identity that they otherwise purport to express are *fabrications* manufactured and sustained through corporeal signs and other discursive means'.

5 It is important to note that Archer's notion of deliberation does not equate to making calculatively, rational, maximising decisions. It simply means that agents often think about their concerns, what they need, what will

enable and constrain them, and what action might be appropriate. This can result in wholly inappropriate action when agents' deliberations are mistaken, to sub-optimal outcomes, and can involve genuine altruism – i.e. not self-interest in disguise.

6 Some researchers on the HRM–P link, like Purcell and Hutchinson (2007), are aware of this – although they do not use critical realist terminology.

7 The terms 'objective' and 'subjective' have become rather fraught in contemporary social scientism. See Fleetwood (2004) for a discussion.

8 A significant point to our argument here is that understanding why certain outcomes do not prevail as a direct consequence of certain organisational HR practices lies in explaining the generative ensembles at work underpinning them (Hesketh and Fleetwood 2006b).

9 But not, we hasten to add, reducible to their diagnoses (cf. Fleetwood 2005).

Bibliography

Ackroyd, S. (2004) 'Methodology for Management Studies: Some Implications of Critical Realism' in S. Fleetwood and S. Ackroyd (eds.), *Realism in Action in Organisation and Management*, London: Routledge.

Ackroyd, S. and Fleetwood, S. (2000) *Realist Perspectives on Organisation and Management*, London: Routledge.

Ahmad, S. and Schroeder, R. (2003) 'The Impact of Human Resource Management Practices on Operational Performance: Recognizing Country and Industry Differences', *Journal of Operations Management*, Vol. 21, 19–43.

Allen, D., Shore, L. and Griffeth, R. (2003) 'The Role of Perceived Organizational Support and Supportive Human Resource Practices in the Turnover Process', *Journal of Management*, Vol. 29, No. 1, 99–118.

Alleyne, P., Doherty, L. and Greenidge, D. (2006) 'Human Resource Management in the Barbados Hotel Industry', *International Journal of Hospitality Management*, Vol. 6, 623–46.

Alleyne, P., Doherty, L. and Howard, M. (2005) 'A Qualitative Study of HRM and Performance in the Barbados Hotel Industry', *Journal of Human Resources in the Hospitality and Tourism*, Vol. 4, No. 2, 27–51.

Applebaum, E., Bailey, T., Berg, P. and Kallerberg, A. (2000) *Manufacturing Advantage: Why High-Performance Systems Pay off*, Ithaca: Cornell University Press.

Archer, M. (1995) *Realist Social Theory: The Morphogenetic Approach*, Cambridge: Cambridge University Press.

(1998) 'Realism and Morphogenesis' in M. Archer, R. Bhaskar, A. Collier, T. Lawson and A. Norrie (eds.), *Critical Realism: Essential Readings*, London: Routledge.

(2000) *Being Human, the Problem of Agency*, Cambridge: Cambridge University Press.

(2003) *Structure, Agency and the Internal Conversation*, Cambridge: Cambridge University Press.

Archer, M., Bhaskar, R., Collier, A., Lawson, T. and Norrie, A. (1998) *Critical Realism: Essential Readings*, London: Routledge.

Argyris, C. (1973) 'Personality and Organization Theory Revisited', *Administrative Science Quarterly*, Vol. 18, No. 2, 141–67.

Aron, R. and Singh, J. (2005) 'Getting Offshoring Right', *Harvard Business Review*, Vol. 83, No. 12, 135–43.

Bacharach, S. (1989) 'Organizational Theories: Some Criteria for Evaluation', *Academy of Management Review*, Vol. 14, No. 4, 495–515.

Bacon, N. and Blyton, P. (2003) 'The Impact of Teamwork on Skills: Employee Perceptions of who Gains/who Loses', *Human Resource Management Journal*, Vol. 13, No. 2, 13–29.

Baker, G., Gibbons, R. and Murphy, K. (1994) 'Subjective Performance Measures in Optimal Incentive Contracts', *Quarterly Journal of Economics*, Vol. 108, No. 8, 1125–56.

Balageur, E., Cheese, P. and Marchetti, C. (2006) *Accenture-High Performance Workforce Study: Research Report*, London: Accenture.

Barber, F. and Strack, R. (2005) 'The Surprising Economics of a "People Business"', *Harvard Business Review*, June, 81–90.

Barney, J. (1991) 'Firm Resources and Sustained Competitive Advantage', *Journal of Management*, Vol. 17, No. 1, 99–120.

(1991) 'Is The Resource-Based "View" a Useful Perspective for Strategic Management Research? Yes', *Academy of Management Review*, Vol. 26, No. 1, 41–56.

Baron, A. and Armstrong, M. (2007) *Human Capital Management: Achieving Added Value through People*, London and Philadelphia: Kogan Page.

Bateira, J. (2006) 'What are Institutions? A Naturalist Approach', EAEPE 2006 Conference, Istanbul, Turkey.

Batt, R. (2001) 'The Economics of Teams amongst Technicians', *British Journal of Industrial Relations*, Vol. 39, No. 1, 1–24.

Becker, B. and Gerhart, B. (1996) 'The Impact of Human Resource Management on Organizational Performance: Progress and Prospects', *Academy of Management Journal*, Vol. 30, No. 4, 779–801.

Becker, B. and Huselid, M. (1998) 'High Performance Work Systems and Firm Performance: A Synthesis of Research and Managerial Implications', *Research in Personnel & Human Resources Management*, Vol. 16, 53–101.

(1999) 'Overview: Strategic HRM in Five Leading Firms', *Human Resource Management*, Vol. 38, No. 4, 287–301.

(2006) 'Strategic Human Resources Management: Where Do We Go From Here?', *Journal of Management,* Vol. 32, 898–925.

Becker, B., Huselid, M. and Ulrich, D. (2001) *The HR Scorecard: Linking People, Strategy and Performance,* Cambridge, MA: Harvard Business School Press.

Beer, M., Spector, B., Lawrence, P. R., Quinn Mills, D. and Walton, R.E. (1984) *Managing Human Assets,* New York: The Free Press.

Bennis, W. and O'Toole, J. (2005) 'How Business Schools Lost Their Way', *Harvard Business Review,* Vol. 83, No. 5, 96–105.

Bhaskar R. (1978) *A Realist Theory of Science,* Hemel Hempstead: Harvester-Wheatsheaf.

(1989) *The Possibility of Naturalism,* Hemel Hempstead: Harvester-Wheatsheaf.

Bhattacharya, M. and Wright, P. (2005) 'Managing Human Assets in an Uncertain World: Applying Real Options Theory to HRM', *International Journal of Human Resource Management,* Vol. 16, No. 6, 929–48.

Bigo, V. (2006) 'Open and Closed Systems and the Cambridge School', *Review of Social Economy,* Vol. LXIV, No. 4, 493–513.

Boselie, P., Dietz, G. and Boon, C. (2005) 'Commonalities and Contradictions in HRM and Performance Research', *Human Resource Management Journal,* Vol. 15, No. 3, 67–94.

Boudreau, J. and Ramstad, P. (1999) 'Human Resource Metrics: Can Measures be Strategic?', *Research in Personnel and Human Resources Management,* Supplement 4, 75–98.

(2007) *Beyond HR: The New Science of Human Capital,* Boston: Harvard Business School Press.

Bourdieu, P. (1998) *Outline of a Theory of Practice,* Cambridge: Cambridge University Press.

Bowen, D. and Ostroff, C. (2004) 'Understanding HRM-Form Performance Linkages: The Role of the "Strength" of the HRM System', *Academy of Management Review,* Vol. 29, No. 2, 203–21.

Bowman, C. and Ambrosini, V. (2000) 'Value Creation Versus Value Capture: Towards a Coherent Definition of Value in Strategy', *British Journal of Management,* Vol. 11, 1–15.

Boxall, P. (2003) 'HR Strategy and Competitive Advantage in the Service Sector', *Human Resource Management Journal,* Vol. 13, No. 3, 5–20.

Boxall, P. and Purcell, J. (2000) 'Strategic HRM: Where Have We Come From and Where Should We Be Going?', *International Journal of Management Reviews,* Vol. 2, No. 2, 183–203.

Brakely, H., Cheese, P. and Clinton, D. (2004) *Accenture-High Performance Workforce Study: Research Report,* London: Accenture.

Brewster, C. (1999) 'Different Paradigms in HRM: Questions Raised by Comparative Research', *Research in Personnel and Human Resource Management,* Supplement 4, Strategic HRM in the Twenty First Century, 213–38.

Brown, S. and Eisenhardt, K. (1998) *Competing on the Edge: Strategy as Structured Chaos,* Cambridge, MA: Harvard Business School Press.

Bruner, J. (1986) *Actual Minds, Possible Worlds,* Cambridge, MA: Harvard University Press.

Budhwar, P. (2000) 'Strategic Integration and Development of Human Resource Management in the UK Manufacturing Sector', *British Journal of Management,* Vol. 11, 285–302.

Burkitt, I. (2002) 'Technologies of the Self: Habitus and Capacities', *Journal of the Theory of Social Behaviour,* Vol. 32, No. 2, 219–37.

Burns, T. and Carson, M. (2002) 'Actors, Paradigms and Institutional Dynamics: The Theory of Social Rule Systems Applied to Radical Reforms' in J. Rogers-Hollingsworth et al. (eds.), *Advancing Socio-economics: An Institutionalist Perspective,* Lanham: Rowman and Littlefield.

Burns, T. and Stalker, G. (1961) *The Management of Innovation,* Oxford: Oxford University Press.

Butler, J. (1990) *Gender Troubles: Feminism and the Subversion of Identity,* London: Routledge.

Cakar, F. and Bititci, U. (2002) 'Modelling the HRM Business Process', *International Journal of Human Resources Development and Management,* Vol. 2, No. 3/4, 223–47.

Caldwell, B. (1991) *Beyond Positivism: Economic Methodology in the Twentieth Century,* Sydney: Unwin Hyman.

Camic, C. (1986) 'The Matter of Habit', *American Journal of Sociology,* Vol. 91, No. 5, 1039–87.

Cantrell, S., Benton, J., Thomas, R., Vey, M. and Kerzel, L. (2005) 'Human Performance Insights: Year in Review 2005', Accenture publication.

Cardy, R. and Selvarajan, T. (2005) 'Competencies: Alternative Frameworks for Competitive Advantage', *Business Horizons,* Vol. 49, 235–45.

Carter, B. and New, C. (2004) *Making Realism Work: Realist Social Theory and Empirical Research,* London: Routledge.

Cartwright, N. (2007) *Hunting Causes and Using Them: Approaches in Philosophy and Economics,* Cambridge: Cambridge University Press.

Cascio, W. (2007) 'Evidence-based Management and the Market-place for Ideas', *Academy of Management Review,* Vol. 50, No. 5, 1009–12.

Chadwick, C. and Capelli, P. (1999) 'Alternatives to Generic Strategy Typologies in Strategic Human Resource Management', *Research in Personnel and Human Resource Management,* Supplement 4, 1–29.

Chalmers, A. (1999) *What Is This Thing Called Science?,* Buckingham: Open University Press.

Cheese, P., Thomas, R.J. and Craig, E. (2008) *The Talent Powered Organization: Strategies for Globalization, Talent Management and High Performance,* London: Kogan Page.

Chick, V. and Dow, S. (2005) 'The Meaning of Open Systems', *Journal of Economic Methodology*, Vol. 12, No. 3, 361–81.

Cho, S., Woods, R., Jang, S. and Erdem, M. (2006) 'Measuring the Impact of Human Resource Management Practices on Hospitality Firms' Performances', *Hospitality Management,* Vol. 25, 262–77.

Chow, I. (2005) 'High Performance Work Systems in Asian Companies', *Thunderbird International Business Review*, Vol. 47, No. 5, 575–99.

Clark, I. (1999) 'Corporate Human Resources and "Bottom Line" Financial Performance', *Personnel Review*, Vol. 28, No. 4, 290–306.

Clegg, S.R. and Ross-Smith, A. (2003) 'Revising The Boundaries: Management Education and Learning in a Postpositivist World,' *Academy of Management Learning & Education*, Vol. 2, No. 1, 85–98.

Cohen, D. (2007) 'The Very Separate Worlds of Academic and Practitioner Publications in Human Resource Management: Reasons for the Divide and Concrete Solutions for Bridging the Gap', *Academy of Management Journal*, Vol. 50, No. 5, 1013–19.

Colakoglu, S., Lepak, D. and Hong, Y. (2006) 'Measuring HRM Effectiveness: Considering Multiple Stakeholders in a Global Context', *Human Resource Management Review*, Vol. 16, 209–18.

Colley, H. (2003) 'Engagement Mentoring for Socially Excluded Youth: Problematising an "Holistic" Approach to Creating Employability through the Transformation of Habitus', *British Journal of Guidelines & Counselling*, Vol. 31, No. 1, 77–99.

Collis, D.J. and Montgomery, C.A. (1995) 'Competing on Resources,' *Harvard Business Review*, July–Aug, 118–28.

Combs, J., Liu, Y., Hall, A. and Ketchen, D. (2006) 'How Much Do High Performance Work Practices Matter? A Meta-Analysis of their Effects on Organizational Performance', *Personnel Psychology*, Vol. 59, No. 3, 501–28.

Connolly, P. (2006) 'The Masculine Habitus: "Distributed Cognition": A Case Study of 5–6 Year Old Boys in an English Inner-city, Multi-ethnic Primary School', *Children and Society*, Issue 20, 140–52.

Contu, A. and Willmott, H. (2005) 'You Spin Me Around: The Realist Turn in Organization and Management Studies, *Journal of Management Studies*, Vol. 42, No. 8, 1645–62.

Dacin, M. Tina (1997) 'Isomorphism in Context: The Power and Prescription of Institutional Norms', *The Academy of Management Journal*, Vol. 40, No. 1, 46–81.

Danermark, B., Ekstrom, M., Jakobsen, L. and Karlsson, J. (1997) *Explaining Society: Critical Realism in the Social Sciences,* London: Routledge.

Danford, A., Richardson, M., Stewart, P., Tailby, S. and Upchurch, M. (2005) *Partnership and the High Performance Workplace: Work and Employment Relations in the Aerospace Industry*, Basingstoke: Palgrave Macmillan.

Datta, D., Guthrie, J. and Wright, P. (2005) 'Human Resource Management & Labour Productivity: Does Industry Matter?', *Academy of Management Journal,* Vol. 48, No. 1, 135–45.

Davenport, T.H. (2005) 'The Coming Commoditization of Processes', *Harvard Business Review,* June, 100–11.

David, M., Ball, S., Davies, J. and Reay, D. (2003) 'Gender Issues in Parental Involvement in Student Choices of Higher Education', *Gender and Education,* Vol. 15, No. 1, 21–37.

Davis, J. (2003) *The Theory of the Individual in Economics: Identity and Value,* London: Routledge.

De Cindio, F., Gentile, O., Grew, P. and Redolfi, D. (2003) 'Community Networks: Rules of Behaviour and Social Structure', *The Information Society,* Issue 19, 395–406.

Delaney, J. and Godard, J. (2001) 'An Industrial Relations Perspective on the High Performance Paradigm', *Human Resource Management Review,* Vol. 11, 395–429.

Delbridge, R. (1998) *Life on the Line in Contemporary Manufacturing: The Workplace Experience of Lean Production and the 'Japanese' Model,* Oxford: Oxford University Press.

Delery, J.E. and Doty, D.H. (1996) 'Modes of Theorizing in Strategic Human Resources Management: Tests of Universalistics, Contingency and Configurational Performance Predictions, *Academy of Management Journal,* Vol. 39, 802–35.

Deloitte/The Economist Intelligence Unit (2007) *Aligned At The Top,* London: Deloitte/EIU.

Demos, N., Chung, S. and Beck, M. (2001) 'The New Strategy and Why It Is New', *Strategy + Business,* Vol. 25, No. 4, 1–5.

Den Hartog, D. and Verburg, R. (2004) 'High Performance Work Systems, Organisational Performance and Firm Effectiveness', *Human Resource Management Journal,* Vol. 14, No. 1, 55–79.

Dipboye, R.L. (2007) 'Eight Outrageous Statements about HR Science,' *Human Resource Management Review,* Vol. 17, No. 2, 96–106.

Donaldson, L. (2003) 'Position Statement for Positivism' in R. Westwood and S. Clegg (eds.), *Debating Organization: Point-Counterpoint in Organization Studies,* Oxford: Blackwell.

Donkin, R. (2002) 'Measuring the Worth of Human Capital', *Financial Times,* 7 November.

(2005) 'Passage to India for Human Resources Function', *Financial Times*, 9 June.

Doornward, H. and Meihuizen, H. (2000) 'Strategic Performance Options in Professional Service Organisations', *Human Resource Management Journal*, Vol. 9, No. 3, 46–62.

Doty, D.H. and Glick, W.H. (1994) 'Typologies as a Unique Form of Theory Building: Toward Improved Understanding and Modeling', *Academy of Management Review*, Vol. 19, 230–51.

Doty, D., Glick, H. and Huber, G. (1993) 'Fit, Equifinality, and Organizational Effectiveness: A Test of Two Configurational Theories', *Academy of Management Journal*, Vol. 36, No. 6, 1196–250.

Dow, S. (2006) 'Themes and Issues: Rejoinder to Steve Fleetwood & Paul Downward', *Journal of Critical Realism*, Vol. 5, No. 1, 169–82.

Downward, P. (2003) *Applied Economics and the Critical Realist Critique*, London: Routledge.

Echambadi, R., Campbell, B. and Agarwal, R. (2006) 'Encouraging Best Practice in Quantitative Management Research: An Incomplete List of Opportunities', *Journal of Management Studies*, Vol. 48, No. 8, 1801–920.

Edgar, F. and Geare, A. (2005) 'HRM Practice and Employee Attitudes: Different Measures – Different Results', *Personnel Review*, Vol. 34, No. 5, 534–49.

Edwards, P. (2006) 'The Challenging but Promising Future of Industrial Relations: Developing Theory and Method in Context-Sensitive Research', *Industrial Relations Journal*, Vol. 36, No. 4, 69–87.

Edwards, P. and Collinson, M. (2002) 'Empowerment and Managerial Labour Strategies', *Work and Occupations*, Vol. 29, No. 3, 272–99.

Edwards, P. and Wright, M. (2001) 'High Involvement Work Systems and Performance Outcomes: The Strength of Variable, Contingent and Context Bound Relationships', *International Journal of Human Resource Management*, Vol. 12, No. 4, 568–85.

Elder-Vass, D. (2006) *'The Theory of Emergence, Social Structure, and Human Agency'*, unpublished PhD thesis, Birckbeck College, London.

    (2007a) 'For Emergence: Refining Archer's Account of Social Structure', *Journal for the Theory of Social Behaviour*, Vol. 37, No. 1, 25–44.

    (2007b) 'Social Structure & Social Relations', *Journal for the Theory of Social Behaviour*, Vol. 37, No. 4, 463–77.

Elias, J. and Scarbrough, H. (2004) 'Evaluating Human Capital: An Exploratory Study of Management Practice', *Human Resource Management Journal*, Vol. 14, No. 4, 21–34.

Elvira, M. and Davila, A. (2005) 'Emergent Directions for Human Resource Management in Latin America', *International Journal of Human Resource Management*, Vol. 16, No. 2, 2265–82.

Evans, P. (1999) 'HRM on the Edge: A Duality Perspective', *Organization*, Vol. 6, No. 2, 325–38.

Ferratt, T., Agarwal, R., Brown, C. and Moore, J. (2005) 'IT Human Resource Management Configurations and IT Turnover: Theoretical Synthesis and Empirical Analysis', *Information Systems Research*, Vol. 16, No. 3, 237–55.

Ferris, G., Hall, A., Royle, M. and Martocchio, J. (2004) 'Theoretical Development in the Field of Human Resources Management: Issues and Challenges for the Future', *Organizational Analysis*, Vol. 12, No. 3, 231–54.

Fey, C., Bjorkman, I. and Pavlovskaya, A. (2000) 'The Effect of Human Resource Management Practices on Firm Performance in Russia', *International Journal of Human Resource Management*, Vol. 11, No. 1, 1–18.

Fleetwood, S. (1995) *Hayek's Political Economy: The Socio-economics of Order*, London: Routledge.

(1999a) 'The Inadequacy of Mainstream Theories of Trade Unions', *Labour*, Vol. 13, No. 2, 445–80.

(2001) 'Causal Laws, Functional Relations and Tendencies', *Review of Political Economy*, Vol. 13, No. 2, 201–220.

(2004) 'The Ontology of Organisation and Management Studies' in S. Fleetwood and S. Ackroyd (eds.), *Critical Realist Applications in Organisation and Management Studies*, London: Routledge.

(2005) 'The Ontology of Organization and Management Studies: A Critical Realist Approach', *Organization*, Vol. 12, No. 2, 197–222.

(2006) 'Themes and Issues: Rejoinder to Sheila Dow and Paul Downward', *Journal of Critical Realism*, Vol. 5, No. 1, 169–82.

(2007) 'Why Neoclassical Economics Explains Nothing at All' in E. Fullbrook (ed.), *Real World Economics: A Post-autistic Economics Reader*, London: Anthem Press.

(2008a) 'Institutions and Social Structures', *Journal for the Theory of Social Behaviour*, Vol. 38, No. 3, 241–65.

(2008b) 'Structure, Institution, Agency, Habit and Reflexive Deliberation', *Journal of Institutional Economics*, Vol. 4, No. 2, 183–203.

(2009a) 'The Ontology of Things, Powers and Properties', *Journal of Critical Realism*, Vol. 8, No. 3, 343–66.

(2009b) 'Laws and Tendencies', currently under review.

(2010a) 'Sketching a Socio-economic Model of Labour Markets', *Cambridge Journal of Economics,* forthcoming.

(2010b) 'Powers and Tendencies Revisited', *Journal of Critical Realism.*

Fleetwood, S. (ed.) (1999b) *Critical Realism in Economics: Development and Debate,* London: Routledge.

Fleetwood, S. and Ackroyd, S. (eds.) (2004) *Realism in Action in Organisation and Management,* London: Routledge.

Fleetwood, S. and Hesketh, A. (2004) 'Facing Certain Death by Numbers', *Financial Times,* 5 July.

(2006) 'Theorising Under-Theorisation: Research on the Human Resources – Performance Link', *Journal of Critical Realism,* Vol. 5, No. 2, 228–50.

(2008) 'Theorising Under-theorisation in Research on the HRM – Performance Link', *Personnel Review, Vol.* 37, No. 2, 126–44.

Foley, M., Maxwell, G. and McGillivray, D. (1999) 'The UK Context of Workplace Empowerment: Debating HRM and Postmodernity', *Participation and Empowerment: An International Journal,* Vol. 7, No. 6, 163–74.

Folger, R. and Turillo, C. (1999) 'Theorizing as the Thickness of Thin Abstraction', *Academy of Management Review,* Vol. 24, No. 7, 742–58.

Freedman, D. (2007) 'Statistical Models for Causation' in W. Outhwaite and S. Turner (eds.), *The Sage Handbook of Social Science Methodology,* London: Sage.

Friedman, M. (1988) 'The Methodology of Positive Economics' in D. Hausman (ed.), *The Philosophy of Economics: An Anthology,* Cambridge: Cambridge University Press.

Galbreath, J. (2005) 'Which Resources matter most to Firm Success? An Exploratory Study of Resource-Based Theory', *Technovation,* Vol. 25, No. 9, 979–987.

Gallo, J. and Thompson, P. (2000) 'Goals, Measures and Beyond: In Search of Accountability in Federal HRM', *Public Personnel Management,* Vol. 29, No. 2, 237–48.

Gant, J., Ichniowski, C. and Shaw, K. (2002) 'Social Capital and Organizational Change in High-Involvement and Traditional Work Organizations', *Journal of Economics & Management Strategy,* Vol. 11, No. 2, 289–328.

Geary, J. and Dobbins, A. (2001) 'Teamworking: A New Dynamic in the Pursuit of Management Control', *Human Resource Management Journal,* Vol. 11, No. 1, 3–24.

Gelade, G. and Ivery, M. (2003) 'The Impact of Human Resource Management and Work Climate on Organizational Performance', *Personnel Psychology,* Vol. 56, 383–404.

Gerhart, B. (1999) 'Human Resource Management & Firm Performance: Measurement Issues and their Effect on Causal and Policy Inferences', *Research in Personnel and Human Resources Management*, Supplement 4, 31–51.

(2007) 'Modeling HRM and Performance Linkages' in P. Boxall, J. Purcell and P. Wright (eds.), *The Oxford Handbook of Human Resource Management*, Oxford: Oxford University Press.

Gerhart, B., Wright, P., McMahan, G. and Snell, S. (2000) 'Measurement Error in Research on Human Resources and Firm Performance: How Much Error Is There and How Does It Influence Size Estimates', *Personnel Psychology*, Vol. 53, 803–34.

Ghemawat, P. (2007) 'Managing Differences: The Central Challenge of Global Strategy', *Harvard Business Review*, Vol. 85, No. 3, 58–69.

Ghorpade, J. (2004) 'Management and the Human Resource Function: A Model Based on Social Systems Theory', *International Journal of Human Resource Management*, Vol. 4, No. 3, 235–55.

Ghoshal, S. (2005) 'Bad Management Theories Are Destroying Good Management Practices', *Academy of Management Learning & Education*, Vol. 4, No. 1, 75–91.

Giddens, A. (1975) *New Rules of Sociological Method*, London: Polity.

(1979) *Central Problems in Social Theory*, London: Macmillan.

(1984) *The Constitution of Society*, Cambridge: Polity.

Gifford, J., Neathey, F. and Loukas, G. (2005) *Employee Involvement: Information, Consultation and Discretion*, IES report 427, Brighton: Institute for Employment Studies.

Godard, J. (1993) 'Theory and Method in Industrial Relations: Modernist and Postmodernist Alternatives' in R. Adams and N. Meltz (eds.), *Industrial Relations Theory: Its Nature, Scope and Pedagogy*, Lanham and London: Scarecrow Press and IMLR Press/Rutgers University.

(2001) 'Beyond the High Performance Paradigm? An Analysis of Variation in Canadian Managerial Perceptions of Reform Programme Effectiveness', *British Journal of Industrial Relations*, Vol. 39, No. 1, 28–52.

(2004) 'A Critical Assessment of the High-Performance Paradigm', *British Journal of Industrial Relations*, Vol. 42, No. 2, 349–78.

Gordon S. (1991) *The History and Philosophy of Social Science*, London: Routledge.

Gould-Williams, J. and Davies, F. (2005) 'Using Social Exchange Theory to Predict the Effects of HRM Practice on Employee Outcomes', *Public Management Review*, Vol. 7, No. 1, 1–24.

Gratton, L. (2000) *Living Strategy: Putting People at the Heart of Corporate Purpose*, London: FT Prentice Hall.

Grimshaw, D. and Rubery, J. (2007) 'Economics and HRM' in P. Boxall, J. Purcell and P. Wright (eds.), *The Oxford Handbook of Human Resource Management*, Oxford: Oxford University Press.

Groff, R. (2004) *Critical Realism, Postpositivism and the Possibility of Knowledge*, London: Routledge.

Guest, D. (1997) 'Human Resource Management and Performance: A Review and Research Agenda', *International Journal of Human Resource Management*, Vol. 8, No. 3, 263–76.

(1999) 'HRM and Performance: Seeking the Missing Link. A Progress Report', paper presented at the BUIRA conference, Cardiff.

(2001) 'Human Resource Management: When Research Confronts Theory', *International Journal of Human Resources Management*, Vol. 12, No. 7, 1092–106.

(2007) 'HRM and the Worker: Towards a New Psychological Contract?' in P. Boxall, J. Purcell and P. Wright (eds.), *The Oxford Handbook of Human Resource Management*, Oxford: Oxford University Press.

(2007a) 'Don't Shoot The Messenger: A Wake Up Call For Academics', *Academy of Management Review*, Vol. 50, No. 5, 1020–6.

Guest, D., Michie, J., Conway, N. and Sheehan, M. (2003) 'Human Resource Management and Corporate Performance in the UK', *British Journal of Industrial Relations*, Vol. 41, No. 2, 291–314.

Guthrie, J. (2001) 'High-Involvement Work Practices, Turnover and Productivity: Evidence from New Zealand', *Academy of Management Journal*, Vol. 44, No. 1, 180–90.

Hackett Group (2007) 'World Class Spend Less, yet Achieve Higher Effectiveness'. Online, available at: www.thehackettgroup.com/portal/site/apresearch/menuitem.6da219fe3fb4100ad91dc21066f069a0 (last accessed 30 August 2007).

Hammond, K. (2005) 'Why We Hate HR', *Fast Company Magazine*, August, No. 97, 40–7.

Hancock, P. (1999) 'Baudrillard and the Metaphysics of Motivation: A Reappraisal of Corporate Culture in the Light of the Work and Ideas of Jean Baudrillard', *Journal of Management Studies*, Vol. 36, No. 2, 155–75.

Harley, B. and Hardy, C. (2004) 'Firing Blanks? An Analysis of Discursive Struggle in HRM', *Journal of Management Studies*, Vol. 41, No. 3, 377–400.

Harney, B. and Dundon, T. (2006) 'Capturing Complexity: Developing an Integrated Approach to Analysing HRM in SME's', *Human Resources Management Journal*, Vol. 16, No. 1, 48–73.

Hausman, D. (1992) *The Inexact and Separate Science of Economics*, Cambridge: Cambridge University Press.

Hayduck, L. and Pazderka-Robinson, H. (2007) 'Fighting to Understand the World Causally: Three Battles Connected to the Causal Implications of Structural Equation Modelling' in W. Outhwaite and S. Turner (eds.), *The Sage Handbook of Social Science Methodology*, London: Sage.

Hendry, C., Learner, E., Poirier, D. *et al.* (1990) 'The ET Dialogue; A Conversation on Econometric Methodology', *Econometric Theory*, Vol. 6, 171–261.

Hendry, C., Woodward, S., Bradley, P. and Perkins, S. (2000) 'Performance and Rewards: Cleaning Out the Stables', *Human Resource Management Journal*, Vol. 9, No. 3, 46–62.

Hesketh, A. (2004) *Adding Value Beyond Measure*, Warwick: AGR.

(2006) *Outsourcing The HR Function: Possibilities & Pitfalls*, London: Accenture.

(2008a) 'Taking Talent Into The Boardroom: A New Executive Metric To Understand Talent's ROI', *CPHR Working Paper 08/02*, Lancaster: CPHR/LUMS Working Papers.

Hesketh, A. and Fleetwood, S. (2006a) 'Beyond Measuring the HRM-Organizational Performance Link: Applying Critical Realist Meta-theory', *Organization*, Vol. 13, No. 5, 677–99.

(2006b) 'HRM-Performance Research: Under-theorised and Lacking Explanatory Power', *International Journal of Human Resources Management*, Vol. 17, No. 12, 1979–95.

Hiltrop, J.-M. (1996) 'The Impact of Human Resource Management on Organisational Performance: Theory and Research', *European Journal of Human Resource Management*, Vol. 14, No. 6, 628–37.

Hirsh, W., Bevan, S. and Barber, L. (1995) 'Measuring the Personnel Function', *The Institute for Employment Studies*, Report 286, Brighton: The Institute for Employment Studies.

Hodgson, G. (1988) *Economics and Institutions: A Manifesto for a Modern Economics*, Oxford: Basil Blackwell.

(2002) 'Reconstitutive Downward Causation: Social Structure and the Development of Individual Agency' in E. Fullbrook (ed.), *Intersubjectivity in Economics: Agents and Structures*, London and New York: Routledge.

(2003) 'The Hidden Persuaders: Institutions and Individuals in Economic Theory', *Cambridge Journal of Economics*, Vol. 27, 159–75.

(2004) *The Evolution of Institutional Economics: Agency, Structure and Darwinism in American Institutionalism*, London: Routledge.

(2006a) 'What are Institutions?', *Journal of Economic Issues*, Vol. 40, No. 1, 1–25.

(2006b) *Economics in the Shadow of Darwin and Marx: Essays on Institutional and Evolutionary Themes*, Cheltenham: Edward Elgar.

Holdsworth, C. (2006) '"Don't You Think You're Missing Out Living At Home?" Student Experiences and Residential Transitions', *The Sociological Review*, Vol. 54, No. 3, 495–519.

Holmstrom, B. and Milgram, P. (1994) 'The Firm as an Incentive System', *American Economic Review*, Vol. 84, No. 4, 972–91.

Hoobler, J. and Brown-Johnston, N. (2005) 'An Analysis of Current HRM Publications', *Personnel Review*, Vol. 33, No. 6, 665–76.

Hoque, K. (1999) 'HRM and Performance in the UK Hotel Industry', *British Journal of Industrial Relations*, Vol. 37, No. 3, 419–43.

Horgan, J. and Muhlau, P. (2003) 'The Adoption of High Performance Human Resource Practices in Ireland: An Integration of Contingency and Institutional Theory', *Irish Journal of Management*, Vol. 24, No. 1, 26–47.

Huczynski, A. (1993) *Management Gurus*, London: Routledge.

Hughes, J. and Sharrock, W. (1997) *The Philosophy of Science Research*, London: Longman.

Hume, D. (1888, 1978) *A Treatise of Human Nature*, Oxford: Clarendon Press.

Huselid, M. (1995) 'The Impact of Human Resource Management Practices on Turnover, Productivity, and Corporate Financial Performance', *Academy of Management Journal*, Vol. 38, No. 3, 635–72.

Huselid, M. and Becker, B. (1996) 'Methodological Issues in Cross Sectional and Panel Estimates of the Human Resource-Firm Performance Link', *Industrial Relations*, Vol. 35, No. 3, 400–22.

Huselid, M., Jackson, S. and Schuler, R. (1997) 'Technical and Strategic Human Resource Management Effectiveness as Determinants of Firm Performance', *Academy of Management Journal*, Vol. 40, No. 1, 171–88.

Ichniowski, C. and Shaw, K. (1999) 'The Effects of Human Resource Management Systems on Economic Performance: An International Comparison of US and Japanese Plants', *Management Science*, Vol. 45, No. 5, 704–21.

Ichniowski, C., Shaw, K. and Prennushi, G. (1997) 'The Effects of Human Resource Management on Productivity: A Study of Steel Finishing Lines', *The American Economic Review*, Vol. 87, No. 3, 291–313.

IDC (2006) 'Worldwide and U.S. Business Process Outsourcing 2006–2010 Forecast: Market Opportunities by Horizontal Business Process', *IDC #204178*, Vol. 1, Framingham: IDC.

Ingham, J. (2007) *Strategic Human Capital Management,* Amsterdam: Elsevier.

Jackson, S. and Schuler, R. (1995) 'Understanding Human Resource Management in the Context of Organizations and their Environments', *Annual Review of Psychology,* Vol. 46, 237–64.

Jackson, W. (2007) 'On the Social Structure of Markets', *Cambridge Journal of Economics,* Vol. 31, No. 2, 235–53.

Jessop, R. and Nielsen, K. (2003) 'Institutions and Rules', *Research Papers, Network Institutional Theory,* No. 11/03: 1.

Johnson, P. and Duberley, P. (2000) *Understanding Management Research,* London: Sage.

Kandel, E. and Lazear, E. (1992) 'Peer Pressure and Partnerships', *Journal of Political Economy,* Vol. 100, No. 4, 801–17.

Kane, J. (2001) 'Towards a Modernized Model of Science', *Human Resource Management Review,* Vol. 1, No. 4, 245–51.

Kaplan, R. and Norton, D. (1996) *The Balanced Scorecard: Translating Strategy Into Action,* Boston: Harvard Business School Press.

(2004) *Strategy Maps: Converting Intangible Assets Into Tangible Outcomes,* Boston: Harvard Business School Press.

Katou, A. and Budhwar, P. (2006) 'Human Resource Management Systems and Organizational Performance: A Test of a Mediating Model in the Greek Manufacturing Context', *International Journal of Human Resource Management,* Vol. 17, No. 7, 1223–53.

Keenoy, T. (1997) 'Review Article: HRMism and the Languages of Representation', *Journal of Management Studies,* Vol. 34, No. 5, 825–41.

Kepes, S. and Delery, J. (2007) 'HRM Systems and the Problem of Internal Fit' in P. Boxall , J. Purcell and P. Wright (eds.), *The Oxford Handbook of Human Resource Management,* Oxford: Oxford University Press.

Khilji, S. and Wang, X. (2006) '"Intended and "Implemented" HRM: the Missing Linchpin in Strategic Human Resource Management Research', *International Journal of Human Resource Management,* Vol. 17, No. 7, 1171–89.

Kim, Y. and Gray, J. (2005) 'Strategic Factors Influencing International Human Resource Management Practices: An Empirical Study of Australian Multinational Corporations', *International Journal of Human Resource Management,* Vol. 16, No. 5, 809–30.

Kingsmill, D. (2003) *Accounting for People, Report of the Task Force on Human Capital Management,* London: Department of Trade & Industry.

Kinnie, N., Hutchinson, S., Purcell, J., Rayton, B. and Swart, J. (2005) 'Satisfaction with HR Practices and Commitment to the Organisation:

Why One Size does not Fit All,' *Human Resource Management Journal*, Vol. **15**, No. 4, 9–29.

Knight, P. (2002) *Small Scale Research: Pragmatic Inquiry in Social Science and the Caring Professions*, London: Sage.

Knox, A. and Walsh, J. (2005), 'Organizational Flexibility and HRM in the Hotel Industry: Evidence from Australia', *Human Resource Management Journal*, Vol. **15**, No. 1, 57–76.

Kurki, M. (2003) 'Re-engaging with Aristotle: Evaluating Critical Realist Philosophy of Causation in Aristotelian Light', paper presented at the IACR conference, August, Amsterdam.

Ladyman, J. (2002) *Understanding Philosophy of Science*, London: Routledge.

Lahteenmaki, S., Storey, J. and Vanhala, S. (1998) 'HRM and Company Performance: The Use of Measurement and the Influence of Economic Cycles', *Human Resource Management Journal,* Vol. **8**, No. 2, 51–65.

Langley, A. (1999) 'Strategies for Theorizing from Process Data', *Academy of Management Review*, Vol. **24**, No. 4, 691–710.

Latham, G.P. (2007) 'A Speculative Perspective on the Transfer of Behavioural Science Findings to the Workplace', *Academy of Management Journal*, Vol. **50**, No. 5, 1027–32.

Lau, C.-M. and Ngo, H.-Y. (2004) 'The HR System, Organizational Culture, and Product Innovation', *International Business Review*, Vol. **13**, 685–703.

Laursen, K. (2002) 'The Importance of Sectoral Differences in the Application of Complementary HRM Practices for Innovation Performance', *International Journal of the Economics of Business*, Vol. **9**, No. 1, 139–56.

Lawler, E.E. (2007) 'Why HR Practices Are Not Evidence Based', *Academy of Management Journal*, Vol. **50**, No. 5, 1033–6.

Lawrence, Paul R. and Lorsch, Jay William (1967) 'Organization and Environment: Managing Differentiation and Integration', Boston: Division of Research, Graduate School of Business Administration, Harvard University.

Lawson, T. (1997) *Economics and Reality*, London: Routledge.

(2003) *Reorienting Economics*, London: Routledge.

Layder, D. (2004) *Social and Personal Identity: Understanding Yourself,* London: Sage.

Leca, B. and Naccache, P. (2006) 'A Critical Realist Approach to Institutional Entrepreneurship', *Organization*, Vol. **13**, No. 5, 627–51.

Legge, K. (2001) 'Silver Bullet or Spent Round: Assessing the Meaning of the "High Commitment Management" / Performance Relationship' in J. Storey (ed.), *Human Resource Management: A Critical Text*, London: Thompson.

(2005) *Human Resource Management: Rhetorics and Realities*, London: Palgrave Macmillan.

Lenz, R.T. (1981) 'Determinants of Organizational Performance: An Interdisciplinary Review', *Strategic Management Journal, Vol.* **2**, No. 2, 131–154.

Lev, B. (2001) *Intangibles: Management, Measurement, and Reporting*, Washington, DC: Brookings Institution Press.

Lewis, P. (1999) 'Metaphor in Critical Realism' in S. Fleetwood (ed.), *Critical Realism in Economics: Development and Debate*, London: Routledge.

(2000) 'Realism, Causality and the Problem of Social Structure', *Journal for the Theory of Social Behaviour*, Vol. 30, No. 3, 249–68.

(2004) *Transforming Economics: Perspectives on the Critical Realist Project*, London: Routledge.

Lewis, P. and Runde, J. (2007) 'Subjectivism, Social Structures and the Possibility of Socio-economic Order', *Journal of Economic Behavior and Organization*, Vol. **62**, 167–86.

Liden, R., Wayne, C. and Sandy, J. (2001) 'Managing Individual Performance in Work Groups', *Human Resource Management*, Vol. 40, No. 1, 63–73.

Lindbladh, E. and Lyttkens, C. (2002) 'Habit Versus Choice: The Process of Decision Making in Health-Related Behaviour', *Social Science and Medicine*, Issue 55, 451–65.

Lipton, P. (1993) *Inference to the Best Explanation*, London: Routledge.

Lopez, J. and Scott, J. (2000) *Social Structure*, Buckingham: Open University Press.

Lounsbury, M. and Ventresca, M. (2003) 'The New Structuralism in Organizational Theory', *Organization*, Vol. 10, No. 3, 457–80.

Lowe, A. and Jones, A. (2004) 'Emergent Strategy and the Measurement of Performance: The Formulation of Performance Indicators at the Microlevel', *Organization Studies*, Vol. 25, No. 8, 1313–37.

Mabey, C., Skinner, D. and Clark, T. (1998) *Experiencing Human Resource Management*, London: Sage.

MacCormick, N. (1998) 'Norms, Institutions, and Institutional Facts', *Law and Philosophy*, Issue 17, 301–45.

MacDuffie, J. (1995) 'Human Resource Bundles and Manufacturing Performance: Organizational Logic and Flexible Production Systems in the World Auto Industry', *Industrial & Labor Relations Review*, Vol. **48**.

Marchington, M. and Zagelmeyer, S. (2005) 'Foreword: Linking HRM and Performance – A Never-ending Search?', *Human Resource Management Journal*, Vol. 15, No. 4, 3–8.

Marks, A. and Lockyer, C. (2005) 'Debugging the System: The Impact of Dispersion on the Identity of Software Team Members', *International Journal of Human Resource Management*, Vol. 16, No. 2, 219–37.

Mason, E. (1939) 'Price and Production Policies of Large-Scale Enterprise', *The American Economic Review*, Vol. 29, No. 1, Supplement, 61–74.

Mayo, A. (2000) *The Human Value of the Enterprise: Valuing People As Assets, Monitoring, Measuring, Managing,* London: Nicholas Brearly Publishing.

Mayson, S. and Barrett, R. (2006) 'The "Science" and "Practice" of HRM in Small Firms', *Human Resource Management Review*, Vol. 16, No. 4, 443–6.

Mazzanti, M., Pini, P. and Tortia, E. (2006) 'Organizational Innovations, Human Resources and Firm Performance: The Emilia-Romagna Food Sector', *Journal of Socio-Economics,* Vol. 35, 123–41.

McDonough, P. (2006) 'Habitus and the Practice of Public Service', *Work, Employment and Society*, Vol. 20, No. 4, 629–47.

McGoldrick, J., Stewart, J. and Watson, S. (2001) 'Theorizing Human Resource Development', *Human Resource Development International,* Vol. 4, No. 3, 343–56.

McKelvey, B. (2003) 'From Fields to Science: Can Organization Studies Make the Transition' in R. Westwood and S. Clegg (eds.), *Debating Organization: Point-Counterpoint in Organization Studies*, Oxford: Blackwell.

McLeod, J. (2005) 'Feminists Re-reading Bourdieu: Old Debates and New Questions about Gender Habitus and Gender Change', *Theory and Research in Education*, Vol. 31, No. 1, 11–30.

McMahan, G., Virick, M. and Wright, P. (1999) 'Alternative Theoretical Perspectives for Strategic Human Resource Management Revisited: Progress, Problems, and Prospects', *Research in Personnel and Human Resources Management,* Supplement 4, 99–122.

Mearman, A. (2006) 'Critical Realism in Economics and Open-Systems Ontology: A Critique', *Review of Social Economy*, Vol. LXIV, No. 1, 493–513.

Meikle, S. (1985) *Essentialism in the Thought of Karl Marx*, Gloucester: Duckworth.

Meyer, A.D., Tsui, A.S. and Hinings, C.R. (1993) 'Configurational Approaches to Organizational Analysis', *Academy of Management Journal*, Vol. 36, No. 6, 1175–95.

Meyer, J. and Smith, A. (2000) 'HRM Practices and Organizational Commitment: Test of a Mediation Model', *Canadian Journal of Administrative Sciences*, Vol. 17, No. 4, 319–31.

Miles, R.E. and Snow, C.C. (1984) 'Designing Strategic Human Resource Systems', *Organizational Dynamics*, Vol. 13, No. 1, 36–52.

Milgrom, P. and Roberts, J. (1990) 'The Economics of Modern Manufacturing', *American Economic Review*, Vol. 80, No. 3, 511–28.

(1995) 'Complementarities and Fit: Strategy, Structure and Organizational Change in Manufacturing', *Journal of Accounting and Economics*, Vol. 19, No. 2–3, 179–208.

Miner, J. (1979) 'Commentary' in D. Schendel and C. Hofer (eds.), *Strategic Management*, Boston: Little, Brown & Company.

Mirowski, P. and Sklivas, S. (1991) 'Why Econometricians don't Replicate (although they do reproduce)', *Review of Political Economy*, Vol. 3, No. 2, 146–64.

Mitchell, T. and James, L. (2001) 'Building Better Theory: Time and the Specification of When Things Happen', *Academy of Management Review*, Vol. 26, No. 3, 530–47.

Moss Kanter, R. (2003) 'Foreword' in Marc Effron, Robert Gandossy and Marshall Goldsmith (eds.) *Human Resources in the 21st Century*, New Jersey: Wiley, vii–xii.

Murphy, G. and Southey, G. (2003) 'High Performance Work Practices: Perceived Determinants of Adoption and the Role of the HR Practitioner', *Personnel Review*, Vol. 32, No. 1, 73–92.

Mutch, A. (1999) 'Critical Realism, Managers and Information', *British Journal of Management*, No. 10, 323–33.

(2000) 'Managers and Information: Agency and Structure', *Information Systems Review*, No. 1, 169–80.

(2002) 'Actors and Networks or Agents and Structures: Towards a Realist View of Information Systems', *Organization*, Vol. 9, No. 3, 477–96.

(2003) 'Communities of Practice and Habitus: A Critique', *Organization Studies*, Vol. 24, No. 3, 383–401.

(2004) 'Constraints on the Internal Conversation: Margaret Archer and the Structural Shaping of Thought', *Journal for the Theory of Social Behaviour*, Vol. 34, No. 4, 429–45.

(2006) *Strategic and Organizational Change: From Production to Retailing in UK Brewing 1950–1990*, London: Routledge.

Mutch, A., Delbridge, R. and Ventresca, M. (2005) 'Critical Realism, Agency and Discourse: Moving the Debate Forward (Response to Hugh Willmott)', *Organization*, Vol. 12, No. 5, 781–6.

Nash, R. (2003) 'Inequality/Difference in New Zealand Education: Social Reproduction and the Cognitive Habitus', *International Studies in Sociology of Education*, Vol. 13, No. 2, 171–91.

Neal, A., West, M. and Patterson, M. (2005) 'Do Organizational Climate and Competitive Strategy Moderate the Relationship between Human Resource Management and Productivity?', *Journal of Management*, Vol. **31**, No. 4, 492–512.

Nielsen, K. (2006) 'Institutional Approaches in the Social Sciences: Typology, Dialogue and Future Challenges', *Journal of Economic Issues*, Vol. **40**, No. 2, 449, 456.

Noble, G. and Watkins, M. (2003) 'So, How Did Bourdieu Learn to Play Tennis: Habitus, Consciousness and Habituation', *Cultural Studies*, Vol. **14**, No. 4, 520–38.

Noon, M. (1994) 'HRM: A Map, Model or Theory?' in P. Blyton and P. Turnbull (eds.), *Reassessing Human Resource Management*, London: Sage.

Nurmi, H. (2006) *Models of Political Economy*, London: Routledge.

O'Mahoney, J. (2005) 'Constructing Habitus: The Negotiation of Moral Encounters at Telekom', *Work, Employment and Society*, Vol. **21**, No. 3, 479–96.

(2007) 'The Diffusion of Management Innovations: The Possibilities and Limitations of Memetics', *Journal of Management Studies*, Vol. **44**, No. 8, 1324–48.

Ostroff, C., Shin, Y. and Kinicki, A. (2005) 'Multiple Perspectives of Congruence: Relationships between Value Congruence and Employee Attitudes', *Journal of Organizational Behaviour*, Vol. **26**, 591–623.

Paauwe, J. (2004) *Human Resource Management and Organizational Performance*, Oxford: Oxford University Press.

(2005) *HRM and Performance: Achieving Long-term Viability*, Oxford: Oxford University Press.

Paauwe, J. and Boselie, P. (2003) 'Challenging "Strategic HRM" and the Relevance of the Institutional Setting', *Human Resource Management Journal*, Vol. **13**, No. 3, 56–70.

(2005) 'Best Practices … In Spite of Performance: Just a Matter of Imitation?', *International Journal of Human Resource Management*, Vol. **16**, No. 6, 987–1003.

Panayotoupoulou, L. and Papalexandris, N. (2004) 'Examining the Link between Human Resource Management Orientation and Firm Performance', *Personnel Review*, Vol. **33**, No. 5, 499–521.

Peacock, J. (2008) '100% Proof: Good HR will Boost your Company Profits', *Personnel Today*, 26 February, 1.

Peccei, R. and Rosenthal, P. (2001) 'Delivering Customer Oriented Behaviour through Empowerment: An Empirical Test of HRM Assumptions', *Journal of Management Studies*, Vol. **38**, No. 6, 831–57.

Pencavel, J. (1994) *Labour Markets under Trade Unionism: Employment, Wages and Hours*, Oxford: Blackwell.

Perry-Smith, J.E. and Blum, T.C. (2000) 'Work-family Human Resource Bundles and Perceived Organizational Performance', *Academy of Management Journal*, Vol. 43, 1107–17.

Pfeffer, J. (1994) *Competitive Advantage through People: Unleashing the Power of the Workforce*, Boston: Harvard University Press.

(1995) 'Mortality, Reproducibility and the Persistence of Styles of Theory', *Organization Science*, Vol. 6, No. 6, 681–93.

(1997) 'Pitfalls on the Road to Measurement: The Dangerous Liaison of Human Resources with the Ideas of Accounting and Finance', *Human Resource Management*, Vol. 36, No. 3, 357–65.

(2005) 'Why do Bad Management Theories Persist? A Comment on Ghoshal', *Academy of Management Learning & Education*, Vol. 4, No. 1, 96.

Pfeffer, J. and Sutton, D. (2006) *Hard Facts, Dangerous Half-truths and Total Nonsense: Profiting from Evidence Based Management*, Boston: Harvard Business School Press.

Porpora, D. (1998) 'Four Concepts of Social Structure' in M. Archer, R. Bhaskar, A. Collier, T. Lawson and A. Norrie (eds.), *Critical Realism: Essential Readings*, London: Routledge.

(2007) 'On Elder-Vass: Refining a Refinement', *Journal for the Theory of Social Behaviour*, Vol. 37, No. 2, 195–200.

Portes, A. (2006) 'Institutions and Development: A Conceptual Re-Analysis', *Population and Development Review*, Vol. 32, No. 2, 233–62.

Potter, G. and Lopez, J. (2001) *After Postmodernism: An Introduction to Critical Realism*, London: Athlone Press.

PricewaterhouseCoopers (2003) *Sustaining Value through People*, PricewaterhouseCoopers Publication, 1–26.

Pullman, P. (1995) *The Northern Lights* (London: Scholastic).

Purcell, J. (1999) 'Best Practice and Best Fit: Chimera or Cul-De-Sac', *Human Resource Management Journal*, Vol. 9, No. 3, 26–41.

Purcell, J. and Hutchinson, S. (2007) 'Front-Line Managers as Agents in the HRM-Performance Causal Chain: Theory, Analysis and Evidence', *Human Resource Management Journal*, Vol. 14, No. 1, 3–20.

Purcell, J. and Kinnie, N. (2007) 'HRM and Business Performance' in P. Boxall, J. Purcell and P. Wright (eds.), *The Oxford Handbook of Human Resource Management*, Oxford: Oxford University Press.

Purcell, J., Kinnie, N., Hutchinson, S., Rayton, B. and Swart, J. (2003) *Understanding the People and Performance Link: Unlocking the Black Box*, London: CIPD.

Purcell, J., Kinnie, N., Swart, J., Rayton, B. and Hutchinson, S. (2009), *People Management and Performance*, London: Routledge.

Rafferty, A.-M., Maben, J., West, E. and Robinson, D. (2005) 'What Makes a Good Employer?', *Global Nursing Review Initiative*, No. 3.

Ramsay, H., Scholarios, D. and Harley B. (2000) 'Employees and High-Performance Work Systems: Testing Inside the Black Box', *British Journal of Industrial Relations*, Vol. 38, No. 4, 501–31.

Reay, D., David, M. and Ball, S. (2001) 'Making a Difference? Institutional *Habituses* and Higher Education Choice', *Sociological Research Online*, Vol. 5, No. 4, available at: www.socresonline.org.uk/5/4/reay. html.

Reed, M. (2001) 'Organization, Trust and Control: A Realist Analysis', *Organization Studies,* Vol. 22, No. 2, 201–28.

(2003) 'The Agency-Structure Dilemma in Organization Theory' in H. Tsoukas and C. Knudsen (eds.), *The Oxford Handbook of Organization Theory*, Oxford: Oxford University Press.

(2007) 'Reflections on the "Realist Turn" in Organisation and Management Studies', *Journal of Management Studies*, Vol. 42, No. 8, 1621–44.

Risman, B. (2004) 'Gender as Social Structure: Theory Wrestling with Activism', *Gender & Society*, Vol. 18, No. 4, 429–50.

Rogers, E. and Wright, P. (1999) 'Measuring Organizational Performance in Strategic Human Resource Management: Problems, Prospects and Performance Information Markets', *Human Resource Management Review*, Vol. 8, No. 3, 311–31.

Rogers, G. (1994) 'Institutional Economics, Development Economics and Labour Economics' in G. Rogers (ed.), *Workers, Institutions and Economic Growth in Asia*, Geneva: International Institute for Labour Studies.

Rogers-Hollingsworth, J. (2002) 'On Institutional Embeddedness' in J. Rogers-Hollingsworth *et al.* (eds.), *Advancing Socio-economics: An Institutionalist Perspective*, Lanham: Rowman and Littlefield.

Rousseau, D. (2007) 'A Sticky, Leveraging, and Scalable Strategy for High Quality Connections between Organizational Practice and Science', *Academy of Management Review,* Vol. 50, No. 5, 1037–42.

Ruben, D.-H. (1992) *Explaining Explanation*, London: Routledge.

Runde, J. (1998) 'Assessing Causal Economic Explanations', *Oxford Economic Papers,* No. 50, 151–72.

Rynes, S. (2007) 'Editor's Afterword – Let's Create a Tipping Point: What Academics and Practitioners Can Do, Alone and Together', *Academy of Management Journal*, Vol. 50, No. 5, 1046–54.

Rynes, S., Colbert, A. and Brown, G. (2002) 'HR Professionals' Beliefs About Effective Human Resource Practices: Correspondence Between Research and Practice', *Human Resource Management,* Vol. 41, No. 2, 149–74.

Rynes, S.L., Giluk, T.L. and Brown, K.G. (2007) 'The Very Separate Worlds of Academic and Practitioner Periodicals in Human Resource Management: Implications for Evidence-Based Management', *The Academy of Management Journal,* Vol. 50, No. 5, 987–1008.

Saari, L. (2007) 'Bridging The Worlds', *The Academy of Management Journal,* Vol. 50, No. 5, 1043–45.

Sandberg, J. (2000) 'Understanding Human Competence at Work: An Interpretive Approach', *Academy of Management Review,* Vol. 41, No. 1, 9–25.

Sayer, A. (1994) *Methodology in Social Science: A Realist Approach,* London: Routledge.

(1998) 'Abstraction: A Realist Interpretation' in M. Archer, R. Bhaskar, A. Collier, T. Lawson and A. Norrie (eds.), *Critical Realism: Essential Readings,* London: Routledge.

(2000) *Realism and Social Science,* London: Sage.

Schmid, G. (1994) 'Equality and Efficiency in the Labour Market: Towards a Socioeconomic Theory of Cooperation' in G. Schmid (ed.), *Labour Market Institutions in Europe: A Socioeconomic Evaluation of Performance,* New York: M.E. Sharpe.

Schuler, R. (1987) 'Matching Effective HR Practices with Competitive Strategy', *Personnel,* Vol. 64, No. 9, 18–20, 22–7.

Schuler, R. and Jackson, S. (1987a) 'Organizational Strategy and Organization Level as Determinants of Human Resource Management Practices', *Human Resource Planning,* Vol. 10, No. 3, 125–41.

(1987b) 'Linking Competitive Strategy and Human Resource Management Practices', *Academy of Management Executive,* Vol. 3, 207–19.

(2005) 'A Quarter of a Century Review of Human Resource Management in the USA: The Growth and Importance of an International Perspective', *Management Review,* Vol. 16, No. 1, 11–34.

Scott, A. (1994) *Willing Slaves: British Workers under Human Resource Management,* Cambridge: Cambridge University Press.

Scott, J. (2001) 'Where is Social Structure?' in J. Lopez and G. Potter (eds.), *After Postmodernism: An Introduction to Critical Realism,* London: Athlone Press.

Scott, W. (1992) *Organizations: Rational, Natural and Open Systems,* Englewood Cliffs: Prentice Hall.

Searle, J. (2005) 'What is an Institution?', *Journal of Institutional Economics,* Vol. 1, No. 1, 1–22.

Sels, L., De Winne, S., Maes, J., Delmotte, J., Faems, D. and Forrier, A. (2006a) 'Unravelling the HRM-Performance Link: Value-Creating and Cost-Increasing Effects of Small Business HRM', *Journal of Management Studies,* Vol. 43, 320–42.

Sels, L., De Winne, S., Delmotte, J., Maes, J., Faems, D. and Forrier, A. (2006b) 'Linking HRM and Small Business Performance: An Examination of the Impact of HRM Intensity on the Productivity and Financial Performance of Small Businesses', *Small Business Economics*, Vol. 26, 83–101.

Shah, S. and Corley, K. (2006) 'Building Better Theory by Bridging the Quantitative-Qualitative Divide', *Journal of Management Studies,* Vol. 43, No. 8, 1821–35.

Sila, I. (2006) 'Examining the Effects of Contextual Factors on TQM and Performance through the Lens of Organizational Theories: An Empirical Study', *Journal of Operations Management,* Vol. 25, No. 1, 83–109.

Skaggs, B. and Youndt, M. (2003) 'Strategic Positioning, Human Capital, and Performance in Service Organizations: A Customer Interaction Approach', *Strategic Management Journal,* No. 25, 85–99.

Sloman, S. (2005) *Causal Models: How People Think about the World and Its Alternatives,* Oxford: Oxford University Press.

Sparham, E. and Sung, J. (2007) 'High Performance Work Practices – Work Intensification or "Win-win"?', Centre for Labour Market Studies, University of Leicester Working Paper. Online, available at: www.clms.le.ac.uk/publications/workingpapers/working_paper50.pdf.

Stavrou, E.T. and Brewster, C. (2005) 'The Configurational Approach to Linking Strategic Human Resource Management Bundles with Business Performance: Myth or Reality?', *Management Revue,* Vol. 16, No. 2, 186–201.

Steele, R. (2003) 'HRMR Special Issue on Methodological Issues in Absenteeism Research', *Human Resource Management Review,* Vol. 13, 153–5.

Stone-Romero, E., Stone, D. and Salas, E. (2003) 'The Influence of Culture on Role Conceptions and Role Behaviour in Organisations', *Applied Psychology: An International Review,* Vol. 52, No. 3, 328–62.

Storey, J. (1992) *Developments in the Management of Human Resources,* Oxford: Blackwell.

Sutton, R. and Staw, B. (1995) 'What Theory is Not', *Administrative Science Quarterly,* Vol. 40, No. 3, 371–85.

Symon, G. and Cassell, C. (2006) 'Neglected Perspectives in Work and Organizational Psychology', *Journal of Occupational and Organizational Psychology,* Vol. 79, 307–14.

Tamkin, P., Cowling, M. and Hunt, W. (2008) *People and The Bottom Line*, IES Report 448, London: Work Foundation.

Taylor, A. (2005) 'Finding the Future that Fits', *Gender and Education*, Vol. 17, No. 2, 165–87.

Thomas, R., Cheese, P. and Benton, J. (2003) 'Human Capital Development', *Accenture Research Note*, Vol. 1, 1–4.

Thompson, M. (2007) 'Innovation in Work Practices: A Practice Perspective', *International Journal of Human Resource Management*, Vol. 18, No. 7, 1298–317.

Tichy, N. M., Fombrun, C. J. and Devanna, M.A. (1982) 'Strategic Human Resource Management', *Sloan Management, 23*, 47–61.

Tomer, J. (2001) 'Understanding High-Performance Work Systems: The Joint Contribution of Economics and Human Resource Management', *Journal of Socio-Economics*, Vol. 30, 63–73.

Toulson, P. and Dewe, P. (2004) 'HR Accounting as a Measurement Tool', *Human Resource Management Journal*, Vol. 14, No. 2.

Townley, B. (1994) *Reframing Human Resource Management: Power, Ethics and the Subject at Work*, London: Sage.

Truss, C. (2001) 'Complexities and Controversies in Linking HRM with Organizational Outcomes', *Journal of Management Studies*, Vol. 38, No. 8, 1120–49.

Tsai, C.-J. (2006) 'High Performance Work Systems and Organizational Performance: An Empirical Study of Taiwan's Semiconductor Industry', *International Journal of Human Resource Management*, Vol. 17, No. 19, 1512–30.

Tsang, E. and Kwan, K.-M. (1999) 'Replication and Theory Development in Organizational Science: A Critical Realist Perspective', *Academy of Management Review*, Vol. 24, No. 4, 759–80.

Tsoukas, H. (2000) 'What is Management? An Outline of a Metatheory' in S. Ackroyd and S. Fleetwood (eds.), *Perspectives on Organisation and Management*, London: Routledge.

(2005) *Complex Knowledge: Studies in Organizational Epistemology*, Oxford: Oxford University Press.

Tsoukas, H. and Hatch, M.J. (2001) 'Complex Thinking, Complex Practice: The Case for a Narrative Approach to Organizational Complexity', *Human Relations*, Vol. 54, No. 8, 979–1013.

Tzafrir, S. Harel, H., Baruch, Y. and Dolan, L. (2004) 'The Consequences of Employing Emerging HRM Practices for Employees Trust in their Managers', *Personnel Review*, Vol. 33, No. 6, 628–47.

Ulrich, D. (1997) *Human Resource Champions, the Next Agenda for Adding Value and Delivering Results*, Boston: Harvard Business School Press.

(2007) 'In The Hot Seat', *People Management*, 28 June, 28–32.

Van de Ven, A. (1989) 'Nothing is Quite So Good as a Practical Theory', *Academy of Management Review*, Vol. 14, No. 4, 486–9.

Van Staveren, I. (2001) *The Values of Economics: An Aristotelian Perspective*, London: Routledge.

Wall, T. and Wood, S. (2005) 'The Romance of Human Resource Management and Business Performance, and the Case for Big Science', *Human Relations*, Vol. 58, No. 4, 429–62.

Walton, R.E. and Lawrence, P.R. (eds.) (1985) *Human Resource Management: Trends and Challenges*, Boston: Harvard Business School Press.

Wan, D., Kok, V. and Ong, C. (2002) 'Strategic Human Resource Management & Organisational Performance in Singapore', *HR Management*, July/August.

Wang, G., Dou, X. and Li, N. (2002) 'A Systems Approach to Measuring Return on Investment for HRD Interventions', *Human Resource Development Quarterly*, Vol. 13, No. 2, 203–24.

Watson, T. (2004) 'HRM and Critical Social Science Analysis', *Journal of Management Studies*, Vol. 41, No. 3, 447–67.

Way, S. and Johnson, D. (2005) 'Theorizing About the Impact of Strategic Human Resource Management', *Human Resource Management Review*, Vol. 15, 1–19.

Wells, A. (1970) *Social Institutions*, London: Heinemann.

Whetten, D. (1989) 'What Constitutes a Theoretical Contribution?', *Academy of Management Review*, Vol. 14, No. 4, 490–5.

Williamson, E.O. (1975) *Markets and Hierarchies: Analysis and Antitrust Implications: A Study in the Economics of Internal Organization*, New York: Macmillan.

Willmott, H. (2005) 'Theorizing Contemporary Control: Some Post-Structuralist Responses to Some Critical Realist Questions', *Organization*, Vol. 12, No. 7, 747–80.

Wright, P. and Boswell, W. (2002) 'Desegregating HRM: A Review and Synthesis of Micro and Macro Human Resource Management Research', *Journal of Management*, Vol. 28, No. 3, 247–76.

Wright, P. and McMahan, G. (1992) 'Theoretical Perspectives for Human Resource Management', *Journal of Management*, Vol. 18, No. 2, 295–320.

Wright, P. and Sherman, S. (1999) 'Failing to Find Fit in Strategic Human Resource Management: Theoretical & Empirical Problems', *Research in Personnel and Human Resources Management*, Supplement 4, 53–74.

Wright, P., Dunford, B. and Snell, S. (2001) 'Human Resources and the Resource Based View of the Firm', *Journal of Management*, Vol. 27, No. 6, 701–21.

Wright, P., Gardner, M. and Moynihan, L. (2003) 'The Impact of HR Practices on the Performance of Business Units', *Human Resource Management Journal*, Vol. 13, No. 4, 21–36.

Wright, P., Gardner, M., Moynihan, L., Park, H.J., Gerhart, B. and Delery, J.E. (2001) 'Measurement Error in Research on Human Resources and Firm Performance: Additional Data and Suggestions for Future Research', *Personnel Psychology*, Vol. 54, 875–901.

Yao-Sheng, L. (2005) 'Business Strategy and Performance: The Role of Human Resource Management Control', *Personnel Review*, Vol. 34, No. 3, 294–309.

Youndt, M. and Snell, S. (2004) 'Human Resource Configurations, Intellectual Capital and Organizational Performance', *Journal of Management Issues,* Vol. **XVI**, No. 3, 337–60.

Zheng, C., Morrison, M. and O'Neill, G. (2006) 'An Empirical Study of High Performance HRM Practices in Chinese SME's', *International Journal of Human Resource Management*, Vol. **17**, No. 10, 1772–803.

Index

Made in the USA
Lexington, KY
21 March 2012